THE MODERN MARKETING PLAYBOOK
Win Digital-First Consumers with Real-World Strategies

THE MODERN MARKETING PLAYBOOK
Win Digital-First Consumers with Real-World Strategies

Doreen Kum
NUS Business School, Singapore

Howie Lau
NCS Group, Singapore

NEW JERSEY • LONDON • SINGAPORE • BEIJING • SHANGHAI • HONG KONG • TAIPEI • CHENNAI • TOKYO

Published by

World Scientific Publishing Co. Pte. Ltd.
5 Toh Tuck Link, Singapore 596224
USA office: 27 Warren Street, Suite 401-402, Hackensack, NJ 07601
UK office: 57 Shelton Street, Covent Garden, London WC2H 9HE

Library of Congress Cataloging-in-Publication Data
Names: Kum, Doreen author | Lau, Howie author
Title: The modern marketing playbook : win digital-first consumers with real-world strategies / Doreen Kum, NUS Business School, Singapore, Howie Lau, NCS Group, Singapore.
Description: New Jersey : World Scientific, [2026] | Includes index.
Identifiers: LCCN 2025030373 | ISBN 9789819819102 hardcover |
   ISBN 9789819820467 paperback | ISBN 9789819819119 ebook |
   ISBN 9789819819126 ebook other
Subjects: LCSH: Marketing | Marketing--Case studies | Marketing--Technological innovations
Classification: LCC HF5415 .K827 2026
LC record available at https://lccn.loc.gov/2025030373

British Library Cataloguing-in-Publication Data
A catalogue record for this book is available from the British Library.

Copyright © 2026 by World Scientific Publishing Co. Pte. Ltd.

All rights reserved. This book, or parts thereof, may not be reproduced in any form or by any means, electronic or mechanical, including photocopying, recording or any information storage and retrieval system now known or to be invented, without written permission from the publisher.

For photocopying of material in this volume, please pay a copying fee through the Copyright Clearance Center, Inc., 222 Rosewood Drive, Danvers, MA 01923, USA. In this case permission to photocopy is not required from the publisher.

For any available supplementary material, please visit
https://www.worldscientific.com/worldscibooks/10.1142/14478#t=suppl

Desk Editors: Kannan Krishnan/Hong Koon Chua/Sandhya Venkatesh

Typeset by Stallion Press
Email: enquiries@stallionpress.com

Printed in Singapore

Endorsements

The Modern Marketing Playbook provides a practicable and insightful read. It helps you deep dive into real business issues, value chain understanding, providing bite size handles for easy application.
—Celine Tan, *Director, Group Marketing, F&N Limited*

Building on Philip Kotler's legacy, this book proves that marketing is not just a function—it's the backbone of modern business. With its deep insights on customer focus, data-driven strategies, and storytelling, there's no doubt it will become a definitive reference for marketing in the digital age.
—Tony Zameczkowski, *Vice President, Netflix APAC*

Destined to become a definitive modern text for marketers. Rich with unique insights and case studies from across the diverse Asian landscape, it inspires the marketing practitioner to hone their craft with a disciplined pursuit of excellence gained from a robust framework of customer focus, data-driven strategies, and storytelling.
—Rob Gilby, *Former Dentsu CEO Asia President, Managing Director SEA, Disney*

The 4Ps of marketing got a boost with 5A's and 5C's! Whether you are a newbie in marketing or an experienced practitioner, the evergreen frameworks shared in this book serve as a great guide.

While product and price remain essential considerations for buyers, the experience with a brand is equally influential in shaping their decisions. Marketing plays a pivotal role in orchestrating emotive brand experience to deliver impactful customer engagement. This book provides insights on how to curate customer experience across various stages of the customer journey, in a manner that is both practical and actionable.

Stacy Seah, *APAC CMO lead, Microsoft*

The Modern Marketing Playbook brings to life the winning strategies for unreasonable growth with marketing. It is the anchor for all marketing professionals against the wave of distractions from shiny object syndrome, fragmentation, technology, and vanity metrics. Start with the cheat sheet at the end of every chapter and learn from the updated case studies to arm yourself with the latest insights.

Jeff Cheong, *CEO, DDB Group Singapore*

The Modern Marketing Playbook isn't just a textbook; it's a mentoring session in print. Learn the winning strategies specific to the New Asia market, understand how AI is transforming the landscape, and acquire the essential skills to not only adapt, but lead in the ever-changing world of marketing. Let Doreen and Howie's passion, experience, and commitment to future generations empower you to thrive.

This book delves into the core principles of marketing, emphasizing the importance of understanding customers in today's dynamic business environment. It explores key concepts like segmentation, targeting, and positioning, providing frameworks and real-world examples to guide effective marketing strategies. The book also examines the challenges and opportunities presented by the digital age, including the shift towards data-driven decision making, the rise of social media, and the increasing importance of customer advocacy.

Glen Francis, *Strategic Advisor, Google Asia*

A gem for marketers and leaders—new or seasoned. This book humanizes strategy, turning cold tactics into warm connections. Learn to speak "with" people, not "at" them. Packed with empathy-driven insights, it bridges theory and action. Craft campaigns that resonate, brands that matter, and growth that includes all. Your compass for marketing with heart.

Daniel Ng, Former CMO APAC, Cloudera, Neo4J, Graphen

In today's digital-first world, marketing is more challenging than ever. Beyond mastering the fundamentals, marketers must stay agile, adapting to an ever-evolving landscape. This book, grounded in real-world experience, highlights how staying nimble and embracing new ways of working is essential—while never losing sight of the core principles of marketing.

Oliver Chong, Head Marketing and Comms, Mediacorp

Lauded as a robust and comprehensive guide, this playbook equips the entire ecosystem—marketers, agencies, media owners, and service providers—with the knowledge and tools to thrive in the complex, ever-evolving world of modern marketing, particularly within the Asian context. Together, we foster innovation, drive growth, and build a vibrant, sustainable future for our industry.

Rowena Bhagchandani, President AAMS
(Association of Advertising & Marketing of Singapore)
CEO & Co-founder, BLKJ HAVAS

The Modern Marketing Playbook is a timely and much-needed contribution to marketing education and practice, especially in the Asian context. It presents a holistic, human-centered view that blends strategic insight with real-world relevance.

With its strong regional case studies and practical approach, this book will no doubt become a go-to reference for marketers seeking clarity, inspiration, and a deeper understanding of how marketing truly works today.

Roger Wang, *President, Marketing Institute of Singapore & First Vice President, Asia Marketing Federation*

About the Authors

Doreen Kum—an Associate Professor at the National University of Singapore, Asia's #1 university and 8th globally—is not just teaching marketing, she's revolutionizing it. Whether it's undergraduates, master's students, or senior executives, she consistently earns rave reviews for making marketing truly click as a business strategy. Doreen brings a powerhouse blend of academic rigor (evidenced by multiple teaching excellence awards) and expertise that goes beyond the classroom. With a career rooted in marketing management in telco and healthcare sectors, she brings a uniquely practical perspective. Her teaching philosophy is deeply shaped by this real-world foundation, making her insights incredibly relevant. She continues to walk the talk as co-owner and Marketing Director of a healthcare distribution company, where she's instrumental in developing go-to-market and branding strategies for diverse brands wanting to compete in the Asian market. This book is your shortcut to her proven strategies. Get ready to transform your marketing game.

**Howie Lau** is a seasoned business leader with three decades of experience in the technology and media sectors. Currently, he serves as Managing Partner, Chief Corporate Development and Synergy at NCS Group, a prominent tech services leader in Asia with over 13,000 employees. In this role, he oversees critical functions including marketing, communications, partnerships, organization development, ESG, and government relations while also leading NCS's Greater China business.

Before joining NCS, Howie was the Assistant Chief Executive of Singapore's Infocomm Media Development Authority (IMDA), a government agency spearheading the nation's technology, telecommunications, media industries, and digital economy. His extensive career also includes leadership positions as Head of Consumer business and CMO at StarHub, and CMO for Lenovo Emerging Markets and Asia Pacific/Latin America.

An alumnus of the National University of Singapore, Howie also holds a postgraduate MA in Asian Art Histories from Lasalle College/Goldsmiths University of London. He has received significant accolades, including IT Leader of the Year 2020, the Philip Kotler Marketing Excellence Award 2018, and the NUS Outstanding Alumni Award 2009.

Contents

Endorsements		v
About the Authors		ix
Chapter 1	Understanding Marketing as a Strategy	1
Chapter 2	The Marketing Process	15
Chapter 3	Segmentation and Targeting	37
Chapter 4	Positioning	65
Chapter 5	Branding	89
Chapter 6	Understanding Consumers	131
Chapter 7	Understanding Business Buyers and Account-Based Marketing	159
Chapter 8	Product Strategy and Value Proposition	185
Chapter 9	Product Management	209
Chapter 10	Price Strategy	235
Chapter 11	Place Strategy	269
Chapter 12	Promotion Strategy	311
Chapter 13	Promotion Mix	333
Chapter 14	A Marketing Career	377
Chapter 15	Marketing Tech Landscape	395
Index		419

Chapter

1

Understanding Marketing as a Strategy

This chapter explores the crucial role of a marketing mindset in today's business landscape. It defines what a marketing mindset entails and explains why marketing is now central to business strategy. Furthermore, it examines how shifts in the business environment and customer behavior are reshaping brand interactions. Think your brand can coast by without marketing? Think again! This chapter is a wake-up call to the modern business world, where understanding customers is as essential as oxygen. In today's dynamic business environment, marketing is not just a department; it is a strategic imperative. This chapter deep dives into the "why" and "how" of a marketing mindset, proving it is not just fancy tricks, but the key to unlocking your brand's true potential.

Understanding Marketing as a Business Strategy

> "Because its purpose is to create a customer, the business enterprise has two – and only these two – basic functions: marketing and innovation."[1]
>
> —Peter Drucker

As Drucker points out, marketing is not just catchy slogans and glossy ads. It is the strategic compass that guides a business toward

---
[1] Drucker, P. F. (1954). *The Practice of Management*, Kindle edn. HarperCollins, New York, p. 416.

sustainable growth and thriving customer relationships. The American Marketing Association (AMA) states that "Marketing is the activity, set of institutions, and processes for creating, communicating, delivering, and exchanging offerings that have value for customers, clients, partners, and society at large."

Understanding this expansive definition is crucial for businesses to make informed strategic decisions. It is about recognizing that marketing is not a siloed department, but a thread woven into the fabric of every company, every function, and every employee and stakeholder. Thus, for brands to succeed, every company, business function, and employee needs to have a "marketing mindset."

Why a Marketing Mindset Matters for Every Company

A marketing mindset is key to unlocking customer-centricity. It is about understanding that every organization needs to be laser-focused on its customers. Why? Because the ultimate goal of any business is to earn the attention, liking, trust, and loyalty of customers. Marketing helps the organization adopt an outside-in perspective, allowing the business to see the world through the eyes of the customers to understand their needs and feeding those insights into innovations for the firm. Marketing is about translating innovations into offerings and experiences that customers find meaningful. Marketing identifies and connects the right customers to the right products. Marketing figures out how to engage with customers amidst the noise and clutter to keep the brand salient and remembered.

All these can only be done through deep customer knowledge and insight. In other words, marketing is the eyes, ears, and mouthpiece of the customer. Marketing sets the strategic direction for the firm and helps attract and retain customers for business success.

Debunking the Myths: Marketing beyond the 4Ps

A common misconception is that marketing is the domain of just the marketing department—those who craft advertisements and design social media posts. Organizations that confine marketing to tactical campaigns fail to tap into its transformative power to drive growth, attract, and retain customers. Marketing is not limited to the "4Ps" of pricing, promotion, product, and place. It is about strategy, innovation, understanding the customer journey, and creating value at every touchpoint. It is about understanding your business's entire ecosystem, from employees and partners to competitors and the larger social context, and being prepared for a constantly evolving marketplace.

It is also not just about selling products. It is about building organic demand, long-term loyalty, and advocacy.

Marketing in the Digital Age: A Double-Edged Sword

Technology has gifted us a toolbox bulging with innovative marketing tools and techniques. We can understand the customer better, micro-target with laser precision, personalize every touchpoint, and track performance in real time. It is a marketer's dream, right?

Not quite. This technological revolution is a double-edged sword. While it empowers, it also disrupts. New products, businesses, and operating models emerge overnight, threatening to outpace even long-standing incumbents. As consumers spend more time online, traditional sources of brand equity, such as store displays, crumble under the digital onslaught. To add to that complexity, all these happen in the face of macroeconomic uncertainty, geopolitical turmoil, and strained global supply chains.

In sum, what we are seeing is a challenging business environment with fierce competition and short product life cycles (PLCs). At the same time, customers are drowning in information, spoilt for choice, and increasingly distrustful. They have digital-first expectations of lightning-fast, hyper-personalized experiences delivered at their fingertips. Capturing their attention, engagement, trust, and loyalty is harder than ever. But the rewards for those who succeed are sky-high.

Clearly, today's marketers have a big job to do. Three large-scale studies have painted a clear picture: Marketing is key to driving business performance.

Forbes[2] highlights the transformative power of Chief Marketing Officers (CMOs). These data-driven visionaries link key performance indicators (KPIs) to business performance, forge strong cross-departmental collaborations, and lead with innovation. Their role? Orchestrating growth, not just managing campaigns.

McKinsey[3] echoes this sentiment. High-growth companies, they note, are laser-focused on growth, and driven by their marketing departments. Advanced analytics fuel their journey, uncovering and seizing opportunities with lightning speed.

Salesforce's State of Marketing survey[4] further confirms the rising stakes. Marketers believe their work is more valuable than ever, and priorities are shifting. Redefining customer engagement, juggling personalization amidst the data privacy maze, fostering collaboration in a distributed world, and aligning with customer values are at the forefront of their minds.

Modern marketing is a high-wire act. Mastering technology, catering to super-savvy customers, and adapting to a volatile world are the new battlegrounds.

Demystifying Marketing Strategy: The Key to Customer-Driven Growth

So, what exactly is marketing? At the core, legendary marketing guru Philip Kotler says it is about doing the homework to figure out what people need and what the company should make.[5] It is a fundamental shift in perspective from inside-out to outside-in.

---

[2] Cameron, N. (2014). Forbes: CMOs are the new transformers of business. CMO. Accessed on 8 December 2023. https://www.cmo.com.au/article/551212/forbes_cmos_new_transformers_business/.

[3] Gordon, J., Liedtke, N., and Timelin, B. (2016). Now new next: How growth champions create new value. 8 September 2016. McKinsey.com. Accessed on 8 December 2023. https://www.mckinsey.com/capabilities/growth-marketing-and-sales/our-insights/now-new-next-how-growth-champions-create-new-value#/.

[4] Salesforce. State of Marketing, 8th edn. Accessed on 11 December 2023. https://www.salesforce.com/content/dam/web/en_us/www/documents/resource-center/State%20of%20Marketing-8th%20Edition-11102022.pdf.

[5] Kotler Marketing Group. Dr. Philip Kotler answers your questions on marketing. Accessed on 14 December 2023. https://kotlermarketing.com/phil_questions.shtml#:~:text=Marketing%20is%20the%20homework%20the,improves%20the%20offering%20over%20time.

Instead of pushing products based on what is convenient for the company to make, we start with the customer. We identify unmet customer needs and who to sell to. This outside-in perspective recognizes that sustainable growth is based on customer-led demand. Imagine you spend months perfecting a new gadget, only to discover so few people need it that your efforts do not pay off. A customer-centric approach, on the other hand, ensures we are not just creating products but also creating solutions with real value and meaning for our customers. Innovation becomes more efficient. Accordingly, the entire go-to-market strategy and usage ecosystem have a higher probability of satisfying your customers, leading to a higher likelihood of repeat purchases and loyalty. (Read the sidebar for an account of how a scientist discovered the hard way that identifying his target market and understanding their needs first was important.)

Strategic decisions

To have a market-centric strategy, three strategic questions first need to be answered:

1. Who should our customers be?

    (This identifies the firm's target market and segment. More will be discussed in Chapter 3.)

2. What makes us important to customers? What do they want from us?

    (This defines the value proposition to customers. More will be discussed in Chapter 8.)

3. What makes us different from our competitors?

    (This determines the positioning of a brand relative to its competition. More will be discussed in Chapters 4 and 5.)

Operational decisions

So where do the good old 4Ps, aka marketing mix (Product, Price, Place, and Promotion), come in? Kotler expands on his definition, saying, "Marketing determines how to launch, price, distribute, and promote the product/service offering in the marketplace. Marketing then monitors the results and improves the offering over time."[6]

After making those big strategic decisions, the 4Ps are the tools you use to carry out the marketing strategy. Each P plays a crucial role:

- **Product:** What features and packaging will delight your customers?
- **Price:** How to find a sweet spot between profits and a price point that resonates with your target customers?
- **Place:** Where should your customers go to encounter your offering?
- **Promotion:** How will you get the right message to the right people?

These 4Ps work in concert, like a well-oiled machine. Nail the product, price it right, make it accessible, and shout it from the rooftops (strategically, of course). But the journey does not end there.

Marketing is a continuous feedback loop. Once you have executed it, it is time to monitor the results. Are customers responding as you expected? Are the 4Ps aligned with your initial strategy? Based on your findings, you can adjust and improve your offering, making it even more irresistible to your target audience.

Beyond Academic Walls: A Scientist's Journey to Market with Phage-Based Antimicrobials

Academic research increasingly focuses on translating basic scientific findings into practical technologies and products that can benefit society, potentially leading to commercialization and market value. For an academic scientist who has developed a technology, navigating its integration into the market poses several crucial questions: Does the technology address a genuine problem? Is there a real unmet need? What is its commercial potential? How can it be brought to market? Who is the target audience? While academic scientists are exposed to innovation and translation principles, the path to market is less illuminated.

---

[6] *Ibid.*

I've spent over 12 years delving into the development and mechanisms of antimicrobials and the challenges of antimicrobial resistance (AMR). AMR has emerged as a critical public health concern, with projections suggesting a staggering toll of over 10 million deaths annually within the next two decades if effective alternatives to failing antibiotics are not found. In recent years, my team identified phages—viruses that target bacteria—as promising alternatives to antibiotics, offering a solution to the pressing issue of antibiotic resistance. However, a significant obstacle arises—arduous regulatory requirements and the costly process to bring anti-infective therapeutics for humans to the market. The question remains: How can we bring our product to market effectively and for whom?

Contemplating these challenges, our thought process and steps unfolded as follows. While AMR is a pressing issue in human medicine, it also significantly impacts veterinary medicine. Through a valuable connection, we were introduced to Sage Healthcare, a leading distributor of medical products in Singapore with expertise in both human and veterinary fields. Leveraging Sage Healthcare's insights and network of key opinion leaders (KOLs), we gained a deeper understanding of the infectious diseases market in companion animals and its challenges. This collaboration allowed us to grasp the regulatory landscape and identify a beachhead market and specific applications for our technology. In the veterinary space, certain indications, such as skin- and wound-related infections in dogs, present urgent needs with limited therapeutic options, making them ideal targets for our novel solution.

Ultimately, this process underscored the importance of integrating market feedback into product development to ensure product–market fit. Integrating market feedback earlier would have certainly influenced our product development strategy. For example, identifying viable market segments and desirable target product profiles would have helped us refine our product design to meet specific needs. Getting early market feedback could improve our competitiveness, potentially helping with speed to market, penetration, and adoption rate. By aligning product development with market demands from the outset, the product would be better positioned for success, maximizing its impact and commercial potential. Through the collaboration with Sage Healthcare, we engaged

> with stakeholders across the value chain, including potential buyers, KOLs, and key players, and eventually aligned our technology with real-world needs and validated its potential in the market.
>
> Wilfried Moreira, PhD
> Principal Investigator and Senior Research Fellow, Singapore-Centre for Environmental Life Sciences and Engineering (SCELSE), Singapore

In Chapter 2, we will dive deeper into this dynamic process, exploring the marketing cycle in all its glory.

Let's have a look at how having a marketing mindset helped Asahi gain market share in the Japanese beer market.

Case: The Thinking behind the Success of Asahi Super Dry

Imagine being stuck in a beer market where your rival holds a crushing 60% share, while you flounder with a single-digit squeak. Sounds bleak, right? That was Asahi in the mid-1980s, facing the Goliath of Kirin. But Asahi was not about to roll over.

Instead, it did what every smart underdog does: listened to its customers. It commissioned a market study to better understand what its customers liked and disliked about beer. The results revealed two golden nuggets: consumers did not like the bitter aftertaste of beer and wished for it to have a stronger punch of alcohol.[7] Boom! Enter Asahi Super Dry in 1987, a crisp, clean-tasting brew with a higher alcohol content. "Super clean, crisp and refreshing," the ads and the packaging (Figure 1.1) declared.

Faced with strong competitors in the market, a great product was not enough. Kirin still reigned supreme in the traditional "beer shop" battleground. Asahi needed to bring this product to customers' attention and bypass the Kirin-dominated beer shops where customers

---

[7] Hoang, V. (2012). The great Japanese beer war. Tofugu.com. 3 May 2012. https://www.tofugu.com/japan/japanese-beer-wars/.

Figure 1.1. Asahi Super Dry packaging stating its positioning as "Super Dry Taste: With a Quick Clean Finish".

were on autopilot, mindlessly grabbing their usual top-of-mind beer brand. Asahi could be lost in the myriad of choices available. So, Asahi sidestepped. Asahi Super Dry entered the scene in sleek, modern cans,[8] infiltrated supermarket aisles, targeting adventurous, non-traditional consumers, trying to catch customers in the frame of mind to give a new product a try.

The launch of Asahi Super Dry in 1987 was a game-changer. The dry, crisp beer resonated with Japanese consumers and sparked a nationwide craze. It went on to solidify the concept of "dry beer" as a major category in the global beer market. Super Dry's success revitalized Asahi, propelling it to become the leading brewery in Japan by the mid-1990s. The beer revolutionized the taste preferences of Japanese consumers and established Asahi as a trendsetter. By the end of 1989, Super Dry accounted for 20% of all beers consumed in Japan. Super Dry's success triggered the "Dry Beer Wars," with

---

[8] Ewer, K. (2014). Asian champions of design: Asahi. Campaign Asia. 6 March 2014. Accessed on 16 December 2023. https://www.campaignasia.com/article/asian-champions-of-design-asahi/374270.

Step 1: Chill thoroughly
Step 2: Fully open the lid! Lift tab vertically straight up towards you.
Step 3: Enjoy "draft beer just like at a bar" to your heart's content

Figure 1.2. Asahi's Nama Jokki.

rivals scrambling to launch their own dry beers. While this diluted some of Asahi's lead, it kept the overall market dynamic in its favor. In 2021, Asahi launched a new packaging called "nama jokki" (which means "fresh beer mug"),[9] where a special coating inside the can produces frothy beer head,[10] and the top of the can comes off entirely (Figure 1.2), so that consumers feel like they are drinking beer from a mug served straight from the tap at a bar.

As they say, sometimes the best way to beat Goliath is to create a whole new battlefield. By listening to its customers, innovating with packaging and distribution, and riding the wave of a new taste preference, Asahi Super Dry did just that. It is a case study in understanding your audience, taking calculated risks, and ultimately owning the market.

The Asahi vs. Kirin case study serves as a reminder that success in the marketplace requires both an understanding of the evolving

---

[9] Japanese beer brewing giant Asahi launches mug-cans. Mainichi. 7 April 2021. https://mainichi.jp/english/articles/20210407/p2a/00m/0bu/011000c.

[10] *Ibid.*

needs of consumers and the ability to adapt and innovate with speed and agility. The following are some key learnings:

- **Understanding consumer shifts:** Asahi identified a growing desire for a drier, crisper beer taste than the traditional malt-heavy lagers prevalent in Japan. It capitalized on this shift by pioneering "dry beer" with Asahi Super Dry, while Kirin initially stuck to familiar territory and missed the trend.
- **Understanding consumer psychology and behavior:** In marketing, this is like having the ability to peek into the minds of your customers, understand their desires and motivations, and then craft offerings and marketing messages that resonate deeply with them. Consumers are not rational decision-makers; they are emotional beings driven by desires, fears, and social influences, who often operate on habits or mental shortcuts. Understanding these psychological factors allowed Asahi to speak to consumers using messaging, product packaging, and a purchase context that motivated them to take action to try a new product.
- **Innovation and agility:** Asahi's new management system fostered closer collaboration between product development and marketing, enabling it to quickly respond to consumer feedback and iterate on Super Dry. Kirin was slower to react and adjust.
- **Targeted marketing and brand positioning:** Asahi's marketing campaign for Super Dry effectively resonated with young professionals by portraying it as a modern, stylish beverage for after-work socializing. Kirin's messaging remained focused on tradition and family gatherings, failing to connect with the evolving consumer base.
- **Distribution and partnerships:** Asahi actively built relationships with distributors and retailers, ensuring widespread availability of Super Dry. Kirin, relying on its existing network, missed the opportunity to capitalize on new demand.
- **Adaptability and continuous improvement:** As the market matured, Asahi continued to innovate, maintaining its market leadership. Kirin eventually introduced its own dry beer but struggled to catch up with Asahi's established brand image and consumer loyalty.

The Asian PoV

The 21st century is shaping up to be Asia's defining era. Home to over half the world's population, the region has undergone a remarkable transformation. Fueled by economic powerhouses like China and India, the region is experiencing phenomenal growth. By 2040, Asia is predicted to generate over half of the world's GDP and account for nearly 40% of global consumption,[11] with a rising middle class driving domestic consumption. The robust intraregional trade and investment networks, coupled with a rising emphasis on innovation and technological advancements, are fostering a dynamic and interconnected Asian market, ultimately establishing Asia as a major global power.

For brands navigating the dynamic landscape of Asian markets, the key takeaways from this chapter are even more critical as Asia is not one market but is made up from many unique markets. Naturally, these principles come with their own set of challenges when applied in the Asian context.

Customer-centricity, while crucial, requires brands to grapple with the vast diversity in cultures, languages, and socioeconomic backgrounds across Asian countries. Understanding and catering to the needs of a heterogeneous customer base can be complex. As an example, Bahasa Indonesia is the official language in Indonesia, but there are over 700 sub-regional spoken languages across the 17,000 islands in Indonesia. Brands must invest in comprehensive market research and cultural sensitivity to truly connect with their target audience. This may involve tailoring products, messaging, and distribution channels to suit local preferences and nuances. Additionally, the digital landscape in Asia is fragmented, with different platforms and channels dominating in various markets. For example, WeChat dominates China while LINE holds a similar position in Thailand and Taiwan. Brands must navigate this complexity to effectively reach and engage their target customers.

---

[11] Seong, J. and Woetzel, J. (2019). We've entered the Asian century and there is no turning back. World Economic Forum. 11 October 2019. https://www.weforum.org/agenda/2019/10/has-world-entered-asian-century-what-does-it-mean/.

Like Asahi, many Asian brands are recognizing marketing as a strategic imperative that is crucial for long-term success. However, there are many different organizational constructs in Asian companies from family-owned businesses, state-owned businesses, and multinationals to Keiretsu and Chaebols. Integrating impactful marketing into the overall business strategy for each of these constructs will require different approaches and tactics. It requires a shift in mindset and culture at all levels of the organization, from leadership to frontline employees.

We opened this chapter with Drucker's words: "Because its purpose is to create a customer, the business enterprise has two—and only these two—basic functions: marketing and innovation." The success of Asahi Super Dry aligns well with Peter Drucker's quote in several ways: With marketing feeding into innovation, the product's popularity and innovative appeal generated organic demand, decreasing the need for aggressive marketing tactics. Consumers actively sought out Super Dry, creating a "pull" effect instead of a "push" one. Indeed, Super Dry "created a customer" for Asahi. The marketing campaign resonated with consumer preference, building a new niche within the market, and attracting a distinct customer base. Overall, the success of Asahi Super Dry demonstrates how effectively combining marketing and innovation can create customer value and drive business success. It aligns with Drucker's point that these two functions are the heart of a business, propelling it to "create a customer" and ultimately generate lasting profitability.

Ultimately, Peter Drucker's quote serves as a powerful reminder that businesses should prioritize understanding and catering to customer needs through creative and innovative approaches. Asahi Super Dry's story stands as a testament to the effectiveness of this philosophy.

Key Takeaways

- **Customer-centricity is key:** Understanding your customers and their evolving needs is fundamental. Your brand should focus on creating products that customers genuinely want and value.
- **Targeted marketing and innovation:** Develop a deep understanding of your target market and craft marketing messages that resonate with your customers. Embrace innovation and agility to adapt to changing consumer preferences and stay ahead of the competition.
- **Marketing is a strategic imperative:** Marketing is not just about promotions; it is a strategic heartbeat that should permeate every aspect of your business. A marketing mindset enables you to make informed decisions, build strong customer relationships, and achieve sustainable growth.
- **From strategy to execution:** The 4Ps are guided by consumer insights. A deep understanding of the target audience is the compass that steers the marketing mix (the 4Ps). By clearly defining who your customers are, what they want, and how you differentiate your offering, you can effectively allocate resources across product development, pricing, distribution, and promotion. This knowledge ensures that every element of the marketing strategy is aligned with the needs and desires of the target market, maximizing its impact and return on investment (ROI).

Chapter

2

The Marketing Process

In Chapter 1, we shared research from Forbes and McKinsey, which showed that organizations that did well had marketers who took ownership for growth and planned for it. Indeed, sustained success is by no means an easy feat or a stroke of luck; it is the product of deliberate action. Companies that neglect marketing planning often end up throwing money at campaigns with frustratingly little to show for it. They become the ones dismissing marketing as a futile expense.

Yet, think of Apple, Singapore Airlines, Samsung, Nike, or Louis Vuitton among others—these are the giants that inspire trust, command premium prices, build anticipation, hold sway over channel partners, and are the employers of choice.[1] They are etched in customers' minds for their distinct value propositions and powerful brand images. That is the power of effective marketing and brand building.

So, how do these titans achieve such dominance? The answer lies in intelligent, agile marketing strategies and plans.

The marketing process is a three-stage process, which we call the "Plan–Implement–Control Cycle," constantly fueled by insightful analysis (Figure 2.1). It empowers companies to unlock opportunities, shape viable business models, and craft winning strategies. This process also serves as a powerful feedback loop, tracking your progress and guiding future efforts. In this chapter, we focus on the "plan" stage of the process.

---

[1] Keller, K. L. (2009). Building strong brands in modern marketing communications environment. *Journal of Marketing Communications*, 15 (April–July), 139–155.

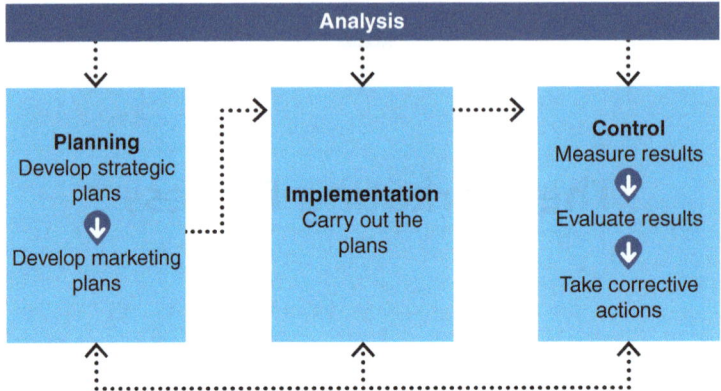

Figure 2.1. The marketing process.

The Roadmap Begins with Identifying the Destination: Linking Marketing to Business Goals

Your marketing strategy is your compass, outlining your marketing objectives and goals. These goals, however, cannot exist in a vacuum. They must harmonize with your overall business strategy, ensuring every marketing move contributes to your company's growth. These goals are also the yardsticks by which you will measure success in the "control" phase later.

Linking marketing goals (common marketing goals include increasing brand awareness, generating leads, boosting sales, enhancing customer satisfaction, and building brand loyalty) to business goals (such as increased revenue, profitability, and market share expansion) is fundamental to aligning your marketing efforts with the overall vision and success of your company. It is like building a bridge between what you want to achieve in the bigger picture and the specific actions you take through your marketing campaigns. Your goals determine your target customer, telling you who to focus on and how to tailor your offerings to acquire and retain them, outpacing your competition. Recall that these are the three strategic marketing decisions we described in Chapter 1. For example, a company that wants to expand its market would look at new customers in new geographies or non-buyers, as opposed to one wanting to fight for more market share. In the latter instance, it would focus on converting its competitors' customers.

The 2023 State of Marketing survey[2] of 6,000 marketing managers, directors, VPs, and CMOs across 35 countries revealed that their KPIs are now closely linked to business performance (Figure 2.2).

Figure 2.2. Marketing KPIs are linked to business performance.[3]

---

[2] Salesforce. State of Marketing. 8th edn. Accessed on 11 December 2023. https://www.salesforce.com/content/dam/web/en_us/www/documents/resource-center/State%20of%20Marketing-8th%20Edition-11102022.pdf.

[3] *Ibid.*

Navigating the Business Jungle: Environmental Scanning Is Your Survival Guide

> "There are three kinds of companies: those who make things happen; those who watch things happen; and those who wonder what's happened."
>
> —Anonymous

The one constant in the business world? Change. Just ask Kodak and Nokia, once towering giants felled by their failure to adapt. That's why understanding the environment where your business operates is vital. It is like having a map through the jungle, revealing where your customers dwell, the dangers lurking in the shadows, and even hidden paths to unexpected opportunities.

That is where environmental scanning comes in. Think of it as constantly scanning the horizon, picking up on the subtle shifts and tremors that could impact your business. This constant vigilance helps you with the following:

- **Decipher customer whispers:** By understanding the intricacies of your customers, their concerns, and the factors influencing them, you can tailor your offerings to their evolving needs.
- **Become a future-reading shaman:** Scanning for trends and anticipating disruptions prepares you to pivot and adapt before the storm hits, turning threats into potential triumphs.
- **Boost your reaction speed:** With early warnings about changes, you can respond swiftly, outmaneuvering competitors who are still scratching their heads in the dust.
- **Embrace the proactive panther:** When you see opportunities before others, you can pounce, leaving the competition scrambling for the leftovers.

The word "scanning" is key here. It is not a one-time expedition; it is a continuous quest for knowledge. To ensure you are not missing a single rustle in the leaves, you need a comprehensive framework.

Enter the 5Cs model, your handy compass for navigating the business jungle. It guides you through five vital realms:

- **Customer analysis:** Unveiling the desires, behaviors, and pain points of your customers, the lifeblood of your business.
- **Company analysis:** Taking a hard look at your own strengths, weaknesses, resources, and capabilities.
- **Collaborator analysis:** Identifying potential allies and partners who can strengthen your hand and open new paths.
- **Competitor analysis:** Keeping a watchful eye on your rivals, their strategies, and vulnerabilities, ensuring you can outsmart and outplay them.
- **Context analysis:** Understanding the broader economic, social, and technological forces shaping your environment, so you can navigate the undercurrents wisely.

With the 5Cs model as your guide and environmental scanning as your constant companion, you can transform your business from a vulnerable prey into a swift, adaptable predator, ready to thrive in the ever-changing jungle.

Customer analysis: Demystifying our target

In the previous chapter, we trumpeted the importance of putting customers at the heart of everything we do. We need to truly understand who they are. Customers are not just numbers on a spreadsheet—they are the very reason for the existence of our business. By taking the time to understand them, we unlock the secrets to long-term success and forge genuine connections that fuel growth and loyalty. This starts with pinpointing our target segment: the specific group of people most likely to resonate with our brand and products.

Imagine your customers (a young professional checking emails on a bustling city street, a family huddled around a kitchen table planning their next vacation, a group of friends laughing over beers at a local bar). What are their passions and pursuits? What problems do they face? What makes them tick?

Next, we delve into their buying habits. Where do they get their information? How do they make decisions? What influences their choices? Understanding their path to purchase is crucial for crafting targeted marketing messages and optimizing the buying experience.

But it is not just about what they buy, it is why they buy. What motivates them to choose our product over the competition? Are they seeking convenience, value, status, or something else entirely? Tapping into these deeper desires allows us to connect with them on a more emotional level and build lasting relationships. Learn more about understanding buyer behavior in Chapters 6 and 7.

Focusing solely on our product can lead us down a tunnel of myopia, blind to the ever-evolving needs and wants of our customers. By prioritizing customer-centricity, we shift our gaze outward, constantly learning and adapting to stay relevant and responsive in a dynamic marketplace. For example, as technologies change, many products become obsolete as new ways to satisfy those needs become available. Businesses were disrupted because they lost sight that these customers really wanted a hole in the wall and not a better drill bit! Many such companies were holding on to the security blankets of the products or ways of doing things that once brought them success.[4] If Kodak had realized that digital photography had many advantages, instead of dismissing it in the 1990s as a niche trend, it would not have been caught flat-footed. Customers didn't want better film, but better ways to capture memories. Likewise, the likes of Nokia and Blackberry failed to recognize the ability of touchscreens to provide a more interactive experience, alienated consumers, and caused their own demise as a result.

These cautionary tales highlight the importance of staying agile and responsive to changing customer needs in today's fast-paced business environment. Companies that fail to adapt risk getting left behind. Remember, customer needs and preferences are

---

[4] Sull, D. (1999). Why good companies go bad. *Harvard Business Review*. July–August. https://hbr.org/1999/07/why-good-companies-go-bad.

dynamic, and businesses must constantly evolve to stay relevant and competitive. The inability to keep up can spell disaster, even for the most established players.

> "People don't want to buy a quarter-inch drill. They want a quarter-inch hole!"
> —Theodore Levitt, Harvard Business School

Our customers will not tell us explicitly what to produce or how to best connect with them. Even with the best intentions, they may lack the imagination or ability to do so. It is those companies that are most sensitive to their needs and interests that reap the biggest harvest when their innovations and marketing campaigns hit the sweet spot for customers. Staying ahead of consumer trends is crucial for any business to thrive in today's dynamic market. Here are some ways you can keep your finger on the pulse of what customers want:

Stay close to your customers

- **Direct feedback:** Conduct surveys, focus groups, and one-on-one interviews with your customers to get their direct feedback and understand their needs, wants, and frustrations.
- **Pay attention to where they spend their time:** Where customers choose to spend their time often reflects their interests, priorities, and values. Observing changes in how consumers engage with different platforms and activities can point to broader shifts in behavior. For example, with 60% of Millennials and Gen Z preferring to spend money on experiences over material goods, luxury brands started to pivot their strategies, offering engaging and personalized experiences.
- **Customer forums and communities:** Create or participate in online forums and communities where your target audience congregates. Tracking online forums, social media groups, and virtual platforms around specific topics can reveal nascent communities and potential areas of interest before they hit the mainstream.

This was how L'Oréal found that there was a trend for ombre hair coloring styles that were expensive for consumers to do at salons. This gave rise to the idea of creating a DIY Ombre hair dye for this unmet need.

- **Be sensitive to cultural differences:** Embrace the fact that Asia is diverse and different in the languages, religions, state of development, and technological advancement. This is further complicated by the rapid pace of change in consumer behavior driven by digitalization and rising affluence. Customer analysis in Asia requires a deep understanding of not just demographics but also psychographics, cultural values, and local trends. It is crucial to move beyond stereotypes and understand the underlying values and social contexts that drive consumer behavior in different regions. This allows for culturally sensitive marketing that resonates with specific audiences, leading to more effective and respectful engagement.
- **Partnerships with influencers:** Follow and/or collaborate with relevant influencers in your industry to tap into their audience and gain fresh perspectives on customer trends.

Focus on data

- **Analyze data about your customers:** This could be first- or third-party data. Utilize existing customer data from different sources, such as sales, surveys, and website interactions, to identify patterns and preferences. If you sell online, analyze website traffic, click-through rates, and purchase patterns to understand how customers navigate your site and what products they are interested in. Look for what products are selling well, what features are most used, and what feedback customers are giving. In case the world changes to be "cookieless", companies that start to collect first-party data from their customers will be well placed to deal with the change.
- **Leverage market research:** Utilize reports, studies, and insights from established market research firms or industry publications to understand broad trends and emerging demographics. If these do not provide you with the necessary answers, conduct your own research.

- **Social listening:** As of February 2025, 5.24 billion of 5.56 billion of internet users are social media users,[5] making social media the largest source of consumer insights and insights. Not only would there be a copious amount of information but social media is also a gateway to honest, non-incentivized, and unprompted consumer opinions. Monitor social media platforms, forums, and review sites to see what people are saying about your brand, your competitors, and industry trends in general.

Embrace technology

- **Trend forecasting tools:** Utilize tools like Google Trends and Trendhunter to gain insights into popular keywords, rising searches, and emerging topics.
- **Experiment with technology:** Explore emerging technologies like virtual reality (VR) and augmented reality (AR) to see how they might impact customer behavior and how you can potentially integrate them into your offerings.

Company analysis: Unveiling a company's true potential and weaknesses

Understanding a company goes beyond a simple tally of strengths and weaknesses. It is about peeling back the layers to reveal its full story.

A detailed analysis starts with financial health, scrutinizing profitability, liquidity, and efficiency ratios like an X-ray to reveal the company's financial pulse. But money isn't the only metric. Analyzing sources and timing of revenue streams paints a more vibrant picture—multiple revenue streams diffuse risk and build in cash flow resilience.

Market share and brand strength become the battle lines in the competitive landscape. Here, we size up the company's position against its rivals, gauging the effectiveness of its marketing strategies, sales, and distribution networks. These can be hidden weapons,

---

[5] Petrosyan, A. (2025). Internet and social media users in the world 2025. Statista. 1 April 2025.

turning weaknesses into unexpected strengths. A firm could be strong at specific areas, but these may not be sufficient to be labeled as competitive advantages. A core competency must provide a meaningful form of value to the customer and be difficult for competitors to imitate.

Leadership also plays a starring role. The experience and track record of the management team, along with the quality of its human capital, form the orchestra that conducts the company's symphony.

Finally, no analysis is complete without delving into the operational engine. Zoom in on production processes, supply chain mastery, and the technological infrastructure that fuels it all. Is R&D churning out innovation that keeps the company in the game? These operational gears grind out the company's real-world performance.

A comprehensive analysis is like a kaleidoscope, turning a single company into a mesmerizing spectrum of strengths, weaknesses, opportunities, and threats (SWOT). Only by understanding all facets can we truly see the company for what it is and, more importantly, what it can become.

Collaborator analysis: Finding allies to journey with

Beyond internal teams, a company's journey to success relies heavily on external partnerships that align with your strategic goals, maximize mutual benefits, and minimize potential risks. Collaborators are partners that the firm can leverage and borrow equity or glean shared resources from. A collaboration is about creating a synergistic partnership that leverages each brand's strengths to create something bigger and better than either could achieve alone.

Collaborators could include financing agents such as banks, investors, venture capital funds, and crowdfunding platforms such as Kickstarter or Indiegogo. Many ideas launched through Kickstarter have given birth to successful companies. Examples include the Oculus Rift, a VR headset company which was acquired by Facebook for $2 billion in 2014, and Exploding Kittens, a casual quirky card game firm which sought only $10,000 in crowdfunding but went on to exceed its fund targets in 10 minutes and eventually received

$8.8 million.[6] These financing platforms often help to not only provide financial resources but at times also provide validation of business ideas or networking resources.

Joint ventures with other companies serving the same target market can open new opportunities and leverage combined resources. Co-branding with complementary brands—bringing together two (or more) brands to create a unique product, service, or experience—can reap numerous benefits for both parties, exceeding what they could achieve alone. Combining both brands' followings broadens reach and exposes both brands to new customers. Partnering with a respected brand can elevate your own image and lend credibility for new positionings. For example, Supreme's collaborations with Louis Vuitton propelled their street style cred into the luxury realm, and vice versa. Such co-branded offerings often create excitement and foster customer engagement. They can also revitalize a brand. Collaboration can spark fresh ideas and lead to innovative products or experiences. Look at Nike's Air Jordan collaborations with musicians like Travis Scott, generating limited-edition hype and pushing design boundaries. Partnering with non-profits can enhance your social impact and attract environmentally conscious consumers.

Manufacturers, suppliers, and distributors/retailers play critical roles in ensuring smooth production, logistics, and access to customers. But in the early stages, when brand recognition is still fledgling, channel collaborators like major distributors can unlock crucial doors. Giant retailers like Best Buy or Target offer much more than just shelf space. They bring with them a well-established brand equity, a stamp of trustworthiness that acts as a magnet for curious customers and minimizes their perceived risk of trying a new brand. This invaluable validation becomes the bridge between an unknown product and a willing buyer, opening doors that might otherwise remain shut. So, when crafting your collaboration strategy, don't underestimate the power of channel partners. Embrace their established reputation and

---

[6] Feldman, A. (2016). Ten of the most successful companies built on Kickstarter. Forbes. 14 April 2016. https://www.forbes.com/sites/amyfeldman/2016/04/14/ten-of-the-most-successful-companies-built-on-kickstarter/.

leverage it to propel your brand into the spotlight, paving the way for sustainable growth and customer loyalty.

Technology providers such as software developers, cloud service providers, or data analytics companies can enhance your technological capabilities. For example, app developers helped firms like Apple scale and provide further customization of their products for users. Likewise, the embedding of the Google Maps application programming interfaces (APIs) within the Airbnb platform allowed for accurate directions, nearby attractions, and estimated travel times. This streamlined the booking process and increased transparency, tremendously improving the user experience. Partnering with the right technology provider can take your business to the next level.

In summary, it is important to consider the full ecosystem of your firm and its collaborators. The key to successful collaboration is finding partners who share your vision, complement your strengths, and help you achieve your goals. Conduct thorough research, assess potential synergies and shared vision, and negotiate clear terms to ensure a mutually beneficial partnership. Consider potential cultural differences and communication barriers that might arise. The right collaborators can be powerful allies in your business journey.

Competitor analysis: Competing with confidence

In the bustling marketplace, knowing your friends is not enough. To truly thrive, you need to understand your rivals. That's where competitor analysis comes in. It is the process of gathering and analyzing information about your direct and indirect competitors.

Competitor analysis is about gaining a comprehensive understanding of the competitive landscape you operate in to inform your own strategic decisions and drive sustainable growth. Understanding your competitors' capabilities highlights areas for improvement and potential differentiation. It is good practice to benchmark against them to track your progress and see how you are stacking up. This data-driven approach keeps you motivated and focused on continuous improvement.

By analyzing your competitors' past behavior and current initiatives, you may spot lucrative gaps in the market that your competitors have not filled. It can also help you anticipate their next steps and prepare your own counterstrategies. Staying one step ahead is key to maintaining your competitive edge.

When analyzing competitors, the definition of *who* constitutes the competition is important. It is not just about who sells the same product as you; it is about understanding who fulfils the same need for your target customers. For example, the competitors to a film camera firm like Kodak could include other film camera makers like Minolta or Polaroid, or digital camera firms like Sony or Nikon. But it could also include smartphone manufacturers such as Apple and GoPro who also provide advanced tools for on-the-go photography.

You may define your direct competition by looking at brands that offer identical or very similar products or services to yours. They directly compete for the same market share and customers. However, competition is not a battle over who makes the "best" widget. True competition lies deeper—in the hearts and minds of your customers. Imagine a gym. Its direct competitor might be other gyms, but its true rivals could be the local running club, pickleball classes, and even parks. All these options compete for the same user's time and attention, vying to fulfil their desire for a healthier lifestyle. Hence, a user-centric approach to competition is crucial.

By shifting our focus from products to people, we unlock a treasure trove of insights:

- **Broader landscape with strategic clarity:** It reveals all players fulfilling your customers' needs, not just those with identical products. Yet, comparing yourself to everyone and everything leads to confusion. A user-centric definition pinpoints your true rivals, allowing you to focus your resources and develop targeted strategies.

- **Hidden opportunities:** Unmet needs become potential battlegrounds. By listening to customers, you discover gaps in the market and opportunities to stand out with innovations that address their true desires.

- **Brand differentiation:** Understanding what resonates with customers helps you craft a unique brand identity that goes beyond product features and speaks directly to their needs and aspirations.

So, next time you think about competition, skip the product comparisons and ask yourself the bigger question: What are we competing for, and in whose eyes? Look at the vast landscape beyond your own offerings. Understand who offers value to your target audience, directly or indirectly, and why customers choose them. Regularly revisit your definition: As your business evolves and the market changes, so might your competition. Adapt your definition accordingly to maintain a clear competitive landscape.

Context analysis: Macro-environmental factors

Lastly, context analysis looks at macro-environmental factors, such as technology, demographic, sociocultural, political, legal, economic, and natural factors. The global is more connected than ever before, so it is critical to look beyond local context for this analysis. Geopolitical tensions could create challenges as well as new opportunities. Global cultural norms, mores, and trends could impact your markets and customers. Growing demands for sustainability could impact demand for your products. Technology shifts like the advancement of artificial intelligence (AI) could greatly impact your company, your competitors, and your industry. One needs to understand where the trends in the environment may lead; for example, a firm like Tesla would need to consider whether the market values carbon footprint and sustainability.

Context analysis is particularly vital in Asia, where political, economic, and sociocultural factors can significantly impact business operations and consumer sentiment. Beyond the ongoing trade tensions between the US and China, it is important for the marketer to understand the other potential tensions and due considerations between countries within Asia (e.g., between India and China).

Understanding the environment deeply would enable one to spot future opportunities and potential threats. Sometimes, the entire business model and value propositions need to be changed. Mediacorp is an example.

Case: The Shifting Sands: How Mediacorp Navigates the Digital Deluge[7]

The once-dominant landscape of television viewership has been undergoing a dramatic transformation. Gone are the days when families gathered around a single screen, united by the limited programming options national broadcasters offered. The digital age has ushered in an era of on-demand content, personalized viewing experiences, and fierce competition for eyeballs. The rise of digital media consumption has fragmented audiences and revolutionized how we watch and engage with content. National broadcasters, once the undisputed kings of the entertainment domain, face a critical challenge: how to adapt and stay relevant in this evolving ecosystem.

One of the most significant shifts is the rise of over-the-top (OTT) or streaming platforms, which deliver content directly to viewers through the internet, empowering viewers to choose what and when they watch, reshaping the landscape of television and film. This shift toward personalized viewing experiences erodes the traditional power of national broadcasters who dictate content and control time slots. The ability to watch content on demand, on any device, is no longer a luxury but an expectation. National broadcasters have had to acknowledge the changing viewing habits of audiences by creating their own streaming platforms.

Singapore's national media network, Mediacorp, responded to this trend in 2013 with Toggle. Its core objective was to make content accessible on digital devices, from computers and laptops to tablets, mobile phones, and even Smart TVs. This groundbreaking platform extended the viewing experience beyond the living room, allowing viewers to engage with their favorite shows and discover new content anytime, anywhere. It served as a complementary extension to Mediacorp's traditional TV broadcasting, offering viewers a chance to catch up on programs they might have missed or delve into exclusive online content.

---

[7] The authors gratefully acknowledge Oliver Chong (Head, Marketing and Communications) and Dawn Ong (Senior Brand Manager) for their invaluable insights and content contributions, which were instrumental in the development of this case study.

As OTTs continued to innovate and ramp up original content production, the challenge extended beyond simply replicating content. These high-quality, original shows and movies became a major draw, attracting new subscribers and establishing OTT platforms as serious competitors to traditional television. Additionally, technological advancements led to improved streaming quality, buffering became less frequent, and platforms began to prioritize user interface design, making navigation and content discovery more intuitive. OTT platforms like Netflix and Hulu soon became a global phenomenon. The market became increasingly saturated, with traditional media companies launching streaming services (Disney+ and HBO Max) to compete for viewers. This diversification led to a wider range of content options, catering to various demographics and interests. Cord-cutting, the phenomenon of canceling cable subscriptions in favor of OTT platforms, accelerated. This shift highlighted the growing consumer preference for on-demand content and the convenience of a single platform housing a vast library of shows and movies.

Mediacorp realized it was time to augment and rebrand Toggle—mewatch was born in 2020 as its successor. While Toggle offered a library of catch-up programs and exclusive online content, mewatch builds on this foundation by becoming the primary video destination, with content released in batches to cater to the binge-watching trend. It seamlessly provides audiences with Mediacorp's free, on-demand access to a rich variety of Made-in-Singapore original productions, including dramas, entertainment, news, live shows, and shorter-form content formats, catering to the on-the-go viewing habits of today's audiences. It also expanded its offerings with subscription-based content from prestigious partners such as HBO Go, Animax + GEM, and TVB Wow, thus broadening its appeal and cementing its role as a central hub for diverse and premium digital video content. This strategic expansion caters to a diverse audience with varying viewing preferences, ensuring there is something for everyone.

Beyond content variety, mewatch prioritizes user experience. The platform boasts a user-friendly interface that allows viewers to easily navigate the extensive library to discover content that piques their interest. Mediacorp also leverages the rich database of content consumption habits. Combining advanced analytics and such user behavior data, mewatch can recommend similar titles based on the content each viewer consumes. Such personalized recommendations not only enhance user experience by making it easier to discover new, relevant content but they also drive retention and loyalty. Additionally, mewatch offers features like high-definition streaming, multi-device compatibility, and offline viewing capabilities. These features cater to the modern viewers' desire for a seamless and convenient entertainment experience, ensuring they can watch their favorite shows anytime, anywhere. To provide convenience to its audiences, Mediacorp introduced meconnect, a single sign-on platform that offers subscribers one-stop access to all its content and services in the digital space.

Mediacorp understands that bringing value to its audience goes beyond developing a good product. It includes marketing mewatch to ensure the rebranded Toggle is widely recognized across all audience segments as the go-to destination for video content. To ensure a smooth transition and excite viewers about the enhanced features, Mediacorp implemented a multifaceted marketing campaign. Eye-catching visuals and catchy slogans emphasized the evolution from Toggle to mewatch, highlighting the wider content library, quality of local content, seamless integration of live TV, and multi-device accessibility. Engaging social media campaigns showcased snippets of popular shows and promoted original content available exclusively on mewatch. Strategic partnerships with local influencers further amplified the platform's reach, allowing them to leverage their established audiences to generate excitement and encourage viewers to explore mewatch's diverse offerings. Recognizing the importance of a strong online presence, Mediacorp also uses social media to foster fan communities and engage with viewers in real time. This allows Mediacorp to promote its shows, generate buzz, and build a more interactive relationship with its audience. This allows viewers to connect with shows and characters beyond the passive experience of simply watching. Additionally, strategic partnerships with telecommunication companies offer bundled subscriptions, making mewatch even more accessible to a wider audience.

The multifaceted marketing approach used by mewatch led to year-on-year growth in brand recall and usage, solidifying the platform as a dominant force in Singaporean entertainment.

The future of this entertainment industry remains dynamic. AI is poised to play a bigger role in recommending content based on viewing habits, mood, and even time of day. This could include personalized content curation, dynamic ad placements based on user data, and even interactive storytelling experiences. Imagine shows with branching narratives influenced by viewer choices, or live events with interactive elements that enhance audience participation. Streaming platforms could integrate cloud gaming services, allowing viewers to seamlessly switch between watching and playing games within the same platform. This caters to the growing popularity of online gaming and the convenience of a single entertainment hub. Additionally, partnerships and mergers between platforms might occur to navigate the increasingly crowded market. The possibilities are endless, but one thing is certain: OTT platforms have fundamentally changed how we consume entertainment, and their continued evolution promises to keep audiences engaged and reshape the media landscape for years to come.

Key lessons learned from Mediacorp

- Technological advancements are a double-edged sword for established industries. While they can bring innovation and efficiency, they can also be disruptive forces, fundamentally altering how businesses operate and consumers engage.
- To avoid losing market share and relevance in the eyes of their audience, national broadcasters must be vigilant in monitoring technological and environmental changes. This includes not just tracking advancements in streaming technology, but also staying abreast of broader consumer trends and the shifting sands of consumer behavior.
- A good product needs to be marketed effectively. Mediacorp's success with mewatch demonstrates the importance of using engaging campaigns, social media presence, and strategic partnerships to reach target audiences and build brand awareness.
- Change is constant. The media landscape is constantly evolving. National broadcasters, like Mediacorp with mewatch, need to be prepared to continuously adapt their offerings and strategies to

stay relevant in the face of ongoing changes in consumer behavior and technological advancements.

SWOT Analysis

Altogether, the 5Cs provide a basis for the firm to do a further SWOT analysis (Figure 2.3). Specifically, SWOT analysis identifies strengths, weaknesses, opportunities, and threats, and helps the firm identify key priorities to focus on. A firm must develop strategies to leverage its strengths and resources to capitalize on opportunities. At the same time, it should minimize threats by developing contingency plans and improving on its weaknesses with proactive solutions.

How to start analyzing? Sources of information for analysis

Marketing research provides the information for analysis. These sources of data could include internal records, secondary research, or primary research.

Internal records include customer data, sales figures, and website analytics—these internal goldmines reveal past performance and customer behavior, helping you understand what is working and what needs tweaking.

Secondary research, such as industry reports, academic publications, and online databases, offer existing data and analyses on

	Opportunities (external, positive)	**Threats** (external, negative)
Strengths (internal, positive)	**Strength-Opportunity strategies** Which of the company's strengths can be used to maximize the opportunities you identified?	**Strength-Threats strategies** How can you use the company's strengths to minimize the threats you identified?
Weaknesses (internal, negative)	**Weakness-Opportunity strategies** What action(s) can you take to minimize the company's weaknesses using the opportunities you identified?	**Weakness-Threats strategies** How can you minimize the company's weaknesses to avoid the threats you identified?

Figure 2.3. SWOT analysis.

your target audience, market trends, and competitor strategies. But remember, just like an old book, check for relevance, timeliness, and potential biases before relying on it.

Alternatively, consider running primary research, where you gather new information firsthand. Exploratory research methods like focus groups, in-depth interviews, and social media listening let you delve deeper into customer thoughts, feelings, and online behavior. Online communities are also information-rich—these groups typically constitute dedicated communities deeply vested in specific interest areas that may be relevant to your firm. These hidden forums buzzing with passionate conversations are ripe with insights. Conducting surveys or focus groups within these communities can provide invaluable perspectives on specific interests relevant to your brand.

Finally, firms could also potentially conduct experiments such as A/B testing or collaborate with academic institutions to unlock data and expertise for more complex research projects.

In the marketing research process, it is important to keep your business objectives in focus. It is easy to get lost in data overload. Define your research goals and tailor your efforts to answer specific questions that advance your strategy. Leverage existing research—use relevant secondary data or qualitative methods to provide exploratory research that can help you ask the right questions should you need to embark on your own investigation. Finally, test your hypotheses through surveys and gather necessary additional information needed to develop your marketing strategy. Ensure your samples are accurate and representative to avoid skewed results.

By navigating the data maze with these tips, you can transform marketing research from a daunting task into a powerful tool for driving informed decisions and achieving sustainable success.

Writing out the blueprint: The marketing plan

The marketing plan translates your strategy into actionable steps. It details the specific tactics and tasks you will execute to support your established strategy. Jumping straight into action without a strategy is like putting the cart before the horse—trying to build a house without a blueprint. It is a recipe for wasted resources and disappointing results.

The specific components of a marketing plan can vary depending on the size and complexity of your business, but the following are some key elements:

- **Executive summary:** A concise overview of the entire plan, highlighting its key points and strategies.
- **Situation analysis:** An assessment of your current market position, including your strengths, weaknesses, opportunities, and threats (SWOT analysis).
- **Target market definition:** A detailed description of your ideal customer, including their demographics, needs, wants, and buying behaviors.
- **Marketing goals and objectives:** Specific, measurable, achievable, relevant, and time-bound (SMART) goals that define what you want to achieve with your marketing efforts.
- **Marketing strategies and tactics:** The detailed actions you will take to reach your target audience and achieve your goals. This could include things like content marketing, social media marketing, email marketing, paid advertising, and promotional activities.
- **Budget and resources:** A breakdown of how you will allocate your financial and human resources to execute your marketing plan.
- **Evaluation and measurement:** A plan for tracking your progress and measuring the success of your marketing efforts. This might involve KPIs and metrics tailored to your specific goals.

The Control Process in Marketing: Steering the Ship

The marketing control process is the compass that guides a marketing strategy toward its intended destination. It involves monitoring and evaluating marketing activities to ensure they align with the overall strategy and deliver the desired results.

Regular monitoring and evaluation are essential for effective control. Once marketing objectives are defined, marketers can develop

KPIs (such as website traffic, social media engagement, sales figures, and customer feedback) to track progress. By comparing actual results against established benchmarks, marketers can identify gaps in performance and implement necessary adjustments. The marketing process model provides a comprehensive guide in evaluating the environment and firms' positions within it. Value is defined from the customers' perspective, and the environment should be analyzed in a manner to identify how the company can work with collaborators to best operate in its context to deliver better value to customers than its competitors. With a robust marketing plan as your blueprint and a clear process to guide you, marketers can finally answer the following question: "Where do I spend my money?" More importantly, they can measure if those resources are building a stronger, more successful brand.

Key Takeaways

- Analysis underscores the marketing process, which constitutes planning, implementation, and control.
- Marketing goals must support business objectives.
- The 5Cs form a useful framework for ensuring that you do not have any blind spots in your environmental scanning. These constitute customer analysis, company analysis, collaborator analysis, competitor analysis, and context analysis.
- It is important to consider what sources of data are used for analysis. Are they relevant to your purposes? Is there any bias?
- The insights from the 5Cs analysis should be integrated with a SWOT analysis to help identify key priorities for the firm.
- A marketing plan details specific tactics and tasks you will execute to support your established strategy.

Chapter

3

Segmentation and Targeting

Recall that the first strategic decision a firm needs to make is to answer the question: "Who should our customers be?". In this chapter, we expand on this question and discuss how best to conduct segmentation and targeting. By the end of this chapter, you should have a firm understanding of target marketing, why it is important, and how to form and choose target segments.

Finding Your Perfect Fit: Why Target Marketing Matters

Have you ever wondered why some brands seem to speak directly to you while others feel like they are shouting into the void? The answer lies in the power of target marketing, a powerful strategy that recognizes customers are not one-size-fits-all and caters to their unique needs and desires.

Before we dive into how to do it right, let's explore why focusing on specific customer groups is crucial for success.

Think of it like shopping for clothes. Would you buy a one-size-fits-all suit? Probably not. The same applies to marketing. Customers are diverse, with unique needs and desires. A generic approach leaves everyone feeling a little ill-fitting. If we recognize and accept that customers are not homogeneous and can be better served differently, segmenting a market into groups so that we market to them differently makes sense.

The next question some may ask is "Why must we choose our customers? Why can't we sell to whoever wants to buy from us?"

Value creation

You cannot add value without knowing who you are adding it for. Imagine designing a product without considering your target customer. You will be stuck chasing after them spending resources on advertisements and promotions, or sales reps cold calling and deflecting buyer hesitation, hoping they will like what you have made. With proper targeting, you can focus your research and development on what your ideal customer truly needs, ensuring they become loyal fans, boosting your bottom line without chasing cold leads.

Playing to your strengths

Companies, just like people, have their own talents and limitations. Targeting allows you to leverage your strengths. By focusing on a customer segment that aligns with your capabilities, you increase your chances of checkmating the competition.

Long-term vision

Who you serve today shapes who you can serve tomorrow. Think about a budget airline. Its focus on affordability builds cost-cutting expertise but might limit its ability to invest in innovation or luxury experiences. It is important to think of the long-term company mission and goals. Choosing your target segment sets you on a specific path, so pick wisely and commit to the journey.

Remember, a brand that tries to be everything to everyone is a recipe for mediocrity. Multiple targets can work, but each needs its own tailored approach.

Next, let's look at various market coverage strategies.

Market Coverage Strategies

Here, we go deeper to introduce five possible market coverage approaches, starting with mass marketing on one end to customization at the other end of the spectrum (Figure 3.1).

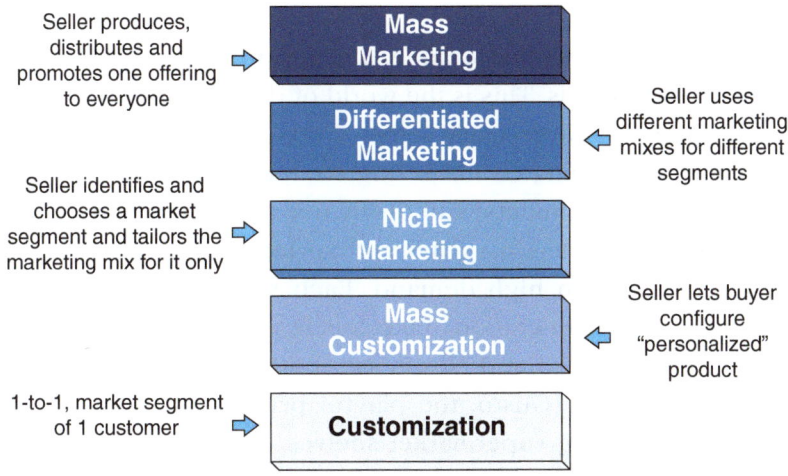

Figure 3.1. Market coverage strategies.

Mass marketing: Big volume, big risks

The mass marketing strategy assumes that the market is homogenous. It is all about volume, churning out one generic offering and blasting it through every channel possible. The advantage of this approach is volume and economies of scale.

While a first-mover might get away with mass marketing in a nascent market, it is often a temporary advantage. As the market evolves, the pressure to segment and personalize becomes irresistible. For example, Mastercard and American Express started with one card in the 1950s. Now, the credit card industry boasts a dizzying array of options catering to every travel habit, spending style, and reward preference. Even toilet paper brands have embraced differentiation, acknowledging that comfort and texture are not one-size-fits-all affairs.

Differentiated marketing: When one size does not fit all

Notice how watch stores are bursting with options? Sporty chronographs for the adrenaline junkie, glittering diamonds for the fashionista, and timeless classics for the heritage enthusiast. Each customer seeks something unique, a value proposition that speaks directly to their needs. This is the world of differentiated marketing, where a single brand stretches across diverse segments with distinct offerings. A differentiated marketing strategy would suit a market that has multiple segments with distinctive needs and preferences.

Differentiation has its gears and springs. Resources, the fuel of marketing, are in high demand. Each segment needs its own forecast, plan, and operation. Take Nestle's coffee kingdom—from Nescafe's Dolce Gusto and Nespresso. Both are capsule-based yet worlds apart. Dolce Gusto, the playful prince, offers variety and affordability, gracing supermarket shelves. Meanwhile, Nespresso, the sophisticated emperor, reigns in dedicated boutiques, catering to coffee connoisseurs.

Here's the rub: This intricate dance can bring two challenges. First, beware of product line overlap. Dolce Gusto and Nespresso can't step on each other's toes—cannibalization, where products steal sales from one another, is a marketing monster. Second, brand images need laser focus to avoid customer confusion. If Nike emblazons its swoosh on both a diamond-encrusted watch and a rugged fitness tracker, the message muddies. But Nike is a masterclass in balancing differentiation and brand image. Nike maintains a premium image across all product lines. This is achieved through high-quality materials, innovative technology, and effective storytelling that reinforces the brand's association with performance, innovation, and inspiration. These core values permeate all sub-brands and products, even if the aesthetics and target audiences differ. This creates a unifying thread that binds everything together under the Nike banner. Nike minimizes cannibalization by clearly positioning each product and avoiding direct overlap in features and target segments. For example, Nike Alphafly running shoes target serious marathoners, while Free Trainers appeal to casual gym-goers. Also, Nike doesn't just slap its swoosh on everything. It uses different brands (within the same company), such as Converse and Jordan (branding strategies are explained in Chapter 5), to avoid dilution to the core Nike brand while offering options for diverse tastes within the athletic umbrella.

As evidenced, if mastered well, differentiated marketing is a symphony of success—the best of both worlds of volume and profit margins. But before you embark on this strategy, weigh the resources needed against the potential rewards. Can you craft product lines that resonate with distinct segments, ensure smooth operation, and keep your brand image crystal clear? If so, the differentiated marketing stage awaits, ready for your bold performance.

Niche power: The allure and limits of focused marketing

Some brands take a laser-focused approach, zeroing in on a single segment of the market and leaving the rest behind. This niche coverage strategy might seem limiting, but it possesses some advantages. It allows the brand to deep dive into one customer segment, intimately understanding their needs and crafting products that resonate with them. This allows the brand to specialize and become the ultimate authority in its chosen domain. Narrowly focused brands enjoy a distinct and readily identifiable position in the market. This simplifies marketing efforts and is easier on the pockets for companies with more limited resources. Furthermore, as the go-to expert in their niche, these brands can often command a price premium.

However, venturing into niche markets is not without its challenges. While starting in a niche can be a smart launchpad, scaling up into broader markets can be tricky. The product or service that excites passionate early adopters might not hold the same appeal for mainstream audiences. Crossing the "adoption gap" requires understanding if the core values resonate with wider demographics. While audiophiles prioritize every tweak that elevates their listening experience, even to the point of using gold cables, for most music lovers, basic fidelity often takes precedence.

Extending your appeal from one segment to another requires a high "coefficient of imitation," which accounts for the "word of mouth" or "social contagion" effects. While innovators and early adopters are initially drawn to new ideas, it is the coefficient of imitation that drives widespread adoption among the "majority" and "late majority" segments. Some customers have a higher ability to influence others into imitating them, hence focusing on influential individuals and communities can maximize the impact of word-of-mouth communication. Take a leaf out of Apple's masterclass book of targeting the young and hip to attract the masses. Early Apple products were often ahead of their time, creating a sense of exclusivity and innovation that appealed to early adopters and trendsetters. Ads focused on emotion and experience rather than technical specifications, creating a lifestyle around Apple products that young people aspired to "Think Different." Their products were statement pieces with minimalist design, premium materials, and user-friendly interfaces, helping Apple cultivate a sleek, desirable image. Apple focused on fostering a loyal community of users who evangelized the brand. This organic buzz amplified their reach and solidified their reputation among the young and hip. Once established with the young and hip, Apple's cool factor began to trickle down to a broader audience. Apple stores were designed to be more than just places to buy products. They were interactive, visually appealing spaces that offered a unique customer experience, further solidifying the brand's cool factor. Their products became a status symbol, desirable not just for their functionality but also for the social cachet they carried. By emphasizing design, innovation, and community, they established themselves as a desirable brand and secured a loyal following. Of course, navigating the demands of a growing and diversifying customer base presents ongoing challenges for the company.

While a niche coverage strategy helps a brand stay true to its identity, when expansion possibilities exist, niche brands also face the temptation to stray from their core identity. Brands such as Ferrari, long synonymous with high-performance sports cars, carefully considered diluting their image by entering the SUV market. Ultimately, the Italian "prancing horse" decided to introduce the Purosangue in September 2022,[1] 20 years after Porsche's successful SUV pivot. This highlights the difficulty of the trade-off between growth and brand integrity.

---

[1] Korn, M. (2023). The secret to a successful sports car company? Build more SUVs. *ABC News*. Accessed on 14 June 2023. https://abcnews.go.com/Business/secret-successful-sports-car-company-build-suvs/story?id=100428714.

Mass customization: Tailoring for the masses

In today's customer-centric world, personalization reigns supreme. Just look at a survey of 1,000 people aged 18–64: a whopping 90% craved custom experiences.[2] Enter mass customization, a strategy where brands flex their innovation muscle by offering personalized products or services at scale, without the exorbitant price tag of bespoke options.

Think of it as a buffet of choices. Customers pick and choose from a carefully curated menu of options, crafting a bespoke product that whispers "me, myself, and I." Sneakers that match your vibe and jackets that sing your style. This personalized touch fosters a sense of ownership and emotional connection, leading to higher satisfaction and brand loyalty. Bonus points for exclusivity, which allows brands to command premium prices.

Mass customization requires careful preparation. Implementing complex customization platforms and managing diverse production processes can be a costly feat. Ensuring quality control, timely delivery, and efficient workflows demands meticulous planning and coordination. Imagine balancing pre-made components with on-demand requests—inventory management becomes a delicate dance, juggling the risk of stockouts and overproduction.

Now, let's savor a real-world example: Nike by You. This platform lets customers customize their Nike shoes and apparel (Figure 3.2), from material and color choices to personalized designs. Imagine choosing textures for your kicks, picking a vibrant sole, and even adding your own artwork—it's a canvas for creativity. This service extends beyond online platforms. Nike retail stores like those in Seoul and Singapore offer in-store customization, letting shoppers add personal touches to clothing, hats, and totes.

Muji and Xiaomi are just two Asian brands proving mass customization is not just for Western giants. Muji, a champion of Japanese

---

[2] Epsilon. (2018). New Epsilon research indicates 80% of consumers are more likely to make a purchase when brands offer personalized experiences. Epsilon. 9 January 2018. Accessed on 27 December 2023. https://www.epsilon.com/us/about-us/pressroom/new-epsilon-research-indicates-80-of-consumers-are-more-likely-to-make-a-purchase-when-brands-offer-personalized-experiences.

Figure 3.2. Personalized design of a Nike Dunk Low shoe.[3]

minimalism, allows furniture enthusiasts to personalize their pieces with wood finishes, handles, and configurations, fostering self-expression within the brand's signature aesthetic. Similarly, Chinese smartphone giant Xiaomi's Mi Mix range caters to the region's tech-savvy consumers by offering customizable back panels, engravings, and themes, enabling them to create phones that reflect their unique personalities.

Mass customization is a potent tool for brands to build deeper customer connections and stand out in the crowded marketplace, if the operational complexities and customer expectations are managed well.

Customization: Crafting uniqueness at a cost

Unlike mass customization, which caters to segments with pre-defined options, pure customization crafts bespoke products or services for each individual customer. This approach comes with a hefty price tag, making it ideal for situations where the need for a perfectly tailored

---

[3] Nike. (n.d.). Nike Dunk Low Unlocked By You [Product page]. Nike Singapore. https://www.nike.com/sg/u/custom-dunk-low-unlocked-by-you-10001549/1688452995834#Builder.

product outweighs cost concerns. Think of a bride dreaming of a one-of-a-kind wedding gown, meticulously designed, and crafted to her specifications.

But customization is not for everyone. It is a resource-intensive strategy, demanding specialized skills, meticulous attention to detail, and often, longer production times. Fortunately, there is a growing toolbox of innovative technologies today that can democratize customization of products and services, and more so, the customer experience. For example, 3D printing and digital fabrication fuel personalization by allowing companies to produce unique items based on individual preferences. Phone cases can be personalized with your pet's face on them, or a water bottle perfectly contoured to your hand grip. The possibilities are endless! AI-powered chatbots or virtual assistants can guide customers through the customization process, offering suggestions and recommendations based on their needs and budget. With big data and AI machine learning (ML) that analyze our browsing history, purchase patterns, and even social media activity to reveal hidden patterns and preferences, brands can offer bespoke products that precisely suit customers' present or even future tastes and needs. Think of a travel app recommending hidden gems in a city based on your interests and past vacation experiences.

For businesses that master this art, the rewards are substantial. The intense collaboration and personalized service build strong, loyalty-forged relationships with customers. These businesses stand out by the unique value propositions they create with each individual client.

In essence, choosing the right market coverage strategy boils down to understanding your resources and objectives.

Segmentation: How to Form and Identify Target Segments

Having explored the different ways businesses can approach the market from niche specialization to mass market domination, we now turn our attention to a crucial next step: segmentation.

Segmentation is the art of slicing the market into groups where individuals share similar needs and preferences yet differ distinctly from other groups. By focusing on segments with internal homogeneity, we gain the power to fine-tune our offerings and messaging. This laser-sharp focus leads to customized products that perfectly fit the segment's specific needs, tailored messages that strike a chord, and an overall experience that feels like it was designed just for them. This is the true beauty of segmentation—it allows us to move beyond cookie-cutter solutions.

The following four "segmentation bases" are often described as the criteria for grouping customers: demographic (or firmographic for business-to-business (B2B) companies), geographic, psychographic, and behavioural segmentation. This may lead many to think that one should divide the market into groups by country, age, gender, etc. Such interpretations of segmentation should be treated with caution.

Instead of focusing solely on grouping customers by easily observable characteristics such as age, gender, or location, effective market segmentation delves deeper into understanding the underlying motivations and needs that drive their choices. While demographics and geography can be helpful starting points, they only truly hold weight when they correlate with distinct benefit preferences among different customer groups.

Here is an example: Imagine a seemingly simple product like toilet paper. While we might initially think of segmenting by demographics or geography, a closer look reveals diverse motivations. Some prioritize softness, others thickness, while some might choose based on eco-friendly materials or fair-trade practices. While certain demographics might correlate with specific preferences, for example, some women might prefer printed designs, it is crucial to remember that not women share the same needs. In contrast, when male customers have different needs from females (e.g., Clear Shampoo targets men because male scalps produce more sebum and more prone to dandruff[4]), gender is the right segmentation variable to use.

This is where profiling variables come in. They help us paint a picture of a typical customer within a segment, but they should not

---

[4] CLEAR Men Collection. Accessed on 14 June 2023. https://www.clearhaircare.com/sg/men.html.

be mistaken for definitive rules. For instance, high-income earners might be more likely to buy multi-ply rolls, but not all will do so.

In summary, first understand the benefits that customers seek. Segment the market based on the differences in the benefits they seek, or why they buy your products. Often, multiple segmentation bases are used.

Unveiling your customers: The power of buyer personas

Once you have identified your segments, the next step is to create a buyer persona. Think of it as a detailed portrait of your ideal customer within that segment, capturing their motivations, desires, and behaviors. This fictional archetypal description becomes a powerful tool for understanding your target audience and tailoring your marketing and sales efforts to their specific needs.

Take speed-seeking sportscar drivers as an example. Statista tells us they tend to have high incomes, value achievement, and recall seeing ads in video games more vividly. A whopping 24% are early adopters, eager for the latest and greatest.[5] This rich profile guides your marketing decisions: what language resonates, where to reach them, and even who to choose as an influencer.

This is the magic of buyer personas. By having a good understanding of your ideal customer, you can craft marketing messages that truly connect, personalize your sales approach, and ultimately drive business success.

So, how do you build these personas? You gather insights from market research, customer interviews, and data analysis. Then, you weave these threads together to create a profile that *typically* encompasses:

- **Demographics:** Age, income, location, profession, etc.
- **Psychographics:** Values, interests, lifestyle, personality traits, opinions, etc.

---

[5] Statista. (2023). Target audience: Sports car owners in the United States. Statista Consumer Insights Report. September 2023. https://www.statista.com/study/123214/target-audience-sports-car-owners-in-the-united-states/.

- **Behaviors:** Shopping habits, media consumption, brand choices, purchase timing, etc.
- **Motivations and aspirations:** What problems they are trying to solve, what they want to achieve and why, and how your product can help.
- **Barriers and frustrations:** What their frustrations and worries are and what stops them from achieving their goals.

The purpose of a buyer persona is to boost the effectiveness of our marketing efforts. To truly harness this power, we need to delve into the drivers and influencers of buying decisions within each segment. This understanding guides us in selecting the right information to include in our personas. In turn, these personas help guide our marketing efforts.

To illustrate, research on hypertensive patients revealed distinct segments with varying adherence to medication regimens, not based on typical demographic or socioeconomic factors, but rather on their psychological and behavioral profiles. These segments, such as the "Skeptical," "Proactive," and "Confused," were defined by their attitudes towards medication, trust in physicians, perceived control over their health, and willingness to adopt lifestyle changes. For instance, the "Proactive" segment demonstrated high adherence, driven by their belief in medication's importance and a strong doctor-patient relationship, while the "Skeptical" segment exhibited low adherence due to mistrust and negative perceptions of long-term health risks of medication. For the "Proactive" segment, reinforcement of their positive beliefs and relying on doctors to manage them would be effective. On the other hand, understanding the "Skeptical" patient's mistrust calls for campaigns emphasizing medication safety and addressing long-term risk concerns. This approach highlighted that understanding patient beliefs allows for the development of strategies that address the root causes of non-adherence.

B2B brands can also profile their customer segments. While B2B personas often draw on firmographics such as company size and industry, they should not stop there. To truly ignite your marketing efforts, delve deeper into the buying process itself. This means understanding the human decision-makers behind the company logo, such as the motivations and challenges that drive decisions within a company. This includes the following:

- **KPIs of decision-makers:** What metrics drive their success? Aligning your offerings with their priorities is key.
- **Buying cycle length:** Do they make quick decisions or require extensive research? Understanding these timeframes and pressures allows you to tailor content and outreach accordingly.
- **Openness to change:** Are they early adopters or risk-averse? Do they crave cutting-edge solutions or prioritize stability? Matching their innovation appetites builds trust.
- **Decision-making structure:** Is the power centralized with one key decision-maker, or spread across a committee? Knowing who influences the purchase allows you to target the right stakeholders.
- **Data-driven vs. intuition:** Does this team rely on cold, hard data to make decisions, or do gut feelings play a role? Aligning your communication style and evidence with their preferences builds trust and credibility.

By going beyond firmographics and embracing the nuanced realities of B2B decision-making, your buyer personas become powerful tools for crafting targeted messages, fostering deeper connections, and ultimately, closing more deals.

A priori vs. post hoc segmentation: Two paths to understanding your market

So far, we talked about segmentation for the purpose of identifying a target market. But there are many other uses for segmentation. As long as you want to understand different groups in your customer base, segmentation can be used since its basic premise is to form meaningful homogeneous subgroups.

Your purpose for wanting to segment will determine that "certain variable" to form these meaningful segments. Let's dive in and understand the two different paths to segmenting:

A priori

There are times when this variable is pre-determined, hence known as *a priori* segmentation. For instance, you want to know the differences between your top spending customers and those who spend very little. In such a case, your segments are categorized by amounts spent. You may also be curious about your loyal customers and want to compare them with defectors. Then, loyalty is the segmentation variable. Likewise, you can analyze the different behaviors by the frequency or duration of website visits. You can even segment your customer base by the nature of their complaints to determine what are their priorities.

A priori segmentation is faster and simpler, without the need for complex data analysis. It can be effective for well-understood markets with readily available data, or if you know who to reach with your marketing efforts from the outset. Recognize, however, that the pre-determined variables are based on a set of assumptions. Those assumptions may not capture the full picture of customer needs and motivations. It can be limiting and might miss out on unexpected relationships between variables. You might overlook valuable segments that do not fit neatly into your pre-defined categories.

Post hoc

There may be times when the variable is not pre-determined. You analyze a large set of data and use statistical analysis to identify groups of customers with similar characteristics, without imposing any pre-defined criteria. For example, you want to discover possible segments of customers for a product category, say fashion. We could use data from surveys and transaction records and statistically classify respondents into relatively homogeneous clusters that are distinct from one another. By analyzing different responses to carefully crafted survey questions, we can identify that the fashion market is made up of trend chasers, comfort seekers, brand name conscious, etc., for example.

If you have access to good-quality data and want an in-depth understanding of your customers, this approach can reveal hidden segments and insights you might not have anticipated. It can lead to more granular and nuanced understanding of your customer base. However, it requires complex data analysis and interpreting data patterns. Defining segments can be challenging. You may not always find clear-cut segments, leading to confusion.

Hybrid approach

Sometimes, combining both methods can be beneficial. You can start with *a priori* segmentation to set a general direction and then use *post hoc* analysis to refine your segments and discover hidden insights.

Targeting: Finding the Perfect Fit in Segment Selection

Now that we have divided our market into segments, it is time to decide on which one(s) to pursue. It is a strategic decision that requires a keen eye for potential through careful consideration of several factors to ensure maximum impact and efficiency.

Choosing your target segment can feel like navigating a treasure map—glittering possibilities lie ahead, but treacherous competition lurks too. While segment size and growth potential are certainly crucial, large, fast-growing segments are often warzones. Fierce competition from established players with deep pockets can quickly drown out your voice. Analyze your competitors' resources, brand strength, and marketing strategies. Can you outmaneuver them and stand out from the crowd? Focus on segments where you can shine. Do you have a unique value proposition that resonates with that segment? Assess your own arsenal: Do you have the budget, marketing team expertise, and channels to effectively reach and engage your chosen segment? Consider if this opportunity would lead you astray from your ultimate long-term goal.

Strategy is about finding the sweet spot. The ideal segment is one where your resources, capabilities, and brand values align perfectly with the segment's needs, characteristics, and competitive landscape.

One-to-one targeting: Tailoring the engagement for each customer

The age of generic marketing is over. Around 65% of today's customers expect companies to adapt to their changing needs and preferences.[6] As such, businesses are embracing a more nuanced approach: one-to-one targeting. This concept focuses on tailoring messages, offers, and experiences to the individual needs and preferences of each customer. No more generic emails—instead your customer receives a personalized message that addresses their specific needs and preferences, or a birthday offer for their favorite restaurant.

Customers will no longer feel like just a number. They will experience a tailored journey from product recommendations to customer service that feels uniquely designed for them. Feeling like a brand understands and caters to your specific needs fosters engagement, boosts conversions, and builds trust and brand loyalty. The numbers speak for themselves: Around 60% of customers will likely buy again after a personalized shopping experience, while 45% are likely to take their business elsewhere if they do not receive one.[7]

One-to-one targeting requires a blend of technology, data, and strategic thinking. First, you need to build a customer data platform. Gather data from various sources, such as customer relationship management (CRM) systems, website interactions, email campaigns, and social media, and even purchase records from partner stores. Publicly available demographic and psychographic data can add extra layers of insight. Ensure that the data is accurate and consistent across platforms. Next, the data needs to be analyzed to identify patterns and trends to reveal preferences and purchase triggers to build an

---

[6] Salesforce Research. (2023, September 9). *State of the Connected Customer* (6th ed.). Salesforce.

[7] Twilio Segment. (2021). *The State of Personalization 2021*. Twilio. https://segment.com/state-of-personalization-report-2021/.

accurate and comprehensive view of our customers. ML algorithms and statistical models can be used. Prescriptive analytics or next-best-action (NBA) models can then identify customer segments and predict their future actions. They can then recommend the optimal move to influence customer behavior to achieve your desired outcomes, whether it is purchases, sign-ups, or other forms of brand engagement. NBA models can prescribe the content and messaging relevant to the customer's segment, buyer persona, industry, and stage in the sales process. Imagine dynamic website and app content based on browsing history, personalized messages, or real-time offers triggered by customer actions.

Besides robust data analytics and marketing automation (MA) tools, implementing one-to-one targeting requires careful consideration of data privacy issues. A thin line exists between personalization and creepiness. People expect full transparency, control, and choice over how their data is shared and used by companies. They will only respond well to personalized communication using the information they have consented to share. Businesses need to show customers that they are worthy of their trust. Not only will customers not do businesses they do not trust,[8] but personalization goes out of the window if they do not trust you enough to give you access to their data. L'Oréal Chief Digital Officer, Lubomira Rochet, could not have said it better: "…consumer trust is the number one currency for brands."[9] More than just compliance with regulations, companies should have "data ethics" that guide ethical and responsible collection and use of customer data.[10] Transparency and clear data management policies are essential.

---

[8] Rama, R. (2020). Brand strategies focused on dependability score highest on customer trust. Gartner. 1 December 2020. Accessed on 4 January 2024. https://www.gartner.com/en/marketing/insights/articles/brand-strategies-focused-dependability-score-highest.

[9] AdNews. (2010). WFA: The world's first guide on data ethics for brands. 1 June 2020. Accessed on 4 January 2024. https://www.adnews.com.au/news/wfa-the-world-s-first-guide-on-data-ethics-for-brands.

[10] Dulberg, R. (2021). Why the world's biggest brands care about privacy. UX Collective. 14 September 2021. Accessed on 4 January 2024. https://uxdesign.cc/who-cares-about-privacy-ed6d832156dd.

Understanding Market Size: Unveiling the Demand Puzzle

In the world of business and marketing, understanding the potential size of your market is crucial. That's where concepts such as Total Available Market (TAM), Serviceable Addressable Market (SAM), and Serviceable Obtainable Market (SOM) come in (Figure 3.3).

TAM is the entire, theoretical market for your product or service, without any limitations. It encompasses everyone who could possibly be interested in what you offer, regardless of whether they can access it, afford it, or even know about it. TAM is often a theoretical number based on macro-level data, such as industry reports, market research, and government statistics. Firms should finetune this market potential by correcting for market movements, for instance, TAM is likely to be lower for luxury goods and cars during recessions. Knowing the TAM helps estimate the potential for growth.

SAM is a subset of TAM, focusing on the segment of the market that you can actually reach and serve. This might involve factors such as geographical limitations, legal restrictions, customer needs, or technological compatibility. For example, if you sell software products, your SAM might include only countries where you have legal distribution rights and where internet access is widespread.

SOM is the most actionable of the three, representing the portion of SAM that you can realistically capture. Your company's SOM is

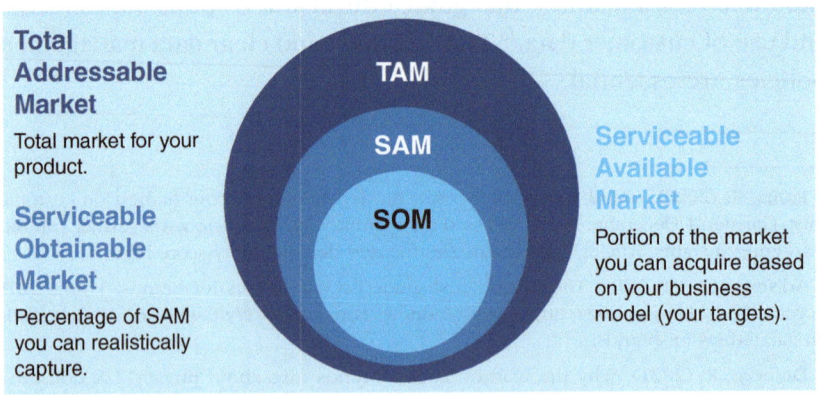

Figure 3.3. TAM, SOM, and SAM.

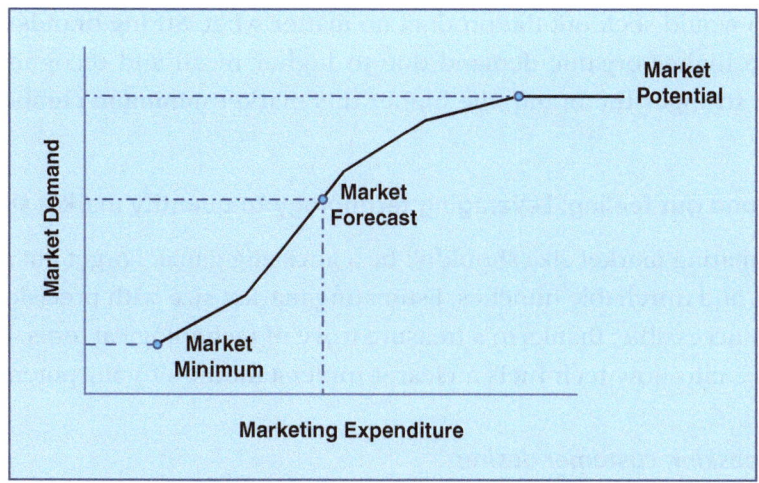

Figure 3.4. Market minimum, forecast, and potential.

essentially the portion of the market which you believe is likely to choose your brand over your competitors'. The competitive landscape within the SAM and your own capabilities (such as marketing resources and execution) determine your SOM.

Figure 3.4 gives us another lens to understand market size, through the market demand function. This function predicts the volume of purchases a specific customer group within a defined geographical area and time frame would make under specific marketing efforts and a particular marketing environment (including competitor activity).

As the market approaches saturation, it will be harder to increase demand. Imagine a scenario where most interested buyers already own your product. To attract the remaining potential customers, you need to invest more to convince them to switch from competitors or reconsider their non-purchase decision. This phenomenon is often seen in mature markets. Eventually, even aggressive marketing efforts won't increase demand when the full market potential is reached.

But there is another side to the coin. Even without marketing magic, there is still a minimum level of demand, like a baseline. This comes from things such as eye-catching packaging, convenient distribution, or even brand loyalty built over time. Think of the loyal fans who would seek out the product no matter what. Strong brands also have higher organic demand due to higher recall and recognition. The stronger the brand, the higher this market minimum climbs.

Beyond gut feeling: Leveraging technology to quantify market size

Estimating market size shouldn't be a guessing game. Forget gut feelings and unreliable hunches. Estimating market size with precision is now accessible, thanks to a treasure trove of technological tools. Let's delve into how tech fuels a clearer understanding of your potential:

Unmasking customer desires

Data scraping tools: The web is a treasure trove of data, waiting to be unearthed. Data scraping tools such as Scrapy and Apify can extract valuable insights from websites, such as competitor pricing, customer reviews, or even news mentions. These data fuel market research, price comparison, and even content aggregation, giving you a deeper understanding of your landscape.

Online surveys: Understanding customer needs, preferences, and willingness to pay provide insights into potential market size and penetration. You can poll your target customers directly. Tools such as SurveyMonkey and Qualtrics simplify creating and distributing surveys, providing insights into needs, preferences, and even willingness to pay.

Social listening tools: Listen to the online chatter. Brandwatch and Sprout Social scan social media, blogs, and forums, revealing customer sentiment toward your brand or competitors. Learn what customers ask about your category and discover untapped opportunities.

Competitive intelligence tools: What your customers feel about the competition affects your market share and reveals untapped opportunities. Tools such as SEMrush help you uncover relevant keywords your target audience searches for, along with their search volume, competition, and potential value.

Mapping your market canvas

Geographical information systems (GIS): Fine-tune your market focus. ArcGIS and similar tools paint the picture with interactive maps overlaid with data layers. Visualize population density, track trends, and pinpoint areas with the highest concentration of your ideal customers. With such insights, you can prioritize marketing efforts and determine optimal locations for your offerings.

Transforming data into knowledge

Data visualization tools: See the story hidden within your data. Software such as Tableau and Power BI transforms raw data into digestible dashboards and charts, revealing patterns in demographics, purchase behaviors, social media engagement, etc. to help you gauge potential demand.

Glimpsing the future

Predictive analytics tools: Predict what's next. Amazon Forecast and Microsoft Azure ML are powerful platforms that harness the magic of ML to accurately predict time-series data, such as product demand, website traffic, or seasonal fluctuations, to forecast future trends and demand. In the fast-paced world of business, predicting what is coming around the corner can be your secret weapon.

By leveraging these tools, you can gain a more accurate and comprehensive understanding of your market potential, paving the way for informed business decisions and sustainable growth. However, tech tools are not magic bullets. A few caveats. Data quality is crucial: garbage in, garbage out! Ensure your data is clean, consistent, and relevant for accurate predictions. Second, technology empowers, but it does not replace human judgment. Use these tools to fuel your analysis, but remember, your domain expertise and industry knowledge are invaluable for interpreting data and translating them into actionable strategies.

Case: Rebooting beauty—Skin Inc's personalized journey to success[11]

Skin Inc.'s journey is a fascinating tale of innovation, adaptation, and unwavering dedication to personalized skincare, which has helped it remain relevant by understanding customer needs. Founded in 2008 by Sabrina Tan, a tech veteran with a passion for beauty, Skin Inc. was launched as the world's first "Skin Supplement Bar," offering customized serum cocktails based on individual skin analyses and concerns.

One of the reasons for Skin Inc.'s success was Tan's eye for identifying an unserved demand. With her passion for beauty, and troubled by her own sensitive and eczema-prone skin, she knew too well that busy professional women wanted convenient solutions designed uniquely for their skincare regimes beyond one-size-fits-all products. They had no time for trial and error in search of a skincare routine that fits their constantly evolving needs. Driven by the frustration of limited skincare options, she addressed the demand for personalized solutions. Tan ensured that Skin Inc's personalized serums used high-quality ingredients and leveraged cutting-edge technologies like encapsulation and microfluidics, ensuring stability and efficacy. Their unique concept and early adoption of technology created a buzz and attracted customer curiosity.

While Skin Inc.'s innovative concept of personalized serums was revolutionary, standing out from the crowd amidst established giants in the beauty industry was no small feat. Personalized serums can be perceived as expensive compared to mass-market products. Skin Inc. needed to communicate the value proposition of tailored solutions and justify the cost. Also, accustomed to pre-made products with established brands, some customers were hesitant to trust a "DIY" approach to skincare. Building trust and demonstrating the effectiveness of personalized solutions was crucial.

Skin Inc. embarked on a multi-pronged approach to overcome these challenges. To back up its claims of efficacy, its products go

---

[11] The authors gratefully acknowledge Sabrina Tan (CEO and Founder) for her invaluable insights and content contributions, which were instrumental in the development of this case study.

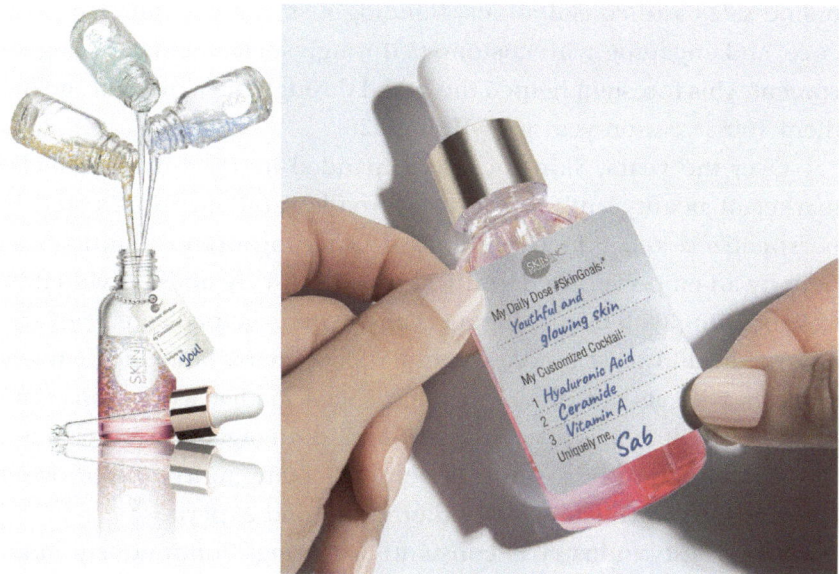

Figure 3.5. Skin Inc's concept store in Ion Singapore.

through rigorous clinical trials and third-party assessments to ensure product efficacy and provide transparency to customers. The interactive flagship store served as an important touchpoint for customer discovery and education. Customers did not just shop; they learned about their skin concerns through consultations and actively participated in crafting their own serums, guided by knowledgeable beauty advisers. This hands-on approach made the concept tangible and exciting and personalized interactions gave customers a deeper understanding of their skin and the concept of customized serums. By focusing on educating customers about personalized skincare (Figure 3.5), Skin Inc. positioned itself as an expert guide, not just another product seller. This built brand trust. Online quizzes, informative blog posts, and educational videos demystified the science behind personalization and helped customers understand their unique skin needs. It even has its own "Sounds like Spa" podcast available on Spotify.

From serums, Skin Inc. branched out to offer a wider range of skincare products while staying true to its belief of "Customize, Don't Compromise." To reach a wider audience, the brand expanded to online sales and consultations, building a strong e-commerce presence, and engaging with customers through social media and digital content. This foresight helped the brand through the pandemic, giving them 400% year-on-year growth in 2020!

Over the years, Skin Inc. has expanded its reach from a niche market of beauty enthusiasts to a broader audience interested in personalized and effective skincare. A strong brand identity was built by an empowering narrative around self-care and individuality. Collaborating with beauty bloggers and experts helped spread awareness and build trust among potential customers. Skin Inc. actively engages with its customers through social media, workshops, and online consultations, fostering a loyal and engaged customer base. The brand carefully fostered a sense of community and allowed customers to learn from each other and brand experts.

The beauty industry is constantly evolving. Continuously innovating and adapting to evolving customer needs and technology advancements was crucial to remain competitive. Leveraging Tan's tech background, Skin Inc. embraced AI and data-driven insights to move the narrative on skincare to wellness. She firmly believes that skincare is a part of self-care, emphasizing the connection between inner well-being and outer appearance. She wants Skin Inc. to stand not just for skincare or bodycare but as a holistic brand where beauty comes from within.

In 2022, they partnered with +SABI AI Corp to develop the +SABI 360°, a comprehensive skin and wellness coach app which can be used in tandem with its new Tri-Light +SABI skintech device.[12] Using AI and a series of algorithms, the app analyzes consumer patterns by leveraging 1.2 million profiles and face scans, to guide customers in tracking and improving their own wellness and skin health according to their own goals. The technology is based on the premise that lifestyle behaviors and environmental stressors affect skin health. Based on diagnostics on these factors (think water and alcohol consumption, sleep and stress levels) and selfies, customers receive

---

[12] Saini, N. (2022). Behind the brand: Sabrina Tan of Skin Inc on the brand's newest AI-powered skin health app. Prestige. 18 April 2022. Accessed on 11 January 2024. https://www.prestige online.com/sg/people/sabrina-tan-skin-inc-ai-powered-skin-app/.

Figure 3.6. Tri-light +SABI device (left) and app (right).

a skin report of skin health markers (Figure 3.6) and prescriptive advice on device settings to use in the Tri-Light device that can help achieve their skin goals. The app includes an optional custom serum subscription, automatically renewing your order.

When asked how she keeps up with big brands and new entrants in the beauty game, Tan confidently said she has a trump card—a database of over 1 million skin profiles! Data-driven insights are how she keeps up with consumer needs! She is confident her brand is built on the solid foundation of loyal customers.

"Skin Inc. was created based on the synthesis between beauty and tech, with the principal tenet that no one individual's wellness and skin is the same. We have known that 80% of your skin health is determined by lifestyle and environmental stressors, with +SABI AI we can provide our customers with a 360 personalized coach to help them improve, not only their skin health but their overall wellness," Tan says. "This is particularly important since your skin, as your biggest organ, is the barometer of your inner wellbeing. It is the first place to show signs of other ailments."

Skin Inc. has garnered international recognition, winning over 150 beauty awards and gracing the pages of renowned publications, such as Vogue and Harper's Bazaar. The brand expanded its presence beyond Singapore, entering markets, such as the US, China, and

Southeast Asia. Skin Inc.'s story is an inspiring example of how a brand can thrive by prioritizing customer needs, embracing innovation, and remaining adaptable. Early adoption of technologies cemented Skin Inc.'s image as an innovative leader in the industry. They innovated but they did not deviate from their commitment to research and development and their purpose to provide "customized solutions" by marrying technology and holistic wellness. By continuing to personalize the skincare experience and push the boundaries of what's possible, Skin Inc. is poised to remain as a brand that matters in the ever-evolving beauty landscape.

Here are some key learnings from Skin Inc.'s journey:

- **Identify and address unmet needs:** Skin Inc.'s success stemmed from recognizing a gap in the market—busy customers left unsatisfied by one-size-fits-all products. It resonated with this segment by meeting diverse skin concerns and offering custom-made solutions, resonating with a market often. Through the years, it stayed focused on its mission to serve customers who saw the value to "customise, never compromise."

- **Playing to strengths:** Tan's unique blend of tech expertise and passion for beauty has kept Skin Inc. ahead of the curve. From the early adoption of technologies such as encapsulation and microfluidics for customized serums, they have consistently leveraged the power of innovation. Today, their vast database of millions of profiles fuels AI-powered diagnostics and recommendations, making customization their unbeatable advantage.

- **Embracing technology to provide customization:** At the start, Skin Inc. used technologies such as encapsulation and microfluidics to formulate customized serums. Now, the brand can use AI and the millions of profiles acquired over the years to create personalized data-driven diagnostics and recommendations. Customization has truly become the brand's competitive advantage.

- **Expanding from niche segmentation:** Skin Inc. actively educated customers about personalized skincare through interactive experiences, online content, and community building. It collaborated with influencers and experts with high coefficients of imitation to build a global community. By delivering real results and building trust, its loyal customers became its best source of word of mouth.

- **Data as a currency, trust as a reward:** Skin Inc. understands the value of transparency. They are open about how they collect, use, and protect customer data.[13] But more importantly, they demonstrate the reciprocal value exchange. Customers readily share data in exchange for personalized diagnostics and insights, empowering them to make informed choices about their skincare journey. The +SABI app and online consultations further solidify this one-on-one engagement, ensuring a continuous feedback loop for personalized solutions.

The Asian PoV

The diversity of Asian markets makes segmentation even more challenging. This necessitates a localized approach to marketing, requiring businesses to invest in market research and adapt their strategies to suit specific regions or even individual countries. For example, McDonald's has localized offerings (e.g., McAloo Tiki burger in India and Teriyaki McBurger in Japan), marketing campaigns, pricing strategies, and even store formats for the different parts of Asia they operate. Alternatively, businesses can leverage technology for data-driven insights and personalized marketing. Successful Asian brands such as Skin Inc. have effectively utilized technology to offer personalized skincare solutions, incorporating AI and data analytics to enhance customer experiences and build brand loyalty.

Finally, segmentation would also require a strong understanding of the channels, go-to-market, tactics, and messaging that would resonate. For example, for upcountry Thailand segments, value-based messaging leveraging traditional channels such as radio, print, and outdoor advertising might be more successful. For Bangkok customers, a trend-based messaging with experiential and digital marketing for the same product might resonate better.

---

[13] Skin Inc. (n.d.). *Privacy Policy*. I Love Skin Inc. https://iloveskininc.us/pages/privacy-policy.

Key Takeaways

- There are various market coverage strategies: Mass marketing, differentiated marketing, niche marketing, mass customization, and customization. Understand the pros and cons of each.
- Businesses need to choose their target customers wisely. This will enable them to add value, play to their strengths, and contribute to the long-term mission and growth of the firm.
- Segment to divide and conquer. Understand your market is not one homogenous blob. Slice it into manageable segments based on the different needs of the market and build a persona for each target segment. Profiling the segments helps tailor your strategy and maximize impact.
- Targeting specific customer segments, based on shared needs and characteristics, leads to laser-focused marketing efforts and optimized outcomes. A firm that attempts to market to everyone may end up being nothing to everyone.
- Choosing more than one target segment (differentiated marketing) is possible. However, for each target segment, a unique marketing strategy should be employed.
- Once you have segmented, prioritize! Target the most promising segments that align with your business goals and resources, ensuring your marketing resonates with the right crowd.
- Hyperpersonalization, or one-to-one targeting, can provide a tailored experience for customers to improve desired outcomes.
- Understand market demand and potential. Technology can provide data-driven insights to accurately size your market.

Chapter 4

Positioning

Building on the previous chapter's discussion of market segmentation and targeting, this chapter delves into the crucial concept of positioning. Segmentation and targeting helped us understand and choose our customers. But now, it is time to paint a picture of who we want to be in their eyes. This chapter unravels the mysteries of positioning—how to differentiate your firm from the competition and carve out a unique space in the minds of your target customers.

The Power of Perception: Why Brand Positioning Matters

Some companies focus their efforts on improving their products. A good product is crucial because branding will not make lemons taste like candy, but it is still a necessary first act. The real magic happens in your customer's mind. Positioning lets your customers know what you stand for, why they should care, and most importantly, claim a distinct spot in their minds. Brand positioning is not about tweaking reality; it is the art of shaping perception.

Think of a crowded party. You want your brand to be the unique personality everyone remembers, not the wallflower lost in the crowd. Perception is your customer's version of reality.

Classical Positioning Strategy

Classical positioning strategy suggests that the brand first identifies its membership category, usually (but not limited to) the product category it belongs to. The idea is to choose a frame of reference for customers to know how to categorize the product. Categorization affects usage occasions. Orange juice is not a breakfast drink by accident. Introducing orange juice as a breakfast table staple in the early 1900s created consumption occasions for the fruit and solved farmers' oversupply problem.[1] Customers apply their beliefs, knowledge, and expectations for the category to judge a product. Category membership also influences the alternatives used to compare it against. Hence, the brand must prove its worth to stay in the game. It must meet the minimum expectations that customers deem to be essential to that category. These are known as "points of parity" (PoPs). Brands that are seen to be inferior on these PoPs are deemed as poor alternatives and will be out of contention.

Second, unleash your points of difference (PoDs) to break free from the pack. What makes you unique, superior, or simply irresistible? Shout your PoDs loud and clear to show customers why you are the one they should crave for.

Finally, craft a memorable slogan that captures your positioning's essence. Think Nike's "Just do it,", Lenovo's "For Those Who Do", or LG's "Life's Good." This brand mantra guides your communication, ensuring every message reinforces your unique place in the customer's mind.

Ensure that your positioning reflects your customers' needs, aspirations, and desired experiences. At the same time, check that your offering is seen to be different from competitors'. Figure 4.1 offers a handy tool to map your positioning strategy. In the diagram, analyze your offerings, your rivals', and your customers' needs. As you fill in the diagram, consider the following questions that pertain to each area as marked out in the diagram.

- A: What are our PoDs? How big and sustainable are these differences? Are they based on distinctive capabilities that are relevant and important to customers?
- B: What are the key attributes that are points of parity (PoPs)? Are we delivering effectively in the areas of parity?

---

[1] Greenwood, V. (2022). How orange juice took over the breakfast table. *BBC*. 28 June 2022 https://www.bbc.com/future/article/20220627-how-orange-juice-took-over-the-breakfast-table.

Positioning | 67

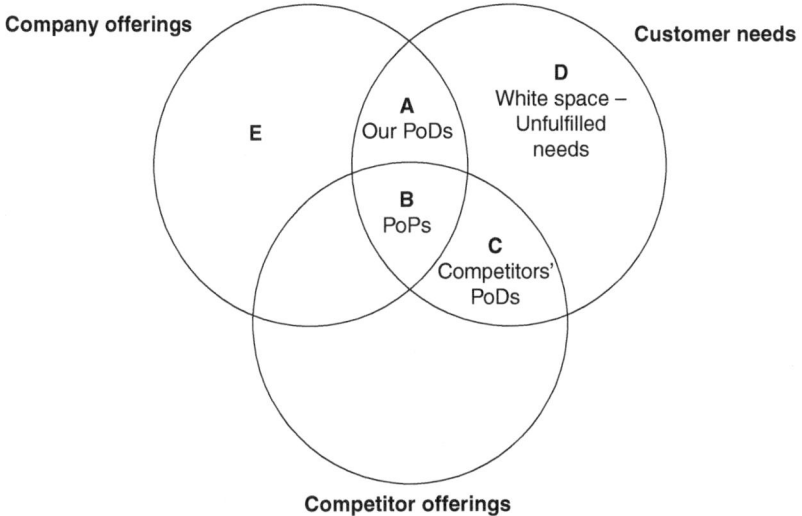

Figure 4.1. Strategic positioning tool.[2]

- C: What are your competitors' PoDs? How can we counter your competitors' advantages? If you can counter your competitors' PoDs, they become PoPs instead and mitigate your competitor's advantage.
- D: Are these unfulfilled needs opportunities for growth? Consider if you have competencies that can address these unfulfilled needs.
- E: If your PoD are not relevant to customer needs, then they would fall in Area E instead. In this case, there could be two scenarios: First, consider if you could educate the current segment on the importance of your PoDs. If you succeed in doing so, you could address latent needs and truly have a competitive edge over your competitors. Second, if lack of knowledge is not the reason, you could be wooing the wrong target segment and would be better off evaluating if there are other customers who may be interested in what you have to offer.

---

[2] Adapted from Urbany, J. E. and David, J. H. (2007). Strategic insight in three circles. *Harvard Business Review*, July, 28–20.

Differentiating your product: Vertical versus horizontal differentiation

Positioning is all about achieving a competitive differentiation. Brands can look at two types of differentiation: vertically or horizontally.

Vertical differentiation is a marketing strategy where companies offer products or services within the same category but at different quality levels and price points, catering to consumers with varying budgets and preferences for quality. Let's illustrate this using two prominent Asian hospitality brands: Shangri-La and OYO.

Shangri-La, a Hong Kong-based luxury hotel chain, is renowned for its opulent accommodations, exceptional service, and world-class amenities. Their properties often feature lavish interiors, multiple dining options with gourmet cuisine, extensive spa and wellness facilities, and personalized concierge services. Shangri-La's strategy lies in its unwavering commitment to luxury, exclusivity, and a premium guest experience, targeting affluent travelers seeking the finest hospitality experience.

In contrast, OYO, an Indian hospitality company, has disrupted the budget hotel segment with its innovative business model. They partner with existing hotels, standardize their offerings, and leverage technology to streamline operations and reduce costs. OYO rooms are typically basic yet functional, offering essential amenities like comfortable beds, clean bathrooms, and free Wi-Fi at affordable prices. OYO's strategy is based on affordability, accessibility, and convenience, appealing to budget-conscious travelers seeking a clean and comfortable stay without breaking the bank.

Shangri-La and OYO have successfully differentiated themselves through distinct price points and quality levels. This vertical differentiation allows both brands to cater to different customer segments based on their budgets and preferences for quality, maximizing their reach and market share.

Horizontal differentiation is a marketing strategy where companies offer similar products or services at the same price point but with distinct characteristics to appeal to varying consumer preferences. An example would be these two prominent Asian brands: Uniqlo and MUJI, both known for their minimalist apparel and lifestyle products.

Uniqlo, a Japanese brand, champions functional and affordable clothing basics. Its LifeWear collection features simple, high-quality garments designed for everyday wear, with an emphasis on comfort and versatility. Its differentiation lies in its focus on functional innovation and affordability, attracting consumers seeking practical and stylish everyday wear.

MUJI, also a Japanese brand, embraces a philosophy of simplicity and "no-brand" quality. Their products, ranging from apparel and household goods to stationery and food, are characterized by a minimalist aesthetic, natural materials, and understated design. MUJI's stationery, for instance, is often praised for its clean lines, functional simplicity, and affordable price. Their differentiation lies in their emphasis on minimalist design and a "no-logo" approach, appealing to consumers who value simplicity, quality, and a sense of understated luxury.

Both Uniqlo and MUJI offer similar product categories, such as apparel and household goods, with comparable price points. However, they have successfully differentiated themselves through distinct brand philosophies and design aesthetics. Uniqlo focuses on functional innovation and affordability, while MUJI emphasizes minimalist design and a "no-brand" quality. This horizontal differentiation allows both brands to attract different customer segments with varying preferences and values, ultimately capturing a larger share of the market.

Another example of horizontal differentiation would be BMW ("The ultimate driving machine") versus Mercedes Benz ("The best or nothing"). Again similar price points but different values and positionings to cater to the diverse tastes and aspirations of their customers.

Positioning Statements

Positioning statements are internal strategy documents that express how a brand wishes to be perceived by customers. By explicitly spelling out the vision for the brand, how it is different from competitors, and how it brings value to the target customers, a positioning statement forms the blueprint for the implementation of the marketing plan. Marketing efforts should align with the brand and value proposition.

A positioning statement typically comprises these elements as shown in this sample template:

> To (the target group and the need to be fulfilled), our (Brand), is (the concept—why the target customer needs your product) among all (competitive frame—which category you claim to be a part of) that (what the Point-of-Difference is).

An example of a positioning statement is one from Gryphon Tea:[3]

> "Gryphon Tea is a company on a mission to make the highest-quality gourmet teas for the discerning tea drinker who is always in search of new taste experiences. Built with passion and fuelled by our founder's love for Asia's rich culinary culture, our tea is crafted with exotic and experimental ingredients to bring out a unique and flavourful pedigree. Each and every blend is a commitment to quality, in which we use only the world's finest tea leaves and herbs. We guarantee a premium tea drinking experience with every sip."

Another example is from Coca-Cola as a company:

> "For quality beverage seekers, Coca-Cola offers a wide range of the most refreshing options. Each creates a great experience for customers when they enjoy a Coca-Cola brand drink. Unlike other beverage options, Coca-Cola products inspire happiness and make a positive difference in customers' lives, and the brand is intensely focused on the needs of consumers and customers."

Here, as a company which owns multiple beverage brands that appeal to various target markets, Coca-Cola uses a positioning statement that works for all customer segments. An alternative is to have individual positioning statements and slogans for each brand and by making sure they don't clash. The Coca-Cola brand has a long history

---

[3] Gryphon Tea Company. (n.d.). *Our Story*. https://www.gryphontea.com/our-story.html.

of various brand slogans that help keep the brand relevant to consumers while staying unified to the theme of inspiring happiness and making a positive difference. For example, in 2021, it launched the "Real Magic" slogan to emphasize the magic of humanity, uniqueness, and connection and to create "a movement to choose a more human way of doing things by embracing our unique perspectives."[4]

A positioning statement is the foundation of your marketing strategy. Every campaign, every message, every interaction should resonate with its essence.

Intended versus Actual Positioning: How Perceptions Shape Reality

Customers don't just see brands, they interpret them. It is a complex mix of what they see (ads, products, prices, experiences, etc.) and their own pre-existing beliefs, biases, and cultural filters. This creates their personal view of a brand, often an altered version of the brand's intended image (Read more about this perception and interpretation process in Chapter 6). As marketers, bridging the gap between what you want your brand to be and how customers actually see it is crucial. Think of it like a story you're trying to tell. You craft the plot, cast the characters, and set the stage, but the audience interprets it through their own lens, drawing on their experiences and emotions. The challenge lies in understanding these influences—the touchpoints that shape perception.

Sometimes a brand is perceived in a certain way because of how successful it has been with its positioning. For instance, Volvo's "safety first" story turned into a narrative of "boxy, boring cars"[5] that lacked the badge value of fellow luxury car brands. Their luxury aspirations

---

[4] Phillips, M. (2023). Why Coca-Cola has had so many different slogans. Mashed.com. 5 April 2023. https://www.mashed.com/1244768/why-coca-cola-has-had-so-many-different-slogans/.

[5] Lee, J. (2010). Volvo breaks out of the boring box by putting consumers in front of the car. *Sydney Morning Herald*. 26 February 2010. Accessed on 16 November 2023. https://www.smh.com.au/business/companies/volvo-breaks-out-of-the-boring-box-by-putting-consumers-in-front-of-the-car-20100225-p5zf.html.

were overshadowed by a perception of practicality. So, they had to reframe the conversation, swapping safety sermons for sleek design and "award-winning Scandinavian style."[6,7]

Another driver of customers' brand perceptions is its association with its customers. What started in the early 1990s as "sexy sneakers" for "hot girls with drama on their mind" endorsed by Britney Spears[8] gradually became perceived as "old people's shoes" as a large percentage of their customer base was made up of baby boomers.[9] This was certainly not what its founder had in mind when he named the brand using teenager lingo where Skechers refers to someone who is "antsy and can't sit still."[10]

Perceptual Maps

Perceptual maps are useful tools to graphically represent customers' perceptions of competing brands. They are mostly commonly presented as a two-axis scatter chart. The two axes should represent the two parameters that are most salient to your product category, that is, the two attributes that customers would typically consider when choosing between you and your competitors. This is the most important step of developing a perceptual map, as the power of the insights you can obtain from it depends on the choice of the axes,

---

[6] White, E. (2002). About advertising: Volvo plays up its dangerous side—car maker equated with safety works to shed its conservative image. *Wall Street Journal*. 14 June 2002.

[7] Bubbers, M. (2017). In search of Scandanavian style: Making Volvo hip, in a Nordic way. *The Globe and Mail*. 23 February 2017. https://www.theglobeandmail.com/globe-drive/culture/commentary/in-search-of-scandinavian-style-making-volvo-hip-in-a-nordic-way/article34108620/.

[8] Telfer, T. (2014). Remember when Skechers were sexy? *Bustle*. Accessed on 9 November 2023. https://www.bustle.com/articles/33000-whatever-happened-to-skechers-they-used-to-be-so-hip-but-today-theyre-justawkward#:~:text=The%20Sketcher%20sneaker%20was%20birthed,ultimate%20oxymoron%3A%20a%20sexy%20sneaker.

[9] The Harris Poll. (2023). Skechers footwear makes serious strides in 2023. The Harris Poll. 8 September 2023. Accessed on 17 November 2023. https://theharrispoll.com/briefs/skechers-footwear-makes-serious-strides-in-2023/.

[10] Bettner, J. (1993). Stepping out in new, successful direction: Shoes: Robert Greenberg, founder of L. A. Gear, has launched a company that's building sales from the popularity of trendy 'Doc' Martens. *Los Angeles Times*. 26 October 1993. Accessed on 14 November 2023. https://www.latimes.com/archives/la-xpm-1993-10-26-fi-49893-story.html.

so spend time analyzing the category and understanding your business. Understanding why customers choose one brand over another helps you identify those parameters that lead to success in your category. Alternatively, some brands may choose to use their points of differentiation to map against competitors. This works if those differentiators are meaningful to customers.

A tell-tale sign of a poor choice of axes is when your brand and competitors fall into one plane or half of the perceptual map (see Figure 4.2). This could be because the unoccupied space represents positionings that are undesirable or unachievable. Ensure your axes are distinct and independent. For example, price and quality are not independent, making them unsuitable as separate axes. Consider creating different maps for different customer segments if their attribute preferences vary significantly.

Next, conduct market research (surveys, interviews) to understand how consumers perceive your brand and its competitors on these chosen attributes. Based on your data, position your brand and competitors on the map. Each brand gets a spot on the map based on its perceived position on these axes. Use your research, customer feedback, and competitor analysis to find their coordinates. Consider using bubble sizes to represent market share or brand awareness.

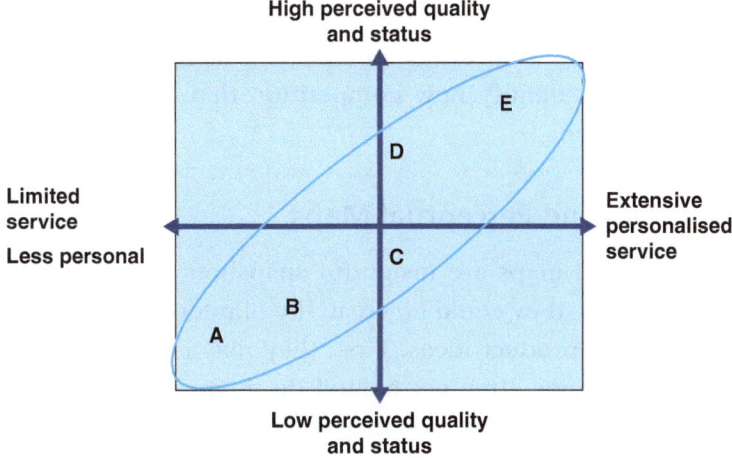

Figure 4.2. Example of poor choice of axes.

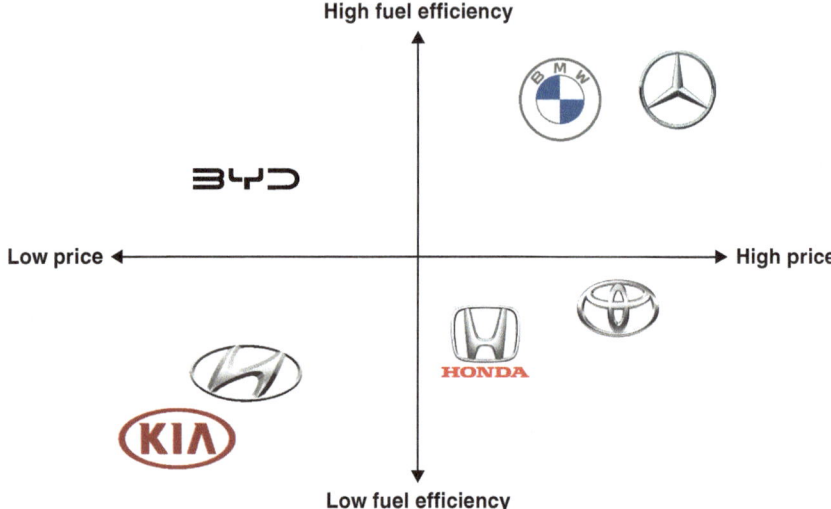

Figure 4.3. Example of perceptual map for car brands.

Here is an hypothetical example of a perceptual map for the car market (Figure 4.3).

Perceptual maps are a powerful tool for understanding brand positioning and identifying opportunities. The process of developing perceptual maps also opens your eyes to important insights too. A competitor analysis will help you understand who customers compare you with and what your strengths and weaknesses are relative to them. Adopting a customer perspective in competitor analysis would help you identify new competition that may be worthy of keeping an eye on.

Thinking beyond Perceptual Maps

While perceptual maps are insightful snapshots for understanding market dynamics, they could be creativity blinders when it comes to groundbreaking product ideas. First, they may cause tunnel vision to rivals. Companies often get fixated on their closest competitors, plotting them and themselves on maps defined by established product categories and customer expectations. This leads to product-centric thinking, missing the bigger picture of alternative solutions or new ways to fulfill needs. Customers, after all, are not confined to defined categories—they might readily turn to substitutes to scratch the same itch.

Companies also may be hyper-sensitive to every move their rivals make, constantly reacting and tweaking their offerings within the map's boundaries. This reactive mindset limits innovation, potentially trapping them in a game of incremental improvements that are easily copied and unsustainable in the long run. Looking for inspiration within existing offerings often leads to minor tweaks—mere "better versions" of the same old thing. These "differentiation points" are weak—easily replicated and unlikely to wow the market. Think about adding new ringtones to a mobile phone instead of envisioning the revolutionary touch-screen iPhone!

In addition, perceptual maps are blind to customer aspirations beyond what is currently available. They fail to capture unspoken needs, emerging trends, and latent desires. They do not consider what customers might want but have not thought of yet, or what technologies or trends might shift their needs in the future. Truly disruptive innovations often come from outside the mapped space, from unexpected sources that don't play by the category's rules. Apple's iPhone did not just improve existing features; it redefined the mobile phone's role in our lives, addressing needs we did not even know we had.

So, how do we break free from the map's limitations?

Look at the category, not just within the category

Forget the endless skirmishes over market share within the same old product category! The real battle for brand dominance lies in understanding the entire category itself. Consider if there are any vulnerabilities, such as consumer dissatisfaction, boredom, or unnecessary augmentation, in that category that the brand can better satisfy. The firm that satisfies its customers better than its competitors wins. Remember the Asahi story we talked about earlier? They listened to the whispers of consumer dissatisfaction, the growing boredom with the same old beer, the unspoken yearning for something clean, crisp, and fresh. They saw what the rest of the market did not—an opportunity to rewrite the rules of the game. And rewrite they did. Inspired by the delicate balance of sake, Asahi Superdry arrived on the scene, not as another bitter brew, but as a revolution in a can. It was a beer for the modern palate, a symphony of refreshing dryness that left the competition's aftertastes in the dust.[11]

Another brand that disrupted its industry by looking at customers' pain points is Owndays. The Japanese eyewear brand knew they had to differentiate themselves and fundamentally change the way people buy glasses. Unlike traditional optical stores with hidden fees and inflated prices, Owndays championed all-in-one pricing. One transparent cost covered frames, lenses, and coating, making budgeting predictable, and eliminated the surprise at the checkout. The brand kept its prices low by offering a curated selection of its own in-house frames, cutting out middlemen through a direct-to-consumer (DTC) model.

Ditching the intimidating atmosphere of frames in glass counters guarded by pushy salespeople, Owndays stores were designed to be inviting and accessible. Open-concept spaces empowered customers to browse and try on frames independently, creating a stress-free environment. In fact, shelves of fashionable frames enticed shoppers into the store even if they may not have been intentionally shopping for new glasses. Trust is earned by offering a warranty of a one-time complimentary change of lens if customers are dissatisfied with their vision.

To top it off, Owndays eliminated the need to wait for weeks. Owndays streamlined the process by investing in machines in each retail store to craft custom eyewear in just 20 minutes, making the experience convenient and instantly gratifying.

Owndays' impact is undeniable. Today, they have hundreds of stores across Asia, serving millions of customers. They dared to challenge the status quo and created a new model for the eyewear industry toward more transparent pricing models, improved customer service, and a focus on creating a positive buying experience.

---

[11] Asahi. (26 March 2020). Asahi Super Dry brand introduction [YouTube channel]. Retrieved 28 September 2023. https://youtu.be/CP7jQj7lF48?si=qUE_iqb8yQg-1_wY.

Break the mold, offer the unexpected

When a product category matures, customer expectations of brands are formed. As companies try to meet those expectations, they reinforce them, hence perpetuating the pressure for brands to meet those points of parity and the cycle goes on. Over time, offerings within the category become more similar over time. Companies that challenge the category norm successfully could have a breakthrough differentiation.

IKEA's story is a masterclass in defying category norms and redefining customer expectations. The Swedish furniture brand threw the category rulebook out the window and crafted a unique customer experience that is anything but ordinary. IKEA carefully taught customers to appreciate its value proposition and supplemented it with unexpected augmentations. Forget the cramped aisles and "Do Not Touch" signs of traditional furniture stores. Instead of playing the "more features, better than you" game, IKEA saw the trap of parity. So, they flipped the script. They ditched the hovering salespeople and let customers explore at their own pace. They succeeded in making their furniture into adult Lego where DIY was made easy so customers could embrace self-assembly as a badge of pride, not a chore. They promised that you didn't have to be rich to be clever, with their a la carte affordability. Customers chose their level of service instead of a one-size-fits-all price tag.

IKEA understood why customers bought furniture, and they did not just sell furniture—they fed the nesting instinct. Their interactive showrooms transformed display spaces into playrooms, where sofas beg to be lounged on and kitchens invite culinary dreams. They understood that furniture was not just about function, it was about creating a home, and homes need more than just sofas. They filled their shelves with vases and bedsheets, candles and plants, transforming shopping into a treasure hunt for homey delights. They orchestrated a sensory feast in their stores that turned shopping into a destination.

By focusing on unexpected value propositions, unconventional augmentations, and a customer-centric approach, IKEA redefined the furniture game and became a household name synonymous with innovation and delight.

Redefine the Game with Category Creation

Breaking free from existing categories is a powerful tool for brands. It allows them to rewrite consumer expectations, escape the limitations of established rivals, and create a market all their own. This is exactly what Apple did with the iPad launch in 2010.

Imagine a sleek device with a touchscreen that whispers possibilities but is trapped in a label like "netbook." Bleh, right? All that comes to mind are low-powered laptop replacements that were yesterday's news. That's the fate Apple could have faced with the iPad, a revolutionary device destined for greater things than spreadsheet crunching on the go. Instead, Apple did the unthinkable. They shattered the category cage and forged a new path, birthing the "tablet" category. This was not just a marketing gimmick; it was a deliberate act of reframing how people saw these devices. Why? Because the iPad wasn't a miniaturized laptop; it was a portal to entertainment, education, and creativity. By creating a new category, Apple redefined the conversation, escaping the limitations of "netbook" and gave consumers a whole new way to experience the world.

This category creation brought several benefits: Price and product stereotypes were shattered. It offered a unique proposition that allowed Apple free play. The iPad ushered in a new era of mobile computing, with Apple as the crowned leader. Apple became the voice of the new category, communicating its value and evangelizing its potential. By reframing the narrative, Apple unleashed a wave of possibilities. The tablet wasn't just about checking email; it was a playground for creativity, entertainment, and education. It could be a canvas for artists, a gateway to learning for students, and a window to the world for anyone with a curious mind. Suddenly, consumers who would not have considered a "netbook" or another piece of tech were suddenly intrigued by the possibilities of a "tablet." This opened the door to a broader audience and increased revenue streams.

The iPad's story is a testament to the power of category creation. It is a reminder that sometimes the best way to win isn't to play by the existing rules but to rewrite them entirely.

Evolve by changing categories

While Apple boldly painted a new picture with the iPad, Microsoft's Surface took a different, equally fascinating path of category evolution. Instead of planting a shiny new flag in the "tablet" territory, they evolved using the very associations of existing categories. Here's how they played the category association game:

Surface was initially positioned in 2012 as a premium tablet to capitalize on the growing tablet market and directly challenge the iPad's dominance. Microsoft aimed to disrupt the tablet market, targeting tech-savvy customers by capitalizing on the perceived limitations of the iPad such as its closed ecosystem and lack of productivity features. Ads showcased its sleek design, versatility (keyboard dock!), and productivity (desktop software!), targeting professionals and creative types. However, the value proposition for Surface's productivity features was not clear to everyone. Furthermore, this being Microsoft's first foray into hardware, these early Windows tablets suffered from compatibility issues and a smaller app selection compared to iOS.

Microsoft decided to capitalize on its strong business presence. In 2014, as the consumer tablet market grew more saturated, Microsoft shifted gears and Surface was presented as the preferred device for business professionals. Ads showcased Surface Pro as the ultimate business tool, touting its compatibility with business applications, highlighting premium design, powerful hardware, enterprise-grade security, and advanced features such as pen support.

Today, Surface has a family of devices (laptops, tablets, and all-in-ones) for diverse productivity needs, from creative professionals to students. Flexibility, power, and seamless integration with Microsoft 365 and cloud services take center stage in its messaging. This diversification of the product line enabled Surface to cater to broader user segments and increased market share and brand awareness, solidifying Surface as a productivity leader beyond just business.

Case: Carousell's Inspiring Journey From Enabling Declutter to Recommerce Marketplace[12]

Tired of having underused items gather dust in their homes, young Singaporeans Quek Siu Rui, Lucas Ngoo, and Marcus Tan dreamt of a world where old items found new life instead of heading to landfills. This spark of inspiration, ignited during their university days, soon became a blazing ambition: Revolutionize the way people sell and buy second-hand goods.

Thus, in 2012, Carousell, the Singapore-born peer-to-peer online classifieds platform, was born. Its mission was "Make secondhand the first choice." It was a win-win proposition for all—sellers decluttered, buyers found treasures, and the environment rejoiced in less waste. The company boldly proclaims its mission: "We dream of a world where people instinctively sell their under-utilized items instead of letting them go to waste, where others buy them as a first choice. 10 years from now, we will make second-hand a way of life."

Fast forward to today, Carousell reigns supreme as a leading online classifieds and recommerce marketplace in Greater Southeast Asia, boasting millions of users and a vibrant marketplace buzzing with diverse products. Their success story attracted the attention and support of renowned venture capital firms, such as 500 Global, Peak XV Partners, and Telenor Group. But growth didn't stop there. Carousell expanded and eventually evolved into Carousell Group, a powerhouse comprising nine companies with footprints in seven markets. From its Singaporean roots, Carousell now flourishes in Hong Kong, Indonesia, Malaysia, the Philippines, and Taiwan.

While it now boasts a thriving community and impressive growth, its initial journey wasn't without its bumps and challenges. Here's a glimpse into their journey:

Carousell's beginnings

Before Carousell, selling pre-loved treasures was a chore. Imagine: 30 minutes just to list a single item! Photos, transfers, uploads from

---

[12] The authors gratefully acknowledge John Huang (Director of Marketing) and Natalie Lim (Senior Communications Manager) for their invaluable insights and content contributions, which were instrumental in the development of this case study.

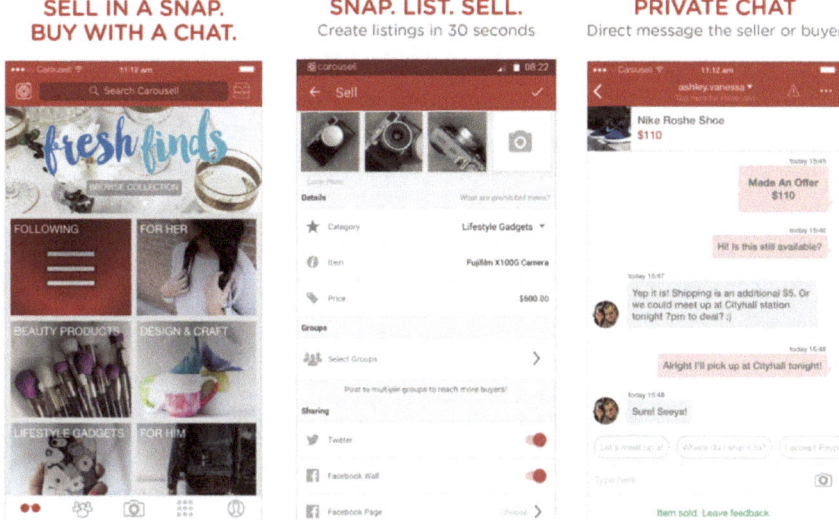

Figure 4.4. Screenshots of Carousell's app interface in the early days.

camera to desktop—the process was enough to make anyone say "nah" to decluttering.

Recognizing the pain points of then-existing methods, they envisioned a mobile-first solution. Launched in 2012, Carousell became the region's first platform to enable peer-to-peer selling via a smartphone app. Their "Snap, List, Sell" approach (Figure 4.4) revolutionized the process, making it extremely snappy and entirely on your phone. Carousell was intuitive and convenient, perfectly aligning with the mobile-first habits of young, tech-savvy Southeast Asians. Selling went from a 30-minute ordeal to a 30-second long breeze, all on one device.

Network effects play a significant role in online marketplaces. To truly thrive, Carousell needed a vibrant community. They targeted millennials and specific user personas (e.g., those interested in textbooks and fashion) to begin with, who were comfortable with online transactions and eager for unique finds. This strategic focus helped them build a loyal user base first within a specific niche.

Carousell knew it needed to foster trust to attract both buyers and sellers to create a vibrant marketplace. It enabled human interaction through an in-app chat function, allowing buyers and sellers

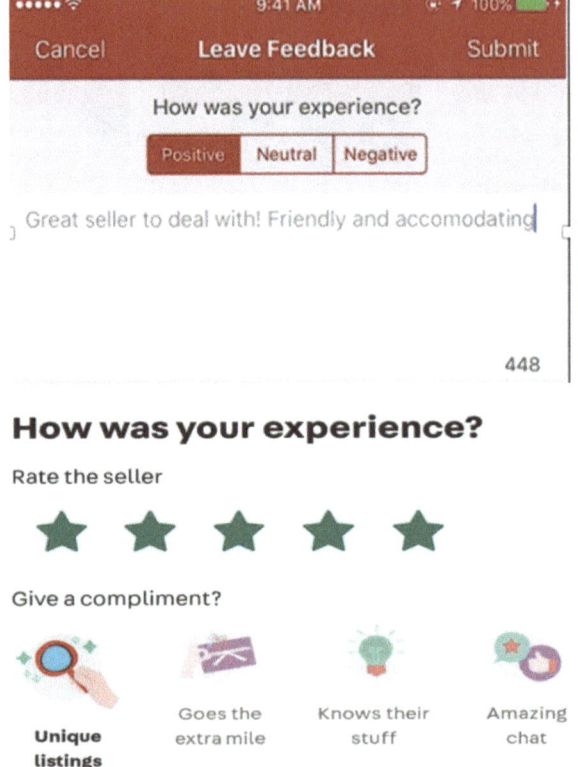

Figure 4.5. Rating and feedback system for users in the early days.

to connect without sharing personal details. This interaction fostered trust and negotiations, making transactions smoother and more enjoyable. Additionally, it added ratings and reviews (Figure 4.5) to provide transparency and help users assess each other's reliability.

Carousell didn't stop at making selling convenient. They knew the power of social media networks. Sharing listings on popular platforms such as Facebook and Instagram allowed sellers to tap into wider networks, increasing reach and driving app adoption, thus they continued to improve their sharing function over the years (Figure 4.6). This clever integration created a virtuous cycle: more users shared, more people downloaded, leading to even more sharing and engagement.

Together with the appeal of allowing users to earn a quick buck while decluttering their homes, Carousell garnered positive responses

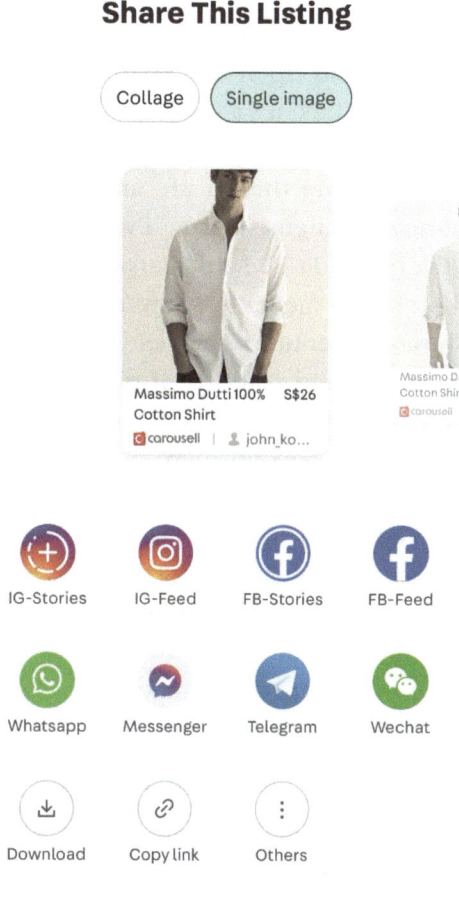

Figure 4.6. Feature that allows users to share their listings on popular social media and messaging platforms.

from the public. But recall, the founders' mission for Carousell was not to just be an online marketplace but to make second-hand a way of life. Let's dive into how they steered the brand in that direction.

Establishing its brand platform of "Everyone Wins"

In 2019, 7 years in on driving the mission of making second-hand the first choice, Carousell established its first-ever brand messaging platform, "Everyone Wins". "Everyone Wins" was derived from deeper insights into the community, accessibility, and empowerment made possible by the platform. Going beyond simply selling and buying pre-loved items, it's about empowering individuals to give new life to their old belongings and open up possibilities for others. Every item listed isn't just a product; it's a chance to help someone in need, forge connections, and discover unique treasures.

And how do they bring this to life among users? Apart from integrated marketing campaigns such as "Everyone Wins", and "Every Kinda Thing for Every Kinda Person", Carousell leverages powerful user stories on their social media to showcase the deeper impact of "carouselling." These authentic narratives highlight the friendships forged, opportunities created, and joy of giving and receiving. This positions Carousell not just as a platform but as an open community where connections bloom beyond mere buying and selling, where "Everyone Wins."

One such heartwarming tale features a Carouseller selling an electric bike. His post caught the eye of an elderly postman, struggling with his daily deliveries on a regular bicycle. Touched by the postman's dedication and need, the Carouseller went beyond a sale and gifted him the e-bike. This act of generosity, captured in a social media post (Figure 4.7), perfectly embodies the "Everyone Wins"

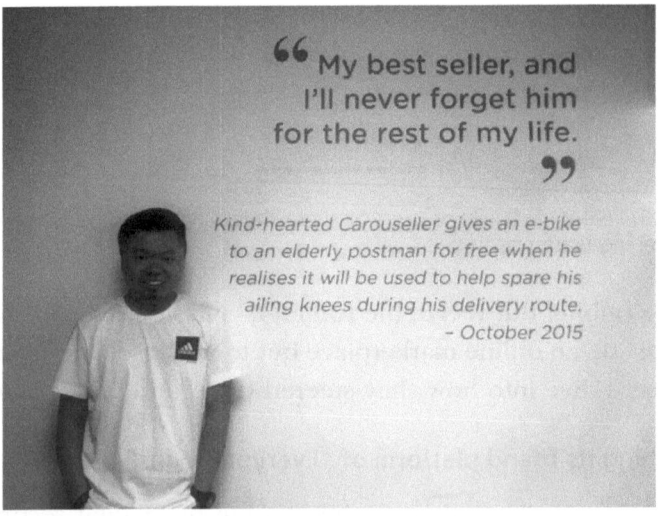

Figure 4.7. Social media post by a postman who received an e-bike for free.

spirit—making a tangible difference in someone's life through the power of second-hand.

Carousell's authentic user stories continue to showcase the heart and soul of the Carousell community and are a regular fixture in their social media content. It's a window into the diverse community that fuels Carousell's success and the impact it has on individuals' lives. Scan the QR code to watch the collection of such stories on Carousell's Instagram account and embark on a heartwarming journey of discovery.

Thriving through the pandemic

The COVID-19 pandemic threw a curveball at everyone. However, Carousell emerged as a platform that not only adapted but also thrived. While some used the shortage in necessities such as masks for short-term gains,[13] a heartwarming counter-movement blossomed on Carousell. Users, driven by the platform's "Everyone Wins" message, started giving away masks for free. The brand saw this as an opportunity for a positive ground-up movement to encourage users to "choose to give" instead. Through Carousell, donors and receivers connected efficiently, and this established a community of individuals who helped each other in times of need. This heartwarming effort wasn't missed by the media. Coverage from Today, Mothership, and AsiaOne (Figure 4.8) generated positive buzz, solidifying Carousell's image as a platform that empowers the community and possibilities.

---

[13] Coronavirus: 5 people arrested for allegedly cheating customers over face masks sold on Carousell. *The Straits Times*. 18 February 2020. Accessed on 5 December 2023. https://www.straitstimes.com/singapore/courts-crime/coronavirus-5-people-arrested-for-allegedly-cheating-customers-over-face.

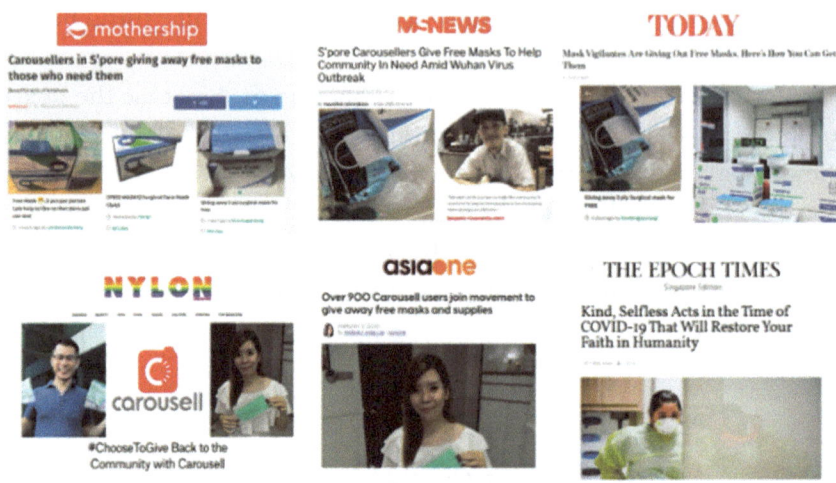

Figure 4.8. PR mentions during the COVID-19 pandemic.

The road ahead

Carousell now boasts millions of users across Southeast Asia and beyond, with vibrant communities exchanging a wide range of pre-owned items. The Singapore-born unicorn's success can be attributed to its understanding of local markets, focus on mobile-first experience, emphasis on community building, and building a strong brand identity. Carousell's story is an inspiration for startups and entrepreneurs.

And this is just the beginning. To further encourage more users to choose second-hand, Carousell has launched recommerce programs in 2023 to make buying and selling even more trusted and convenient. To make peer-to-peer transactions on the marketplace even safer, Carousell has the Buyer Protection program for users to enjoy payment and delivery services without leaving the platform, and enjoy protection should their orders not be delivered or differ greatly from the listing.

Hearing user concerns about buying lemons or fakes online, Carousell also launched the Carousell Certified program to provide an even more assured experience. Under the Certified program, cars, luxury bags, and mobile phones are thoroughly checked for quality and authenticity by experts before being listed for sale. All Certified Luxury bags and Certified Mobile listings come with money-back guarantee, while Certified Mobile and Certified Cars also come with warranties.

Additionally, some users want to participate in the circular economy but lack the time to sell on their own. Hence, Carousell launched "Sell to Carousell" where users can sell cars, clothes, luxury bags, and mobile phones directly to Carousell and get paid. This service was broadened in 2024 to bicycles with a Decathlon partnership.

As Carousell continues to make second-hand better by empowering individuals and redefining the way we consume, it will have to constantly anticipate and address evolving user needs. Based on what we've read so far, we learned the following:

- New ideas can be obtained from looking at the inadequacies and pain points of current options.
- Carousell differentiated from incumbents by offering a solution based on user-driven needs such as a seamless mobile experience catered to the region's smartphone-centric habits and in-app chat and reviews to build trust for the online marketplace.
- Carousell used a simple brand mantra of "Snap, List, Sell" to educate the market about what it is about and how to use it.
- It first targeted millennials and specific user personas (e.g., textbooks and fashion), who were more inclined to use online transactions and social media and facilitated word of mouth by embedding features to allow them to share their experiences and listings on their own social media. This is a classic example of getting into "earned media."
- Carousell carefully shaped public perception of what it stands for and wants to achieve with its company mission with the use of clever storytelling via its "Everyone Wins" brand messaging platform.

Key Takeaways

- Positioning defines how your brand wants to be perceived by customers, differentiating it from competitors and highlighting its unique value proposition. A strong position sets you apart from the competition and attracts the right customers.
- Customers may not necessarily see your brand as you intended. It is crucial to see what they see and identify the touchpoints that influence their perceptions. This will allow you to think of ways to address the gaps between the actual and intended positionings.
- A positioning statement should specify the category membership and clearly identify the points of parity and PoDs that give the brand an edge over its competitors. It should specify "who are we, what we stand for, why you should care, and why should you choose us over others?"
- Perceptual maps are snapshots of where you stand vis-à-vis competitors in your customers' minds. They can also reveal potential gaps in the market where your brand can offer better solutions. Carefully chosen attributes and accurate data determine the effectiveness of the maps.
- Be mindful of the limitations of the classical positioning strategy. Don't be afraid to break the mold! Some of the most successful brands defied conventional thinking and created new categories or redefined existing ones.

Chapter

5

Branding

Having established a clear brand positioning, the next crucial step is to bring it to life through a robust brand identity. While positioning determines where your product or service sits in the market, branding is about crafting emotional and perceptual connections with your target audience. In this chapter, we explore how to build a powerful brand, encompassing its benefits, strategies, and holistic application, including the critical aspect of employer branding.

What Is a Brand?

> "Products are made in a factory but brands are created in the mind."
>
> —Walter Landor

As this quote suggests, brands are abstract concepts that exist in the minds of consumers. They are built through perceptions, emotions, and associations that customers develop with the company and its offerings. The value of a product often goes beyond its physical attributes. It is the brand that ultimately drives purchase decisions and builds long-term loyalty. Hence, a brand must add other dimensions that differentiate it from other products designed to satisfy the same need.[1]

---

[1] Keller, K. L. (1993). Conceptualizing, measuring, managing customer-based brand equity. *Journal of Marketing*, 57(1), 1–22.

A brand is a multifaceted distinctive entity that encompasses a variety of elements:

- **The identity:** This includes the branding elements such as logo, colors, sonic, and typography, as well as the brand name itself.
- **The personality:** This is the emotional and human side of the brand, defined by its values, mission, and voice.
- **The promise:** This is what the brand offers to its customers, including the benefits, experiences, emotional rewards, and values it stands for.
- **The perception:** This element recognizes that a brand is the collective perceptions and emotions people associate with a company or product, based on their own experiences and interactions with it.

The accumulated value of a brand's image, reputation of unwavering quality, trust, and emotional connection with its customers amounts to an intangible asset known as brand equity. A strong brand is a valuable investment in a business' future, and brand equity is the return on that investment, measured in the hearts and wallets of your customers.

The Power of Brand Equity

In today's crowded marketplace, differentiation is key. While product quality and price are important factors, it is a company's powerful brand that can truly elevate it above the competition. Brands that succeed in doing so have positive brand equity, which is defined as "a value premium that a company generates from a product with a recognizable name when compared to a generic equivalent."[2] The benefits of positive brand equity are multifaceted and far-reaching.[3] Let's delve into some of them:

---

[2] Hayes, A. (2023). Brand equity: Definition, importance, effect on profit margin, and examples. Investopedia, 27 October 2023. Accessed on 19 February 2024. https://www.investopedia.com/terms/b/brandequity.asp.

[3] Hoeffler, S. and Kevin L. Keller (2003). The marketing advantages of strong brands. *Journal of Brand Management*, 10(6), 421–445.

Quality perceptions

Brand reputation is known to affect quality perceptions.[4] This "halo effect" arises from a collective consensus, built not on one voice but on thousands of consistent customer experiences over time. This consensus enables individuals to infer that the brand is of good quality even if they have not had their own personal experiences with it. Brand reputation precedes itself and extends to new product launches too.[5]

Marketing muscle

First, customers are more likely to buy from familiar brands.[6] Strong brands reduce choice conflict as they reduce the perceived risk of a wrong decision. People are also more likely to notice, engage with, and remember your marketing messages, even in the face of information overload. The resulting superior (top-of-mind) recall helps you stand out from the competition in a world overflowing with options. This translates to increased market share and revenue, as your brand cuts through the noise and resonates with your target audience.

Cultivates trust and loyalty

A strong brand fosters trust and emotional connections with its audience, building a loyal following that goes beyond simple transactions. Research shows that a new customer costs at least five times more than retaining an existing one and increasing customer retention rates by 5% increases profits by 25–95%.[7,8] Imagine pouring marketing

---

[4] Dodds, W. B., Monroe, K. B., and Grewal, D. (1991). Effects of price, brand, and store information on buyers' product evaluations. *Journal of Marketing Research*, 28, 307–319.

[5] Aaker, D. A. and Keller, K. L. (1990). Consumer evaluations of brand extensions. *Journal of Marketing*, 54(1), 27–41.

[6] Laroche, M., Kim, C., and Zhou, L. (1996). Brand familiarity and confidence as determinants of purchase intention: An empirical test in a multiple brand context. *Journal of Business Research*, 37, 115–120.

[7] Reichheld, F. F. and Phil, S. (2020). The economics of e-loyalty. Harvard Business School Working Knowledge: Business Research for Business Leaders. Accessed on 14 December 2023. https://hbswk.hbs.edu/archive/the-economics-of-e-loyalty.

[8] Rioux, P. (2020). The value of investing in loyal customers. *Forbes*. 29 January 2020. Accessed on 6 June 2023. https://www.forbes.com/sites/forbesagencycouncil/2020/01/29/the-value-of-investing-in-loyal-customers/?sh=75d80e9e21f6.

dollars into a leaky bucket—that's what neglecting customer retention is like. To truly grow, businesses must prioritize both attracting new customers and keeping the ones they already have.

Breeds advocacy

These loyal customers become brand advocates, spreading the word through trusted word-of-mouth recommendations, boosting organic reach. People are 90% more likely to trust and buy from a brand recommended by a friend[9] because word-of-mouth impressions are trusted above all forms of advertising.[10] It results in 5x more sales than a paid media impression.[11] This organic reach is particularly potent in the digital world where skepticism reigns.

A shield in times of crisis

When unforeseen challenges arise, a strong brand acts like a protective shield. A well-established reputation built on trust and transparency can help navigate negative publicity and recover more quickly during difficult times.[12] Think of it as a reserve of goodwill, earned through consistent action, ready to be drawn upon when needed.

Premium pricing power

Leading brands command a premium. An astounding 87% of customers are willing to pay extra for brands they love,[13] drawn in by the

---

[9] *Ibid.*

[10] Nielsen. (2012). Consumer trust in online, social, and mobile advertising grows. April 2012. Accessed on 22 January 2024. https://www.nielsen.com/insights/2012/consumer-trust-in-online-social-and-mobile-advertising-grows/.

[11] Marinova, I. (2023). Word of mouth marketing statistics, fun facts and tips in 2023. Review 42. 20 May 2023. Accessed on 22 January 2024. https://review42.com/resources/word-of-mouth-marketing-statistics/.

[12] Bhattacharya, C. B. and Sen, S. (2004). The effect of brand strength on a firm's ability to recover from negative publicity. *Journal of Marketing Research*, 41(2), 225–238.

[13] Gartner. (2022). How to position your brand to drive preference. 7 October 2022. Accessed on 14 December 2023. https://emt.gartnerweb.com/ngw/globalassets/en/marketing/documents/gartner_position_your_brand_to_drive_preference_final.pdf?_gl=1*1lk9wil*_ga*Mjk1MDkzNjU2LjE3MDIyODIwODI.*_ga_R1W5CE5FEV*MTcwMjUzODgzMi40LjEuMTcwMjUzODg0Mi41MC4wLjA.

value and emotional connection. Apple, for instance, boasts a cult-like following and commands premium pricing on its products, thanks to its carefully crafted brand image. A PWC study further confirms this, showcasing a willingness to pay up to 16% more.[14]

Talent magnet

A strong brand does not just attract customers; it attracts top talent. Employees want to work for companies they believe in and are proud to be associated with.[15] This leads to a more engaged and productive workforce, contributing to overall business success, For example, Google's innovative and playful brand image consistently attracts top tech talent in Silicon Valley.

Financial returns

The impact of a strong brand goes beyond intangibles. Strong brands have a direct impact on financial performance. Familiar brands enjoy a higher market share.[16] Even a 1-point gain in brand metrics, such as awareness and consideration, drives a 1% increase in sales.[17] Over time, this commitment to brand building yields impressive returns, as showcased by the outperformance of the top 40 brands in Figure 5.1—these brands deliver nearly twice the return to shareholders compared to the market average.

---

[14] Puthiyamadam, T. and José R. (2018). Experience is everything: Here's how to get it right. PwC.com. Accessed on 24 January 2024. https://www.pwc.com/us/en/advisory-services/publications/consumer-intelligence-series/pwc-consumer-intelligence-series-customer-experience.pdf#page=10.

[15] Adams, B. (2012). Make your employer brand stand out in the talent marketplace. *Harvard Business Review*. 8 February 2022. Accessed on 24 January 2024. https://hbr.org/2022/02/make-your-employer-brand-stand-out-in-the-talent-marketplace.

[16] Park, C. S. and Srinivasan, V. (1994). A survey-based method for measuring and understanding brand equity and its extendability. *Journal of Marketing Research*, 31 (May), 271–288.

[17] Nielsen. (2021). When it comes to brand building, awareness is critical. June 2021. Accessed on 14 December 2023. https://www.nielsen.com/insights/2021/when-it-comes-to-brand-building-awareness-is-critical/#:~:text=At%20the%20end%20of%20the,was%20exceptionally%20strong%20(0.73).

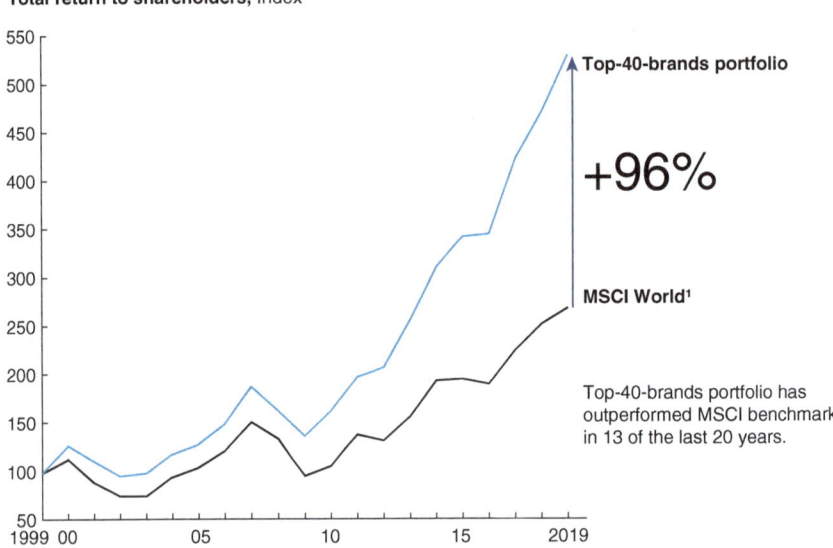

Figure 5.1. Strong brands outperform the market.[18]
Source: McKinsey Marketing & Sales Practice.

The above discussion about the payoffs of strong brands is not just theory—a global survey confirms it (Figure 5.2). Shining brands illuminate trust, guiding customers toward them.

Branding transcends the physical boundaries of products and companies. It is a powerful tool that can be applied to anything that seeks to be perceived, remembered, and valued. Whether it is a sleek new phone, a charismatic politician, a revolutionary movement, or a nation with a rich history, branding crafts a narrative, shapes perception, and builds emotional connections. It involves identifying core values, crafting a compelling story, and consistently communicating that narrative across all touchpoints. Ultimately, branding is the art of shaping how the world perceives something, and its potential extends

---

[18] Lehmann, S., Nils, L., Phyllis, R., and Eloy, T. (2020). The future of brand strategy: it's time to go electric. McKinsey & Company. 27 May 2020. https://www.mckinsey.com/capabilities/growth-marketing-and-sales/our-insights/the-future-of-brand-strategy-its-time-to-go-electric.

Figure 5.2. What customers would do for strong brands they trust.[19]

far beyond the confines of traditional marketing. Read how branding is used in Singapore's journey as a country, from third to first world.

Case: From Humble Port to Global Hub—Singapore's Journey of Branding and Transformation[20]

Author Buck Song Koh said, "Without nation branding, there would be no Singapore."[21] In fact, he claims "nation branding is the lifeblood of any nation."[22] Indeed, in an increasingly interconnected world, nations are no longer passive players in the global arena. They actively compete for talent, investment, and influence, and the tool they wield is nation branding. One of the most important functions of national branding is building trust and fostering a sense of national identity. A strong brand image can attract foreign investment, tourism, and talent, contributing to economic growth and development. It can

---

[19] Marketingcharts.com. (2021). The importance of brand trust. 14 May 2021. Accessed on 13 December 2023. https://www.marketingcharts.com/brand-related/brand-metrics-117111.

[20] The authors gratefully acknowledge Brandon Chew (Deputy Director for International Branding, Ministry of Trade and Industry) and Jerine Lee (Brand, Marketing and Communications, EDB) for their invaluable insights and content contributions, which were instrumental in the development of this case study.

[21] Koh, B. S. (2017). *Brand Singapore : Nation Branding after Lee Kuan Yew, in a Divisive World*, 2nd edn. Marshall Cavendish, Singapore.

[22] *Ibid.*

also create a sense of pride and unity among citizens, especially in a globalized world where cultural identities are increasingly fluid.

In 1965, Singapore was an improbable young nation, struggling to find its identity on the world stage. A fledgling economy with limited resources that relied on manufacturing. Fast forward to the 21st century, and Singapore is the fourth wealthiest city in the world.[23] Its economic miracle, fueled by trade and industry, had left behind the image of a sleepy port city. Its per capita GDP rose from S$1,600 in 1965 to S$113,779 in 2023.[24] This meteoric rise wasn't accidental; it was meticulously orchestrated, with branding playing a transformative role.

Branding Singapore is a decades-long effort that intensified in the 21st century. The year 2010 marked the birth of crafting a national narrative for coherence and coordinated identity. Launched in March 2010, the "Your Singapore" campaign by the Singapore Tourism Board (STB), showcased the city-state's vibrant multi-culturalism and welcoming atmosphere of dining, shopping, and cultural attractions. Visitors from overseas were invited to share their personal experiences, adding an emotional touch to the brand narrative. Meanwhile, the Singapore Economic Development Board (EDB) launched "Future Ready Singapore," highlighting its aspiration to be a partner for global businesses. It encapsulated the benefits that Singapore offered to businesses powered by the country's brand truths of collaboration, forward-looking, can-do spirit, and ingenuity to develop future-forward solutions. These initial efforts were crucial in building a foundation of trust and establishing Singapore as a reliable business partner.

In 2017, Singapore's brand strategy evolved: Both agencies came together to create the unified Brand SG, while retaining the flexibility to run their own marketing campaigns and activities that brought the

---

[23] Tan, A. (2024). Singapore is world's 4th wealthiest city, overtaking London: Report. *The Straits Times*. 7 May 2024. https://www.straitstimes.com/business/singapore-is-world-s-4th-wealthiest-city-overtaking-london-report.

[24] Department of Statistics Singapore. (2024). National accounts. https://www.singstat.gov.sg/find-data/search-by-theme/economy/national-accounts/latest-data.

Figure 5.3. The Singapore (SG) Mark.

"Passion Made Possible" brand narrative to life. This campaign showcased Singapore's ability to turn seemingly impossible dreams into reality, attracting talent and businesses seeking fertile ground for innovation. Singaporean brand ambassadors shared their stories about how they could pursue their passions in Singapore. The Singapore (SG) Mark (Figure 5.3) is the logo and the key visual signifier of the Singapore brand.

From 2018, EDB built on the Singapore business brand to position it as one of the world's most desirable places to start and grow a business. "The Impossible Story" was a global campaign that showcased the country's achievements proving the world wrong. A series of short stories by innovators, entrepreneurs, and trailblazers told their stories of success, challenging the very notion of what was possible. It celebrated Singapore's spirit of innovation, collaboration, and can-do spirit, reflecting the "Passion Made Possible" narrative that "no dream is too big for Singapore."

Then came the world-altering pandemic. Faced with a global crisis, Singapore pivoted with agility.[25] The "Dear World" campaign in 2020 showcased the nation's agility and resilience amidst the global pandemic. The video highlights how Singapore overcomes adversity with grit and resolve to "not (looking) at what if, but what's next." Singaporeans are "a people who stare impossible challenges in the face and say no, we won't be beaten," the video's narrator adds. This campaign portrayed Singapore's proactive response, including its early and decisive moves like securing crucial vaccine agreements and being

---

[25] EDB. (2020). Turning lemons into lemonade: Five lessons from COVID-19 for businesses. 7 August 2020. https://www.edb.gov.sg/en/business-insights/insights/turning-lemons-into-lemonade-five-lessons-from-covid-19-for-businesses.html.

among the first to receive the Pfizer-BioNTech vaccine. Furthermore, BioNTech's strategic decision to establish Singapore as its Southeast Asia headquarters and first Asia-Pacific hub further underscored the nation's strong standing and effective pandemic management. Beyond its intended international audience, the campaign resonated deeply with Singaporeans, even being shared by the then Prime Minister Lee Hsien Loong on social media. The campaign fostered deep emotional resonance and ignited national pride by showcasing Singapore's proactive global positioning through early vaccine agreements, effectively serving as a powerful rallying cry that reinforced solidarity and boosted morale during a period of uncertainty.

In 2021, EDB started positioning Singapore as a force for good. This initiative positioned Singapore as a prime destination for businesses seeking to navigate the new normal, emphasizing its commitment to sustainability and social responsibility. It marks Singapore's commitment to balance profits and purpose to create a better future for generations to come. This campaign resonated with a post-pandemic world seeking solutions and partnerships. This was followed by "Your Business Needs Singapore", a global campaign that highlights Singapore's secure, stable, and open economy as an ideal environment for global trade and business expansion, particularly amidst global volatility and challenges. It emphasizes Singapore's trustworthiness and stability, positioning it as a place where companies can innovate and take calculated risks.

These campaigns, woven together, created a powerful brand identity for Singapore. Today, Singapore stands tall, a global hub for business. It punches above its weight class among the world's best and ranks top in Asia for talent, innovation, sustainability, and digital competitiveness. Its economic transformation is a story of strategic vision and a testament to the power of branding, of a nation finding its voice and place in the world. As the world navigates an ever-changing landscape, one thing remains certain: The story of Singapore's brand, its constant evolution and adaptation, will continue to inspire and shape its future.

Here are some takeaways from EDB:

- Nation branding shares similarities with product branding in its aim to create a distinctive and meaningful differentiation. Both aim to build trust and foster identity. Both employ storytelling, messaging strategies, and visual elements to attract a target audience.
- Both product and nation branding are not just about creating catchy slogans and beautiful advertisements. Both require a holistic approach that aligns internal policies and practices with the desired brand image.
- Nation-building also has an important internal dimension. Internal branding is the way the country brand is communicated to, and shaped in the minds of, the citizens of that country—the people who are, or are supposed to be, "living the brand." A shared national brand narrative fosters a sense of belonging and national pride, uniting citizens behind a common goal. This is analogous to the way that a company or product brand is promoted to the employees of that corporation. A company that prides itself on top-quality products must first convince its own employees of the brand attributes.
- The world is constantly evolving, and brands, including nation brands, must constantly evaluate and refine the brand narrative to reflect changing realities and address emerging challenges. Singapore, for example, has successfully adapted its brand story to focus on sustainability and innovation in recent years, reflecting the evolving priorities of the global community.

From Strategy to Perception: How Branding Bridges the Gap

Positioning, the internal compass guiding a brand's direction, holds little power if customers are oblivious to its essence. This is where branding steps in, acting as the translator, educator, and storyteller. Through consistent messaging and engaging experiences across all touchpoints, branding shapes and solidifies the brand image in the minds of consumers.

Think of it like teaching: Positioning is the curriculum, a carefully crafted plan for what you want students to learn. Branding is the actual teaching, the engaging lessons, the interactive exercises, and the classroom atmosphere that bring that curriculum to life. This teaching process requires both clarity and consistency. A clear message about what the brand stands for acts as the curriculum, while consistent delivery through every touchpoint reinforces the lessons learned. This consistency encompasses not just verbal communication but also the entire customer experience, from product quality to interaction styles. Each element must resonate with the brand's DNA, delivering on its promises and shaping positive associations in the minds of customers.

In essence, branding is about making your positioning real. It is not enough to simply declare who you are; you must show it, live it, and breathe it into every customer interaction. Only then can you bridge the gap between your internal strategy and the hearts and minds of your audience. Here are a few ways to brand:

Building an identity with brand elements

Brand elements are the building blocks of identity, the bricks and mortar that identify and make your brand stand out in the crowd. These iconic tools—from the catchy name to the vibrant logo—act as flags, waving in the marketplace and saying, "Here we are! This is who we are!"

Choosing these elements, especially the brand name, deserves careful consideration. The logo, colors, and typography paint your brand's visual identity. These elements should be instantly recognizable, forming a memorable visual language that speaks volumes about your values and personality. And let's not forget the emotional connection. A brand's personality, its tone of voice and interactions, breathes life into its image. Is it playful and energetic? Sophisticated and elegant? Authentic and relatable? This personality should shine through every touchpoint, forging an emotional bond with your audience beyond mere transactions.

At the heart of this structure lies the brand name, the cornerstone that anchors everything. It should roll off the tongue with ease, leaving a lasting impression. Think meaningful, likable, and adaptable. Ensure your name is unique and legally protected. If international expansion is on your horizon, choose a name that translates well and has positive connotations in other languages. Avoiding potential pitfalls early on can save you from the headache (and expense) of rebranding or confusing customers later.

Brand name strategies

A brand name is often the first thing a consumer encounters, shaping their initial perception and influencing their decision to engage. The name becomes synonymous with the brand, embodying its values, personality, and target audience. A well-chosen name can be a springboard for building brand equity, and increasing brand awareness, recall, and loyalty over time.

Choosing a brand name strategy is not just about picking a fancy moniker; it is about navigating your brand on a map of market segments and customer desires. Weigh the pros and cons of each approach, considering brand equity, synergy, customer loyalty, and market demands. Let's explore the possibilities:

- **Family branding/umbrella branding/branded house:**

  Imagine a powerful, trusted name such as Sony, Samsung, or Tata. This is the essence of family or umbrella branding, where all products nestle under the warmth of a single parent brand. For example, Samsung uses the same brand name across its entire range of products from TVs, audio, and smartphones to household appliances. Strong brand equity, along with the brand's associations (such as brand image, USPs, or whatever consumers know of the brand), spill over to new products, creating instant recognition and trust. Consistency fosters memorability and simplifies marketing efforts. This is especially so when products are synergistic—Apple's loyal fans embrace its entire ecosystem, happily hopping from Macs to iPhones.

The historical significance of family branding for family-owned businesses in Asia

The branded house strategy is commonly used in Asia, where some 85% of businesses are family-owned.[26] In fact, two-thirds of the largest family businesses are based in Asia.[27] The use of family brands by family-owned businesses is deeply intertwined with their history and holds significant cultural and economic importance.

Take, for instance, the chaebols in South Korea. In the aftermath of the Korean War, chaebols played a crucial role in rebuilding the nation's economy. The Korean government actively encouraged chaebols to grow, viewing them as drivers of economic development. This support often extended to promoting their family brands as national champions. Their family brands, often synonymous with the founders' names, became symbols of trust and national pride. With a scarcity of established brands, family brands offered a sense of familiarity and security to consumers. This fostered loyalty and helped chaebols rapidly expand.

Chaebols used their family brands to expand into diverse industries, leveraging their established reputation and brand recognition to enter diverse markets and achieve rapid diversification. Family brands served as a powerful tool for centralizing control within chaebols. Unifying diverse businesses under one name also facilitated resource sharing, economies of scale, and cross-selling opportunities. This created a perception of reliability and helped them gain market share. The family brand became a tool for acquiring smaller companies and integrating them under the same umbrella, further solidifying their dominance. Chaebol brands became deeply embedded in Korean society, sponsoring cultural events, and influencing consumer preferences. This further cemented their image as national icons.

---

[26] Wright, M. (2018). 4 things to know about family-owned businesses in Asia. 6 December 2018. Accessed on 19 February 2024. https://www.imperial.ac.uk/business-school/ib-knowledge/entrepreneurship-innovation/4-things-know-about-family-owned-businesses-asia.

[27] *Ibid.*

> Today, chaebol brands are increasingly used to promote innovation and compete on the global stage. They are adapting their brand identities to resonate with international audiences. In contrast, while the Tata Group in India remains a family-owned business, it uses different brands for different segments and businesses. Founded in 1868, the company has grown from a trading company to a global conglomerate with business in steel, automotive, consultancy, consumer products, and hospitality, amongst others. Whilst most of its businesses remain under the umbrella of the Tata brand, it acquired some foreign brands (e.g., Jaguar, Land Rover, and Tetley) to capture the hearts of customers who prefer imported brands and to penetrate overseas markets.

Brands contemplating a family branding strategy should consider if the existing brand's strength can catapult new products to success. Or might they weigh each other down? This double-edged sword requires careful wielding. Remember, Lexus soared in luxury away from the bindings of Toyota, while the Infiniti launched as a new model under the Nissan brand sputtered.

But sometimes, variety is the spice of life. In this case, it is better off letting brands fly solo. Understand customers' desires for the product category—do they seek brand consistency or freedom of choice? Also, all brands are in one boat: While a family brand can offer a springboard, poorly performing new products can drag down the entire ship (known as brand dilution).

- **Multi-branding/house of brands:**

    Laneige, Sulwhasoo, Innisfree, Etude House, and Aestura each has a distinct personality based on clear segmentation under the same AmorePacific roof (Figure 5.4). This is multi-branding. This strategy is the flipside of family branding. Each brand is built from scratch to target specific consumer segments with tailored messaging and distinct identities. This strategy demands more resources, and the new brand can't leverage the reputation of a more established

Figure 5.4. A collage of advertisements from AmorePacific brands.[28]

brand, but its advantage is its freedom to cater to diverse segments, offering variety, and maximizing market reach. The risk of brand dilution is reduced. A multi-brand approach can increase your retail footprint.

---

[28] Schimminger, M. (2024). Laneige launches the Dreamy Skin Campaign with a little help from actress Sydney Sweeney. *Fashion Times*. https://www.fashiontimes.com/laneige-dreamy-skin-campaign-10822; Chong, C. (2016). Journey of the Green Tea Seed Serum by Innisfree flies to Malaysia!. Lipstiq. https://www.innisfree.my/event/main1-green-tea-seed-serum; AESTURA. (n.d.). AtoBarrier365 Lotion for normal to dry skin. https://www.amazon.com/AESTURA-Atobarrier-Lotion-Normal-Skin/dp/B07S5K16W7; K-Pop Life. (n.d.). SHINee Etude House Replay Collection. KpopLife. https://kpoplife.com/shinee-etude-housereplay-collection/; Sulwhasoo US. (n.d.). Sulwhasoo Rebloom × Rosé. https://us.sulwhasoo.com/pages/sulwhasoo-rebloom-x-rose.

For multi-branding, the primary challenge lies in the complexity and resource intensity of managing multiple brands simultaneously. Each brand requires dedicated marketing efforts, separate positioning strategies, and potentially different distribution channels. This can strain resources and increase the risk of internal competition or cannibalization between brands. Moreover, maintaining distinct brand identities and ensuring consistent messaging across multiple brands can be demanding, requiring careful coordination and strategic planning.

Read about how Lenovo uses a multi-brand strategy in Japan in the case study later in this chapter.

- **Sub-branding:**

This is a combination approach where the parent brand endorses the product brand. Think 3M Scotch-brite for its cleaning products or 3M Command for its adhesives or "Frank by OCBC," which the bank started to target youths and young working adults. These sub-brands leverage the parent's long-established reputation while establishing their own unique space to offer specialized expertise and diversification. Sub-branding aims to segment the market without diluting the core brand. But each sub-brand needs a distinct identity, a clear moat separating it from its siblings. Avoid the murky confusion of brands that blend into each other, leaving customers wondering, "Which one am I buying?"

- **Cobranding:**

Cobranding is like a marriage between two brands that join forces, combining their strengths and audiences to create something new and exciting. As both brands are leaders in their own categories, this is a synergistic strategy that helps bring the best of both worlds to customers in one product. This strategy can also help both brands acquire new customers as loyal customers from one brand may be more open to trying out the products from the other brand in the future. It can also be useful for firms that lack expertise in one area and may need to borrow associations from partnering brands for new products (e.g., Huawei, a Chinese tech giant, partnered with German camera maker Leica to co-engineer (and co-brand) camera systems for their high-end smartphones in 2016). This collaboration aimed to leverage Leica's renowned optics expertise and brand prestige to enhance Huawei's smartphone photography capabilities and appeal to photography enthusiasts.

Adidas' collaborations are sweet examples of this strategy. Starting as early as 1972, long before the word "collab" became a hip word, Adidas collaborated with tennis star Stan Smith, to name the shoe after him. It was a marriage of perfect fit between a brand championing athletic performance and a personality embodying effortless cool, allowing it to become a symbol of individuality and understated style. Its versatility allowed it to adapt to countless trends, from punk rock rebellion to preppy chic, retaining its core appeal throughout. Then, in 2003, Adidas in collaboration with Japanese designer Yohji Yamamoto, formed Y-3, the first brand to blend high fashion with sportswear. The Y-3 Stan Smith (Figure 5.5) was born in 2016, injecting Yamamoto's signature deconstructivist approach into the classic silhouette. The Stan Smith's journey through Y-3's lens demonstrates its enduring relevance. It is a statement piece that represents the intersection of sportswear, fashion, and high-end design.

Selecting partners with complementary brand values, target audiences, and synergistic offerings is crucial for co-branding success. Aligning brand visions, managing potential conflicts of interest, and ensuring a seamless integration of brand identities can be challenging. Additionally, co-branding initiatives require effective communication and coordination between partners to

Figure 5.5. Adidas-Y3's Stan Smith.

maintain consistent messaging and avoid diluting individual brand strengths.

- **Private label branding ("house brand"):**

    Amazon's and RedMart's private labels, popularly known as "house brands", show how retailers can build their own empires. By creating their own products, they gain control over pricing, presentation, and customer data. House brands are a force to reckon with. By directly sourcing and selling to the retailer's existing customer base without having to incur marketing and advertising costs associated with other brands, house brands typically offer high profit margins even though they are priced more competitively. Retailers have complete control over shelf space and promotional activity for their house brands. This allows them to strategically place products and incentivize purchases, maximizing marketing and sales effectiveness. House brands provide valuable data about customer preferences and demand. Retailers can track sales and feedback to understand what resonates with their audience and adjust their product offerings accordingly. Another example is National Trades Union Congress (NTUC) FairPrice, Singapore's largest grocery retailer with over 230 outlets (Figure 5.6).

Figure 5.6. Examples of NTUC FairPrice private label products.

By understanding the pros and cons of each brand name strategy, marketers can make informed decisions that align with their overall brand goals, target audience, and market dynamics. Read how Lenovo strategically uses brand names to segment its markets in Asia.

Case: A Symphony of Brands—Lenovo's Strategic Approach across Asia[29]

Lenovo, a Chinese technology giant, adopts a "protect and attack" strategy. While it builds scale by using a single brand in China, it navigates the diverse Asian market with a strategic symphony of brands, tailoring its approach to each region's unique landscape.

In its home market, Lenovo builds and protects its "moat" as China generates most of the company's revenue. As the dominant PC and server leader, it enjoys economies of scale and strong relationships with key institutions in commercial and public sector markets. It focuses on localization, R&D, and enterprise partnerships, solidifying its domestic dominance. Perhaps its most impressive advantage is its immense network of distribution channels, the majority of which are exclusive distributors of Lenovo products. Its local expertise also secures its place in the hearts and minds of Chinese consumers that its non-Chinese competitors find difficult to unseat. It uses its local insights to dominate the rural markets where most Chinese consumers are, before its competitors. For example, it distributed its most affordable desktops that were pre-loaded with applications to help farmers price their crops. It also launched a "wedding computer" in auspicious red and emblazoned with the Chinese character for "double happiness" (a word that is commonly used in weddings), which became a popular gift for brides and grooms.[30]

Simultaneously, it leverages its success at home to fuel global expansion in its "attack" strategy, acquiring brands and diversifying

---

[29] The authors gratefully acknowledge Ken Wong (President, Solutions and Services Group) and Tom Cheng (Chief of Staff, Solutions and Services Group) for their invaluable insights and content contributions, which were instrumental in the development of this case study.

[30] Salter, C. (2011). Protect and attack: Lenovo's new strategy. *Fast Company*. 22 November 2011. Accessed on 15 February 2024. https://www.fastcompany.com/1793529/protect-and-attack-lenovos-new-strategy.

its portfolio. Its success in China reflects Lenovo's deep understanding of its home turf and its ambition to become a global force. Across the diverse tapestry of the rest of Asia, Lenovo adopts a flexible approach, demonstrating Lenovo's ability to cater to diverse regional nuances. In fast-growing Southeast Asia, it emphasizes affordability and online accessibility, while in developed economies such as South Korea, it competes in the premium segment with innovative offerings.

In Japan, where brand loyalty and local preferences reign supreme, the market leader, Lenovo, employs a multi-brand strategy. The Lenovo brand caters to the mainstream consumer and small business segment, offering value and reliability. The ThinkPad brand positions itself as a premium business tool for professionals and enterprises, emphasizing its performance and security. Meanwhile, the acquired NEC brand targets the corporate and government sectors, leveraging its long-standing relationships and local compliance expertise. Finally, the acquisition of Fujitsu in 2017 adds another Japanese brand name to its portfolio. Lenovo can leverage Fujitsu's capabilities in global sales, customer support, and R&D, while Fujitsu will benefit from Lenovo's global scale and presence. This strategic harmony allows Lenovo to capture a wider market share through differentiated targeting of diverse segments while maintaining distinct brand identities.

Here are some learnings from Lenovo:

- **Global markets are not monolithic entities:** A brand that works in one country might not resonate in another due to cultural differences, income levels, or preferences. Adapting to regional nuances is crucial for success in diverse markets.
- **Lenovo's success hinges on its ability to adapt its brand strategy to each region's unique landscape:** The Chinese strategy focuses on dominance and expansion in China, while it uses a multi-brand strategy in Japan. The rest of Asia sees a flexible adaptation to regional dynamics.
- **Brands play a crucial role as a segmentation tool:** Each brand can have its own distinct identity, messaging, pricing, and channels that resonate with its specific target audience. By using a multi-brand

strategy to address the needs of different segments, businesses can capture a larger portion of the overall market.
- However, managing multiple brands requires significant resources and expertise.

Communicating through secondary associations

Beyond their own identities, brands can leverage secondary associations to enhance their images and attract new customers. These are connections with other entities, events, or experiences that "rub off" on the brand, enhancing its image and perception. Brands can leverage secondary associations in a variety of ways.

Celebrities with strong personal brands can transfer their popularity and images to your product, boosting its perceived value and appeal. Nike partnered with Michael Jordan, creating an iconic association with basketball and athletic excellence. Shu Uemura's choice of brand ambassador, Naomi Watanabe, not only taps into her influence on millennials, but the collaboration with her stance for body positivity also aligns with the brand's mission to promote and respect differences.[31] Choose wisely, though, as mismatched endorsements can backfire.

Sponsoring relevant events or causes that resonate with your target customers puts your brand in the spotlight, associating it with shared sentiments and experiences and tapping into the event's audience. Think Red Bull with extreme sports, Rolex with Wimbledon, and Razer. Founded in 2015, Singapore brand, Razer was selling gaming mouse and keyboards under a Microsoft/Razer co-brand. With a laser-sharp focus on its core audience—gamers, the brand knew it needed to offer more than the precision and speed it built into its products. Razer recognized the power of esports and its potential to reach its target audience directly. The brand started by sponsoring small local tournaments, building relationships with the community, and showcasing their products to passionate players.

---

[31] Marchese, K. (2019). Naomi Watanabe serves body positivity as a platform for Shu Uemura Cosmetics. *Designboom*. 26 July 2019. Accessed on 29 January 2024. https://www.designboom.com/design/naomi-watanabe-shu-uemura-now-me-yuni-yoshida-07-26-2019/.

As the brand gained traction, it moved on to bigger events such as the International Dota 2 Championships (The International) and the Electronic Entertainment Expo (E3). Pro gamers, convinced by the performance and community, increasingly favored Razer mice. Watching professional gamers dominate with Razer mice became a powerful advertisement, influencing aspiring players and solidifying Razer's reputation as the "mouse of the pros," which translated into mainstream popularity for serious gamers. The impact of Razer's sponsorship strategy was undeniable. Their market share soared, with the Razer DeathAdder becoming the best-selling gaming mouse globally. Their sponsorship approach fueled their expansion into other gaming peripherals, establishing them as a complete high-performing solution for dedicated gamers.

Associating your brand with cultural heritage can evoke nostalgia, foster community engagement, and add a layer of authenticity. Being successfully paired with a cultural event helps a brand take ownership of the occasion and increase top-of-mind awareness of its products. Guinness Stout, born in Dublin in 1759, embodies the Irish spirit through and through. Its rich, dark brew has become synonymous with Irish pubs and celebrations, making it a natural fit for St. Patrick's Day. While not initially associated with the holiday, Guinness had solidified its role as the unofficial drink of the day. Guinness's clever marketing campaigns further cemented the link. Slogans such as "St. Patrick's Day: A Guinness Thing" and iconic green-hued advertising have solidified the brand's ownership of the holiday in many minds. Today, Guinness celebrates St. Patrick's Day with global campaigns, hosting events, limited-edition brews, and partnerships with pubs that bring the Irish spirit to diverse audiences far beyond the Emerald Isle.

Some countries have positive connotations that can enhance brand image and attract customers seeking specific qualities. For example, Swiss watches are renowned for precision and craftsmanship, Germany for its engineering standards, and of course, the Korean Hallyu that has taken the world by storm. The Korean Wave, or Hallyu, has not only captivated international audiences with K-pop, K-dramas, and Korean cinema but also acted as a powerful catapult for Korean brands to successfully infiltrate international markets. Hallyu has created a global fascination with Korean culture, including its beauty trends, fashion, and cuisine. Korean brands have capitalized on this by tapping into this cultural appetite. Korean dramas and music videos became prime real estate for showcasing Korean products. From smartphones to cosmetics, brands such as Samsung, Hyundai, and Laniege seamlessly integrated their products into narratives, offering subtle yet effective product placements. This exposure familiarized global audiences with Korean brands, fostering curiosity and brand recognition. Food and beverage brands such as Nongshim and Bibigo capitalized on the growing interest in Korean cuisine fueled by K-dramas. Their products became synonymous with the shows, creating a desire to experience the taste of Korea firsthand. The global adoration for Korean celebrities, known as K-stars, also became a powerful marketing tool for brands. From global ambassadors such as BTS and Blackpink to popular actors and actresses, K-stars adorned themselves with Korean products, generating immense buzz and desire among their dedicated fan bases. This endorsement, coupled with celebrities' impeccable fashion sense, made Korean products highly sought-after worldwide. The Hallyu wave serves as a testament to the power of cultural influence in shaping global markets.

Brands can also align themselves to values that customers care about. For example, Coke associates its products with happiness. Coca-Cola's advertising has consistently focused on evoking positive emotions and associating the drink with simple pleasures and everyday moments of happiness. From iconic campaigns such as "Open Happiness" to newsjacking happy events such as the royal wedding, Coca-Cola has built a strong narrative of shared joy and celebration. Coca-Cola's global presence means that its association with happiness transcends cultural boundaries. The brand has adapted its messaging and marketing strategies to resonate with diverse audiences while still maintaining its core message of joy and connection. Such storytelling is instrumental in humanizing the brand to connect on an emotional level to its customers.

Communicating with brand purpose

Around 88% of customers believe that trust becomes more important in times of uncertainty.[32] Trust in a brand refers to the confidence customers have that the brand will consistently deliver on its promise and live by the values that are aligned with what customers want to support. Companies wanting to build trust and humanize their brands may consider adopting a brand purpose. Brand purpose sends the message that the brand goes beyond just selling products or services. It is the core set of values and beliefs that typically embody the broader theme of supporting human good, and shapes how the brand interacts with customers and the society they live in. A brand purpose is about how brands can solve an external broader challenge and in so doing, make the brand more familiar and favorable to its customers.

Brands with brand purposes that align with customers' personal values offer them a platform to achieve something they may not be able to do individually. It speaks to their values and aspirations and makes them feel like they are part of something bigger than themselves. It gives them a reason to care about your brand and to connect with it on a deeper level than just price or features.

Finding your brand purpose is not about chasing trends or copying others. It must be authentic to your core identity. It starts with an introspective journey of understanding your company's history, values, and unique strengths. What makes you different? What impact do you want to make on the world? Talking to employees, customers, or the stakeholders in the community you operate in will help you understand their needs and aspirations. What problems can you help them solve? For example, Changi General Hospital (CGH) used a visioning exercise to find out what matters to their employees (read more about it in the case in this chapter).

---

[32] Solis, B. (2022). The new role of marketing: Drive business growth by reimagining customer engagement. *Forbes*. 1 November 2022. Accessed on 12 December 2023. https://www.forbes.com/sites/briansolis/2022/11/01/the-new-role-of-marketing-drive-business-growth-by-reimagining-customer-engagement/?sh=c53c0c7431c7.

SK-II's Change Destiny campaign is a prime example of brand activism done right. It tackled a sensitive social issue, resonated with its target audience, and delivered tangible business results. Launched in April 2016, SK-II's "Change Destiny" campaign was not just another beauty ad blitz. It was a bold statement challenging the belief that destiny is set at birth and moving the brand from a product-centric narrative of reversing aging to wider societal issues women face. Its most notable example was a campaign for China, where the label "leftover women" stigmatized unmarried women over 25. The campaign's relatable stories and authentic portrayal of women's experiences fostered a strong emotional connection with the audience. It led to over 50% sales increase in the nine months following the campaign's launch, demonstrating its commercial success. The campaign sparked widespread engagement and discussion online. Social media platforms saw millions of views and shares of campaign videos and testimonials. All these raised awareness for the brand.

The campaign's success led SK-II to launch additional initiatives promoting female empowerment, self-acceptance, or resilience—all unified by "#ChangeDestiny." The hashtag also allowed the brand access to user-generated content (UGC) about issues they feel challenged by. In March 2021, the brand launched SK-II Studio,[33] an in-house film studio that uses the brand's voice to drive conversations about social issues and pressures currently affecting women. SKII did more than talk. They also launched a "#ChangeDestiny" fund, which contributes US$1 for every view garnered on each SK-II studio film. These funds were used to support women-owned small businesses and entrepreneurs that were impacted by the COVID-19 pandemic in Tokyo.

The integration of this brand purpose and the authentic follow-through demonstrated by their brand communication and activities help differentiate SK-II from the other products in an extremely competitive makeup and skincare market.

---

[33] Wu, W. (2021). SKII launches a new film studio to explore brand storytelling. *Jing Daily*. April 2021. Accessed on 26 January 2024. https://jingdaily.com/posts/sk-ii-film-studio-explore-brand-storytelling.

Communicating with 360-degree branding

To create the right brand image, we must construct ideal brand encounters or experiences that leave customers, or potential customers, with positive thoughts, emotions, and convictions.[34] These brand encounters or "touchpoints" are not limited to advertisements and other marketing efforts, especially in today's environment where consumer-driven sources such as reviews, recommendations from family and friends, and past experiences[35] (recall how we may have sworn never to fly with a certain airline because of a horrible in-flight experience) are more trusted than advertisements. Many of these touchpoints are not under the purview of marketers. Hence, marketing cannot be done by marketers alone.

Instead, everyone in the organization is a marketer or has a marketing mindset. McKinsey[36] suggests that companies "become marketing vehicles, and the marketing organization itself needs to become the customer-engagement engine, responsible for establishing priorities and stimulating dialogue throughout the enterprise as it seeks to design, build, operate, and renew cutting edge customer-engagement approaches." In other words, the marketing unit architects the branding strategy for customer engagement, and it must make sure that potential customer touchpoints are informed about it so they can accurately let customers experience the brand as intended.

Let's learn more about 360-degree branding through an excellent demonstration by CGH.

The Asian POV

We mentioned that diversity in Asia can be challenging for marketing. Branding can be a segmentation tool to cater to such diversity.

---

[34] Keller, K. L. (1993). Conceptualizing, measuring, managing customer-based brand equity. *Journal of Marketing*, 57(1), 1–22.

[35] Court, D., Dave, E., Susan, M., and Ole, J. V. (2009). The consumer decision journey. *McKinsey Quarterly*, 3.

[36] French, T., Laura, L., and Paul M. (2011). We're all marketers now. *McKinsey Quarterly*. July 2011.

As shown in this chapter, several branding strategies have proven successful in engaging diverse consumer segments in Asia.

By using a family brand in its home market where it is trusted and dominant, brands such as the Korean chaebol brands and Lenovo maximize their brand strength to gain market leadership. On the other hand, multi-branding, as exemplified by Lenovo using four distinct brands in Japan, allows companies to effectively cater to diverse preferences while maximizing effective reach through to target different market segments with tailored messaging and distinct brand identities. This approach recognizes that Asian markets are not monolithic and that consumers have varying preferences and needs. Lenovo's use of four distinct brands in Japan showcases how this strategy can effectively cater to diverse customer segments while maximizing market reach.

Another successful strategy is co-branding, where two brands join forces to tap into each other's expertise to create something new and exciting, such as the case study of Adidas' collaborations with figures like Stan Smith and Yohji Yamamoto. This approach can help brands tap into new customer segments and enhance their brand image by associating with partners that resonate with their target audience. We saw how this was executed by the partnership between Huawei and Leica. Leveraging Leica's renowned optics expertise and brand prestige enhanced Huawei's smartphone photography capabilities and premium positioning.

Case: From "Cannot Go Home" to "Caring General Hospital"—A Story of Employee Engagement and Brand Transformation[37]

In the service industry, and especially in a hospital, brand understanding among employees is not a luxury, it is an absolute necessity. It is the difference between a clinical transaction and a compassionate

---

[37] The authors gratefully acknowledge Professor Ng Kee Chong (Chief Executive Officer), Lee Keng Min (Director, Corporate Planning) and Teo Yin Yin (Deputy Director, Corporate Communications) for their invaluable insights and content contributions, which were instrumental in the development of this case study.

journey of healing. Patients are not just customers; they are entrusting their well-being to the hospital's care, making every touchpoint an opportunity to build trust and embody the hospital's brand values. This is where 360-degree branding comes in, ensuring every aspect aligns with the hospital's vision, resulting in improvements in patient experience, hospital reputation, and employee engagement.

CGH, Singapore's first regional general hospital serving the community in the east, faced a double whammy: low staff morale and a negative public perception fueled by persistent online narrative on the hospital name with "cannot go home" jokes. This stemmed from heavy workloads, caused by a rapidly aging population in the community it serves, and exacerbated by the COVID-19 pandemic. During the pandemic, hospitals faced such a severe bed crunch that a doctor said "Inpatient doctors can't find their patients as they are all over the place. Patients are stacked like sardines..."[38] Staff were getting burnt out and felt under-recognized by the community they were serving.

CGH saw the need for a holistic approach that addressed both internal and external perceptions, to engender trust and confidence in patients, their families, as well as staff. Recognizing the need for immediate action, CGH embarked on a multi-pronged strategy in 2020 focused on employee engagement and brand transformation.

First, to show appreciation for colleagues' efforts and achievements in lifting morale during the pandemic, the team introduced a special internal communications series "Face off with COVID-19," which recognized staff contributions during the pandemic, fostering a sense of community, acknowledging diverse roles within the hospital, and appreciating staff for their courage and contributions in the fight against the virus amidst the pandemic.

Next, CGH embarked on a collaborative visioning exercise in July 2021 (Figure 5.7 shows a summary of the insights). Through this inclusive exercise, a new vision—"Your Trusted Care Partner, Innovating Healthcare for Tomorrow"—was born, reflecting staff aspirations and

---

[38] Khalik, S. (2022). Bed crunch at Singapore hospitals: Some patients are stuck in emergency departments. *The Straits Times*. 21 October 2022.

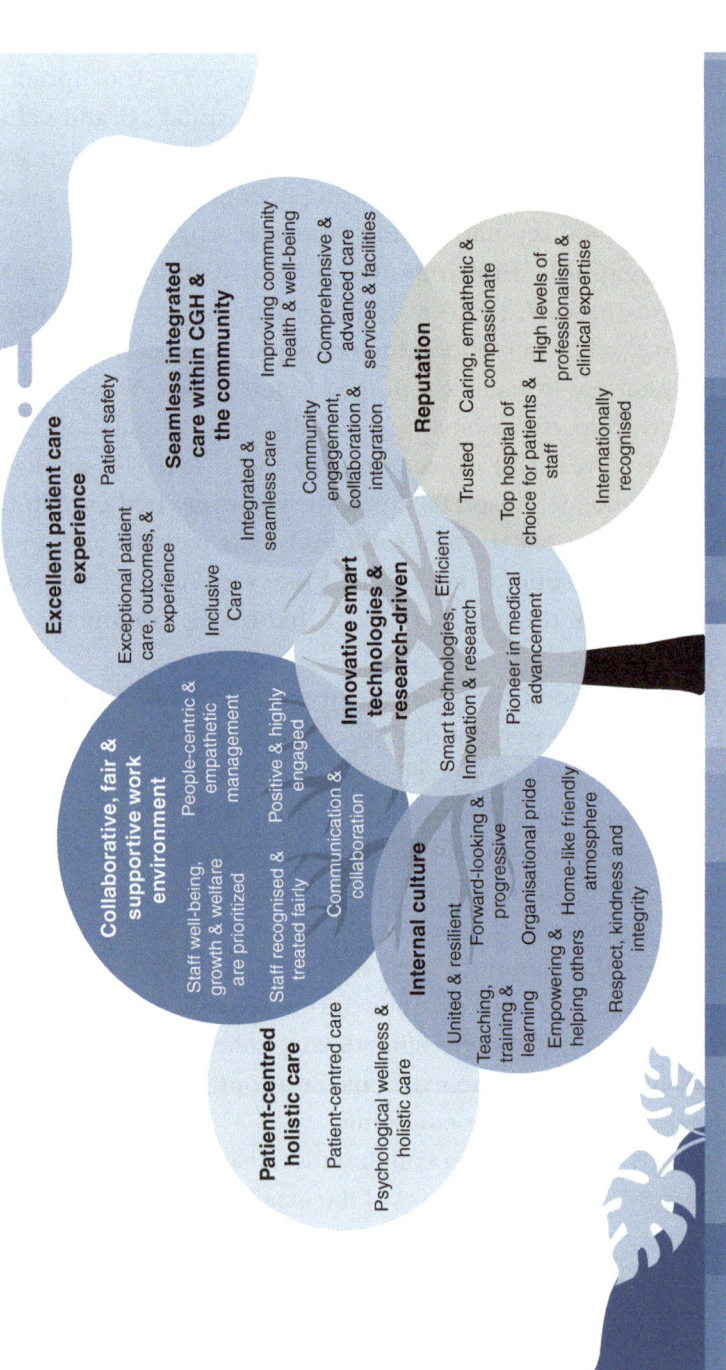

Figure 5.7. Summary of insights from visioning exercise.

future goals. This vision became the guiding light in their daily work, improvement efforts, and creation of strategic initiatives.

This new vision was launched on 23 March 2022 through a town hall meeting. Again, the management team understood that for staff to live and breathe this vision, it takes more than a vision statement. CGH invested in training, communication initiatives, and branding activities to ensure everyone understood and embraced the new vision. But this was not an easy feat given a highly diverse staff population that spans a wide range of ages and education levels, who has varying access to information and are mostly involved in the day-to-day frontline provision of healthcare services. An integrated approach using online and offline platforms ensured no one was left out of the loop. To raise awareness, meal boxes, mugs, and magnets carrying the new vision statement were distributed to all staff. Large and bold premise branding visuals were put up at various locations across the hospital.

Furthermore, a vision cascading exercise was carried out through division/department engagement activities from May 2022 to January 2023. All divisions appointed trainers, and train-the-trainer sessions were conducted for further cascading to their respective departments and teams. Staff reported that the cascading sessions helped them better understand the vision and what they must do in their jobs, and shaped how they should treat patients and caregivers and their colleagues, to achieve the vision. The new vision was also regularly featured in external communication efforts such as social media posts, and CGH publications and website to raise awareness of its commitment to innovating healthcare for tomorrow. The management team also invested in efforts to keep staff informed about the hospital's developments and initiatives toward the vision. From January 2020 to December 2022, there were over 920 leadership engagement initiatives.

These intensified communications and engagement efforts kept staff informed and valued. This was evident as early as CGH's Employment Engagement Survey (EES) in 2021. Around 99% of hospital staff participated in this survey, which is the highest rate of participation CGH had ever seen—this in itself was a good indicator of employee engagement. The EES results showed significant improvements: 90% of staff indicated they understood how their work contributed to organizational purpose, 84% felt proud to belong to CGH, 80% felt they were well-informed about matters affecting staff, and 73% felt there was sufficient interaction between senior management and staff. These results were sustained in the EES held in 2023. Additionally, a significant improvement was observed in the perception of senior management's interest in employees' well-being. In 2023, 81% of staff felt that senior management was interested in employee's well-being, up by 10% from the results in 2021.

"It was an unprecedented swing to positive results and the more recent EES held in 2023 continued to show the confidence and belief in our staff for the work that CGH does. Our staff is the most vital asset of the hospital—people on the frontline and many more working behind the scenes have demonstrated strength in vulnerability, courage in adversity, and selfless and tireless caring for patients and the community. In consistently engaging, empowering, and communicating with our staff, they, in turn, are motivated to take good care of our patients and of each other. This turns into the virtuous cycle of caring and carries on the narrative of the Caring General Hospital and its culture of empathy and compassion," said Associate Professor Ng Kee Chong, Chief Executive Officer, CGH.

The positive internal transformation translated externally. The "Cannot Go Home" narrative shifted to "Caring General Hospital," reflecting improved patient experience and staff confidence. Around 92.7% of patients surveyed in 2022 would recommend CGH to their friends and family members, up from 89.3% in 2019. This turnaround demonstrates the power of employee engagement and brand alignment. In 2023, CGH was ranked 32nd as Singapore's Best Employers.[39] It was the first time CGH was placed in this ranking. It was also consistently ranked internationally in the Newsweek rankings, most recently for the World's Best Hospitals 2024, World's Best Smart Hospitals 2024, and Best Specialized Hospitals Asia Pacific 2023.

"The hospital leadership took the bull by the horns to dispel misperceptions about the hospital with its internal communications,

---

[39] Statista. (2023). Singapore's best employers. Accessed on 15 February 2024. https://r.statista.com/en/employers/best-employers-singapore-2023/ranking/.

public messaging and branding efforts, including a new hospital Vision Statement cascaded to staff. Over a relatively short period of two years or so, this has borne much fruit. There is a palpable change in perception of CGH, with many patients saying that CGH now stands for "Can Go Home" and the CGH care team is acknowledging their good work and the hospital's capabilities in providing trusted care for patients," said Professor Ng Wai Hoe, immediate past CEO of CGH and currently Group CEO of SingHealth.

A hospital's brand reputation is built not just by its advertising but by the work they do, and the stories whispered in waiting rooms and shared on social media. Employees are not just cogs in a machine; they are the living embodiment of the brand. Their interactions with patients, families, and colleagues directly impact perceptions of the hospital. When employees are aligned with and understand the brand's values, they feel connected to a larger purpose. They are more engaged in their work, more motivated to make a difference, and less likely to experience burnout, resulting in better patient care. This leads to a happier and more productive workforce, which ultimately benefits everyone. When employees become brand ambassadors, they become champions of the hospital's good work, spreading positive word-of-mouth and solidifying the brand's image in the community. This helps attract top talent too.

In conclusion, CGH understood that branding that truly lives through every interaction within and beyond the hospital walls translates into more positive patient experiences, a stronger brand reputation, and ultimately, a more successful and sustainable hospital. By prioritizing employee brand understanding through a comprehensive 360-degree approach, hospitals can create a healthier environment for both patients and staff, fulfilling their mission and achieving true success.

Here are some key learnings from CGH:

- **Prioritizing employee engagement:** Investing in employees fosters a positive work environment, directly impacting patient care and brand reputation.
- **Aligned vision and communication:** Transparent communication and a shared vision backed by concrete actions unite staff, fostering purpose and motivation.

- **Authenticity:** Authentic brand values lived by staff create a positive and sustainable culture.

Building the Employer Brand: A Beacon in the Competitive Talent Landscape[40]

In today's competitive job market, attracting and retaining top talent is more crucial than ever. This is where a strong employer brand comes into play. It's not just about having a fancy logo or website; it's about crafting a compelling narrative that showcases your company as a desirable place to work.

According to the Chartered Institute of Personnel Development (CIPD), an employer brand refers to a collection of characteristics and features that distinguish an organization, offering a specific work experience and attracting individuals who would excel in its environment.

Think of your employer brand as your company's reputation as an employer. It encompasses everything from your work culture and values to your employee development opportunities and social responsibility efforts. A positive employer brand attracts high-caliber candidates who resonate with your company's mission and offerings. They see themselves not just filling a job but becoming part of a community that fosters growth and inspires purpose.

Social media has amplified the importance of employer branding. Job seekers can easily research potential employers online, reading employee reviews and getting a glimpse into your company culture. A strong employer brand ensures these online interactions paint a positive picture, attracting talent who are a good fit for your organization.

But it's not just about attracting new hires. As we saw from CGH's experience, employees are a company's most valuable asset, and that value extends far beyond their core job duties. They are, in essence, the face of the company, constantly interacting with customers, stakeholders, and the wider public. Their behavior, attitude, and

---

[40] The authors gratefully acknowledge Gerard Koh (Vice-President, People, Experience and Culture, Singtel) for his invaluable insights and content contributions, which were instrumental in the development of this section.

approach to work all directly influence how the brand is perceived. A strong employer brand fosters employee pride and loyalty, creating a company where people are not just working but feel valued and engaged. When employees feel valued, appreciated, and proud to be part of the team, they're more likely to be productive and innovative and stay with the company for the long haul. This translates to a more stable and successful workforce.

Furthermore, employees possess a unique advantage in promoting the company's offerings. Through daily interaction with products and services, they develop a deep understanding of their value proposition. This firsthand experience translates into genuine testimonials and recommendations that hold significant weight with potential customers. Social media platforms such as LinkedIn provide a powerful platform for employees to share their positive experiences and become vocal advocates for the company they represent. (Read more about "social selling" and how Maersk's passionate employees advocate for the brand in Chapter 13.)

Investing in employer branding is an investment in your company's future. It allows you to attract the best talent, build a strong company culture, and ultimately achieve your business goals. In a world overflowing with job options, a strong employer brand can be the tipping point that convinces top talent to choose you. In today's world, every strong brand has to be built from the inside out, with employer value proposition (EVP) being a cornerstone.

The EVP: A cornerstone of employer branding

A strong EVP is vital for attracting and retaining top talent. It acts as the foundation of your employer branding strategy, similar to how a product's functions and unique qualities anchor its brand positioning.

What makes a compelling EVP?

An EVP is a promise you make to potential employees in exchange for their skills and experience. It should detail the benefits and rewards they can expect, along with opportunities for professional growth and meaningful work. Ultimately, it's your invitation to convince them to choose your company over competitors.

Developing an authentic EVP

Building a compelling and authentic EVP requires understanding your company's purpose, culture, and what makes you unique as an employer. Here are the key steps:

Understand your organization's purpose and mission

The EVP should go beyond just making money and showcase what makes working at your company special. This could include commitment to development, work–life balance, or diversity and inclusion. For instance, as a technology services leader in Asia Pacific, NCS's purpose is as follows: "We advance our communities by partnering with governments and enterprises to harness technology. We do this by bringing people together to make the extraordinary happen."

Identify what makes your organization unique

Define your company culture and identify tangible aspects that set you apart. This could be the chance to work on innovative products, deliver exceptional customer service, or experience diverse work opportunities.

Gather employee perspectives

Conduct surveys or focus groups to understand what your employees value about working at your company. Singtel, for example, uses regular "Pulse Surveys" to gather employee feedback, including new joiners, and those exiting the company.

Craft a clear and unique EVP statement

It should be inspirational, align with employee and organizational expectations, and differentiate you from competitors. NCS' EVP, for instance, is "BIG-ID" (Figure 5.8): Belonging and inclusiveness in a caring work environment, opportunities to do Impactful work, Grow and achieve personal mastery, work with Inspiring teams, Discover one's career passions and track.

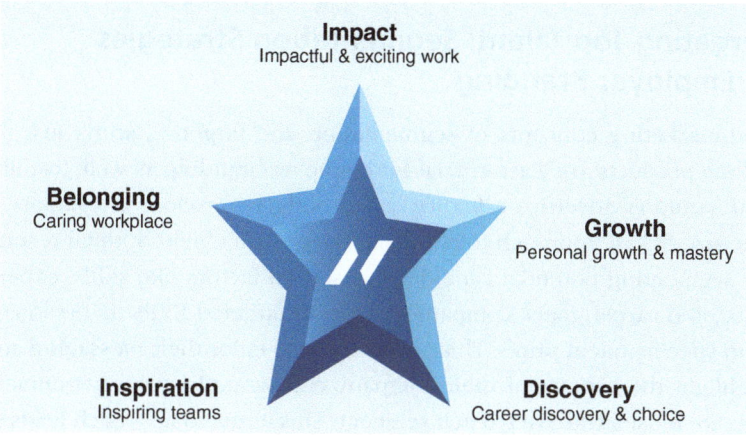

Figure 5.8. NCS' BIG-ID.

Validate and refine your EVP

Get feedback from employees and potential candidates to ensure it resonates with your target audience. NCS uses employee feedback from the annual YVS (Your Voice Survey) to continually improve employee engagement and EVP.

Integrate the EVP into existing HR policies

Make it a reality throughout the employee experience, from recruitment to retirement, including areas such as compensation and development. For instance, NCS delivers on its EVP to enable employees to discover their passions by designing its HR policy to allow employees to explore and choose from an online listing of internal roles and projects.

Develop an employer brand strategy

The EVP forms the foundation for your employer brand message. Reflect on it in job postings, your career site, and all communication channels. NCS's is as follows, "Create the extraordinary and impact millions every day. Be part of our multi-talented team and work across different industries as we innovate for our tomorrow. We're creating an environment that maximizes your potential as innovators. It's more than a job at NCS. From skill courses to having a dedicated career roadmap, your growth matters to us. Join us and equip yourself with the skills you need to excel with our various talent development programs. Our Commitment to our people is BIG-ID:"

Targeting Top Talent: Segmentation Strategies in Employer Branding

The marketing concepts of segmentation and targeting aren't just for selling products; they are crucial for employer branding as well. Just like you wouldn't advertise a luxury car to budget-conscious consumers, a one-size-fits-all approach to attracting talent won't yield optimal results. By segmenting potential candidates based on factors like skills, experience, and career goals, companies can craft targeted EVPs that resonate with specific talent pools. This allows them to tailor their messaging and highlight the aspects of their company culture and work environment that are most attractive to each segment. This targeted approach leads to a more efficient recruitment process and attracts candidates who are a good fit for the company's needs and culture, fostering a win-win situation for both employer and employee.

Just like marketers create detailed profiles of their ideal customers, talent acquisition teams can leverage candidate personas to attract ideal candidates. These personas delve into the motivations, goals, and even preferences of your target talent pool. Details can range from demographics, professional aspirations, and preferred communication channels.

Developing candidate personas goes beyond simple brainstorming. Focus groups with current employees and market research can provide valuable insights. Here are two studies on employee segments:

NTUC and Worker Aspirations

The NTUC in Singapore provides a real-world example. Through their #EveryWorkerMatters Conversations, they engaged over 42,000 workers across various demographics. This extensive research identified distinct worker groups with unique needs and aspirations (Figure 5.9):

- **Youths:** Entering the workforce, they value career development and a dynamic work environment.
- **Mid-career workers:** Seeking advancement, they prioritize job security, upskilling opportunities, and work-life balance.
- **Caregivers:** Balancing work and family, they value flexible work arrangements.
- **Older workers:** Older workers are individuals approaching retirement age. They value job security, benefits, and opportunities to continue making contributions in the workforce.

Branding | 127

- **Vulnerable workers:** Facing potential disadvantages, they prioritize job security, fair wages, and upskilling opportunities.

The findings from NTUC's stakeholder analysis provide valuable insights into the needs and aspirations of the workers in Singapore. These insights can guide the development of policies and initiatives to better meet the needs of the workers, thereby enhancing the employer brand.

Figure 5.9. Worker groups from NTUC's stakeholder analysis.

> Bain and Company identify six worker archetypes from a different perspective:
>
> - **Operators:** They find meaning outside of work. They see work as a means to an end. They don't feel a burning desire to always stand out, which makes them excellent team players.
> - **Givers:** They care about work that helps others. They feel rewarded by seeing their actions make a positive impact in someone else's life. They bring a human touch to their organizations.
> - **Artisans:** They seek work that inspires them and pursue mastery. They are always on the lookout for ways to perfect their skills—for them, learning is a lifelong journey.
> - **Explorers:** They want excitement and variety from work. They help make their organizations more adaptable in a rapidly changing world.
> - **Pioneers:** They are on a mission to change the world. They tend to form strong views about the way things should be and seek opportunities to turn their visions into reality.
> - **Strivers:** They are driven by a powerful desire to make something of their lives. They set high standards for themselves and can be quite competitive.

Key Takeaways

- Brands are abstract concepts built through perceptions and emotions that exist in the minds of consumers.
- Brand equity is the accumulated value of a brand's image and reputation.
- Positive brand equity yields benefits such as quality perceptions, marketing muscle, customer trust, loyalty, advocacy, crisis resilience, premium pricing power, and financial returns.
- Branding bridges the gap between internal strategy and consumer perception through consistent messaging and engaging experiences.
- Brand elements such as names, logos, and personalities are the building blocks of brand identity.

- There are several brand name strategies, including family branding, multi-branding, sub-branding, co-branding, and private label branding.
- Secondary brand associations, such as celebrity endorsements or event sponsorships, can enhance brand image.
- Successful branding involves authenticity, consistency, emotional connection, and a clear brand purpose.
- Brand purpose, aligned with customer values, fosters trust and loyalty.
- Marketing cannot be done by marketers alone. 360-degree branding ensures consistent messaging and experiences across all touchpoints. One such important touchpoint is employees. Employees need to be taught what the brand stands for and how they should implement the brand's strategy in their work. CGH showed us how they did it.
- A strong employer brand, built on a compelling EVP, attracts and retains top talent.
- Targeted employer branding, using segmentation and candidate personas, reaches the right talent pools.

Chapter 6

Understanding Consumers

Consumer behavior is the study of buyers and why and how they form impressions, learn about brands, and eventually make purchasing decisions. By delving into consumer behavior, marketers can develop effective strategies to attract, retain, and satisfy customers. In this chapter, we discuss how consumers have changed due to digitization and what this implies for consumer behavior theories and decision journeys. We also discuss how Asian consumers have changed.

How Consumer Behavior has Transformed in the Digitized Marketplace

The rise of digital technologies has fundamentally reshaped how consumers interact with information and brands. Understanding these changes is crucial for navigating the modern marketplace and achieving success.

Empowered customers

Gone are the days when brand messaging dictated product perception. Consumers no longer need to rely on shop assistants or passively receive information through advertisements. Today, they are empowered by ubiquitous Internet access and mobile devices. They actively research products, compare prices across multiple platforms, and leverage online reviews and social media interactions to inform their decisions. This pre-purchase research becomes their "moment of truth", shaping their initial impression and influencing their final decision. Google coined this stage of the customer journey the "Zero Moment of Truth" (ZMOT).[1] Its macro study revealed that even in 2011, 84% of consumers researched online before buying. This shift of power dynamics from passive receivers in the past to active explorers necessitates a consumer-centric approach to marketing strategies. Consumers today demand "always-on engagement", expecting seamless and readily available service across various touchpoints. Brands need to ensure they meet customers' needs as they arise, with informative and engaging content that addresses their needs and expectations. Brands need to build trust and prioritize transparency, authenticity, and UGC to win over savvy customers.

Paradox of plenty

A result of the ease of information access is information overload and an overwhelming abundance of choices. A simple Google search can yield thousands of results, each vying for our attention. Just imagine Lazada Singapore has 1,214 sellers of bird breeding boxes! This paradox of plenty, while empowering, can also be paralyzing. Consumers often experience decision fatigue, struggling to navigate the vast array of options and ultimately abandoning their purchase journey altogether. Businesses need to strategize to overcome help consumers with choice uncertainty and trade-off conflict.

"Shorter" attention span

While consumers may spend significant time in online activities where it interests them, many times people adopt a "scanning mentality" by quickly assessing information snippets before moving on. Gaining their sustained focus on detailed information or lengthy processes is challenging. Marketers face a smaller window of opportunity to grab attention. The average time spent on a webpage is 54 seconds, but it varies by industry.[2] Digital tools also encourage multitasking,

---

[1] Google. (2011). The zero moment of truth macro study. Google/Shopper Sciences. April 2011. Accessed on 13 February 2024. https://www.thinkwithgoogle.com/consumer-insights/consumer-journey/the-zero-moment-of-truth-macro-study/.

[2] Contentsquare (2021). *Digital Experience Benchmark Report 2021.*

which can fragment attention and reduce depth of focus. Brand messages must be concise, impactful, and cut through the clutter to hold consumers' interest before they click away. This demands a deeper understanding of their audience, their needs, and their preferred content formats.

New expectation of speed

Furthermore, digital platforms have instilled an expectation of immediacy. Consumers accustomed to instant access to information now expect the same level of speed across various touchpoints. Platforms such as TikTok and Instagram, with their short-form content, cater to this preference for rapid consumption. Slow-loading websites, delayed customer service responses, and lengthy processes can lead to frustration and disengagement.

New expectation of relevance and personalization

Digitization paves the way for hyper-personalization driven by advancements in AI, data analysis, and the availability of diverse touchpoints (especially mobile). This allows brands to cater to consumers' desire for unique experiences. This also changes consumers' expectations and raises their benchmark for relevance. This shift toward personalization requires businesses to move beyond a one-size-fits-all approach and embrace data-driven strategies that provide tailored experiences and build stronger customer relationships. However, as discussed in Chapter 3, a balance with data privacy is critical. This balance is a complex and evolving issue, with cultural, legal, and ethical considerations constantly changing.

Omnichannel consumption

Consumers do not compartmentalize their online and offline experiences. They expect a seamless omnichannel journey, seamlessly transitioning between online research, in-store purchases, and mobile interactions. This demands a unified approach from businesses, requiring alignment across online and offline channels to ensure consistent messaging, branding, and customer service.

Global consumption

Even physical borders have blurred in the digital realm. Consumers can now access products and services from around the world with a few clicks, expanding their buying horizons and challenging traditional market segmentation. This presents both opportunities and challenges for businesses. While the potential customer base has exploded, so has competition. Brands need to be mindful of cultural nuances, adapt their offerings to international markets, and leverage the power of digital marketing to reach global audiences effectively.

Mobile-first

The world is witnessing a mobile-first consumer revolution, where individuals primarily access the Internet and consume information through their smartphones. Mobile payments, ride-hailing apps, e-commerce, and social media platforms are widely used, further strengthening the dependence on smartphones. This trend is particularly pronounced in Asia, home to 62% of the world's mobile subscribers.[3] Among these, 68% access the internet through their mobile.[4] Some Asians also have multiple SIM cards—Singapore has a 170% mobile penetration rate,[5] for example. This mobile-first phenomenon necessitates a shift in marketing strategies to cater to the needs and preferences of mobile-centric consumers. Mobile users often switch between apps and activities, making the user journey more fragmented. Aside from optimizing content for small screen sizes and divided attention, marketers need to develop multi-touchpoint and omnichannel strategies that reach users on various platforms and maintain brand consistency across the touchpoints. But mobile platforms offer granular targeting capabilities based on

---

[3] Statista. (2024). Mobile subscriber penetration rate in the Asia-Pacific region from 2015 to 2022, with a forecast for 2030. Accessed on 26 February 2024. https://www.statista.com/statistics/376702/mobile-subscriber-penetration-asia-pacific/.

[4] Statcounter. (2024). Desktop vs mobile vs tablet market share Asia Jan 2023–Jan 2024. Accessed on 26 February 2024. https://gs.statcounter.com/platform-market-share/desktop-mobile-tablet/asia.

[5] Statista. (2023). Penetration rate of mobile subscriptions in Singapore from 2013 to 2022. Accessed on 26 February 2024. https://www.statista.com/statistics/542918/mobile-phone-penetration-in-singapore/.

demographics, location, and user behavior. This allows marketers to deliver personalized and relevant messages to specific user segments, increasing campaign effectiveness. Mobile has also been found to be a channel of discovery bringing new visitors to websites.[6]

The digital marketplace enables ongoing engagement and connection-building between brands and consumers. A customer-centric approach that prioritizes long-term value creation over short-term gains is essential. Understanding human psychology is no longer optional but vital in the digital age. This understanding allows brands to interpret data, anticipate trends, and create meaningful connections to keep up with the ever-changing expectations of modern consumers.

Cracking the Code of Consumer Behavior

Consumer behavior studies the psychology of consumers; it encompasses a holistic view of what drives individuals to choose, use, and dispose of products and services. Understanding consumer behavior is like having a superpower in the business world. It is the ability to peek into the minds of your customers, understand their desires and motivations, and then craft your marketing to resonate deeply with them. After all, Amazon CEO Jeff Bezos' famous words are to "obsess over customers."[7]

Consumers are not rational decision-makers; they are emotional beings driven by desires, fears, and social influences. Understanding these psychological factors allows you to connect with them in a language they understand. Knowing what triggers customers to buy or avoid certain products helps you anticipate their needs and tailor your marketing strategies accordingly. You can identify the pain points they are facing and position your product or service as the ultimate solution. Even after purchase, by understanding what resonates with your target audience, you can build genuine connections with them to turn fleeting customers into passionate brand advocates.

The study of consumer behavior asks what, who, how, when, where, and most importantly, why people buy. While today's digital

---

[6] Contentsquare. (2023). Digital Experience Benchmark Report 2023.

[7] Murphy Jr., B. (2023). Jeff Bezos: 'The most important single thing is to focus obsessively on the customer'. *Inc.* 4 February 2023. Accessed on 16 December 2023. https://www.inc.com/bill-murphy-jr/bezos-most-important-single-thing-focus-obsessively-on-customer.html.

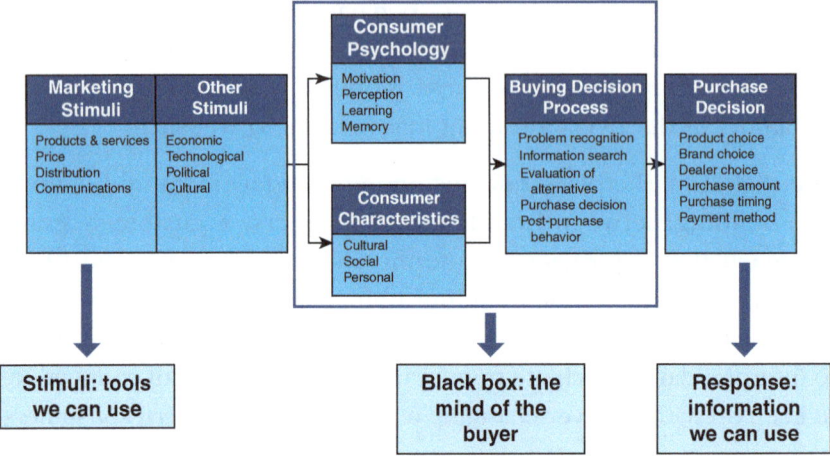

Figure 6.1. Model of consumer behavior.

world enables firms to collect an expanding amount of data on customers, this data analytics can only provide some predictive elements of future behavior. It often falls short of telling us *why* consumers behave in specific ways. We need a deeper understanding of human psychology to get at the "why." This is especially important when the context changes; evidenced by how the COVID-19 pandemic changed the supply and demand environment we operated in, and wreaked havoc to existing forecasting models.

Think of consumers' minds as a "black box": We can't directly observe their thoughts, but by analyzing their choices and drawing on psychological knowledge, we can make informed inferences about their responses to marketing stimuli. Figure 6.1 depicts our model of consumer behavior. Consumer psychology (read "How consumers perceive, learn, and form attitudes") and their characteristics ("Cultural and social understanding of the Asian consumer") influence how they make buying decisions.

How Consumers Perceive, Learn, and Form Attitudes

Perception

So, what goes on in this black box, the minds of customers? We start by understanding how we form perceptions. Our perception is not simply a passive recording of the world around us; it is an

Figure 6.2. The subjectivity of perception.

active and selective process of paying attention to, organizing, and interpreting incoming information. Perception is the process where we give subjective interpretations and meanings to what we see (Figure 6.2). It lays the foundation for every step that follows in the buying journey. Whether it is an advertisement, a logo, or a friend's recommendation, these stimuli are shaped by individual perceptions to trigger associations and ultimately influence our response. Let's delve into the three perception processes:

Selective attention

Our journey starts with sensory receptors capturing information from the environment (sight, sound, touch, taste, and smell). But not everything is given attention. Our perception is a fascinatingly selective process, choosing which stimuli get our attention and which fade into the background. Our perceptual filters act as our mental gatekeepers to prevent us from being overwhelmed by sensory overload from the environment, allowing us to focus on what is important instead.

So, what determines what gets "chosen" by our perception? Anything that stands out from the usual grabs our attention. Loud sounds, bright colors, or movement can trigger this involuntary selection. Additionally, our internal state (such as tiredness, stress, and moods) can influence the selection. We tend to prioritize information that is relevant to our current needs, goals, or interests. Hunger piques us to notice food smells or advertisements for restaurants; likewise, if you are planning a trip, you will be more attuned to travel brochures or airline deals. Recent experiences and exposure also prime our attention to specific things. Our existing knowledge and expectations create frameworks for processing information. We are more likely to notice information that fits within these frameworks and ignore those that contradict them. Societal norms and expectations are good examples of such influences on what we deem important or relevant. Such confirmation bias can create echo chambers and hinder rational decision-making.

Selective organization

Following selecting what we want to pay attention to, our brains arrange the raw data from our senses into meaningful patterns. There are a few ways we typically organize information. First, we naturally group similar elements together—cars with cars, dogs with dogs. This way of categorization helps us be more efficient in interpreting new information as we apply what we know of that category (schemas) to the new stimuli. Hence, what we already know shapes how we organize new information. Second, we use proximity to cluster items together. Objects close together tend to be perceived as belonging together. For example, in a retail setting, a new brand placed with luxury brands may be perceived as also upmarket. Lastly, we distinguish between the foreground (what we focus on) and the background (everything else).

Selective interpretation

Once organized, information is interpreted and meaning assigned. This interpretation process is highly subjective as it can be influenced by emotions, cultural background, social factors, and consumer characteristics (such as demographics, personality, emotions, and past experiences). For instance, shared beliefs and values of your culture influence how you interpret things. A hug might mean a friendly hello in one culture but disrespect in another. Our emotions and the context we are in (such as the company we are with) can also color our interpretation, making us perceive things differently when we are happy or sad.

We also use existing mental frameworks, called schemas, formed by past experiences and learning, to interpret new information. If you see a dog, your "dog schema" activates. So, someone who had been bitten by a dog before would likely associate dogs with danger and fear and respond by screaming or running away.

As much as we would like to believe otherwise, we are not always guided by pure logic and rationality. Faced with numerous choices, time constraints, and an onslaught of information, our brains rely on mental shortcuts called heuristics to help us make those decisions swiftly. These heuristics are often generalizations or rules of thumb that ease our cognitive load. They shape how consumers perceive brands and products. Marketers must be aware of these biases. Read the sidebar for some commonly used heuristics that we use in our daily lives.

How Heuristics Shape Your Decisions

Let's delve into a few common heuristics that might be secretly influencing your shopping habits:

Availability heuristic: Our minds tend to believe that things that come to mind easily are more common or important. For instance, if you've seen multiple ads for a particular brand of yogurt, you might believe it's the most popular option, even if that's not necessarily the case. Marketers often exploit this by using flashy packaging and repeated advertising to increase their brand's mental availability.

Representativeness heuristic: When making judgments, we often rely on stereotypes or prototypes. You might assume a product is of higher quality because it has sleek packaging, aligning with your expectations of premium products. Conversely, you may avoid a brand with a generic label, assuming it's inferior.

Anchoring heuristic: We tend to rely heavily on the first piece of information we receive as a reference point for subsequent judgments. Such anchoring tendencies give rise to what we refer to as "first impressions." See a sale sign proclaiming "50% off!"? You might feel compelled to purchase, even if the original price was inflated to create the illusion of a bargain.

Confirmation bias: Confirmation bias describes our tendency to favor information that confirms our existing beliefs while simultaneously downplaying or ignoring information that challenges those beliefs. This bias helps us make a quick decision and avoid the uncomfortable feeling of being wrong. Imagine you are interested in a particular brand of skincare products. You might spend time reading positive reviews on blogs and watching influencer recommendations while ignoring articles raising concerns about certain ingredients or the product's efficacy. That's confirmation bias at play!

Loss aversion: Loss aversion describes our stronger preference for avoiding losses than acquiring equivalent gains. In other words, the negative emotional impact of losing something feels greater than the positive impact of gaining something new. This bias makes us more likely to hold onto something we already own rather than risk switching to a potentially better alternative. It can also make us more sensitive to price increases than equivalent discounts.

Social proof heuristic: We are social creatures, and this instinct influences our buying decisions. Positive reviews, celebrity endorsements, or trends on social media can make a product seem more desirable. We tend to trust recommendations from others, often without directly verifying the information ourselves.

Affect heuristic: Emotions play a powerful role in decision-making. Advertisers know this and often create campaigns that evoke positive feelings, hoping to associate their brand with those emotions. You might be more likely to buy something because an ad made you laugh or feel nostalgic.

Scarcity heuristic: This shortcut taps into the fear of missing out. Phrases such as "limited time offer" or "only a few left in stock" create an illusion of scarcity, motivating consumers to take immediate action and purchase a product before missing out when it is gone.

In essence, perception is not a passive reflection of reality; it is a dynamic dance between the external stimuli (consisting of marketing stimuli and external environmental factors) and our unique internal lenses (culture, social, and personal factors), constantly shaping our understanding and experience of reality. We must recognize that there is no absolute reality, but each of us has our subjective interpretation of reality, even if it is biased and erroneous. Yet we act based on our perceptions and beliefs.

Our best bet to understanding our customers better is to understand what tinted lens they are looking through. If there are incorrect beliefs, we need to understand how we can correct those beliefs or bring about new understanding. This is where understanding consumer learning comes in.

Learning and attitude formation

Every encounter with a brand—experiences, brand messages, word-of-mouth, and even emotions—gets associated with the brand. Whatever new information and brand experience encountered will be associated with the brand in their memories, confirming what they know or overwriting previous beliefs. This knowledge leads to an attitude—a summary evaluation ranging from love (positive) to dislike (negative).[8] Positive attitudes translate to stronger purchase intentions, making them the holy grail for any business. The more your customers know and understand your brand, the stronger and more robust their attitude. This is why branding is essentially about teaching customers. Make their liking for your brand more than a fleeting whim by building a foundation of knowledge and trust. This is why it is important to understand how customers learn and how their memory impacts brand perceptions and decisions.

Information that makes it past our perceptual filters undergoes encoding—a process that transforms information into a format the brain can store. Initially, it enters short-term memory, easily accessible but fades quickly without reinforcement. For long-term storage, it needs to be encoded properly and sufficiently elaborated on to be transferred to long-term memory. When needed, these stored

---

[8] American Psychological Association. (2018). Attitude. 19 April 2018. https://dictionary.apa.org/attitude.

memories are retrieved, influencing future perceptions and ultimately, our decisions. Information that cannot be retrieved is "lost" in the abyss of long-term memory and has no impact.

Recognizing that learning depends on how well the information is encoded and retrieved suggests some ways we can help our customers learn better. First, spark their motivation to learn by connecting your message to their needs, interests, and past experiences. Help them learn better by factoring in personal relevance in your message. Stories are powerful tools to create a relatable context and emotional connection.

Repetition helps solidify memory but be careful of overdoing it till customers tune you out (known as "advertising wearout"). Reinforce creative variations of consistent key messages across different channels. If possible, use active learning through hands-on activities and discussions, or incorporate interactive elements to promote deeper understanding and memory consolidation. Ride on the gamification trend, for example: Use game mechanics such as points, rewards, and challenges to motivate learning. Engage sight, sound, touch, and even smell to create immersive experiences that enhance encoding and recall.

Building a strong brand is about teaching your customers, not just selling to them. By understanding their learning process and tailoring your approach to your customers' interests, needs, media habits, and preferred learning styles, you can create lasting memories, positive attitudes, and ultimately, loyal brand advocates.

Cultural and Social Understanding of the Asian Consumer

The Asian consumer landscape is a vibrant mosaic, reflecting the continent's rich cultural tapestry and rapid economic evolution. From the dynamic digital hubs of China and South Korea to the emerging markets of Southeast Asia, the diversity is staggering.

The need to go beyond demographic profiling and the search for an elusive "Asian strategy" is profound. For example, to understand the youth market in China, the marketer would need to transverse across traditional values to global perspectives, across different provinces and states. China's youth culture is rich with diverse subcultures with groups such as ACGN (Animation, Comics, and Games), Hanfu (traditional Chinese clothing enthusiasts), and Cyberpunk (fans of a science fiction genre) thriving. These subcultures are fueled by China's social and technological advancements, with social media playing a key role in fostering online communities around these shared interests. Marketers also need to recognize that values change with the rapid developments in the region. For instance, the mindset transitions from "996" to "tang ping" (躺平), literally meaning "lying flat," is a social phenomenon and lifestyle choice in China that emerged as a reaction to the intense pressures of modern society, particularly the grueling "996" work culture (working from 9 am to 9 pm, six days a week).

To succeed, brands must move beyond generalizations and delve deep into the unique nuances of each market. Here are some effective approaches:

- **Immersive cultural experience:** Spending time in the target market is invaluable. Experiencing the local culture firsthand provides deep insights into consumer behavior, values, and preferences.
- **Local partnerships:** Collaborating with local partners who possess in-depth cultural knowledge can accelerate understanding and provide access to valuable networks.
- **Market research:** Conducting thorough market research, including qualitative and quantitative studies, is essential to uncover consumer insights and preferences.
- **Digital ethnography:** Leveraging online platforms to observe and analyze consumer behavior can provide valuable insights into cultural trends and preferences.
- **Continuous learning:** The Asian market is dynamic, so staying updated on cultural shifts and trends is essential for long-term success.

There are, however, some trends observed in the Asian market:

- Incomes are rising across Asia, but wealth inequality remains pronounced with as many as 1.4 billion consumers with low income in 2030.[9]
- Urban consumers in Asian cities drive 85% of the consumption growth.[10]
- Households are getting smaller with singles making up more than 30% of households in advanced Asia.[11]
- By 2030, seniors (aged over 60) are expected to make up about 40% of the Asian population. This will be the Insta-granny generation—seniors who are online. In Korea, it is estimated that there will be 9 seniors for every 10 working-age persons in South Korea by 2060.[12]
- Mobile-first is a must. Asia is a mobile-centric market. This was discussed earlier in this chapter.
- Social media plays a significant role in shaping brand perception.[13] Businesses must actively monitor and respond to online conversations, leveraging positive sentiment and addressing negative feedback with empathy. But platforms and associated behaviors on social media are different across countries.
- Being at the frontline of climate risk, Asian consumers have a rising awareness of ESG issues, influencing their lifestyles and choices.[14]
- Asian consumers are more willing to share data for personalization purposes than their Western counterparts.[15]

---

[9] Tonby, O., Jonathan, W., Rohit, R., Wonsik, C., Sven, S., Naomi, Y., Jeongmin, S., and Tiago, D. (2021). Beyond income: Redrawing Asia's consumer map. McKinsey Global Institute.

[10] *Ibid.*

[11] *Ibid.*

[12] Jones, K. (2020). These countries are aging the fastest—here's what it will mean. World Economic Forum. 12 February 2020. https://www.weforum.org/agenda/2020/02/ageing-global-population/.

[13] Cheng, M. and Rakish, M. (2024). Voice of the consumer survey 2024: Asia Pacific. PWC. 24 June 2024. https://www.pwc.com/id/en/pwc-publications/industries-publications/consumer-and-industrial-products-and-services/consumer-survey-2024-asia-pacific.html.

[14] Tonby *et al.* (2021), *Op. cit.*

[15] Yeong, B., Bodin, B., Nguyen, T. B. T., and Lydia, S. (2023). Tapping the potential of the new Asian consumer. *Business Times*. 1 February 2023. https://www.businesstimes.com.sg/international/global/tapping-potential-new-asian-consumer.

How Consumers Make Decisions

Psychological factors and consumer characteristics influence how we make decisions. Typically, the buyer decision process consists of five steps (Figure 6.3):

1. **Need/problem recognition:** Motivation is the driving force behind consumer behavior. It starts with the realization of a desire or problem that sets the customer on the path of seeking a solution. The larger the gap between the ideal and actual states, the stronger the motivation to act. This could be triggered by internal factors such as hunger or external cues such as advertising. Whether it's a practical need, an emotional desire, or a social aspiration, motivation plays a pivotal role in shaping consumer choices and purchase decisions. Marketers need to understand the needs customers are trying to fulfill and what drives them to pursue these ideal states.
2. **Information search:** Armed with this awareness, they recall brands they know of or embark on a quest for information. This involves researching online, asking friends, reading reviews,

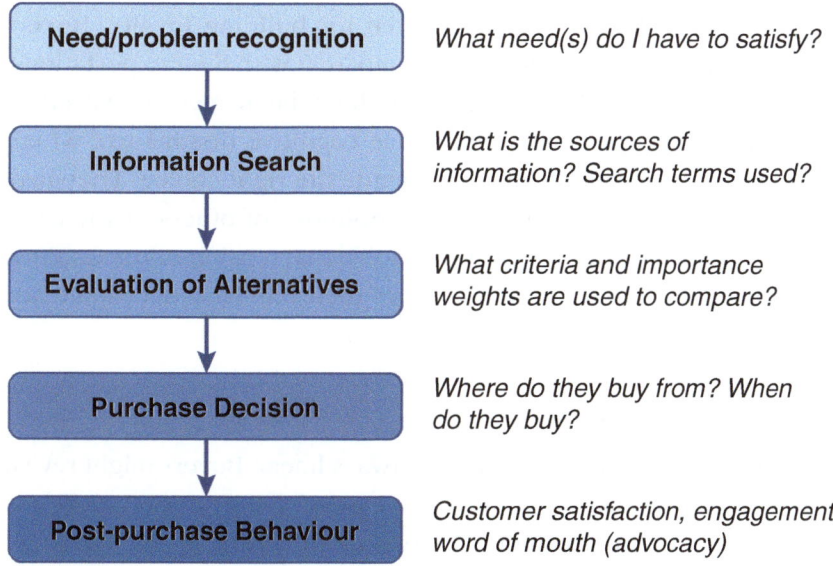

Figure 6.3. Buyer decision-making process.

and in-store shopping. We should identify our target customers' typical questions, media habits, and information sources, so we know where to reach them to address their need for information. Typically, customers use commercial sources (e.g., company-driven information such as advertisements and websites) for facts such as product information and prices, while they rely on personal (e.g., friends, family, or personal experience) or third-party consumer-driven sources (e.g., reviews) to evaluate or legitimize purchase decisions.

3. **Evaluation of alternatives:** With the information gathered, they begin to weigh their options. This involves factors such as price, features, brand reputation, and personal preferences. Knowing what criteria are salient and important to our customers helps us with our positioning strategy.
4. **Purchase decision:** Based on their evaluation, they decide to buy, postpone, or abandon the purchase altogether. Making the purchase process as frictionless as possible- offering convenient buying options, efficient checkout processes, and clear return policies- helps prevent them from changing their minds.
5. **Post-purchase:** The journey does not end with the purchase. The post-purchase stage is crucial for building loyalty. Buyers reflect on their experience and compare it with their expectations. They are satisfied if expectations have been met or exceeded. Alternatively, they may experience cognitive dissonance, where they feel uncertain if they have made the right choice. They may do further research and seek the opinions of others or the company for after-sales support to resolve that tension of uncertainty. A failure to convince themselves of their purchase decision leads to regret and dissatisfaction.

Role of involvement

The decision-making process is not always linear. Buyers might revisit stages or skip some altogether. The extent of the process depends on the level of involvement. Involvement refers to the personal significance and motivational intensity associated with the purchase. The level depends on factors such as how risky they think the decision is (perceived risks are higher for more expensive purchases, or those that involve physical danger or social embarrassment), or how interested they are in the category. It determines how much time, effort, and thought a consumer is willing to invest in making the decision.

High-involvement decisions are characterized by extensive decision-making where consumers are highly engaged, actively researching, seeking out diverse information sources, comparing options, and carefully evaluating multiple product features, quality, and brand reputation. The process takes more time, with consumers likely to go through all stages (need recognition, information search, evaluation, purchase, and post-purchase evaluation) thoroughly.

Conversely, consumers are less engaged when involvement is low. They are likely to skip stages or be condensed, with less emphasis on research and detailed evaluation. Consumers might rely on readily available information or heuristics, such as brand reputation, price cues, convenience, or habit. They may even buy on impulse.

Researchers found that we pay attention to different information under different levels of involvement.[16] The elaboration likelihood model proposes that persuasion occurs via the central route for high-involvement situations; we carefully consider the arguments, evidence, and logic presented in the message. In such instances, marketers should provide detailed information, address concerns, and highlight unique selling propositions through educational content, interactive tools, and customer testimonials. However, when involvement is low, persuasion occurs via the peripheral route where we rely on cues that are easy to process, such as the source's attractiveness, celebrity endorsements, packaging, or emotional appeals. While peripheral cues can quickly influence us, these effects are more susceptible to change.

---

[16] Petty, R. E. and Cacioppo, J. T. (1986). *The Elaboration Likelihood Model of Persuasion*. Advances in Experimental Social Psychology, Vol. 19. Elsevier, London, England, pp. 124–129.

Farewell Funnel: Unraveling the Modern Consumer Decision Journey

In their article, "The Consumer Decision Journey,"[17] McKinsey challenges the outdated "funnel" model of buying behavior. The one-way flow where brands push messages down and consumers passively receive them simply does not reflect the reality of today's digital landscape. Instead, it proposes (Figure 6.4) a circular process with four phases: initial consideration; active evaluation, or the simultaneous process of information search and evaluation of potential choices; purchase; and post-purchase.

The model posits that consumers do not make decisions in a linear fashion starting with a basket of brands and sequentially eliminating them as they go through the funnel from awareness to consideration before finally deciding on one to purchase. Instead,

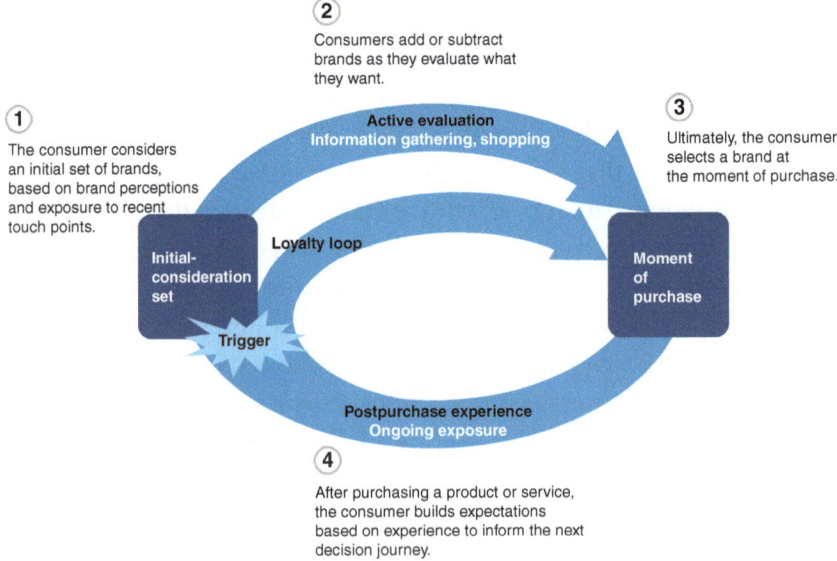

Figure 6.4. Adapted from McKinsey's consumer decision journey.[18]

---

[17] Court, D., Dave, E., Susan, M., and Ole J. V. (2009). The consumer decision journey. *McKinsey Quarterly*, 3, 1–11.

[18] *Ibid.*

they consider brands they can recall when needs are triggered, giving established players a head start. These brands have up to three times more likelihood of being chosen. Being top-of-mind matters more than ever.

But established brands are not guaranteed victory. If a purchase is not made at that point, active evaluation begins. Consumers actively research, finding out more about the category and potentially discovering new brands that make an impact, or realizing some familiar ones no longer fit their needs. Brands can enter or exit the consideration set here. This implies that it is more of a level playing field with new brands vying for attention alongside established players.

This journey emphasizes consumer control. People actively seek information and want to reach decisions on their own. To thrive in this environment, brands cannot just solely rely on "push" marketing. McKinsey found that it only had 39% influence on the initial consideration set, 26% during active evaluation, and 22% at the closure stage.[19] Instead, embrace consumer-driven information: reviews, recommendations, and genuine connections.

McKinsey's article highlights that store interactions are the most significant influencers at the moment of purchase. Dealers and retailers are no longer just sales channels; they become brand ambassadors, directly shaping customer experiences. Do they truly understand your brand strategy? Marketers must actively collaborate with dealers and retailers to ensure they understand the brand's values, messaging, and target customers. Training and support must be provided to equip retailers with the knowledge and skills to engage customers authentically and deliver a brand-aligned experience.

The most radical transformation in the consumer journey lies in post-purchase behavior. The Internet empowers consumers to delve deeper, seeking information to ease any doubts (recall cognitive dissonance). But that is not all. They have also found their voices—and powerful ones at that! Unboxing videos, detailed blog reviews, and passionate social media discussions are the new reality. Reviews,

---

[19] *Ibid.*

testimonials, and social proof shape future decisions and impact others. Advocacy takes center stage for marketing in the digitized world.

The post-purchase phase presents a golden opportunity for brands to engage with customers, address concerns, and offer ongoing support. Building positive relationships is key. Identifying and nurturing loyal advocates is crucial, as word-of-mouth is too important a driver of purchase decisions to be left to chance. Seizing a viral social media moment to demonstrate brand values and build goodwill is a perfect example of proactive post-purchase engagement. The case study on Charles & Keith highlights the potential of turning challenges into opportunities and building lasting customer relationships (read the case at the end of this chapter).

Loyalty also fuels repeat purchases. It connects past satisfaction to future sales. Fail to deliver a good brand experience and customers are thrust back into the treacherous waters of active evaluation. The fight for their business restarts, with competitors waiting to snatch them away. By investing in building loyalty, you move beyond the constant struggle for new customers and build a thriving community

The 5As Model: What does this all mean for marketers?

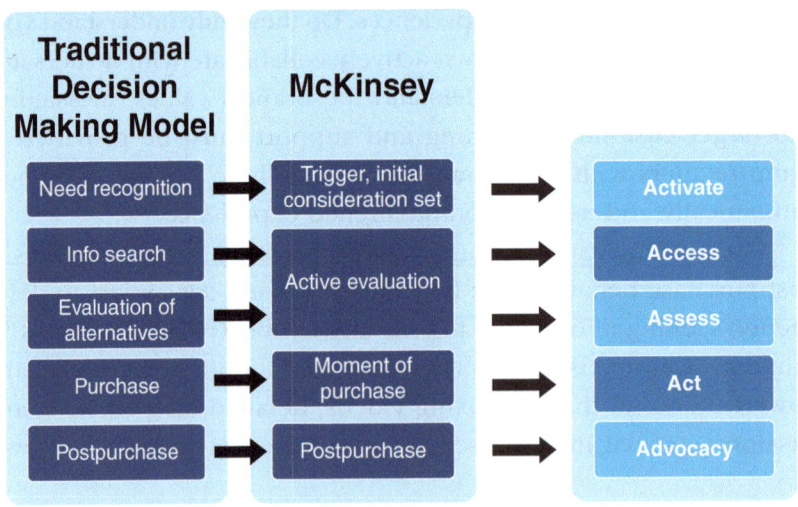

Figure 6.5. Marketing's role in consumer decision journeys.

of advocates who keep your brand at the top of their minds, purchase after purchase. Every positive interaction strengthens the loop, solidifying brand preference and reducing susceptibility to competitors' siren calls. Nurturing loyalty is a proactive strategy.

Both the traditional and McKinsey's models point to a few takeaways for marketers (Figure 6.5). First, we need to understand customers' needs and motivations to *activate* the first step in the buying process. As they embark on finding out more, we need to ensure easy *access* to our brand information. Third, we must teach customers how to *assess* the value of our products, and why we stand out from the rest. Lastly, we should facilitate them to *act* to complete the purchase and advocate for the brand.

Customer Journey Mapping Strategy: Navigating the Customer's Experience

Customer journey mapping is a strategic exercise that visually depicts the entire customer experience with your brand, from initial awareness to post-purchase interactions. It helps businesses understand how customers interact with their brand at every touchpoint, identify areas for improvement, and ultimately, design a more compelling and satisfying customer experience.

Here's how you can develop a customer journey map: break down the customer journey into key stages, such as awareness, consideration, purchase, and post-purchase. For each stage, gather customer feedback through surveys, interviews, or focus groups to understand real customer experiences to list the interaction points the customer has with your brand, including online channels, physical stores, customer service, etc. Evaluate each touchpoint for its effectiveness and potential for improvement. Consider factors such as ease of use, information clarity, and emotional response. Look for areas where the customer experience is subpar or could be enhanced. Based on your findings, create concrete steps to address pain points and capitalize on opportunities. Regularly test your improvements and iterate on the map based on new data and feedback. Use the map to track the impact of your improvements and measure success against your goals.

Customer Journey Map
Example of an online grocery store

STAGE	AWARENESS	CONSIDERATION	DECISION	DELIVERY & USE		LOYALTY & ADVOCACY	
CUSTOMER ACTIVITIES	Hear from friends, see offline or online ad, read from newspapers	Compare & evaluate alternatives	Add groceries to shopping cart	Make an order	Receive or pick up on order	Contact customer service	Enjoy groceries	Order again and/or order more	Share experience
CUSTOMER GOALS	No goals at this point	Find the best solution to buy food	Find and select products easily, get inspired	Order effortlessly	Receive or pick up an order effortlessly and when needed	Get help if problems appear, request for refund	Have the right and good quality ingredients	Repeat good customer experience	Share feelings, give feedback
TOUCHPOINTS	Word of mouth, traditional media, social media	Word of mouth, website, brick & mortar store, social media		Website, app, order confirmation email	Delivery service, packing, messages (email, SMS, phone call)	Phone, email, chat	Food products, packages, other materials		Word of mouth, social media
EXPERIENCE	Interested, curious	Requires effort but excited	Excited	"Payment is painful"	Require effort, happy when received	Frustrated	Satisfied	"This is easy"	"I have to share this"
BUSINESS GOAL	Increase awareness and interest	Increase number of website visitors	Increase shopping cart value & conversion rate	Increase online sales and conversion rate	Deliver on time and minimise the delivery window	Increase customer service satisfaction, minimise waiting time	Make products to match expectations	Increase retention rate and order value and/or frequency	Turn customers into advocates, turn negative experiences into positive
KPIs	Number of people reached	New website visitors	Shopping cart value, conversion rate	Online sales, conversion rate	On time delivery rate, average delivery window	Customer service success rate, waiting time	Product reviews	Retention rate, order value and frequency	Customer satisfaction
ORGANISATIONAL ACTIVITIES	Create marketing campaigns and content both offline and online, PR	Create marketing campaigns and content both offline and online	Optimise grocery shopping experience	Optimise online purchase funnel, order handling	Picking & delivery	Organise customer service	Develop products & product range	Target marketing make re-ordering easy, upselling and/or cross-selling	Manage feedback and social media, develop sharing/inviting possibilities
RESPONSIBLE	Marketing & Communications	Marketing & Communications	Online development, Customer service	Online development, warehouse, logistics	Warehouse, logistics	Customer service	Product development, purchasing	Marketing, online development	Customer service, online development
TECHNOLOGY SYSTEMS	CRM, analytics, programmatic buying platform, social media	CRM, analytics, CMS, marketing automation	CRM, analytics, CMS, ecommerce platform, PIM	CRM, analytics, CMS, ecommerce platform, PIM, inventory system, marketing automation	CRM, analytics, order & delivery system, marketing automation	CRM, analytics, help desk, ticketing system, chat	CRM, analytics, vendor management system, PIM	CRM, analytics, marketing automation, ecommerce platform	CRM, analytics, marketing automation, ecommerce platform, social media analytics

Figure 6.6. Example of a customer journey map.

By understanding customer pain points and preferences, you can design experiences that are more enjoyable and effective. The map helps you focus on what matters most to your target customers. By identifying bottlenecks and inefficiencies in your customer journey, you can also optimize your operations and improve resource allocation.

A positive seamless customer experience needs the organization to look beyond departmental silos and isolated KPIs. Customer journey maps underscore the importance of collaboration between different departments because they paint a complete picture of the customer experience, encompassing all touchpoints and interactions, not just individual department responsibilities. By integrating business goals into each stage of the map, everyone understands how their role contributes to the overall customer experience and the desired business outcomes. Securing buy-in from key stakeholders across the organization is crucial for successful implementation. This means involving different departments from the get-go. Not only does this foster a sense of ownership, but it also brings valuable diverse perspectives to the table, ensuring the map accurately reflects the customer's reality.

Figure 6.6 is an example of a customer journey map.

Case: From "Luxury Bag" to Brand Ambassador—Zoe Gabriel and Charles & Keith

Charles & Keith, the Singaporean footwear and accessories brand, has carved a unique niche in the fashion landscape. It occupies the sweet spot between high-street brands and luxury labels. Offering trend-driven designs at accessible price points, it caters to the modern woman who is independent, confident, fashion-conscious, and craves variety without breaking the bank. Their marketing campaigns and brand messaging encourage consumers to express their individuality and style through their choices.

The fast-paced fashion industry requires continuous innovation and adaptation to stay relevant. Additionally, competition from other affordable fashion brands is fierce. Maintaining the balance between trendy and affordable can also be challenging. Charles & Keith must continuously stay ahead of the curve while ensuring the right brand identity.

In January 2023, 17-year-old Zoe Gabriel's innocent TikTok post sparked a viral debate when she excitedly unboxed a Charles & Keith bag, calling it her "first luxury bag." Some netizens mocked Gabriel's definition of luxury. Comments such as "Who's gonna tell her?" and "There's a difference between affordable and luxury, honey. This ain't it" reflected this viewpoint. Some felt her excitement was materialistic ("That's not even famous or expensive #tryinghard."). Other criticisms were targeted at the brand: "Don't fall for the marketing ploy! This is fast fashion disguised as luxury, targeting young and impressionable audiences." and "…it is not a luxury brand, it is what it is, No excuse. Btw I don't like C n K brand cause quality is bad."

Instead of shying away from the negativity, Gabriel immediately addressed the comments head-on, revealing her family's financial struggles and emphasizing her genuine excitement for the bag. She shifted the focus from brand labeling to individual experiences, stating, "Luxury is what makes you feel good, not a price tag." This challenged the narrow definition of luxury and resonated with many, making her story a relatable example of aspiration and appreciation for seemingly small luxuries.

Impressed by Gabriel's authenticity, Charles & Keith acted swiftly. They invited her to their headquarters for lunch with one of the founders and presented her with a personalized handbag. This gesture solidified their support and further legitimized Gabriel's experience. The brand's spokesperson said, "A community that shows kindness and compassion is exactly what the world needs today and what the brand stands for."

Netizens applauded this response. In four days, Gabriel's original video had 6.7 million views.[20] This incident was mentioned on multiple news and online platforms, reaching a global audience. The

---

[20] Cheong, C. (2023). A teen TikToker who was mocked for calling a $60 bag 'luxury' responded to online hate in a tearful video: 'Growing up, I did not have a lot'. *Business Insider*. 12 January 2023.

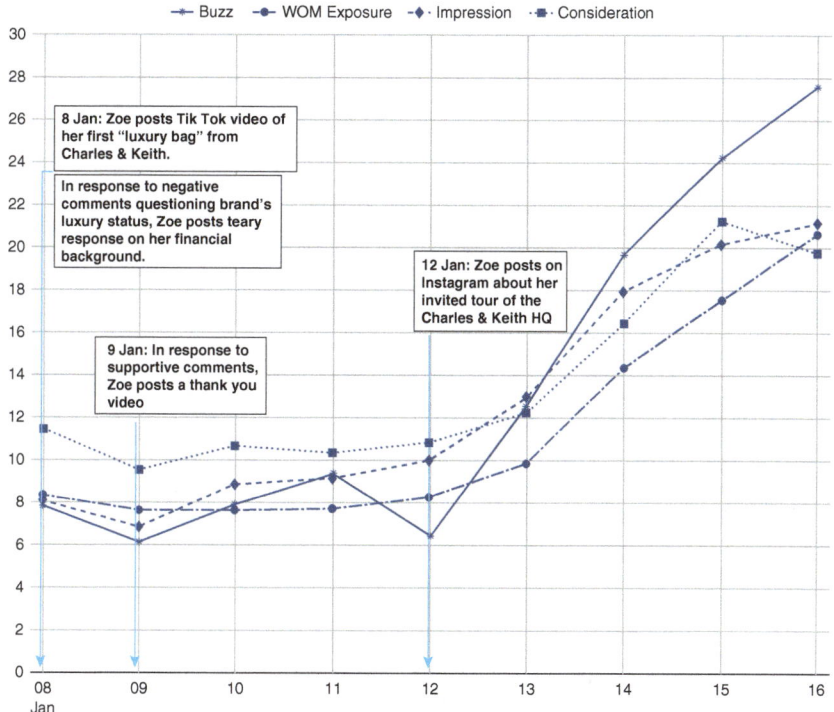

Figure 6.7. Charles & Keith's response resulted in positive brand mentions.[21]

brand's impression and purchase consideration scores also improved sharply (Figure 6.7). This incident was also featured in media globally till months later.

Two months later, they appointed her as a brand ambassador for International Women's Day campaigns (Figure 6.8). This collaboration was met with praise by many, highlighting the brand's responsiveness and appreciation for diverse narratives.

---

[21] Tan, S. (2023). Charles & Keith's luxury controversy—How has its recent actions reshaped consumer perceptions? YouGov. 18 January 2023. Accessed on 9 February 2024. https://business.yougov.com/content/45007-Charles-and-Keith-luxury-Gabriel-Jan2023.

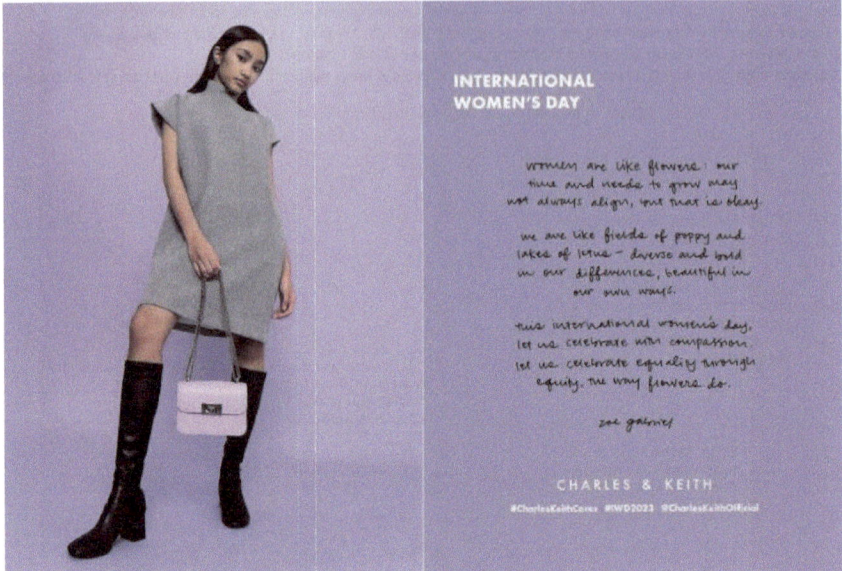

Figure 6.8. Gabriel as a Charles & Keith brand ambassador.[22]

Here are some key learnings from Charles & Keith:

- This incident exemplified that consumers have their own "conversations" on social media about brands and incidents related. The virality of the event demonstrated the significant potential of post-purchase activities on social media in shaping public opinion and brand perception.
- Brands may not be "invited" to join this chatter. However, social listening is an important part of environmental scanning. Brands need to manage their online reputation and those who are vigilant and respond appropriately benefit greatly from gaining positive brand mentions in earned media. Charles & Keith's response showcased the importance of listening to customer sentiment and responding with empathy, turning potential negativity into a positive opportunity.

---

[22] @zoeaaleah. (n.d.). Instagram. https://www.instagram.com/zoeaaleah.

Key Takeaways

- The digital marketplace has undoubtedly changed consumers' behavior and expectations of brands.
- Understanding consumer behavior helps make sense of why consumers behave in specific ways, so we can design better marketing strategies that resonate with them.
- Consumers' perceptions are their reality. Consumers selectively pay attention to stimuli and give meaning to them to subjective interpretations of reality. These perceptions inform preferences and attitudes toward products and brands.
- By knowing how consumers process information, you can create content that is informative, engaging, and easy to understand. Knowing what they know, brands can correct misbeliefs or provide new knowledge that builds on their current brand perceptions.
- The 5As model: The customer decision-making process starts when customers recognize that they have an unfulfilled need. Only when this is triggered will they go on to search for more information and compare alternatives. Marketers to understand how best to *activate* this need recognition stage. Thereafter, ensure that customers can *access* their information and help them *assess* their product against alternatives. They also need to influence consumers to *act* and purchase. Lastly, marketers need to take a proactive approach in the post-purchase stage to promote *advocacy*.
- Developing a customer journey map identifies customers' touchpoints with the brand so resources can be focused on the areas that are most important to them. This document can also be used as a collaboration tool to bring other functions together to provide a seamless customer experience.

Chapter

7

Understanding Business Buyers and Account-Based Marketing

Navigating Two Worlds: Demystifying B2C vs. B2B Buying Behavior

The world of commerce is a diverse landscape and understanding the distinct nuances of business-to-business (B2B) buying behavior is crucial for navigating its complexities.

The core drivers behind business-to-consumer (B2C) and B2B purchases differ significantly. B2C decisions can often be emotionally charged, and influenced by personal preferences, impulses, and aspirations. For many product categories, consumers often rely on heuristics, mental shortcuts such as brand recognition, to navigate the overwhelming amount of information available. Social proof, in the form of online reviews and influencer recommendations, heavily influences B2C decision-making, as consumers seek validation and trust before making a purchase. Speed and convenience are paramount in the B2C world. Consumers expect seamless online shopping experiences with easy navigation, quick checkout processes, and readily available customer service.

B2B buying decisions, on the other hand, are typically described to be conducted with rationality and careful deliberation. Businesses prioritize total cost of ownership (TCO), ROI, risk mitigation, and the product's ability to address specific business needs. Extensive research, comparative analysis, and negotiations are commonplace, involving multiple stakeholders within the organization. Technical specifications, white papers, case studies, and testimonials were believed to resonate more with B2B buyers compared to emotional appeals.

Is this indeed so distinctively different? Let's explore if B2B and B2C are really two different worlds, and if so, how should businesses manage B2B marketing?

The human element in B2B buying

While B2B transactions may seem less susceptible to whims compared to B2C purchases, they remain fundamentally human-to-human interactions. Individual decision-makers are not simply calculating machines. They navigate complex landscapes with their own interests and motivations. Some might prioritize "safe" choices that minimize career risk, opting for established solutions. Conversely, others might champion high-profile purchases, aiming to climb the corporate ladder. This highlights the limitations of solely relying on traditional, purely rational models to understand B2B buying behavior.

Bain & Company's research reinforces this notion. Their framework identifies 40 "elements of value"[1] that influence B2B decisions, categorized into five groups (Figure 7.1). Notably, the "individual" and "inspirational" categories hold significant weight. Factors such as reducing personal risk, enhancing career prospects, or contributing to the company's social responsibility can significantly impact decision-making. Interestingly, the research suggests that purely product-related factors might not be as strong a differentiator as previously assumed. They are low in importance or may even fall under "table stakes"—the baseline expectations for any B2B offering.

This complexity underscores the intricate nature of B2B selling. Success hinges not just on highlighting product features but on developing a nuanced understanding of both the rational and emotional aspects that influence individual decision-makers within the buying unit.

---

[1] Almquist, E., Jamie, C., and Lori, S. (2018). The B2B elements of value. *Harvard Business Review*, March–April 2018, 1–11.

Understanding Business Buyers and Account-Based Marketing | 161

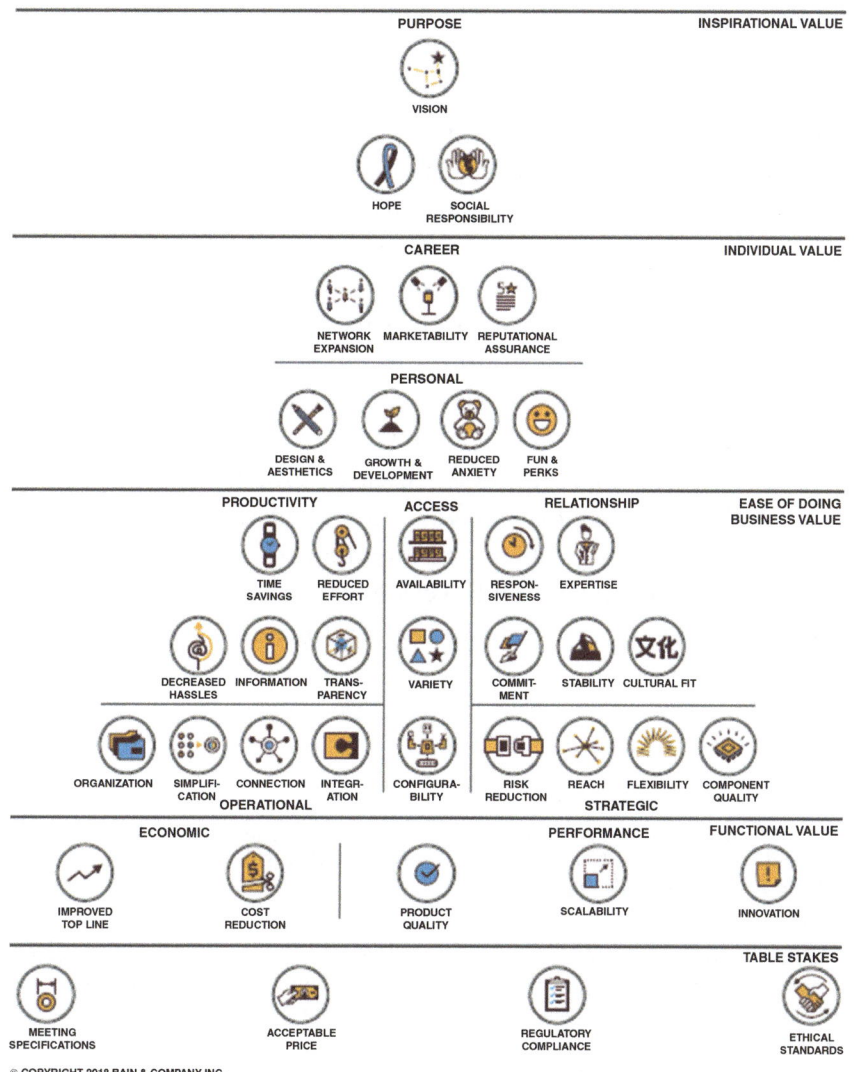

Figure 7.1. Elements of value for B2B customers.[2]

Self-directed buyers

Like B2C buyers, B2B customers can easily gather information online. We bring our personal habits to the job: We take to the search engine

---

[2] Bain & Company. (2018). Explore the B2B elements of value. https://www.bain.com/insights/explore-the-b2b-elements-of-value-interactive/.

automatically to find information. This is especially so when 73% of decision-makers for B2B purchases are now digitally native millennials.[3] Hence, our discussion in the previous chapter about today's customers being more empowered, more informed, and expecting more personalized experiences applies here as well. They are self-directed and are less trusting toward marketing messages.

Research by Gartner[4] and Forrester[5] dovetail nicely contending that the majority of B2B buyers prefer self-directed research and a rep-free sales experience, preferring to do their own, largely online, research. In fact, by the time they contact vendors, 70% of their buying journey doing their own research is completed[6] (see Figure 7.2). They only spend 17% of their purchase process talking with potential suppliers.[7] Clearly, they have largely made their decisions or at least have established their requirements before they initiate contact with vendors. In fact, a Bain & Co. survey found that almost all buyers have a set of vendors in mind before they do any research, and 90% ultimately choose a vendor from that list.[8]

---

[3] Van Eeden, A. (n.d.). The new B2B consumer and what it means for marketing and sales. Accessed on 26 February 2024. https://www.foleon.com/blog/what-the-rise-of-the-new-b2b-consumer-means-for-marketing-and-sales.

[4] Gartner. (2023). Gartner 2023 B2B Buying Report.

[5] Wizdo, L. (2017). The ways and means of B2B buyer journey maps: We're going deep at Forrester's B2B forum. 21 August 2017. Accessed on 26 February 2024. https://www.forrester.com/blogs/the-ways-and-means-of-b2b-buyer-journey-maps-were-going-deep-at-forresters-b2b-forum/.

[6] 6sense Research. (2023). Out of sight, almost out of time: Why buying cycles are usually over long before you ever know about them. Accessed on 26 February 2024. https://6sense.com/report/buyer-experience/.

[7] Adamson, B. (2022). Sensemaking for sales. *Harvard Business Review*. January-February 2022, 1–9.

[8] Sherrard, S., Rishi, D., and Molly, P. M. (2022). What B2Bs need to know about their buyers. *Harvard Business Review*. 20 September 2022. Accessed on 26 February 2024. https://hbr.org/2022/09/what-b2bs-need-to-know-about-their-buyers.

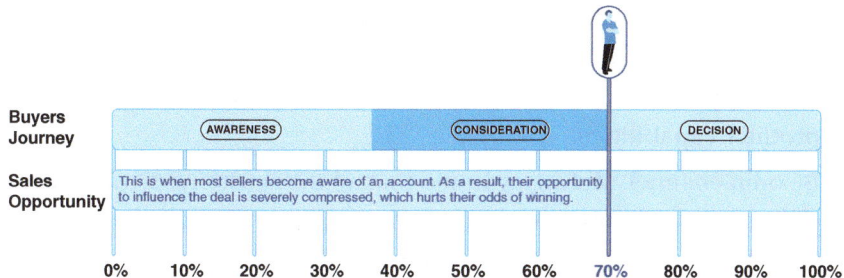

Figure 7.2. Sales opportunity decreases further in the buying journey.[9]

If you are thinking of getting in contact with them before they have made up their minds, think again, because buyers want to initiate contact on their own time.[10] They may not respond until they are satisfied with their research. What is worse is early direct outreach by sellers reduces the chance of landing the deal![11]

So, where does this leave us? Following are a few key implications:

- Think about how buyers form their top-of-mind vendor list, which is their consideration set. Previous experience with vendors, recommendations from trusted colleagues or industry contacts, and reputation for expertise count a lot toward that. Building strong relationships with vendors and establishing a proven track record remain crucial in B2B marketing.

- Like B2C, ZMOT also applies to B2B. B2B businesses must rely on content marketing to do much of the selling for them. This content needs to be relevant and accessible to buyers and meet their needs as they arise through their buying journey. They may be searching for information about the category before they know enough to search for brands. Ensure there is content that addresses their questions while they are still figuring things out.

---

[9] 6sense Research (2023), *Op. cit.*

[10] *Ibid.*

[11] *Ibid.*

- Content need not be stuffy and product-centric. B2B buyers now expect the same B2C experience in the B2B content they consume. Use copy that focuses on buyers' needs and solutions instead of product capabilities.
- Be omnichannel. McKinsey found that all B2B customers want "more channels, more convenience, and a more personalized experience."[12] Look beyond the company website as a channel for communication. When researching potential solutions, many buyers use a range of digital sources, such as industry publications, industry influencers, and review websites. Reaching customers through their preferred channels and formats, whether it is social media, email marketing, webinars, or white papers, ensures they receive information in a way that is convenient and accessible to them. Video content was found to be highly effective giving the highest ROI[13] and social media was rated by B2B marketers as their most effective marketing channel.[14] Gartner's research (Figure 7.3) shows us where buyers go to acquire information.

Being omnichannel requires marketers to know which channels their customers use throughout the decision journey to provide the right information at the right time. In some markets, B2B businesses use over ten channels.[15] Follow where your customers' eyes and ears are. Also, remember that mobile usage is a big part of B2B buyers' lives: Over 40% use mobile devices during the purchase process,[16] whether it is comparing prices, researching, contacting vendors, or purchasing.

---

[12] Arora, A., Liz, H., Candice, L. P., Max, M., and Jennifer, S. (2022). The new B2B growth equation. McKinsey & Company. February 2022.

[13] Hubspot. (2024). The state of marketing 2024: Navigating business growth with technology and creativity for more human marketing.

[14] Ackerman, T. (2018). How B2B and B2C marketing are converging today. *Forbes*. 26 July 2018. Accessed on 1 March 024 https://www.forbes.com/sites/forbescommunicationscouncil/2018/07/26/how-b2b-and-b2c-marketing-are-converging-today/#44363b9054ce.

[15] Arora *et al.* (2022), *Op. cit.*

[16] Snyder, K. and Pashmeena, H. (2015). The changing face of B2B marketing. Think with Google. March 2015. Accessed on 28 February 2024. https://www.thinkwithgoogle.com/consumer-insights/consumer-trends/the-changing-face-b2b-marketing/.

Where Should Marketing Create Digital Value?

Percentage of Buyers Who Engaged With Digital Supplier Interactions in Purchase Process

Figure 7.3. Where buyers engage with vendors.[17]

Case: Maersk's Maiden Voyage on Social Media—B2B Content Can Be Like B2C Too!

In 2011, the world of social media was abuzz with conversations, connections, and cat videos. It was in this vibrant landscape that Maersk Line, a global shipping giant traditionally known for its stoic professionalism, took a bold step: dipping its toes into the uncharted waters of social media. Spearheaded by Jonathan Wichmann, their Head of Group Marketing, this venture marked a turning point for the company, injecting a dose of unexpected personality into its brand image.

Its initial foray, documented on Wichmann's blog, focused on sharing insightful and engaging content relevant to their industry. It delved into topics such as the impact of global trade on everyday life,

---

[17] Gartner. (2023). Navigating successfully through the evolving B2B buying journey. Accessed on 28 February 2024. https://www.gartner.com/en/sales/insights/b2b-buying-journey. GARTNER is a trademark of Gartner, Inc. and/or its affiliates.

the intricacies of the shipping industry, and even the challenges and opportunities posed by emerging technologies such as e-commerce. This content wasn't just informative, it was thought-provoking and sparked conversations among industry professionals and unexpected interest groups from the public.

The shipping giant realized people followed them for various reasons other than business: photography, marine life, love for ships, etc. The team engaged with the different audiences on the topics they were interested in, replying actively to their comments, and slowly developed more relevant content for these audiences. In one post, a Lego figure was featured with a Maersk ship in the background. The text stated "Last year #MaerskLine moved more than 300,000 containers of #toys and #gadgets". These posts helped humanize the brand and communicated its brand core values of reliability, simplicity, and focus on the environment (Figure 7.4).

Beyond informative content, Maersk Line also used social media to foster a sense of community. It engaged with followers, responded to comments and questions, and even posted live updates about how one of their ships had an accident with a whale. This human-centric approach helped bridge the gap between the often-perceived faceless corporation and its stakeholders, fostering a sense of transparency and approachability.

The results were positive. Maersk Line saw a significant increase in brand awareness and engagement. Its social media presence helped it connect with new audiences, build stronger relationships with existing customers, and position itself as singular within the shipping industry. It even earned recognition for its innovative approach, winning awards such as the Guggenheim Social Media Award.

Maersk Line's foray into social media changed the perception of a traditionally conservative industry. By embracing the power of social media and human connection, they demonstrated that even a global giant could be approachable, insightful, and even a little bit human. This pioneering move paved the way for other B2B companies to explore the potential of social media, proving that even the most established organizations can benefit from injecting a touch of personality into their digital presence.

Understanding Business Buyers and Account-Based Marketing | 167

Figure 7.4. Screenshots of Maersk's LinkedIn posts.

Sense-making

The abundance of information in today's digital world presents a significant challenge not just for consumers but also for enterprise customers. B2B buyers, bombarded with product brochures, case studies, and competitor claims, are increasingly overwhelmed and struggle to make informed decisions. The 2023 Gartner B2B Buying Journey Report[18] highlights this challenge, stating that "B2B buyers are overwhelmed with information and lack the time or expertise to evaluate all of it." This information overload can lead to decision paralysis and hinder the buying journey. For those who were gung-ho enough to buy based on purely self-service modes, some 43% expressed regrets over their purchases[19] (Figure 7.5).

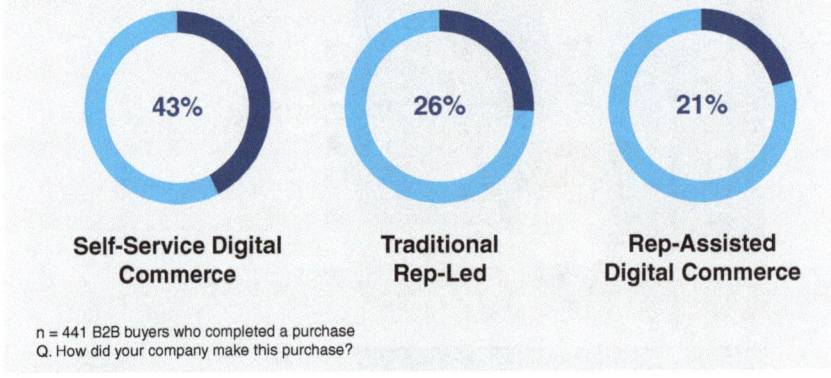

Figure 7.5. Percentage of buyers who reported high purchase regret.[20]

Note: Percentages calculated based on stated level of agreement with a series of questions associated with purchase regret. Colored segments represent the proportion of respondents who scored at least a 6 "Agree" out of a 7-point scale.

Gartner's research highlighted the benefits of a hybrid mode with digital and human integration. McKinsey's research also supported this approach, emphasizing its effectiveness. While digital channels gave buyers control, the human element was superior in providing empathy and helping with contextual adaptations and judgments.

---

[18] Gartner (2023), *Op. cit.*

[19] *Ibid.*

[20] *Ibid.*

Two criteria were found to reduce the likelihood of buyer regret: decision confidence and trust in the seller.[21] Buyers who believed they had made sense of the information, considered the right issues, and prioritized the most important ones were more likely to complete high-quality, low-regret deals. Conversely, regret is more likely when buyers are skeptical of sales representatives' claims.

Sellers who help customers make sense of the overwhelming and sometimes contradictory information are more likely to be trusted and complete deals that are perceived to be of high quality. These "sense makers" guide customers to useful information, instead of drowning them with comprehensive detail, to help them along with their purchase journeys. They understand that customers face competing perspectives, help them evaluate and reconcile conflicting information, and quantify trade-offs. Sense-makers empower customers to come to their own decisions with assurance and confidence to buy. In a nutshell, sellers must help customers understand how to use a solution to help them improve in their job or company performance (value framing) and validate that the purchase is the right decision (value affirmation). Around 80% of sellers who use the sense-making approach closed high-quality, low-regret deals.[22]

Here's how B2B marketers can step up to be a sense-maker:

- **Becoming trusted advisors:** Building trust and establishing themselves as reliable sources of information allows B2B marketers to guide customers through the sea of information and recommend the most relevant and insightful resources.

- **Curating high-quality content:** Instead of adding to the noise, B2B marketers should focus on and/or curating high-quality content that is actionable, insightful, and tailored to the specific needs and challenges of their target audience. Figure 7.6 is a useful guide with

---

[21] Adamson (2022), *Op. cit.*

[22] Blum, K. (2019). Why B2B sellers need a sensemaking sales strategy. Gartner. 5 November 2019. Accessed on 4 March 2024 https://www.gartner.com/smarterwithgartner/b2b-sellers-need-sense-making-sales-strategy.

some suggestions on the types of content for the various stages of the buying journey:

	Problem Identification	Solution Exploration	Requirements Building	Supplier Selection	Solution Ownership
Value Framing	Article on top industry challenges	Peer benchmarking data	Video product demo	Product specifications chart	Video showing how to deploy product
Value Affirmation	Calculator to estimate problem costs	Product selection tool	Product configuration visualizer	Ratings and reviews	Prompts for service based on usage data

Figure 7.6. Content types to match buyers' user journeys.[23]

- **Leveraging data and analytics:** By utilizing data-driven insights, B2B marketers can personalize their communication and content, delivering information that is most relevant to individual customer needs and stages in the buying journey.

- **Simplifying and storytelling:** Presenting complex information in a clear, concise, and engaging manner can make it easier for B2B buyers to understand and retain key messages. Utilizing storytelling techniques can further enhance comprehension, build emotional connections, and show empathy for buyers' pain points. Use interactive digital tools, such as cost calculators, product comparison and selection tools, and product visualizers, to help buyers navigate through options.

- **Know customers' expectations:** McKinsey's large-scale research showed that there were some elements that were deal breakers—if these "must-dos" are missing (Figure 7.7), buyers would actively look for another vendor.

Stakeholder management

B2B buying usually involves complex buying centers. A B2B buying group typically consists of three tiers: approvers who own the decision, a core buying committee that does the research and buying, and influencers including end-users who provide feedback on vendors and

---

[23] Gartner (2023), *Op. cit.*

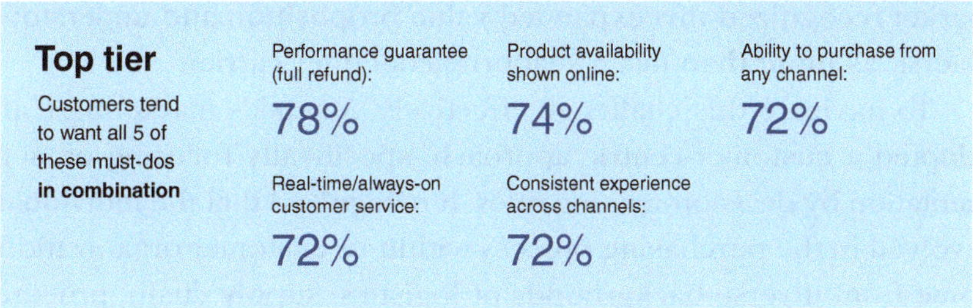

Top tier	Performance guarantee (full refund):	Product availability shown online:	Ability to purchase from any channel:
Customers tend to want all 5 of these must-dos **in combination**	**78%**	**74%**	**72%**
	Real-time/always-on customer service:	Consistent experience across channels:	
	72%	**72%**	

Figure 7.7. Expectations from B2B customers.[24]

products.[25] There could be five to eleven stakeholders, who represent an average of five distinct business functions.[26] Each member has their own interests, performance deliverables, and concerns. Content should be tailored to each of their priorities, such as technical presentations for engineers, ROI analyses for finance folks, and solutions-focused information for end-users.

B2B marketers must understand the buying unit's structure and potential power dynamics. This helps identify key decision-makers and their goals, allowing for a more focused and customized approach that addresses the company's needs.

Maersk shares with us how it manages the different levels in its marketing efforts.

Case: Maersk Tailors Engagement Strategy to Bridge the Integration Gap[27]

In 2016, Maersk embarked on a significant transformation, evolving from a traditional shipping line to a provider of comprehensive, integrated logistics solutions. This shift necessitated a strategic shift in its marketing approach. Its primary challenge became ensuring the

---

[24] Arora *et al.* (2022), *Op. cit.*

[25] Sherrard *et al.* (2022), *Op. cit.*

[26] Gartner (2023), *Op. cit.*

[27] The authors gratefully acknowledge Maersk Asia Pacific's Ross Gearing (Regional Head of Marketing) for his invaluable insights and content contributions, which were instrumental in the development of this case study.

market recognized this expanded value proposition and understood Maersk as more than just a seaborne container carrier.

To navigate this challenge effectively, Maersk's marketing team adopted a customer-centric approach, specifically focusing on segmentation by decision-making roles. It recognized that the individuals involved in the purchasing process within its customer organizations come from diverse backgrounds of logistics, supply chain, procurement, transformation, and IT personnel.

The final decision often rests with senior executives such as Presidents or Chief Experience Officers (CXOs) in global offices. These approvers rely on a panel of deciders who evaluate proposals from various logistics service providers (LSPs). This panel, typically comprising Global Vice Presidents or Directors, plays a crucial role in recommending LSP choices and typically remains consistent across projects.

The selection panel further seeks influencers, from managers to end-users, to shortlist LSPs through multiple rounds of evaluation. These influencers, often from different departments, provide practical user insights and perspectives. By understanding these diverse roles and responsibilities, Maersk can tailor its messaging and engagement strategies to each segment effectively (Figure 7.8).

To illustrate, Maersk identified a gap in awareness and understanding regarding its integrated logistics solutions across different levels within potential client companies. This gap manifested in varying degrees of knowledge, mindset, and attitude toward data and operational integration. Recognizing this diversity, Maersk devised a multi-layered engagement strategy with tailored approaches for each group:

1. Approvers and Deciders—Senior Executives and VPs:
   - **Existing awareness:** Familiar with Maersk as an integrator.
   - **Mindset:** High acceptance of strategic data and operational integration.
   - **Engagement goals:** Deepen engagement, understand solution benefits, and convert interest into purchase intent.

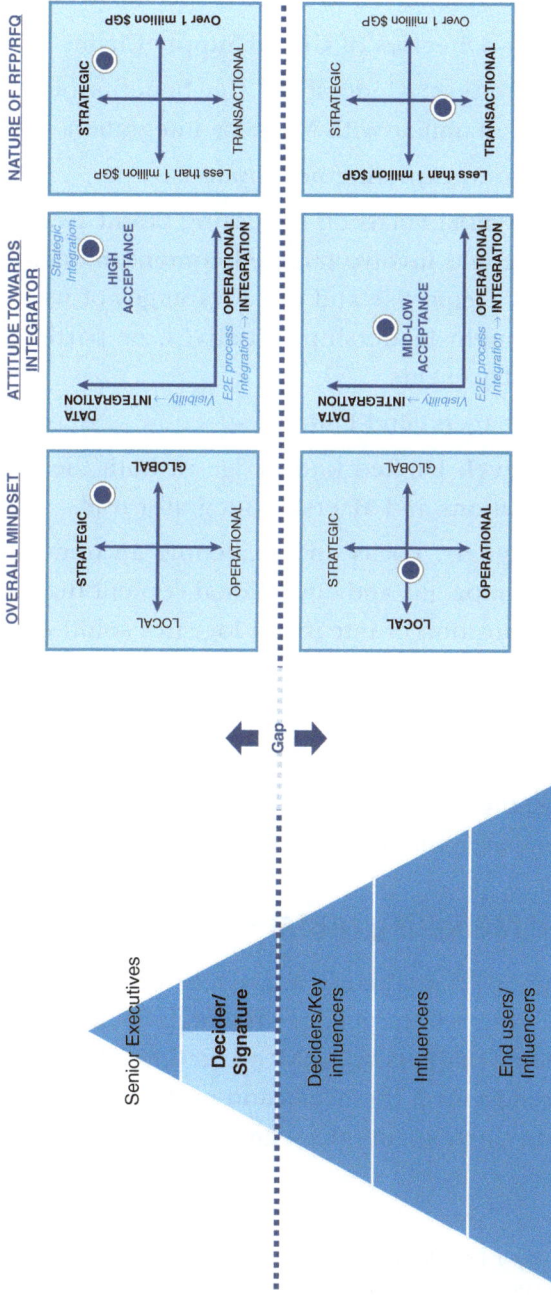

Figure 7.8. Understanding target audience segments.
Source: Ross Gearing, Regional Head of Marketing, APA, Maersk.

- **Approach:** One-on-one interactions to showcase the benefits of their integrated solutions and address specific needs.
2. Key Influencers—Directors of Global Supply Chain:
    - **Limited awareness:** Understand the benefits of integrated solutions but unfamiliar with Maersk's integration capabilities.
    - **Mindset:** Open to exploring new options.
    - **Engagement goals:** Focus on increasing brand awareness and interest. This could involve targeted content marketing showcasing Maersk's expertise and the advantages of its integrated approach, thought leadership initiatives, or participation in relevant industry events.
3. Influencers (Managers) and End-users:
    - **Knowledge level:** Limited knowledge of both the benefits of integrated solutions and Maersk's integrator role.
    - **Engagement goals:** Focus on broadening awareness through mass media campaigns and educational content that highlights the value proposition of integrated logistics solutions.

This multi-layered approach ensures Maersk effectively communicates with each audience segment using the most appropriate channels and messaging. By tailoring their engagement strategy, Maersk can bridge the existing knowledge gap and ultimately convert awareness into meaningful business relationships.

Account-Based Marketing (ABM)[28]

ABM is a strategic B2B marketing approach where marketing and sales teams collaborate to target specific, high-value accounts as if they were individual markets. In ABM, marketing efforts are personalized and tailored to meet the needs and preferences of individual accounts, treating them as unique segments.

---

[28] The authors gratefully acknowledge Joe Escobedo (CEO, Escomedia) for his invaluable insights and content contributions, which were instrumental in the development of this section.

ABM programs can be one-to-one, where a very small number of high-value accounts, typically the most critical and strategic ones for the business are targeted. Here, personalization is the highest. ABM can be used to protect and grow existing accounts, or to win new business from specific target accounts.

Here's how ABM works:

- **Account selection:** Marketing and sales teams collaborate to identify a list of high-value accounts that have the potential to generate significant revenue and long-term partnerships. Factors such as industry, size, revenue, and growth potential are considered.
- **Deep account research:** In-depth research is conducted on each target account to understand their specific needs, challenges, buying committee structure, and decision-making process.
- **Personalized campaigns:** Based on the research, personalized marketing campaigns are developed that address the specific pain points and goals of different stakeholders in the target account. This may involve customized content targeting specific roles or departments, targeted advertising, or direct outreach to contacts on LinkedIn or emails. Content on websites and email campaigns is also dynamically adjusted according to the target's browsing history, purchase behavior, or inferred interests.
- **Marketing and sales alignment:** Marketing and sales teams work closely together throughout the entire process to ensure a unified approach. Marketing creates targeted content, nurtures leads, and provides sales with insights about the accounts (such as stage of readiness and types of content consumed). Sales teams follow-up to engage with qualified leads and close deals.

By customizing the marketing approach for each account, ABM aims to foster stronger relationships with key decision-makers in target accounts and be positioned as trusted advisors. Its personalized outreach and content can increase engagement and aims for faster deal closure. By focusing on high-value accounts, ABM can generate a higher ROI compared to traditional marketing strategies.

Around 76% of B2B marketers reported that ABM programs generate a higher ROI compared to any other marketing strategy.[29] The success of ABM hinges heavily on two key issues: having enough insights on the target accounts, and getting marketing and sales aligned to work collaboratively.

Gaining insights into target accounts

Here's how companies can learn more about their target accounts beyond direct sales relationships with the target clients:

Account research and profiling

Companies could invest in research to understand their target accounts' needs, pain points, and preferences. This can involve studying public information, website interactions, and social media activity to build comprehensive profiles.

Surveys and interviews

Directly engaging with key stakeholders from target accounts through surveys and interviews can provide invaluable insights. Companies can conduct customer interviews, user surveys, or even gather feedback from lost deals to identify areas of improvement.

Inbound marketing

Inbound marketing involves creating content for potential customers to find through organic or paid search or social media. Such content can pique the interest of contacts of targeted ABM accounts. Inbound marketing goes hand in hand with ABM. By tracking which pieces of content these contacts have consumed, ABM marketers can infer where these prospects are in the buying journey.

Intent data and predictive analytics

By monitoring online activities and engagement signals, companies can identify accounts actively researching or displaying buying signals. For

---

[29] Adobe. (2023). Your guide to account-based marketing (ABM). Adobe Experience Cloud. 26 July 2023. Accessed on 7 March 2024. https://business.adobe.com/blog/basics/account-based-marketing.

example, say you are a software company targeting a specific hospital. Through intent data (such as the frequency of website visits, search queries, and social media activity), you identify that the hospital had downloaded a white paper on one of your products and conducted several searches related to implementing a new system. Predictive analytics, considering these data and historical trends, might then predict that the hospital has a high probability of making a purchase within the next quarter. With these insights, the ABM team can proactively reach out to the hospital with personalized communication, highlighting relevant case studies, offering a demo tailored to their specific needs, and connecting them with the appropriate sales representative.

Alignment between marketing and sales

ABM is most effective when there is a close collaboration between marketing and sales teams. By aligning marketing and sales objectives, ABM ensures that both teams work toward a common goal—targeting and converting high-value accounts.

1. **Establish shared goals and KPIs:**
   - **Cultural misalignment and building trust:** Address any cultural barriers between marketing and sales. Foster a culture of collaboration, mutual respect, and shared responsibility for achieving revenue goals. Build trust between the two teams through transparency, shared successes, and accountability.
   - **Revenue and sales pipeline:** Align marketing and sales around the same business goals and definition of success. Shared targets ensure both teams work towards the same outcome: converting high-value accounts into customers.
   - **Establish roles and expectations:** Document what each team is responsible for. Communicate what each team needs to succeed and ensure that both teams agree on tasks and participation. Agree on a common pipeline process and definition of a qualified lead. Without standardized definitions, it is easy to have misaligned expectations of responsibilities, leading to a blame game.
   - **Collaborative persona development and journey mapping:** Marketing and sales must agree on whom to target (the key

customer targets) and the prioritization of various targets. By sharing an understanding of the target accounts' needs, pain points, and preferences, both teams can craft the buyer personas collaboratively. Map out the touchpoints and interactions at each stage of the journey, from the initial awareness phase to the final decision-making phase, to develop buying journeys. This is useful for creating personalized messages and experiences.

- **Unified data and analytics:** Implementing a shared CRM system and MA platform can provide a unified view of target accounts and their interactions. This shared data allows marketing and sales teams to understand which accounts engage with specific marketing efforts and when they are ready for sales engagement. Breaking down data silos provides transparency that helps foster trust between marketing and sales.
- **Message alignment check:** An aligned team will have a unified messaging approach from the initial digital touchpoint to a live demo and beyond. Determining where the messaging starts to break down can help you identify where alignment may have broken down.
- **Opportunity and deal conversion rates:** Track the conversion rates and progress of leads in the common pipeline process. These would usually include rates of qualified leads and close/win rates. Monitoring these rates helps identify areas for improvement and collaboration between marketing and sales.

2. **Implement regular communication and feedback loops:**
   - **Regular communication and collaboration:** Companies should foster regular communication and collaboration between marketing and sales teams to review progress, discuss challenges, and adjust strategies accordingly. This can be achieved through joint meetings, shared dashboards, and coordinated planning sessions.
   - **Feedback loops:** Creating feedback loops between marketing and sales is essential. Sales teams can provide valuable insights into the pain points and objections encountered during client conversations. Marketing can use this information to refine messaging and content, ensuring they resonate with the specific needs of the accounts.

3. **Utilize ABM technology:**
   - **ABM platforms and tools:** Invest in ABM-specific technology to enhance collaboration and alignment. ABM platforms can provide insights into account engagement, facilitate personalized content delivery, and enable joint workflows.

ABM Technology

ABM technologies are a diverse set of tools designed to streamline and enhance the effectiveness of your ABM strategy. Here are some key categories and their applications:

1. **Data management and insights:**
   - **Function:** Collects, cleans, and organizes data from various sources (CRM, website analytics, and intent data platforms) to build comprehensive profiles of target accounts and their decision-makers.
   - **Benefits:** Enables effective targeting, personalization of messaging, and identification of high-potential accounts.
2. **Account identification and prioritization:**
   - **Function:** Utilizes data and analytics to identify and prioritize target accounts based on specific criteria such as firmographics, buying intent signals, and fit with your ideal customer profile (ICP).
   - **Benefits:** Streamlines resource allocation by focusing on the most promising accounts.
3. **Personalization and engagement:**
   - **Function:** Creates personalized content (e.g., emails, landing pages, and social media posts) tailored to the specific needs and interests of each target account and its decision-makers.
   - **Benefits:** Increases engagement and conversion rates by delivering relevant, valuable content.
4. **Orchestration and automation:**
   - **Function:** Automates repetitive tasks such as campaign execution, lead scoring, and multi-channel engagement across various platforms (email, social media, and website).

- **Benefits:** Improves efficiency and frees up time for more strategic activities.
5. **Measurement and reporting:**
   - **Function:** Tracks campaign performance and provides insights into key metrics such as engagement rates, conversion rates, and ROI.
   - **Benefits:** Enables data-driven decision-making and optimization of ABM strategies.
6. **Intent data integration:**
   - **Function:** Integrates intent data from external platforms to identify accounts actively researching solutions related to your offerings, indicating potential buying intent.
   - **Benefits:** Enables early engagement with accounts demonstrating purchase interest, increasing the likelihood of successful conversion.
7. **Social media management:**
   - **Function:** Manages social media outreach and engagement with target accounts on various platforms, allowing for personalized interactions and brand building.
   - **Benefits:** Expands reach, fosters deeper connections with decision-makers on their preferred social media channels, and enhances brand awareness.

Case Study: Adobe Chats—B2B Marketing Demystified Asia Edition[30]

This case study demonstrates how marketing and sales work together to use a marketing campaign to engage with targeted leads. Led by Emily Wong from Adobe's Field Marketing team and Joe Escobedo, CEO of Escomedia, the campaign titled "Adobe Chats—B2B Marketing

---

[30] The authors gratefully acknowledge Joe Escobedo (CEO, Escomedia) and Emily Wong (Field Marketing, Adobe) for their invaluable insights and content contributions, which were instrumental in the development of this case study.

Demystified Asia Edition" aimed to generate new leads in Southeast Asia by targeting specific accounts based on industries, personas, and pain points.

Campaign idea and inspiration: Emily Wong derived campaign ideas from three main sources:

1. **Sales team insights:** Collaboration with the sales team to gather insights on prospects' requests when seeking solutions. This input helped identify relevant topics such as "Rethinking Third-Party Cookies" that were crucial for B2B marketers and the target audience.
2. **Market trends and media buzz:** Emily monitored market trends and media discussions to identify topics making waves in the B2B marketing landscape. Subjects such as "ABM Marketing Attribution" and "Third-Party Cookies" emerged as hot topics, indicating high interest and relevance to the target audience.
3. **Vendor collaboration:** Emily worked closely with vendors, including her co-host Joe, to explore event agendas and identify topics that could resonate with the audience.

Campaign process: The campaign process was methodical, ensuring alignment with marketing objectives and stakeholder goals:

1. **Alignment with marketing plan:** Emily started by aligning the campaign's objectives with the annual marketing plan, setting key metrics, such as the number of marketing-qualified leads, sales-qualified leads, and pipeline generation.
2. **Stakeholder alignment:** Emily engaged with key stakeholders, including her manager and the regional marketing team, to ensure alignment on the campaign plan, budget, and objectives to avoid duplication of efforts and maximize results.
3. **Vendor selection and briefing:** Emily carefully selected a trustworthy and dependable vendor, in this case, Joe, for the podcast series. She emphasized the importance of providing a clear and detailed brief to enable vendors to effectively bring the campaign idea to life.

4. **Channel setup and promotion:** Emily used a mix of channels, including paid media campaigns, email sponsorships, and paid search, to target both existing prospects and net new leads. Additionally, she leveraged internal stakeholders, such as sales and customer success teams, to promote the campaign through their social networks.

Strategy implementation:
- With inputs from the sales team, 300 target accounts across Asia were selected based on their intent and need for Adobe's solutions. These accounts were categorized into five verticals for a tailored approach. The content creation focused on addressing the challenges and growth opportunities identified through interviews with key buyers and influencers.
- Sponsored emails and paid ads were used to reach the 300 selected accounts, ensuring focused and effective marketing efforts.
- Weekly marketing reports kept the sales team updated on prospect engagement. Marketing and Salesforce reports were utilized to highlight interactions. Unique UTM tags helped track the impact of different content pieces. Such communication reinforced the alignment between marketing and sales efforts.

Campaign launch and key learnings: The campaign successfully gained traction with industry-level prospects. Emily noted two key learnings during the campaign:

1. **Scaling content with industry focus:** Emily found that scaling content by focusing on industry verticals proved effective. By addressing common challenges within specific industries across Southeast Asian countries, she achieved wider reach and resonance with the target audience without creating redundant content for each market.
2. **Importance of passionate and knowledgeable speakers:** Selecting passionate and knowledgeable speakers who were

experts in their fields contributed to the campaign's success. The speakers' enthusiasm and expertise resonated with the audience and generated positive engagement and interest in the campaign.

The Adobe Chats–B2B Marketing Demystified Asia Edition campaign exemplified how a well-thought-out strategy, collaborative efforts, and audience-centric content can result in a successful B2B marketing campaign. Emily's meticulous planning, efforts to ensure alignment with stakeholders, and industry-specific content strategy, combined with well-planned execution, helped create an impactful and engaging campaign that generated valuable results for Adobe in Southeast Asia.

The Asian PoV

Asian companies exhibit a wide range of organizational constructs, including family-owned businesses, state-owned enterprises, multinationals, Keiretsu (Japan), and Chaebols (South Korea). These diverse structures can influence decision-making processes and require ABM strategies to be adapted accordingly. Understanding the unique dynamics of each type of organization is essential for effective targeting and engagement.

Relationships in B2B businesses are critical but building these relationships in Asia will require a stronger understanding with a more delicate and nuanced approach. Understanding and respecting cultural differences is paramount. This includes communication styles, business etiquette, decision-making processes, and the importance of personal relationships. Building strong relationships in Asia often involves investing time and effort in getting to know your partners on a personal level. This can involve social gatherings, shared meals, and demonstrating genuine interest in their business and culture. It is often viewed as a long-term commitment where patience and persistence are key. For some cultures in Asia, face-to-face meetings and interactions are highly valued. And worthwhile to note that gift-giving is a common practice in many Asian cultures, but it's essential to understand the local customs and etiquette to avoid causing offense. It is useful to research the appropriate types of gifts, occasions, and presentation methods.

Finally, government, business regulations, and practices can vary significantly across Asian countries and impact B2B relationships and engagement. Staying informed about local laws and regulations is crucial to avoid legal complications and maintain compliance.

Key Takeaways

From this chapter, we can see how B2B marketing and B2C marketing have similarities. While sales are being conducted between businesses, involving a formal buying unit with the firm, the process is ultimately human-to-human. Hence it evokes similar characteristics and requirements as B2C marketing, such as using storytelling to humanize a brand and engage with their customers.

In summary:
- While B2B marketing may involve sales between businesses to businesses, the process is human-to-human.
- For more effective B2B marketing, marketing and sales must work closely. Marketing can help qualify leads and provide sales with the necessary information to provide more targeted and personalized solutions.
- B2B buying requires assisting with the sense-making of information and change enablement to push through purchases in the buying organization.
- Using storytelling in B2B marketing can help humanize a brand, create deeper engagement and connection with its customers, and act as a point of differentiation for the firm against its competitors.

Chapter

8

Product Strategy and Value Proposition

A product is the main way brands articulate their brand positioning and deliver their value proposition. One's product experience is what makes a brand important and determines repeat purchases. No matter what reason drove customers to buy, their direct experience with the product would validate or nullify the brand promise. A well-defined product strategy translates a company's vision into a tangible offering that resonates with target customers and solves their unique problems.

But there is more than just offering a good product. Product strategy involves managing the product over time. So, product managers wear many hats and their decisions significantly impact a product's success in the market. The key decisions for a product manager would include the following:

(i) Defining the product vision;
(ii) Identifying the elements of value;
(iii) Developing new products;
(iv) Redefining products in a connected world;
(v) Managing the PLC; and
(vi) Managing the product portfolio.

In this chapter, we focus on the decisions for new products. In the next, we discuss the management of existing products.

Product Vision

A product vision is a concise and aspirational statement that outlines the long-term direction and purpose of a product. It serves as a guiding principle for everyone involved in the product's development, from conception to market launch, so they are aligned and focused on the same goal. It clearly articulates the value proposition of the product and the benefit(s) it offers to its ideal customer. Bearing in mind the needs and aspirations of the users the product is designed to serve, the product vision describes what the product aspires to be in the long term, not just its current features. Having a clear product vision would come in handy when making crucial decisions about product features and roadmap priorities.

For example, Grab's product vision is to drive Southeast Asia forward by creating economic empowerment in the ecosystem of users, driver-partners, businesses, and service providers. It then created the superapp to include deliveries, mobility, financial services, and enterprise solutions, connecting consumers to everyday entrepreneurs and solving logistical needs for businesses and individuals.

Elements of Value

The true value of a product goes beyond its price tag. It is the sum of all the benefits a customer receives minus the cost they pay. These benefits can be functional, like solving a problem, but also extend to emotional, social, and experiential aspects. Think of it this way: Exceptional customer service or a unique shopping experience can add significant value. Similarly, aligning with a brand community through a purchase can fulfil a social need. Likewise, costs to a customer are not just limited to the monetary outlay to acquire the product. Costs could also be in the form of discomfort, inconvenience, delays, or the social cost of a bad haircut leading to embarrassment.

By understanding these diverse value drivers, businesses can think outside the box and create products that resonate more deeply with their target audience. Case in point: Scrub Daddy.[1]

---

[1] Godio, M. (2023). Scrub Daddy: The Shark Tank breakout brand that makes cleaning much more fun. *NBC News*. 28 February 2023. Accessed on 29 March 2024. https://www.nbcnews.com/select/shopping/scrub-daddy-sponges-ncna1303149.

Product Strategy and Value Proposition | 187

Figure 8.1. The Original Scrub Daddy.

This sponge costs more than competitor brands but is a brand worth over USD 240 million with 4M followers on TikTok. Its iconic bright yellow smiley face design offers functional benefits, shaped to fit in the palm, with eyes for fingers to fit into for a better grip (Figure 8.1). It also stands out visually, adding a playful element to the often mundane chore of cleaning. The combination of functionality, design, and hygiene benefits creates a positive user experience, encouraging repeat purchases and word-of-mouth recommendations.

A deep customer understanding of the motivation behind a purchase helps us identify what truly matters to our target customer. Why do customers buy your product? Harvard Professors recommend a few ways to add elements of value.[2]

What are the jobs customers want to get done? Is it problems they want to solve or aspirations they want to achieve? Are there "negative jobs" that people hate having to do? How can you help make these negative jobs more pleasant? Take a leaf out of Scrub Daddy's book.

---

[2] Christiansen, C., Hall, T., Dillon, K., and Duncan, D. S. (2016). Know your customers' "jobs to be done". *Harvard Business Review*. September 2016.

Customers derive more than functional benefits from a product. Don't neglect the potential for powerful social and emotional connections. Who would have imagined a dishwashing sponge that customers hold funerals for when they throw theirs away (watch "Scrub Daddy Death" videos on TikTok)? The brand understood that the job to be done to get dishes cleaned is often a chore. It made the chore a little nicer, a little brighter, and a little less mundane. It was a welcome change to boring rectangular sponges that were often gross, smelly, and ugly. Instead, Scrub Daddy users put them out on display.[3]

Understanding the reasons and barriers that stop non-users from buying available solutions can often reveal opportunities. What are the workarounds non-buyers use to get the job done instead? When celebrities were flaunting ombré hair, L'Oréal found that consumers were searching online for DIY alternatives to achieve that same look without having to spend a few hundred dollars at the salon. This insight led them to launch the world's first DIY ombré hair color kit.[4]

Examining unusual uses for existing products may also reveal opportunities to add value. Arm and Hammer would not have lasted till today if it had not realized that consumers were using baking soda to remove bad smells from their refrigerators.[5] Today, the brand has product lines for deodorizing, laundry, cat litter, and oral and personal care.

A starting point to gain such an understanding could be from market research (surveys, focus groups, and user interviews to identify target customers' needs, challenges, pain points, and aspirations) or through customer journey maps to identify touchpoints where value can be delivered.

---

[3] Taylor, D. (2017). Scrub Daddy's Daddy tells how the brand reached $150 million in just 5 years. Taylor Brand Group. 18 December 2017. Accessed on 1 March 2024. https://www.taylorbrandgroup.com/scrub-daddys-daddy-tells-brand-reached-150-million-just-5-years/.

[4] Think with Google (2014). L'Oréal Paris discovers the beauty of search for building brand love. Accessed on 1 March 2024. https://www.thinkwithgoogle.com/marketing-strategies/search/loreal-paris-builds-brand-love-with-search/.

[5] Anand, V. (2023). Arm and Hammer—Discontinuous positioning saved the day. Medium.com. 18 December 2023. Accessed on 1 March 2024. https://medium.com/@onlykutts/arm-hammer-discontinuous-positioning-saved-the-day-a22edf0eca8e.

Product Strategy and Value Proposition | 189

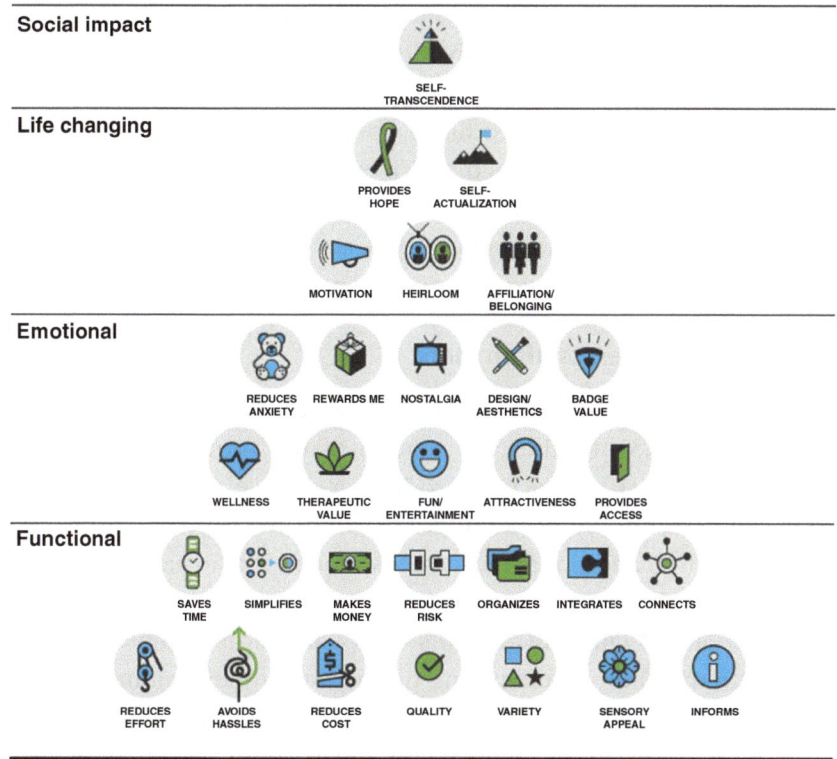

Figure 8.2. Elements of value for B2C customers.[6]

Another useful way to get ideas for new products or product improvements is to understand the elements of value that consumers want, in order to meet functional, emotional, life-changing, and social impact needs. Like Maslow's Hierarchy of Needs, this framework works on the basis that some functional elements must be delivered before higher-level ones can be offered. Based on Bain's research[7] (Figure 8.2), while many brands compete on fundamental aspects

---

[6] Bain & Company. (2016). Explore the B2C elements of value. https://www.bain.com/insights/elements-of-value-interactive/.

[7] *Ibid.*

like saving time, money, and effort, as well as quality, variety, and sensory appeal, the truly differentiating factors are the higher-value elements. These higher-value elements are rooted in a product's capacity to deliver emotional benefits (e.g., reducing anxiety, offering badge value, bestowing attractiveness and access), life-changing benefits (e.g., providing hope, motivation, self-actualization), and social impact benefits (through self-transcendence). In essence, beyond basic functionality, it's a product's ability to connect with deeper human needs and aspirations that drives true competitive advantage. In general, brands that consumers perceive to be doing well in four or more elements lead to higher advocacy and revenue. Emotional elements were found to have the greatest effect on word of mouth.

The feature trap: Less is often more

Marketing managers may think about their product offerings on three levels (Figure 8.3): (i) the core benefit of the product/service that buyers are after; (ii) the actual product or service such as the brand name, features, quality, packaging, or styling; and (iii) the augmented benefits, such as additional consumer services, like installation, after-sales service, delivery, and warranty.

In the race to innovate and outshine competitors, businesses often fall prey to the allure of cramming products with new features. While adding a single feature might seem like minimal incremental cost, the cumulative effect can be detrimental. Overstuffed products become expensive to produce, leading to squeezed margins or price hikes for consumers.

Here's the surprising truth: Research shows that post-purchase satisfaction hinges on ease of use, not an abundance of features. Consumers initially crave options, but the reality is, many struggle to navigate complex functionalities. Imagine the frustration of trying to decipher a feature-laden oven manual instead of intuitively making a delicious meal. Feature fatigue[8] sets in, reminding us that "more is not always merrier."

---

[8] Thompson, D. V., Hamilton, R. W., and Rust, R. T. (2005). Feature fatigue: When product capabilities become too much of a good thing. *Journal of Marketing Research*, 42(4), 431–442.

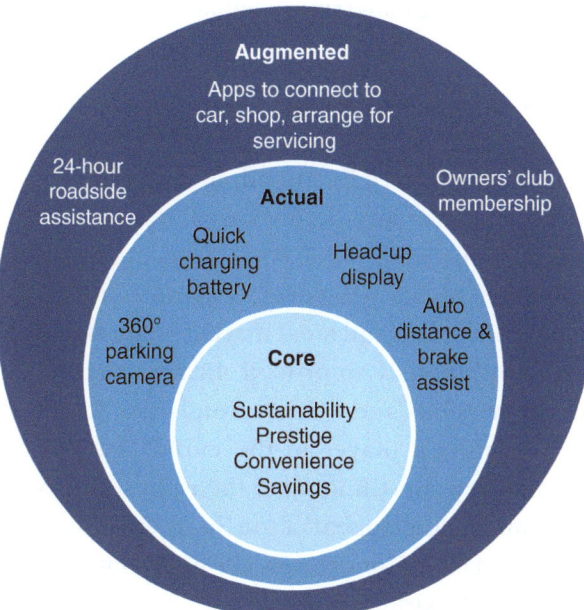

Figure 8.3. Three levels of product for an electric vehicle.

Marketers, this is a better approach: Instead of a one-size-fits-all approach, consider what features truly resonate with customers and what they are willing to pay for. This understanding can be used to develop product lines tailored to the specific needs of distinct customer segments. This allows for targeted value propositions and avoids the "one-size-fits-all" approach. Each product could boast a streamlined set of well-appreciated features, clearly communicated as its key selling points. By focusing on value propositions tailored to distinct segments and including only features that are genuinely appreciated by customers within each product segment, businesses can optimize costs and achieve better product differentiation.

By adopting a customer-centric approach and focusing on features that deliver value, businesses can avoid the feature trap and create products that are not only cost-effective but also resonate with their target customer, leading to greater customer satisfaction and long-term success.

The constant challenge of sustaining value

While intellectual property like patents can temporarily extend a product's competitive advantage, the business landscape is constantly evolving. Remember the 5Cs (Company, Customers, Competitors, Collaborators, and Context). Even with a valid patent, a shift in any of these Cs can alter the very definition of value for your product.

Brand equity can also provide some protection, offering a buffer against immediate threats. However, it is not an invincible shield. A superior competitor can still steal market share if your value proposition is not continuously improved. Brands that fail to adapt to evolving customer needs and market trends risk losing momentum. BlackBerry, a dominant player in the early days of smartphones, serves as a cautionary tale. Clinging to their physical keyboard design while underestimating the appeal of touchscreens and app ecosystems proved fatal. Their lack of innovation allowed competitors like Apple and Android to steal market share.

To navigate this dynamic environment, businesses must remain vigilant, constantly monitoring how the 5Cs are changing. This awareness allows for proactive adaptation of product offerings and value propositions. This could involve introducing entirely new product lines or categories.

New Product Development (NPD)

Innovation is a top priority for organizations to keep up with trends and stay relevant to customers, as well as to keep up with competition. New products also help to diversify product offerings and create new revenue streams. But let's be honest about how it is not a walk in the park, with new products reaching high failure rates of 50% or greater[9] (Gasp! A McKinsey poll reported a failure rate of 94%[10]). Common reasons[11] include launching a product that fails to sway customers either because of a lack of education or because its differences didn't

---

[9] Ogawa, S. and Pillar, F. T. (2006). Reducing the risks of new product development. *Sloan Management Review*. 1 January 2006.

[10] Almquist *et al.* (2016), Op. cit.

[11] Schneider, J. and Hall, J. (2011). Why most product launches fail. *Harvard Business Review*. April 2011.

meet the "so what?" factor. Some failures were because products were launched before they could meet marketed claims or production could not ramp up quickly to cater to fast growth. These reasons point to one commonality: a bad understanding of the market and customer needs. This speed to failure is especially apparent in the technology sector. An example is the Humane AI pin, which was launched with great fanfare and raised over $240 million of funding. But the new product did not meet the marketing hype and prompted the company to exit the market.[12]

Undeniably, there are conflicting demands on the development of a product with superior value. Ideally, it should meet all criteria of optimal time, optimal cost, and optimal quality (Figure 8.4). But how should "optimal" be defined? Value is subjectively determined by the customer, hence "optimal" should be defined by the target customer. By focusing on customer needs, companies can significantly increase their odds of launching successful new products that resonate with the market and generate sustainable growth.

While not foolproof, having a customer-centric systematic process to take out the guesswork and reliance on gut feel or fixation on someone's "pet project" may help minimize the risks of launching products that fail. The NPD process is a roadmap

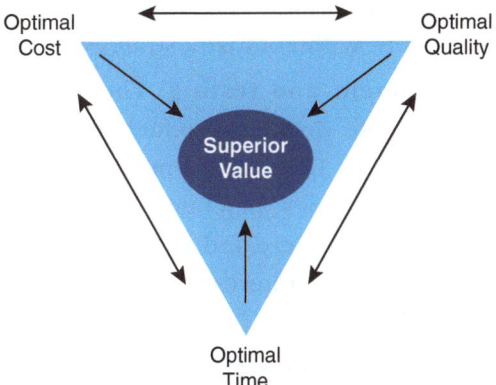

Figure 8.4. Conflicting demands for new products.

---

[12] Snelling, G. (2024). Humane's AI Pin was never going to be great. Fast Company. 12 April 2024. https://www.fastcompany.com/91092156/humanes-ai-pin-was-never-going-to-be-great

that takes an idea from conception all the way to market launch. The specific steps involved in the NPD process may vary depending on the industry, company size, and complexity of the product. The following is a breakdown of the typical stages involved:

1. **Idea generation:** Based on the direction that the company has decided to embark on, the first stage focuses on sparking creativity and generating a wide range of new product ideas. Techniques like market research, competitor analysis, and internal brainstorming sessions are used to identify potential opportunities. In today's digital economy, a treasure trove of resources exists for marketers seeking ideas for new products: Marketers can leverage various data sources—website analytics, social media listening tools, customer surveys, and loyalty program data—to gain valuable insights into customer behavior, trends, preferences, and pain points. The digital age also fosters a collaborative innovation environment where marketers can tap into partnerships with start-ups, universities, and research institutions. They can also crowdsource for ideas from potential customers to tap into the creativity and ingenuity of the public.

2. **Idea screening:** Not all ideas are feasible or have market potential. At this stage, ideas are evaluated and filtered based on various criteria like market fit, profitability, sustainability, technical feasibility, and alignment with company strategy.

3. **Concept development and testing:** The shortlisted ideas are further developed into detailed product concepts. This involves defining the product's features, benefits, target segment, and pricing strategy. Prototypes, mockups, or even minimum viable products (MVPs) may be created to be presented to potential customers to gauge their interest and feedback. Concepts may be refined accordingly.

4. **Business analysis and development:** In this next stage, companies analyze their target market to understand competitors, pricing, and potential sales. They also estimate costs and project financials to assess profitability. Finally, a go-to-market plan is

developed, outlining the strategy for launching and selling the product, including target market, value proposition, pricing, distribution, and launch activities.

5. **Product development:** Once the green light is given, this stage focuses on the actual creation of the product. This might involve engineering, design, packaging, and development of any necessary manufacturing processes. Quality control measures are implemented throughout the process to ensure the final product meets desired specifications and safety standards.

6. **Test marketing:** Before a full-scale launch, a limited test launch might be conducted in a specific target market, such as in a small city for a limited time, to test the waters for the purpose of estimating the potential sales for a full-scale rollout. Alternatively, firms may consider doing a simulated lab approach, which involves recruiting research participants and simulating a retail environment to assess their purchase decisions. Test marketing may be omitted in some situations, especially when confidentiality and speed to market are priorities.

7. **Product launch and commercialization:** This is the official introduction of the product to the market. Marketing and sales efforts are ramped up to generate awareness and drive initial sales. Public relations (PR) campaigns, influencer marketing, and promotional activities might be used to create buzz and excitement around the new product. When a product fails, not only are time and resources wasted but these failed introductions may potentially cause reputational damage and cause consumer confidence to waver in the parent brand (this is known as brand dilution).

Overall, a well-structured NPD process provides a roadmap for navigating the complexities of NPD. A well-defined NPD process significantly reduces the risk of new product failure in several ways:

- **Increased focus and prioritization:** The NPD process provides a structured framework for evaluating ideas, ensuring resources are directed toward concepts with the highest potential for success.

- **Early customer feedback and iteration:** Integration of user testing throughout the process allows companies to gather valuable customer insights early on. This feedback loop identifies potential issues and helps refine features and functionalities to better align with customer needs and preferences. This can significantly reduce the risk of launching a product that misses the mark.
- **Risk identification and mitigation:** The NPD process provides for a proactive and comprehensive analysis of potential risks associated with a new product, including technical challenges, market competition, and potential cost overruns. This allows the development of mitigation strategies and contingency plans.
- **Improved resource allocation and efficiency:** The structured approach of the NPD process fosters better resource allocation throughout the development cycle. Teams have a clear understanding of the tasks involved, timelines, and dependencies, enabling them to work more efficiently and avoid costly delays or rework.
- **Data-driven decision-making:** The NPD process emphasizes data-driven decision-making throughout all stages. Market research, customer feedback, and test marketing results provide concrete data points to inform decisions about product features, marketing strategies, and pricing. This data-driven approach reduces the risk of relying on intuition or guesswork, leading to more informed and successful product launches.

Redefining Products in a Connected World

The marketplace is undergoing a metamorphosis, driven by powerful forces like ubiquitous data, environmental concerns, and the rise of a sharing economy. Consumers are no longer passive recipients of products; they are active participants in a connected, borderless world. In this dynamic landscape, the very notion of a product needs to be redefined. Here are some key trends:

1. **Data-driven products:** In today's data-driven world, companies are wielding a powerful arsenal for creating hyper-personalized

product experiences: behavioral data, AI algorithms, and real-time analytics. This confluence enables companies to personalize offerings to an unprecedented degree, predict and prevent product failures, and foster a continuous cycle of improvement.

Companies collect data through smart appliances, website interactions, app usage, search queries, and purchase history. The data provide insights into user preferences, browsing habits, and pain points. AI capabilities can identify patterns, predict user needs, and even anticipate future behavior from this data. They can segment users based on demographics, interests, and past interactions, allowing for personalized product recommendations and features. Today, e-commerce platforms already recommend products based on your past purchases, browsing history, and even your social media activity. Finally, real-time analytics allows companies to analyze user behavior and adapt product experiences in real time. For example, a streaming service might recommend a movie based on what you're currently watching or the time of day. Similarly, a fitness tracker might adjust its workout suggestions based on your real-time heart rate data.

AI algorithms can also analyze sensor data in connected products to predict potential failures before they occur. This enables companies to implement preventive maintenance measures, reducing downtime and improving product reliability.

The beauty of this data-driven approach lies in its cyclical nature. Behavioral data fuel AI algorithms, which personalize the product experience. Real-time analytics then provide insights into user behavior and product performance, informing further iterations and improvements. This continuous cycle ensures the product remains relevant, user-centric, and constantly evolving to meet the ever-changing needs of the customer base.

While such a data-driven approach creates better insights-driven customer engagement and offerings, navigating data privacy concerns, maintaining data quality, and effectively reaching niche audiences remain key challenges to address for successful implementation.

2. **Ecosystems and integration:** The rise of the Internet of Things (IoT) has ushered in an era of connected products. These products transcend their physical form, evolving from standalone entities to becoming interconnected nodes within vast ecosystems, exchanging data and interacting with other devices and services. Smart homes and connected appliances are examples. The focus for companies is no longer on selling a single product, but on creating an integrated ecosystem that can personalize user experiences, automate tasks, and offer greater functionality. Some companies might create closed ecosystems, limiting user choice and restricting interoperability with other products and services. This can lead to vendor lock-in, where users feel compelled to stick with a specific brand to maintain functionality within the ecosystem.

3. **Platforms as products:** Platforms create an ecosystem enabling interactions and value creation between third-party developers and users, fostering innovation and expanding the product's potential beyond a single functionality. Essentially, the platform itself becomes the product, facilitating connections and fostering a network effect. Examples include operating systems (Android is a platform for developers to create and distribute software applications), e-commerce marketplaces (Carousell and Shopee are platforms connecting buyers and sellers for product discovery, transactions, and reviews), and cloud computing (AWS and Azure offer on-demand computing resources, allowing businesses to build and deploy applications without managing physical infrastructure). Platform models allow for rapid scaling. The value (monetization) of a platform increases as more users participate. This creates a virtuous cycle, attracting new users and developers, further enriching the ecosystem. Hence, platform businesses must do what they can to ensure openness and connectivity by providing APIs and Software Development Kits (SDKs) that allow developers to build integrations and expand the platform's functionalities. Platforms must also foster a vibrant community of users and developers through forums, events, and support channels. Providing anonymized data insights to developers helps create more targeted and valuable integrations. Various monetization strategies include

freemium models, subscription fees, or transaction-based revenue models to incentivize participation and generate income.

4. **Customer collaboration through co-creation and crowdsourcing:** The one-way flow of innovation from companies to consumers is being disrupted by the rise of online communities and social media. Companies can leverage the collective intelligence of online communities to co-create and refine products. Open-source platforms allow users to submit ideas, provide feedback on prototypes, and even contribute to the development of new features. This collaborative approach fosters a sense of community and ownership among consumers, leading to products that are more aligned with their needs and desires. Read about how MediaCorp leveraged the collective creativity and feedback of Wattpad's user base.

5. **Iterative product development:** In today's dynamic marketplace, customer needs and preferences seem to evolve at a breakneck pace, requiring a faster speed to market. According to research, the median time to market for new products is 18 months.[13] Iterative development, championed by the concept of a MVP, empowers businesses to adapt rapidly and thrive in a changing landscape. An MVP is a stripped-down version of the product that includes only the core features necessary to validate the core concept and gather user feedback. By getting the MVP into users' hands early, companies can validate their product idea before significant resources are invested. User feedback helps identify what resonates and what needs improvement. The MVP also forces companies to focus on the essential features that deliver value to users. This helps avoid feature creep and ensures the product addresses a genuine user need. Iterative development, with its emphasis on quick iterations and testing, allows companies to get products to market faster, capitalizing on emerging trends and staying ahead of the competition. This agility allows start-ups, which heavily leverage this approach, to experiment, iterate, and refine their product vision based on real-world user data, not just

---

[13] Lindner, J. (2023). Must-know product development statistics [current data]. Gitnux. 24 December 2023. Accessed 18 April 2024. https://gitnux.org/product-development-statistics/.

assumptions. By focusing on the core functionalities first, they can quickly validate their ideas, secure funding, and refine their product based on user feedback.

6. **Immersive experiences:** Technology is enabling immersive experiences that redefine how consumers interact with products. AR and VR are being used to showcase products in a realistic and interactive way, blurring the lines between the physical and digital worlds. Imagine virtually trying on clothes before purchasing them online or taking a 360-degree tour of a future home using VR. These immersive experiences enhance product discovery and engagement, personalize the buying journey, and create a deeper connection between the product and the user.

7. **Technology merges industries and product categories:** Consumers today seek convenience and a seamless user experience, and companies are increasingly looking at the bigger picture to see how their products can fulfil a broader range of user needs. The merging of different technologies creates entirely new possibilities, often blurring the lines between traditional industries and product categories. For instance, the combination of AI, sensor technology, and connectivity allows TVs to morph into entertainment hubs, offering fitness apps, video conferencing capabilities, and even health-tracking features. Traditional ride-hailing apps, initially focused on transportation, have become multi-service platforms. They now offer food delivery, courier services, mobile payments, etc., allowing users to fulfil multiple needs with a single app. For businesses, while this merging enhances customer experience and gives room for more innovative offerings, companies are no longer limited by traditional boundaries. The blurring of lines can lead to new players entering established markets, challenging traditional industry leaders. Companies need to be agile and adaptable to survive in this evolving landscape.

8. **Sustainability now a core value:** Sustainability has become a paramount concern for consumers, companies, employees, and

investors alike.[14] Asia Pacific consumers were found to care about sustainability issues as much as their Western counterparts. Companies are expected by employees, investors, and regulators to place more emphasis on ESG and follow sustainable business practices. 90% of APAC consumers say they are willing to pay more for sustainable products but not all follow through with purchase. Bain's research revealed one of the challenges is consumers have a nascent understanding of what constitutes sustainability. They are overwhelmed and confused by multiple and often conflicting sources of information. Figure 8.5 shows other factors contributing to this "say–do" gap. Companies need to make bolder moves to incorporate sustainability into the core of their business to close the say–do gap. Those that do that well are rewarded, as four out of five environmentally and socially conscious consumers in Asia-Pacific actively recommend sustainable products that they like.

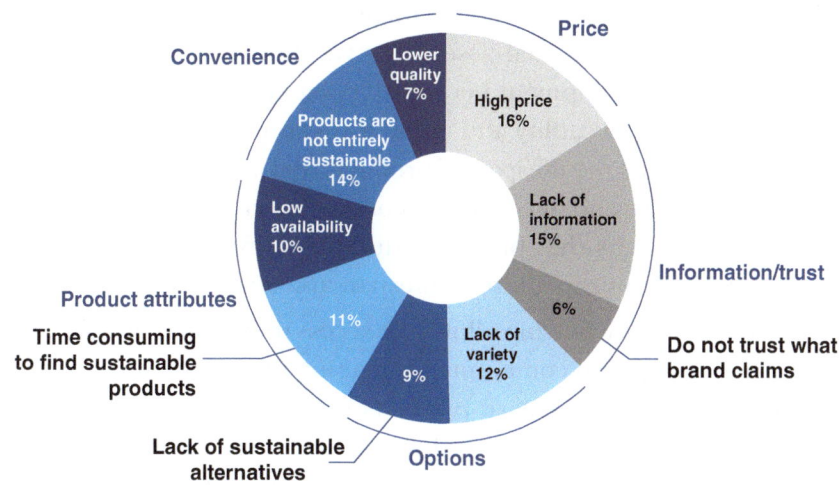

Figure 8.5. Factors that prevent consumers from buying sustainable products.[15]

---

[14] Lightowler, Z., Mattios, G., Yang, J., and Zehner, D. (2022). Unpacking Asia-Pacific consumers' new love affair with sustainability. Bain and Company. 3 June 2022. Accessed on 19 April 2024. https://www.bain.com/insights/unpacking-asia-pacific-consumers-new-love-affair-with-sustainability/.

[15] *Ibid.*

Seven sustainability elements were found to be important to consumers: healthy ingredients, natural, additive/chemical free, organic, sustainable packaging, sustainability symbols, and local sourcing.[16] Products must also minimize environmental impact throughout their life cycle. This includes using design for durability and repairability and employing energy-efficient production processes. The concept of a product's life cycle is expanding, with companies exploring possibilities for product take-back programs and refurbishment services.

9. **Fractional ownership:** The concept of ownership is transforming. Driven by factors like affordability, access, lifestyle, and sustainability, fractional ownership models—including timeshares, equipment rentals, clothing subscriptions, and car-sharing services—are rapidly gaining popularity. These models allow individuals to access and enjoy the benefits of a product without the burden of full ownership.

    Fractional ownership encourages using products to their full potential. Underutilized assets like vacation properties or infrequently used equipment become accessible to a wider audience, maximizing their utility and reducing overall waste. This business model extends the lifespan of products, reduces waste, and caters to a growing trend of conscious consumption. This shift demands product designs that prioritize durability, modularity, and ease of repair to cater to a longer lifespan and shared usage patterns.

    Fractional ownership allows for access to products and services without long-term commitments, making previously unattainable experiences or expensive products more accessible. People can now enjoy luxury vacations through timeshares, utilize high-end equipment for specific projects through rentals, or experience the latest fashion trends via clothing subscriptions, all without the burden of full ownership costs.

    However, addressing data privacy concerns, mitigating algorithmic bias, and promoting equitable access are critical for this

---

[16] *Ibid.*

model to reach its full potential. Fractional ownership models often require users to share personal data regarding usage patterns and preferences, hence requiring robust data privacy measures. Moreover, platforms with fractional ownership opportunities may utilize algorithms to match preferences and personalize offerings. However, these algorithms can potentially perpetuate biases, limiting access for certain demographics or creating unfair pricing structures. While fractional ownership can increase access for some, barriers like subscription fees, membership costs, and digital literacy can create barriers for participation by certain demographics.

Example: Product-as-a-Service

Product-as-a-Service (PaaS) is an example of how businesses can address some trends and deliver value in the digital age. It refers to selling benefits/outcomes from the product, rather than selling the product itself. Customers pay a subscription fee for access to the product and ongoing services. From a business perspective, PaaS transitions product sales from a one-time transaction to a recurring revenue stream. This provides companies with more predictable cash flow, facilitating financial planning and resource allocation.

PaaS companies typically have a strong focus on maximizing customer retention through high customer satisfaction. PaaS companies are thus motivated to be more customer-oriented by delivering ongoing value (through offering support, continuous updates, and potential service upgrades) than their traditional counterparts.

PaaS models generate valuable data on customers, their usage patterns, and preferences. Companies can leverage the data to improve product development, marketing efforts, and overall customer experience. Guided by data-driven insights, companies can offer tiered subscription plans or bundle services with the product, creating opportunities for upselling and cross-selling, potentially increasing revenue per customer.

Offering PaaS could be an excellent way to distinguish yourself from competitors, especially in an age where sustainability is becoming an indicator of quality. Products are used for more extended periods, reducing waste. Customers also save money from having to keep buying new products or making big outlays to own the product.

Case: Lights, Camera, Wattpad: Unveiling Singaporean Stories[17]

Singapore's National Media Network, Mediacorp, has long been a household name, synonymous with local news and entertainment. But in 2019, it embarked on a new chapter, partnering with the global online platform Wattpad.

Wattpad, unlike traditional publishing houses, thrives on a unique model. It functions as a social writing platform, where aspiring authors can upload their stories chapter by chapter. Readers, captivated by a gripping plot or relatable characters, can "like" chapters, leave comments, and even participate in online discussions with authors and fellow readers. This creates a vibrant community, fostering a sense of shared journey between writer and audience. Stories with high engagement and readership gain visibility, attracting the attention of literary agents, publishers, and, in this case, content creators like Mediacorp.

Understanding the reader and building a compelling proposition:
Choosing the right stories from Wattpad's vast library of UGC, teeming with vibrant narratives from Singaporean and international authors, is key to this collaboration. The teams use a combination of art and science, looking at both data insights and editorial considerations when aligning on the stories with proven appeal. Mediacorp then leverages its production expertise to translate these online stories into compelling video content with themes that resonate with both local and global audiences.

Targeted data-driven marketing:
By analyzing reader engagement metrics like comments, shares, and search trends for a particular story, both Wattpad and Mediacorp

---

[17] The authors gratefully acknowledge Oliver Chong (Head, Marketing and Communications) and Dawn Ong (Senior Brand Manager) for their invaluable insights and content contributions, which were instrumental in the development of this case study.

can delve into reader profiles. The data paint a clear picture of the story's appeal—the characters that resonate, the themes that generate discussion, and the emotional core that keeps readers hooked. By understanding the audience's preferences and expectations, the marketing team can craft targeted ads that focus on themes that resonate with specific demographics.

Marketing for multiple screens:
With a clear understanding of the reader base, the collaboration then focuses on crafting a marketing proposition that extends beyond the original Wattpad audience. This involves identifying "lookalike audiences"—potential viewers who share similar interests and demographics with the existing reader base. Utilizing these data, marketing efforts shift to targeted platforms and activities. This might involve leveraging platforms like TikTok for content marketing or organizing exclusive previews and social media takeovers to generate buzz and attract the "lookalike audience." Social media teams and creative agencies then collaborate to develop tailored content and marketing assets that resonate with both the existing and potential audiences.

Expanding the reach:
Mediacorp works closely with Wattpad to utilize their respective extensive databases of users and their established promotional platforms. This can involve targeted geographical collaboration, with Mediacorp focusing on Singapore and Malaysia, while Wattpad expands outreach to other regions where it has a strong user base. Building upon an existing author's fan base can be another powerful tool. Mediacorp and Wattpad can organize live interactive sessions with the author or release exclusive content, further fueling audience engagement. Additionally, based on data points and genre similarities, Wattpad can expose its audience to other Mediacorp productions, widening the appeal and viewer base.

In essence, the Wattpad and Mediacorp collaboration unlocks the potential of audience-centric data-driven script development and targeted marketing to breathe life into Wattpad stories, taking them from readers' personal screens to a national media network. By combining audience insights, strategic marketing, and the power of established platforms, popular stories are transformed into engaging video content, expanding their reach and captivating viewers across diverse platforms.

The partnership benefits Mediacorp and Singapore's entertainment industry. By showcasing local stories on a national platform, the collaboration fosters a sense of cultural identity and encourages the development of a uniquely Singaporean style of storytelling. It provided Mediacorp access to Wattpad's pool of millions of users worldwide, many harboring dreams of seeing their stories come alive on screen. This collaboration allowed Mediacorp to bypass traditional scouting methods and tap directly into a community brimming with fresh ideas and diverse voices. Additionally, Wattpad authors gain valuable exposure and see their work reach a wider audience, potentially kickstarting their careers in the field of professional writing.

The success of the first project, a series based on the Wattpad novel "Slow Dancing," paved the way for further collaboration. This innovative partnership between a media giant and a social writing platform signifies a shift toward a more open and data-driven approach to content creation. It empowers aspiring writers, provides valuable audience insights, and allows established production houses to stay at the forefront of storytelling in a rapidly evolving media landscape.

Here are some marketing lessons gleaned from the Mediacorp and Wattpad case study:

1. **Leverage UGC to build a strong value proposition:**
   - **Tap into audience insights:** The case study highlights the power of UGC platforms like Wattpad to uncover hidden gems of creative storytelling. They provide valuable insights into audience preferences and interests. By analyzing data on popular stories, characters, and themes, and understanding the emotional connections readers form with stories, companies can create compelling narratives that resonate with audience needs and aspirations.

2. **Data-driven decision making:**
   - **The power of data analytics:** The success of the Wattpad–Mediacorp collaboration underscores the importance of data-driven decision-making in the creative process. By analyzing user data, companies can identify trends, predict audience preferences, and make informed decisions about product development and marketing strategies.
3. **Shared experiences enhance the value proposition:**
   - **Creating shared experiences:** The collaboration between Wattpad and Mediacorp demonstrates the power of creating shared experiences through interactive storytelling. By engaging with audiences through social media and live events, companies can foster a sense of community and build stronger brand loyalty.
4. **Expanding reach and building partnerships:**
   - **Leveraging existing networks:** By partnering with other companies and platforms, businesses can expand their reach and tap into new markets. The Wattpad–Mediacorp collaboration demonstrates the power of leveraging existing user bases and distribution channels.

The Asian PoV

Striking the right balance between localization (adapting products to local preferences) and standardization (maintaining global consistency) is a key challenge in Asia. Over-localization can be costly, while under-localization can lead to missed opportunities. But this is often necessary, as many Asian markets are home to strong local products that enjoy high levels of consumer loyalty. Competing with these established players requires differentiation, innovation, and localization.

In many Asian markets, price sensitivity is a major factor influencing consumer behavior. Balancing product quality with affordability is essential, especially in emerging markets with lower purchasing power. Sachet product offerings are prevalent in cost-sensitive markets in Asia due to their affordability and convenience. This has proven to be a successful strategy for reaching consumers with limited budgets, providing them with access to essential goods and services in a manageable and affordable way. Some of the products and brands that have executed this product play include personal care products (e.g., Sunsilk, Lifebuoy, Colgate, Gillette), food and beverages (e.g., Nescafé, Milo, Maggi, Knorr), and household products (Surf Excel, Rin). Global brands not only compete with one another but also compete with domestic brands that know the consumers and cultural practices better (e.g., Ayurvedic and Traditional Chinese Medicine) as well as know how to convince consumers in rural markets to buy instead of make.

Key Takeaways

- A well-defined product strategy, focusing on the customer, is crucial for a product's success.
- Product managers wear many hats: defining the product vision, identifying value, developing and redefining products, and managing the PLC and portfolio.
- A product vision is a long-term, aspirational statement guiding product development.
- Elements of value encompass functional, emotional, social, and experiential benefits, minus costs.
- Understanding customer needs and motivations is vital for identifying value drivers.
- The feature trap highlights the risk of overcomplicating products; focus on features customers value and will pay for.
- Sustaining value is an ongoing challenge due to evolving customer needs and competition.
- NPD is a systematic process to reduce the risk of failure.
- In the connected world, products are redefined by data, ecosystems, platforms, co-creation, and sustainability.

Chapter

9

Product Management

> In this chapter, we explore the intricacies of managing a product throughout its lifecycle, from the initial spark of an idea to its eventual sunset. We examine the various stages of the PLC, understanding the challenges and opportunities at each juncture. Additionally, we delve into the art of managing a product portfolio, where you learn how to strategically allocate resources and make informed decisions about which products to invest in, maintain, or potentially phase out, ensuring a healthy and sustainable product ecosystem.

Managing a Product through its Life Cycle

Products, such as humans and companies, have a life cycle. The PLC, a journey from conception to decline, presents distinct challenges and opportunities at each stage. The introduction stage begins as a product is commercialized after the product development phase. Thereafter, it enters the growth, maturity, and decline stages as it becomes obsolete or irrelevant. Figure 9.1 shows a typical PLC curve. Note that product categories and brands have their own PLCs. For instance, Amazon launched the Fire Phone in 2014 in an obviously mature smartphone category.

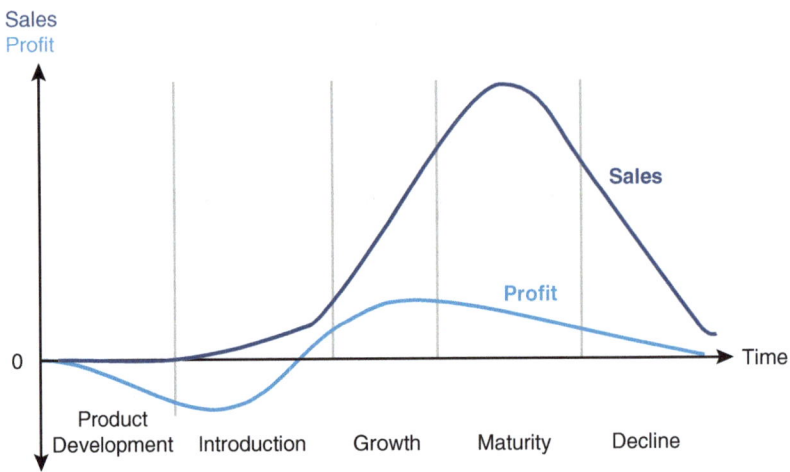

Figure 9.1. A typical PLC curve.

Introduction

The introduction stage, the first chapter in a product's life cycle, is a period of immense anticipation and uncertainty. It is the moment a brand unveils its creation to the world, hoping to spark excitement and establish a foothold in the market. The focus during this critical stage is twofold: building brand awareness and generating initial sales to lay the foundation for future success.

Marketers entering the introduction stage face a unique challenge. They must introduce a product to a potentially unfamiliar audience, educate them about its benefits, and convince them to take a chance on something new. This necessitates a comprehensive go-to-market strategy that revolves around creating a compelling narrative that clearly communicates the product's value proposition, highlighting how it solves a specific problem or fulfills an unmet need. Effective messaging should not only inform but also pique customer curiosity and generate excitement. However, overhyping a product's capabilities can lead to disappointment and negative reviews upon launch. As market acceptance is still uncertain, brands can take a conservative approach to offer one basic product in this stage.

Circles.Life[1] provides a good example of how a value proposition that fits the target segment helps a brand succeed in the introduction phase. In 2016, Circles.Life stormed into the Singapore market dominated by traditional giants, such as Singtel, M1, and StarHub. They recognized the frustrations of traditional telco plans with hidden fees, complex contracts, and limited data allowances. Recognizing the shift toward data-driven activities such as streaming and social media, Circles.Life countered this with transparent, competitively priced data-centric mobile plans that allowed customers to customize their data packages according to their needs. For example, its social media post announced a new data plan, urging users to "#NeverRunOutOfData" that lets customers add 20 GB for $20 on top of their base plan without being tied to a contract. The post directly addresses customer demand for more data and positions Circles.Life as the provider of the largest and most flexible data solutions. Additionally, the online platform provided a user-friendly interface for customers to manage their plans, track data usage, and access customer support—all from the convenience of their mobile devices. This focus on flexibility and user control resonated with a generation accustomed to on-demand services and personalized experiences. Through engaging social media campaigns and partnerships with popular influencers, Circles.Life established itself as a youthful, innovative brand that challenged the stodgy image of traditional telcos.

WeChat offers another example of successful differentiation from incumbents to become the titan it is today (find out more about WeChat in the case study in this chapter)

The choice of who to target in the introduction phase is a crucial decision in a go-to-market strategy. While typically innovators are the best bet for new products, these innovators should also be influential to imitators in terms of their ability to generate word of mouth or social pressure (such innovators are said to have high coefficients of imitation[2]). Brands that fail to clearly define their target audience

---

[1] Kaur, T. (2018). How Circles.Life created the Netflix of Telco in Singapore. *Forbes*. 19 July 2018. Accessed 11 March 2024. https://www.forbes.com/sites/tarandipkaur/2018/07/19/how-circles-life-created-the-netflix-of-telco-in-singapore/?sh=4a3dd8de584e.

[2] Bass, F. M. (1976). A new product growth model for consumer durables. *Management Science*, 15(5), 215–227.

or communicate the product's value proposition risk a lukewarm reception. A prime example of this is Google Glass. This wearable technology aimed to revolutionize communication, but its high price tag, limited functionality, and privacy concerns resulted in a lack of consumer interest. The marketing campaign failed to resonate with a poorly defined target audience, leading to a confusing message and ultimately, the product's demise.

Securing positive media coverage can significantly amplify brand awareness and build initial trust with potential customers. Influencer marketing, where established figures within a specific niche endorse the product, can also be a powerful tool for reaching a targeted audience and generating organic excitement. Recall we talked about Skechers in Chapter 4. The brand rose to popularity by having Christina Aguilera and Britney Spears, the top pop stars of that time, show consumers that sneakers were not just for sports and nerds (Figure 9.2).

Figure 9.2. Skechers' advertisements in the early 1990s.[3]

---

[3] Telfer, T. (2014). Remember when Skechers were sexy? *Bustle*. Accessed on 9 November 2023. https://www.bustle.com/articles/33000-whatever-happened-to-skechers-they-used-to-be-so-hip-but-today-theyre-.

How fast an innovation is adopted and spreads from one consumer to another (diffusion rate) also depends on product characteristics. Products with these characteristics have a higher likelihood of quicker adoption[4] and move into the growth phase sooner:

1. **Relative advantage:** How superior customers perceive it to be compared to existing products.
2. **Compatibility:** How closely it fits with customers' needs, value systems, norms, culture, behavior, and lifestyle patterns.
3. **Observability:** The ease with which the benefits of the product can be observed.
4. **Complexity:** The ease of understanding, purchase, and use.
5. **Trialability:** The ease with which it can be tested.

Another crucial aspect of the introduction stage is establishing distribution channels. Making the product readily available to potential customers is paramount. This might involve partnering with retailers, online marketplaces, or even creating your own DTC channels. Many brands are not accepted by major retailers till they have proven demand. After GoPro was first launched at the Action Sports Retailer trade show in September 2004, its sales were only through surf shops and specialty retailers. Its founder and his roommate ran a two-person shop calling surf retailers across the country to persuade them to sell the cameras in their shops.[5]

Case: From Messaging App to All-Encompassing Platform—The Rise of WeChat

WeChat's meteoric rise to dominance in the Chinese mobile landscape is a story of strategic innovation and a deep understanding of the target segment. Launched in 2011, it faced established players such

---

[4] Gourville, J. T. (2005). Note on innovation diffusion: Rogers' five factors. Harvard Business School Background Note 505–075, May 2005 (Revised April 2006).

[5] Marcovitch, A. (2013). The early years of GoPro and founder Nicholas Woodman. *Forbes.* 28 February 2013. Accessed on 11 March 2024. https://www.forbes.com/pictures/54f4e70eda47a54de8244f8b/gopros-first-hire-neil-da/?sh=730f39e137e2.

as QQ Messenger and faced the uphill battle of carving out a niche. However, WeChat's creators, Tencent, took a multi-pronged approach that propelled them to become the ubiquitous platform it is today.

First, WeChat recognized the limitations of being just another messaging app. While competitors such as WhatsApp offered basic messaging, WeChat recognized the growing need for a more comprehensive platform. They integrated features such as voice and video calls, photo, and video sharing, and even a "Moments" feed similar to Facebook, creating a one-stop shop for communication and social connection. These features resonated with the mobile-first generation.

Second, WeChat understood the power of social integration. They seamlessly linked their platform with Tencent's existing social network, QQ, allowing users to leverage their existing connections. This not only boosted their user base but also fostered a sense of familiarity and encouraged network effects. The more people joined, the more valuable the platform became for everyone.

Third, WeChat recognized the importance of cultural relevance. They incorporated features that resonated with Chinese users. This included voice messaging, which was more popular than text messaging in China. Additionally, WeChat prioritized group chats, reflecting the collectivist nature of Chinese society, and integrated features such as "red envelopes"—a digital way to send money as a traditional gift-giving practice during holidays and celebrations. This cultural touchstone fostered social interaction and engagement within the platform.

Finally, WeChat went beyond communication, becoming a one-stop shop for daily needs. They introduced innovative features such as "WeChat Pay," enabling mobile payments, and "Moments," a microblogging feature akin to a social feed. They fostered a vibrant ecosystem of third-party developers, allowing users to access a vast array of services within the WeChat platform, from booking taxis to playing games. This "super app" approach addressed a variety of user needs within a single platform, eliminating the need to download and manage multiple apps. Furthermore, WeChat prioritized user experience. Their interface was clean, intuitive, and constantly updated.

This focus on user convenience and a constantly expanding feature set kept users engaged and coming back for more.

Continuous innovation played a vital role in WeChat's sustained growth. They did not rest on their laurels after the initial success. They constantly introduced new features, from mini programs (essentially lightweight apps within WeChat) to official accounts for businesses, allowing brands to directly connect with consumers. This constant evolution ensured that WeChat remained relevant and indispensable for users.

By combining all these strategies, WeChat effectively outmaneuvered its competitors. They captured the zeitgeist of a mobile-driven society that craved convenience, social connection, and a seamless digital experience. Their focus on innovation, integration, and user-centricity allowed them to evolve from a simple messaging app to an all-encompassing platform deeply woven into the fabric of Chinese daily life.

Today, WeChat boasts over 1.2 billion monthly active users, making it one of the most influential digital platforms globally. It has transcended the realm of a social app, becoming a vital tool for communication, commerce, and information dissemination. It serves as a testament to the power of understanding user needs, prioritizing innovation, and constantly adapting to the ever-evolving digital landscape.

WeChat's phenomenal success in China offers valuable insights for launching and growing a social media platform. Here are some key lessons to be learned:

- **Focus on a specific need:** WeChat identified a clear gap in the Chinese market: a single platform that could cater to messaging, social media, payments, and other functionalities. By addressing this unmet need, their value proposition was hard to resist making them an essential tool for daily life.
- **Ease of use:** WeChat did not reinvent the wheel. Recognizing the growing mobile phone penetration, WeChat prioritized a mobile-first design. This ensured a seamless user experience optimized

for the most prevalent mode of Internet access in China at the time. They linked with QQ. This facilitated rapid user acquisition by leveraging existing social connections. They built upon existing mobile payment and social media habits, making it easy for users to integrate WeChat into their daily routines.

- **Compatibility:** WeChat also understood the importance of localization and cultural practices. The platform was designed with local preferences in mind, incorporating features such as voice messaging and group chats that resonated with Chinese communication styles. This focus on localization played a crucial role in WeChat's widespread adoption in China.
- **Adaptability and innovation:** WeChat continuously adapted to evolving user needs and technological advancements, integrating new features such as mini-programs (lightweight apps within the platform) and social commerce capabilities.

Growth

The growth stage, following a successful introduction, is a period of exhilarating expansion and brand solidification. Here, customer acceptance has been achieved, so this period witnesses a surge in demand, brand recognition, and ultimately, profitability. The growth stage requires a strategic shift in focus from initial awareness to scaling production, combating intense competition, building brand loyalty, and navigating a rapidly expanding market. Meeting the surge in demand requires an agile approach to production and distribution. This might involve expanding manufacturing capabilities, forging partnerships with new distributors, or venturing into online marketplaces, to ensure consistent product availability across diverse channels to a wider customer base.

While it signifies initial success and market acceptance, the growth phase also ignites a firestorm of competition. As customer demand surges, existing players might launch similar products, while new entrants, enticed by the market potential, may introduce innovative alternatives. This surge in competition intensifies the battle for market share and brand loyalty. The initial euphoria of a successful launch can lull brands into complacency. However, in the growth stage, even a slight misstep can be exploited by competitors eager to capitalize. Brands that rest on their laurels risk losing their edge.

Here, strategic differentiation becomes the key weapon. Brands must go beyond simply highlighting their initial value proposition. This might involve expanding product lines with new features or functionalities that cater to diverse customer segments. Expanding on our earlier discussion on GoPro, GoPro branched out to make the camera suitable for other sports besides surfing to achieve widespread popularity. It capitalized on its rising popularity by forging partnerships with sporting goods retailers, adventure enthusiasts, and athletes to amplify brand reach. These influencer marketing campaigns showcasing the camera's capabilities propelled GoPro to the forefront of the action camera market. Additionally, GoPro expanded its product line, offering models catering to different price points and user needs, ensuring broader market appeal.

Similarly, after its successful launch, Circles.Life did not rest on its laurels as competitors also started offering data-centric packages. In 2019, it launched a bold campaign titled "A World Without Telco Contracts"[6] highlighting the drawbacks of long-term contracts, such as hidden fees, limited flexibility, and difficulty switching plans. Circles.Life positioned itself as the alternative, offering plans on a month-to-month basis, giving them the freedom to adjust their plan or switch providers without penalty. To further disrupt the industry and demonstrate their commitment to customer empowerment, Circles.Life launched a global crowd-funding campaign with the goal of raising $1 million. This money was used to "bail out" customers trapped in expensive contracts with traditional telcos.

However, growth is not just about quantity; it is about fostering brand loyalty. Customers who have positive experiences with a brand are less likely to defect to competitors. This can be achieved through exceptional customer service, loyalty programs, and a commitment to quality. Leveraging data-driven insights allows for targeted messaging, resonating with different customer segments and fostering a sense of community around the brand. CRM becomes paramount. Nurturing

---

[6] Youtube. (2019) A world without Telco contracts. https://youtu.be/8CAozyBNBYs?si=tV065E0AN1EplHtm.

relationships through personalized communication, addressing feedback swiftly, and offering exceptional customer service are key to converting buyers into loyal brand advocates. This is exemplified by companies such as Sephora, which offer loyalty programs, personalized beauty consultations, and a seamless online and in-store shopping experience.

Maturity

Following the exhilaration of growth, this phase is characterized by stable sales and the need for strategic adaptation to maintain market share. Here, the brand is established and generating more sales and profits than it ever had. Marketers now have a cash cow in their hands. Yet, competitors are strong ones who also survived the onslaught in the growth stage. Brands must become masters of efficiency—optimizing production processes and renegotiating with suppliers and distributors—to maintain competitive pricing and profitability.

Sales have reached its peak. Hence, the focus for marketers in this stage shifts from rapid expansion to solidifying their positions through customer retention to achieve brand longevity. Understanding evolving customer needs and adapting marketing strategies accordingly are crucial for maintaining brand relevance. Flashy brand awareness campaigns might give way to targeted customer loyalty programs and value-added services. For instance, offering extended warranties, subscription models for product upgrades, or bundling complementary products can incentivize repeat purchases and enhance customer lifetime value (CLV). Amazon Prime, which offers expedited shipping, exclusive deals, and access to streaming services for a subscription fee, incentivizes customers to not only remain with the platform but also increase their spending within the ecosystem.

Product innovation remains crucial, albeit with a renewed focus on incremental improvements and line extensions that cater to evolving customer needs. Dove, a mature brand in the personal care industry, exemplifies this approach. They consistently innovate within their core product line, offering new formulations and catering to diverse customer needs, while simultaneously launching targeted social media campaigns to remain relevant to their customer base.

However, the maturity stage is not merely about maintaining the status quo. Having survived the risky and tough battles in the early stages, marketers would strive to maximize returns from the established brand equity for more growth. Identifying new customer segments or untapped markets can also breathe new life into a maturing product. This might involve international expansion or targeting new customer segments within the existing market. For markets that are approaching saturation, brands may look at revitalization strategies (described in the Decline stage). Some may start to plan for the next PLC with new offerings in this stage.

By strategically navigating the maturity stage, brands can not only maintain market share but may also possibly lay the groundwork for future growth and reinvention. The maturity stage is a test of resilience and adaptability—a chance to solidify a brand's legacy or succumb to the pressures of a saturated market.

Decline

Sales begin to dwindle, competition intensifies, and technological advancements or shifting consumer preferences render the product less relevant. While this decline stage signifies a potential downturn, it is not necessarily the end of the road. For marketers, the focus shifts from growth strategies to managing profitability and exploring options for the product's future. Marketers who recognize the signs of decline and adopt strategic approaches can either manage the decline gracefully or even attempt a revitalization.

The focus in the decline stage should shift from maximizing sales to optimizing profitability and resource allocation. Cost-cutting measures become paramount. Analyzing marketing expenditures for efficiency is a crucial step in preserving profit margins during a period of declining sales. Additionally, marketers can explore maximizing revenue from existing customers through price promotions or bundled product offerings.

However, simply managing decline might not be the only option. In some cases, revitalization strategies can breathe new life into a declining product. One approach is to explore product innovation. This might involve introducing new features or functionalities to the existing product or even launching a revamped version that caters to evolving customer needs. For example, the classic children's toy, Barbie, has undergone numerous transformations over the years, introducing new career options, ethnicities, and body types for the dolls. In 2023, Barbie the movie was released. It was instrumental in keeping the brand relevant to consumers by achieving a crucial cultural reset. It deftly addressed and subverted long-standing criticisms of Barbie's outdated ideals, portraying a self-aware brand willing to engage with complex themes like feminism, identity, and societal expectations. This not only resonated deeply with long-time fans and parents but also captivated a new, broader audience, including adults and younger generations who might have previously dismissed the doll. By sparking global conversations and becoming a pop culture phenomenon, the movie brilliantly repositioned Barbie as a contemporary icon, fostering renewed interest and ensuring her continued presence in the consumer consciousness beyond just a toy.

Another strategy for revitalization is to explore new market segments. Sometimes, being closely associated with a cohort of consumers may make a brand be perceived as "the oldies' brand", particularly in beauty and lifestyle brands. Such brands need to target a younger demographic to give a fresh lease on life for a declining product. Let's go back to our Skechers example mentioned in Chapter 4 and earlier in this chapter. Once a prominent name in the 1990s, the footwear brand found itself facing a decline in popularity in the early 2000s. Fast forward to 2023, Skechers is the third most popular shoe brand in the US and has topped its sales with over $2 billion in quarterly sales.[7] One key element of Skechers' resurgence was their embrace of the comfort trend that resonated with a growing consumer preference for casual and athleisure wear. Skechers capitalized on their existing reputation for comfortable shoes. They invested in innovative technologies such as Skechers Goga Mat insoles and Skechers Arch Fit technology to further enhance comfort and support. To attract younger consumers, Skechers rode on the growing popularity of pickleball. By launching a line of shoes dedicated to pickleball before major athletic shoe brands, they positioned themselves as a brand attuned to evolving athletic trends.

---

[7] The Harris Poll. (2023). Skechers footwear makes serious strides in 2023. Accessed on 14 November 2023. https://theharrispoll.com/briefs/skechers-footwear-makes-serious-strides-in-2023/.

Brands faced with a declining product also have the option of harvesting the remaining value. This involves scaling back marketing efforts, focusing on existing customers, and milking the remaining profitability before phasing out the product entirely. When a product becomes unprofitable and offers little strategic value, removing it from the market frees up resources and allows brands to focus on their core offerings.

Case: From Relic to Resurgence—How Pechoin Reclaimed Its Glory in China

Pechoin (百雀羚), a once-dominant Chinese cosmetics brand, faced a period of decline in the early 21st century. Being primarily associated with affordability and a mature audience, the brand was overtaken by international players and failed to resonate with the younger generation. The brand risked fading into obscurity. However, a remarkable turnaround story emerged, with Pechoin experiencing a resurgence in popularity.

The most significant factor in Pechoin's resurgence was its strategic use of influencer marketing. Known as "wanghongs (网红)/KOLs", influencers in China have the power to connect with their target audience and are able to "zhongcao (种草)" which means to be a brand evangelist to recommend something to others. In a country with over 1 billion people in different regions and with different preferences who are cynical of mass media and advertisements, using influencer marketing helped the brand cut through the clutter of too many choices and reach these KOLs' target audience quickly and easily.[8]

The brand partnered with a strategic selection of Chinese influencers, including celebrities, beauty bloggers, and social media stars. These influencers, particularly those popular with younger demographics, showcased Pechoin products using engaging visuals, interactive tutorials, and live streams to showcase the benefits of Pechoin products in engaging and relatable ways. They integrated Pechoin into their beauty routines and shared their honest experiences.

---

[8] Duadarenok, A. G. (2018). Influencer marketing in China: No longer an option, now a necessity. *China Economic Review*. 21 December 2018. Accessed on 12 March 2024. https://chinaeconomicreview.com/influencer-marketing-in-china-no-longer-an-option-now-a-necessity/.

This transparency fostered trust and credibility with viewers. This approach allowed Pechoin to "tap into the trust that millennials and Gen Z place in online recommendations.[9]" On Singles Day 2018, 127 KOLs mentioned the brand, reaching 143 million followers, leading to more than 160,000 engagements on online platforms, such as Weitao, Weibo, WeChat, Xiaohongshu (Little Red Book) (Figure 9.3), and Douyin.[10] Pechoin was the best-selling cosmetic brand that day.

To adapt to changing consumer preferences, Pechoin embraced product innovation. They reformulated existing products with high-quality ingredients and modern aesthetics, ensuring they remained competitive in a rapidly evolving market. Additionally, they launched new lines catering to current beauty trends, such as serums and sheet masks.

Another key element of Pechoin's revival was its reconnection with its heritage. The brand delved into its rich history, established in 1931, and emphasized its status as a "national brand." This resonated with a growing sense of national pride among Chinese consumers as shown by preference for domestic brands over foreign ones.[11] According to a report by Premium Beauty News, Pechoin capitalized on this by "leveraging its heritage and emotional connection with older generations to build trust with younger consumers." This approach fostered a sense of nostalgia and authenticity, positioning Pechoin as a brand deeply rooted in Chinese culture.

The brand also cleverly capitalized on 2024's most popular TV drama series *Blossoms Shanghai* (繁花) which fits its brand for clever marketing campaigns. The drama chronicles how Shanghainese beauty and fashion brands were abandoned by wealthy locals for international luxury labels. The domestic brands continued to improve relentlessly, eventually allowing them to compete with foreign brands. The drama's lead actress is now the brand ambassador. This plot triggered emotional resonance amidst the awakening of Chinese culture and national confidence. More importantly, it reflected Pechoin's fate.

---

[9] Corbin, M.-H. (2019). China: Pechoin or the resounding return of a sleeping beauty. *Premium Beauty News*. 27 September 2019. Accessed on 12 March 2024. https://www.premiumbeautynews.com/en/china-pechoin-or-the-resounding,15632.

[10] *Ibid.*

[11] Duadarenok (2018), *Op. cit.*

Product Management | 223

Figure 9.3. China's first Chinese virtual influencer "Ling" in Pechoin's XiaoHongShu advertisements.[12]

The brand's decisive move to swiftly market the brand with elements drawn from the drama made the brand talked about as well.[13]

The results of Pechoin's revitalization strategy were undeniable. Sales soared, particularly among younger demographics. The brand, once teetering on the brink of obscurity, re-established itself as a major player in the Chinese cosmetics market. By understanding their target audience, leveraging a strong brand identity, and partnering with the right influencers, Pechoin not only revitalized their brand but also carved a niche for themselves in the ever-evolving beauty landscape of China.

From Pechoin's story, we learned the following:

- Not all brands facing decline or stagnation need to be phased out.
- With clever alignment with popular cultural trends and leveraging the power of KOLs, it is possible to gain visibility and connect with consumers again.

---

[12] Daxue Consulting. (2022). How Pechoin, China's oldest skincare brand, remains a top beauty player after nearly 100 years. 11 April 2022. Accessed on 13 March 2024. https://daxueconsulting.com/pechoin-market-strategy/.

[13] Chaileedo. (2024). Chinese skincare brand Pechoin launches first marketing campaign of 2024. Medium.com. 12 January 2024. Accessed on 13 March 2024. https://chaileedo.medium.com/chinese-skincare-brand-pechoin-launches-the-first-marketing-campaign-of-2024-e6e37708415d.

- A good product is still necessary even with the help of KOLs, as authentic user experiences are shared. The brand continuously analyzed and adapted to evolving consumer preferences in terms of ingredients, aesthetics, and product categories.
- A complete overhaul of the brand image may not have been credible. Instead, Pechoin emphasized its brand history and encouraged young consumers to reconnect with its heritage to evoke a sense of nostalgia and build trust.

The PLC is a valuable tool for marketers to inform their strategies across all stages of a product's journey. The first step is to identify the current stage of your product in the PLC. Is it a new launch in the introduction stage, a well-established brand in the growth stage, or a mature product facing increased competition? Each stage requires a different marketing focus. By understanding the specific stage, marketers can tailor their strategies to achieve optimal results. The PLC also helps with resource allocation. During the introduction stage, a larger portion of the marketing budget might be dedicated to brand awareness campaigns. As the product matures, resources might shift towards customer retention and product development. Recognizing signs of decline allows them to develop exit strategies or revitalization plans.

However, it is important to remember that the PLC is a simplified model. Some brands might experience a resurgence in popularity due to social trends before the brand reaches decline, while some may have extended maturity stages. The transition between stages can be gradual, and not all products follow a linear path. The timing of each stage can vary depending on the industry and product category. External factors such as economic conditions, competitor actions, and technological advancements may also disrupt the PLC. Regardless, the PLC remains a valuable tool for marketers. Figure 9.4 provides a summary of the key characteristics of each stage and the accompanying PLC strategies.

Product Management | 225

	Introduction	Growth	Maturity	Decline
Characteristics	• Low sales • Few competitors	• Rapidly rising sales • Growing number of competitors	• Peak sales, high profits • Strong competitors	• Declining sales • Declining competition
Focus	• Create brand awareness • Generate interest and trial • Communicate value proposition	• Increase market share • Differentiate from competition	• Defend market share • Optimise profitability • Maintain brand relevance	• Prune weak products • Reduce price to serve laggards • Phase out low volume distribution channels/outlets • Reduce marketing spend • Revitalisation strategies
Strategies	• Offer a basic product • Target innovators with influence on others • Build distribution channels	• Offer product improvements or variants • Build interest in mass market • Ensure distribution channels can serve new segments	• Encourage more usage among current users • Attract competitors' customers • Convert non-users • Brand extensions	• Encourage more usage among current users • Attract competitors' customers • Convert non-users • Brand extensions

Figure 9.4. Summary of the stages in a PLC.

Navigating Growth: A Strategic Look at Ansoff's Growth Matrix

In the ever-evolving landscape of business, achieving sustainable growth is a constant pursuit. Marketers grapple with the question of "what's next?" after a product successfully launches and establishes itself in the market. Simply riding the initial wave of popularity is not a sustainable strategy. Customers become accustomed to the product, competition intensifies, and market saturation looms large. This is where Ansoff's Growth Matrix steps in (Figure 9.5), providing a structured approach to navigate these challenges and unlock new avenues for growth.

The matrix proposes four distinct strategies:

- **Market penetration:** This strategy focuses on increasing sales of existing products within the existing market. This might involve aggressive marketing campaigns, promotional offers, or intensifying distribution efforts to reach new customers within the established market. Some brands encourage higher consumption through new usages or usage occasions. While it carries a relatively low risk as it leverages the existing product and market understanding, the potential for significant growth might be limited, especially in a saturated market.

- **Market development:** This strategy involves selling existing products to entirely new markets. This could entail entering new geographical territories and targeting new customer segments with alternative applications for the product. Market development becomes relevant when the existing market segment reaches a saturation point. Understanding customer needs and preferences in the new market segment(s) is crucial for success.

- **Product development:** This strategy focuses on introducing new products to the existing market. This might involve leveraging existing brand recognition and customer base to launch new product lines or variations of the existing product that cater to evolving customer needs. The existing market understanding mitigates some of the risks associated with introducing a new product, while the growth potential can be significant.

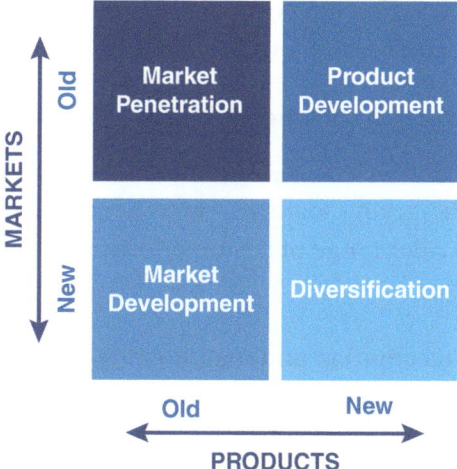

Figure 9.5. Ansoff's growth matrix.

- **Diversification:** This strategy involves introducing new products to entirely new markets. This is the riskiest of the four strategies as it requires significant investment in both product development and market research. This strategy is often considered during the later stages of the PLC when growth within the existing market and product becomes limited.

The selection of the most appropriate strategy from Ansoff's Growth Matrix hinges on a thorough analysis of the market landscape, competitor activity, and the company's own resources and capabilities.

Managing a Product Portfolio

A brand needs a portfolio of products for several reasons:

Mitigate risk and ensure long-term growth

Individual products eventually enter the decline stage of the life cycle, experiencing falling sales and diminishing profits. A portfolio of products ensures that a brand is not solely reliant on a single product. While some products decline, others might be in the growth or maturity stage, generating revenue and offsetting the decline of older products. A diversified portfolio also ensures a more consistent flow of revenue and fosters long-term brand growth.

Catering to diverse customer needs and preferences

Consumers have diverse needs and preferences. By offering a portfolio of products with varying features, price points, and styles, a brand can cater to a broader range of customers, increasing its market share and brand loyalty.

Leverage brand recognition and customer loyalty

Developing a new brand from scratch is a risky, resource-intensive endeavor. A strong brand portfolio leverages existing brand recognition and customer loyalty. Customers who trust a brand for one product might be more likely to try new products within the same brand, especially if they cater to similar needs or share a cohesive brand identity. A portfolio of products creates opportunities for cross-selling and upselling. For example, a brand selling athletic shoes might also offer socks, sports apparel, or fitness accessories. By recommending these complementary products during the purchase process, brands can increase their average order value and boost overall profitability.

Stretching the Brand: Line versus Brand Extensions

In the ever-competitive world of marketing, brands constantly seek new ways to expand their reach and maintain market share. Two prominent strategies for achieving this are line extensions and brand extensions.

Line extensions involve introducing new variations of an existing product category under the same brand name. An example of line extensions would be the different laptop models offered by various brands, such as Dell, Lenovo, and HP. Line extensions leverage existing brand recognition, reducing marketing costs needed to introduce a new product. Additionally, established distribution channels can be readily utilized, ensuring faster product availability. For consumers, line extensions offer a sense of familiarity and trust, as they are already acquainted with the core brand. Introducing too many line extensions can confuse consumers. Maintaining a clear focus and ensuring each extension offers a unique value proposition is crucial. Line extensions can inadvertently cannibalize sales of existing products when multiple products within the portfolio compete for the same customer base and sales. Careful analysis of product positioning and target customers is essential to minimize this outcome. The consideration is if the extension brings positive profits even where there is some level of cannibalization.

Brand extensions, on the other hand, involve introducing a completely new product category under the same brand name. This could involve a footwear company launching a line of bags, a fashion brand venturing into cosmetics, or a technology company introducing a home appliance. Brand extensions carry a higher risk than line extensions. Launching a successful brand extension requires significant marketing efforts to establish the brand's credibility within the new category as brand recognition may not be translated automatically. If customers fail to see the connection between the established brand and the new product category, the brand will be negatively impacted. However, brand extensions can open doors to entirely new customer segments and markets, fostering significant growth opportunities and mitigating risk associated with the decline of a single product category. Successful brand extensions can strengthen a brand's image by showcasing its innovation and versatility. Examples of brand extensions would be Xiaomi and Prism+ extending from smartphones and computer monitors to various household electronics appliances.

While line and brand extensions are popular strategies, brands should also consider alternative approaches. Co-branding, often referred to by Millennials and Gen Zs as "collabs", is extremely popular these days. It allows brands to tap into each other's customer bases, effectively reaching a wider audience. It allows for unlikely unions that can lead to unique and exciting products that might not have been conceived by either brand independently. The limited-edition nature of many collaborations creates a sense of urgency and excitement among consumers. Read how Omega and Swatch used a co-branding strategy to revitalize both brands.

Case: A Moonshot for the Masses: Omega–Swatch's Collaboration Takes the World by Storm

Launched in March 2022, Omega and Swatch sent watch enthusiasts into a frenzy, with queues snaking around stores for a chance to own a piece of this unexpected union. By marrying the iconic design of Omega's Speedmaster Moonwatch with Swatch's signature bioceramic construction and playful color palette, the collaboration offered a unique and affordable entry point to the world of luxury timepieces. Previously, the Omega Speedmaster Moonwatch, a watch steeped in space exploration history, was out of reach for many. The MoonSwatch, priced at a fraction of the original, opened the door for a new generation to experience the Moonwatch's legacy (Figure 9.6).

The collaboration's success was not just about affordability or aesthetics; it revitalized both brands. For Omega, the MoonSwatch injected a youthful energy into its brand image, demonstrating its willingness to adapt and cater to a broader audience. This collaboration helped them connect with a new generation of potential customers who might aspire to own an Omega Speedmaster in the future. In fact, the release of the collaboration boosted sales of the original Omega Speedmaster by about 50%.[14] For Swatch, the association with Omega elevated its brand perception. The MoonSwatch transcended the typical Swatch image, positioning it as a brand capable of collaborating with luxury giants. This association with heritage and quality strengthened their brand image. This collaboration also raised brand awareness among young consumers. Swatch witnessed a resurgence in brand perception. Three months after the launch, not only were they regaining the attention of a new generation, but a report also indicated a significant 41% increase in sales of other Swatch models (excluding Moonswatches) within Switzerland itself.[15]

---

[14] Hoffman, A. (2022). Omega Moonwatch surges after cheap Swatch version goes wild. *Bloomberg*. 8 July 2022. Accessed on 12 March 2024. https://www.bloomberg.com/news/articles/2022-07-08/omega-moonwatch-sales-surge-after-cheap-swatch-version-goes-wild.

[15] Dholakia, U. (2023). Pricing case study: The Moonswatch success story (plus a typology of collabs). The Pricing Conundrum. 15 September 2023. Accessed on 12 March 2024. https://thepricingconundrum.substack.com/p/the-moonswatch-success-story-plus?utm_medium=reader2.

Figure 9.6. Omega Speedmaster Moonwatch (left), Omega-Swatch MoonSwatch (right).[16]

The long queues and instant sell-out of the MoonSwatch serve as a testament to the success of this collaboration. Over a million MoonSwatches were sold in 2022 earning the company over $275 million in revenue.[17] The MoonSwatch collaboration was a calculated move that successfully revitalized two brands by reaching new target segments. It serves as a shining example of how creative collaborations and innovative marketing strategies can breathe new life into established brands.

Here are some lessons learned from this case study:

- Collaborations can open doors to new demographics and customer segments, expanding brand reach (e.g., MoonSwatch made luxury accessible).
- Collaborations can inject fresh energy and innovation, revitalize brand images, keeping brands relevant to evolving preferences. Partners should bring complementary strengths to the table

---

[16] *Ibid.*

[17] Dholakia (2023), *Op. cit.*

(e.g., Omega—heritage and prestige, Swatch—affordability and playful image).
- Collaborations should result in something new and exciting for consumers, not just a rehash of existing products (e.g., MoonSwatch offered a unique color palette and material).
- Successful collaborations can generate positive sales lift for both partners (e.g., increased sales of the original Speedmaster and other Swatch models).
- The hype and media coverage for a well-crafted marketing strategy can amplify the impact of a collaboration and drive sales.

Pruning for Growth: When and How to Streamline Your Brand Portfolio

Just as a gardener judiciously prunes overgrown branches to ensure the health of the entire plant, brands must strategically prune their product portfolios to maintain focus, optimize resources, and foster long-term growth.

The most compelling reason to prune a brand portfolio is the presence of products that consistently underperform, failing to generate significant sales or contribute to brand value. Their continued presence not only burdens resources but also dilutes the overall brand image. Identifying these products through sales data, customer feedback, and competitor analysis is crucial.

Another telltale sign that pruning is necessary is an overextended brand. Having too many products resulting in product proliferation results in higher inventory management costs, forecasting complexities, and increased risks of stockouts. Product proliferation also results in consumer confusion and increased risk of cannibalization. This internal competition not only dilutes marketing efforts but also hinders the potential of each product. Pruning in this instance involves carefully analyzing which product resonates more strongly with the target audience and eliminating the weaker competitor.

Not all products can be eliminated simultaneously. Phasing out products with minimal impact on customer base and brand image can be prioritized initially, followed by the removal of more significant offerings. Existing inventory can be sold at discounted prices, and clear communication with distributors and retailers ensures a smooth transition. Brands should also consider offering alternative products to existing customers of discontinued products to ensure a smooth transition.

The resources freed up from pruning can be strategically redeployed. Investing in the remaining core products through marketing, innovation, and product development fuels further growth. Additionally, resources can be directed toward exploring new market opportunities that align with the brand's core values.

Key Takeaways

- Understanding a product's life cycle is crucial for effective marketing.
- The introduction stage focuses on building brand awareness and generating initial sales.
- In the growth stage, scaling production, building brand loyalty, and navigating competition are key.
- The maturity stage requires strategic adaptation to maintain market share and brand relevance.
- The decline stage involves managing profitability and exploring options for the product's future.
- A brand portfolio helps mitigate risk, cater to diverse needs, and leverage brand recognition.
- Line extensions involve new variations of an existing product, while brand extensions are in new product categories.
- Co-branding allows brands to tap into each other's customer bases and create unique products.
- Pruning a brand portfolio involves eliminating underperforming products to optimize resources. It also reduces product proliferation which can result in consumer confusion and cannibalization.

Chapter

10

Price Strategy

> Crafting a successful pricing strategy requires careful consideration as it will directly impact a company's bottom line. It determines demand and ultimately, how much money a business generates. This influence extends far beyond the initial transaction, shaping consumer perception, profitability, and even channel strategy.

The Balancing Act of Pricing

Setting the right price requires a delicate balancing act. A lower price tag can entice customers, potentially leading to increased sales volume. This volume-based strategy can be particularly effective when a company benefits from economies of scale, where production costs decrease as output increases. However, a race to the bottom in pricing can have detrimental effects. Consumers often associate price with quality, and excessively low prices can lead to the perception of an inferior product. This, in turn, erodes brand equity and weakens a company's premium positioning.

Price directly affects a company's break-even point, the volume at which total costs are recovered. A lower price necessitates selling more units to reach profitability. This can put pressure on distribution channels, as channel partners are motivated by profit margins. If a product's price point offers them minimal profit, they may be less inclined to actively promote or stock it.

In addition, companies must ensure their pricing strategy aligns seamlessly with their overall marketing mix. Imagine a company positioning a product as a luxurious, high-end item. Frequent sales promotions or drastically reduced prices would send conflicting messages to consumers. Over time, this inconsistency would erode the brand's planned image of premium quality.

The key lies in effectively communicating a product's value proposition. Companies should focus on highlighting unique features, benefits, and the overall brand experience that justify the price tag. Investing in branding and educating consumers about the product's value can foster a greater willingness to pay a premium for its perceived quality and differentiation in the market. By prioritizing value over price, companies can cultivate loyal customers who appreciate the unique offering and are less susceptible to price-driven competition.

Price is a powerful tool in a marketer's arsenal. It directly impacts revenue, shapes consumer perception, and influences channel strategy. By carefully considering the interplay between price, product positioning, and overall marketing efforts, companies can establish a pricing strategy that fosters long-term success and brand loyalty. Focusing on value creation and effective communication paves the way for companies to move beyond price wars and secure a sustainable competitive advantage.

Factors Affecting Price

Price sits at the intersection of several key factors: product costs, external market factors, internal company objectives, and customer perception of value.

Price floors and ceilings

Product costs establish the foundation for pricing, acting as the price floor. This represents the minimum price a company can set without incurring losses. Costs encompass fixed expenses (e.g., rent, salaries) and variable costs (e.g., materials, labor) associated with production. Companies meticulously monitor unit variable costs and marginal costs (the cost of producing one additional unit) to determine optimal production volume and the breakeven point at which total revenue equals total costs. Cost curves, however, are not always linear. Experience and economies of scale, achieved through production efficiencies, can bring down overall costs. Setting a price below the price floor, however, leads to negative profits, where a company loses money with every unit sold.

Despite the price floor, there are strategic situations where companies might choose to operate at a temporary loss. Introductory offers aim to attract new customers by allowing them to experience the product at a lower price point. Similarly, perishable goods such as food, or time-sensitive services such as airline seats have a limited window of opportunity. Selling them below cost is preferable to losing the sale entirely. Excess capacity is also perishable. If a company has unused production capacity, selling below cost can generate some revenue rather than none. More is discussed in the section on Sales Promotions.

On the other side of the price spectrum lies the price ceiling, dictated by customer perception of value. This represents the maximum price a customer is willing to pay for a product. Brands must consider their target segment's value perception. Value pricing aims to set a price that aligns with the perceived benefits and utility a customer receives from the product. Extensive marketing efforts, strong brand recognition, and the right value proposition can elevate the perceived value, allowing companies to command a higher price. Conversely, weak brand image or features that fail to resonate with customers often force companies to lower prices to attract customers who might otherwise be hesitant. But frequent sales or discounts risk further erode brand equity in the long run. Understanding and influencing customer value perception, a topic explored in detail in value-based pricing strategies, is crucial for companies to set prices that resonate with their target audience.

The exact price that is right is somewhere between the price floor and ceiling, determined by other considerations, such as marketing objectives and external factors.

Marketing objectives

Brand positioning

Pricing plays a crucial role in communicating a product's positioning. Luxury brands often rely on prestige pricing, where high prices reinforce the association with exclusivity and craftsmanship. Conversely, brands that want to maximize market share may need to emphasize affordability.

Customer acquisition and retention

Companies can leverage various pricing strategies to incentivize customer acquisition and retention. Bundled pricing, offering multiple products at a discounted price, can attract new customers. Loyalty programs with tiered pricing based on purchase history can reward repeat customers and encourage continued engagement with the brand. Additionally, price discrimination strategies, where different customer segments are charged varying prices based on factors such as willingness to pay, can be used to maximize revenue while still catering to a broader customer base.

Short-term gains

Marketing strategies can also be influenced by the desired timeframe. Companies seeking to stimulate immediate sales might resort to temporary price reductions or promotional offers. These tactics can be effective for clearing out inventory or attracting customers during slow periods.

External factors affecting price

While internal factors such as production costs and marketing objectives undoubtedly influence a company's pricing strategy, the external environment plays an equally critical role. Market forces, ever-shifting and dynamic, create a complex landscape that companies must navigate to set optimal prices.

At the heart of external considerations lies the fundamental relationship between demand and competition. Understanding how much consumers are willing to pay for a product, and how competitors are positioning themselves, is crucial. High demand for a unique product allows companies to command premium prices, as seen with innovative tech gadgets or designer clothing lines. Conversely, a saturated market with numerous competitors offering similar products forces companies to price competitively, often leading to price wars and slimmer profit margins. Furthermore, understanding how sensitive customers are to price changes is crucial. For products with inelastic demand (where price changes have little impact on demand), companies have more flexibility in setting higher prices. Conversely, products with elastic demand (where price changes significantly impact demand) require a more price-sensitive approach.

The broader economic climate also casts a long shadow on pricing decisions. Booming economies with rising disposable income allow companies to raise prices with less resistance from consumers. However, during economic downturns, consumers tighten their belts, becoming more price-sensitive. Companies need to adapt their pricing strategies in response, potentially offering discounts or promotions or introducing more affordable brands to attract customers facing financial constraints. Understanding economic trends and consumer spending habits is crucial for navigating these turbulent waters.

Regulations and government policies also impact pricing decisions. Governments might impose price controls on certain essential goods and services to ensure affordability for consumers. Additionally, taxes and import duties can add to the final price paid by the customer, influencing the company's profit margins and overall pricing strategy.

The type of market a company operates in exerts a profound influence on its pricing strategy. Understanding the level of competition, the ability to differentiate, and government regulations empowers companies to make informed pricing decisions that ensure their survival and success within their specific market landscape. Let's explore how four major market structures—monopoly, oligopoly, monopolistic competition, and pure competition—shape a company's ability to set prices. Figure 10.1 provides a summary.

Monopoly

In a monopoly, a single seller reigns supreme. The absence of competition grants them immense control over the market. This translates to significant pricing power. Monopolies can set prices based on factors such as production costs, profit targets, and even consumer demand elasticity. However, this power is not absolute. Monopolies are often subject to government regulations to prevent them from exploiting consumers through excessive price hikes. The threat

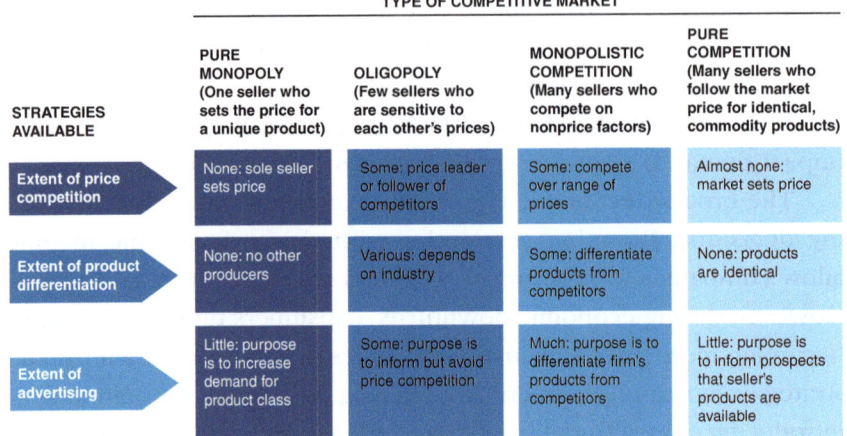

Figure 10.1. The impact of the types of competitive markets on price, product differentiation, and advertising.

of government intervention or the introduction of substitutes can incentivize monopolies to maintain a balance between maximizing profits and keeping prices somewhat reasonable. An example would be Changi Airport in Singapore.

Oligopoly

An oligopoly features a small number of dominant players. These companies are highly interdependent, meaning that the pricing decisions of one significantly impact the others. Price wars can erupt in oligopolies, as companies compete for market share by lowering prices. However, this race to the bottom can be detrimental to profitability for all players. To avoid such destructive competition, oligopolies often engage in tacit or explicit price coordination, where companies unofficially agree on a price range to maintain stability within the market. This form of coordination allows companies to maintain some level of control over pricing without resorting to detrimental price wars. Alternatively, sellers try to make it hard for consumers to compare prices by offering differentiated bundled services. An example would be the few telecommunication providers in each country.

Pure competition

A vast number of sellers offer identical products, with perfect market transparency for both buyers and sellers. This intense competition eliminates any individual company's ability to influence the price. Companies in this market structure act as price takers, forced to accept the market price determined by the forces of supply and demand. Their primary focus becomes cost control and production efficiency to maximize profit margins within the constraints of the market-determined price. Any attempt to deviate from the market price will likely result in lost sales, as consumers can easily find identical products from other sellers at the prevailing price. Commodities, forex, and stock trading are examples of pure competition.

Monopolistic competition

Monopolistic competition features a large number of sellers offering similar, but not identical, products. This creates a sense of differentiation, allowing companies to influence pricing based on factors such as brand image, product features, services, and quality. Unlike a pure monopoly, companies in monopolistic competition do not have complete control over pricing. However, they can leverage their unique selling propositions to justify premium prices compared to close substitutes. Pricing strategies in this market often involve heavy marketing and advertising to establish brand recognition and build customer loyalty, which allows companies to command slightly higher price points. Most businesses operate with such structure, differentiating from one another to justify different prices. For example, tuition centers offer similar services (e.g., math and science tutoring) but compete on teaching methods, reputation, and track record.

Pricing New Products

When introducing a new product, companies face a crucial decision: How to price it for optimal market penetration and revenue generation to be aligned with its brand position? Two key strategies emerge in this context—price penetration and price skimming—each with its own advantages and ideal applications.

Penetration pricing to maximize market share

Price penetration prioritizes attracting a large customer base by setting a low introductory price. This approach is particularly suitable for products that benefit from economies of scale (such as those with high fixed costs), where production costs decrease as output increases. The lower price incentivizes higher volume sales, which in turn keeps the per-unit cost low, allowing companies to maintain low prices and sustain sales volume. This strategy also works well in price-sensitive markets, where customers are highly responsive to price changes. A well-executed price penetration strategy can create a barrier to entry for competitors, making it difficult for them to compete against a company with established market share and low prices.

Price skimming for premium/innovative brand image

Brands which want to signal a premium or innovative brand image may enter the market with a price skimming strategy, where a high initial price point is set to capitalize on early adopters willing to pay a premium for novelty and maximizing revenue before broader competition enters the market. As the product matures and competition increases, prices are gradually lowered to reach a broader audience. Finally, during the decline stage, price reductions can become necessary to clear out the remaining inventory before the product is phased out. This approach is effective when a product boasts superior quality or a unique image that justifies the higher price point. Additionally, it is suitable when production costs for smaller initial volumes are not excessively high, ensuring profitability despite the limited output. Finally, price skimming is most successful for products that competitors cannot copy and undercut prices (such as products that are patented or difficult to replicate). Figure 10.2 shows Samsung Galaxy's price skimming strategy.

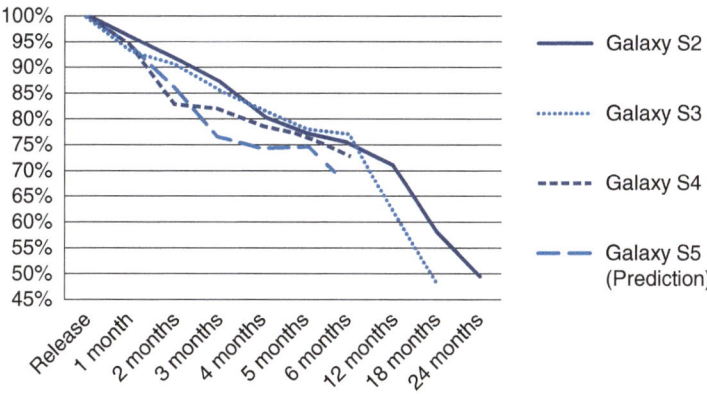

Figure 10.2. Price trends of Samsung Galaxy models after launch.[1]

Pricing Strategies

When a decision has been made to either penetrate or skim the market, there are various approaches to deciding on the actual price amount.

Cost-based pricing

Cost-based pricing takes a bottom-up approach, starting with the internal costs associated with bringing a product to market. This includes factors such as raw materials, labor, manufacturing overhead, and marketing expenses. Companies employing this method add a desired profit margin to the total cost to arrive at a final selling price. This approach is straightforward and relatively easy to implement, ensuring that all production and operational costs are covered. However, it fails to consider the value proposition of the product from the customer's perspective. If the price point is set solely based on internal costs without considering market demand or competitor

---

[1] Katy. (2014). Samsung Galaxy S5: Prices expected to fall by 24% after 3 months. Idealo. 12 February 2014. Accessed on 23 April 2024. https://www.idealo.co.uk/magazine/technology/samsung-galaxy-s5-prices-expected-to-fall-by-24-after-3-months-2.

pricing, it might alienate customers who perceive the product as overpriced or miss out on profits if it is underpriced. Companies with highly commoditized products with little differentiation might benefit from the simplicity of cost-based pricing. In highly competitive markets with numerous substitutes, cost-based pricing might be necessary to stay competitive.

The formula for cost-plus pricing is quite simple:

Selling Price = Total Cost per Unit + Desired Profit Margin

Here's a breakdown of the formula's components:

- **Total Cost per Unit:** This includes all the expenses associated with producing and selling one unit of your product or service. It factors in direct costs such as materials and labor, as well as indirect costs like overhead expenses and marketing.
- **Desired Profit Margin:** This represents the percentage of profit you want to earn on each unit sold. It can be a fixed percentage or vary depending on the product, market conditions, or your overall business goals.

Imagine you run a bakery and want to determine the selling price for your cupcakes:

- **Total Cost per Unit:** The cost of ingredients, cupcake liners, baking time (including labor costs for the baker), packaging, and any other expenses associated with making a single cupcake comes to $1.50.
- **Desired Profit Margin:** You decide you want a 40% profit margin on your cupcakes.

Here's how to calculate the selling price using the formula:

$$\text{Selling Price} = \$1.50 + (40\% \times \$1.50)$$
$$= \$1.50 + \$0.60$$
$$= \$2.10$$

Target return pricing

Unlike cost-plus pricing, which simply adds a markup to production costs, this approach focuses on the desired profit margin, working backward to determine the necessary selling price. At its core lies a formula that considers several key factors:

- **Target ROI:** This represents the desired percentage profit a company seeks to earn on its investment in a particular product or service.
- **Investment cost:** This includes all the expenses associated with bringing the product to market, encompassing research and development, production costs, marketing expenses, and distribution channels.
- **Sales volume:** This refers to the projected number of units the company expects to sell within a specific timeframe.

The formula for target return pricing can be expressed as

$$\text{Selling Price} = (\text{Investment Cost} + (\text{Target ROI} \times \text{Investment Cost})) / \text{Sales Volume}$$

Imagine a company developing a new fitness tracker. Their target ROI for this project is 20%, and the total investment cost associated with research, development, manufacturing, and marketing is estimated at $1 million. The company forecasts selling 20,000 units in the first year.

Plugging these figures into the formula:

$$\text{Selling Price} = (\$1{,}000{,}000 + (0.2 \times \$1{,}000{,}000)) / 20{,}000 \text{ units}$$
$$= \$60 \text{ per unit}$$

Value-based pricing

Value-based pricing starts with understanding the value a product delivers to customers, the benefits it offers, and how it addresses their needs or solves their problems. Value, as discussed in an earlier chapter, is often subjectively defined and goes beyond a product's functions or cost. Read the case on Salvator Mundi to see the mystique behind value perceptions and how a (high) price itself may even increase a product's value even more.

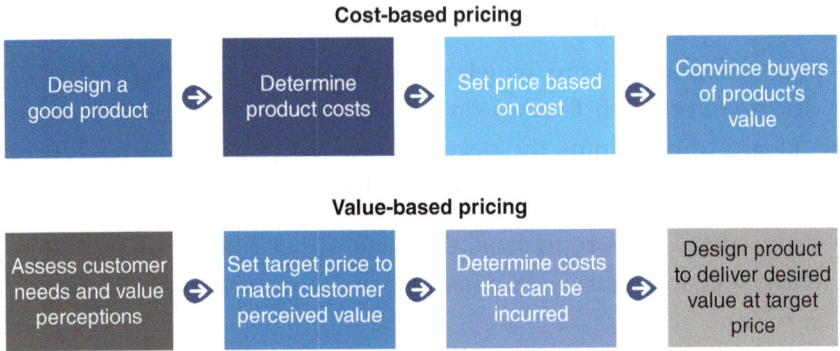

Figure 10.3. Cost-based vs value-based pricing.

Companies employing this approach conduct market research, analyze competitor offerings, and assess customer willingness to pay to determine a price that reflects the perceived value of the product. This customer-centric approach can lead to higher price points than a purely cost-based strategy if customers perceive the product as worth the premium price. Furthermore, value-based pricing allows companies to differentiate themselves from competitors by highlighting the unique value proposition of their offerings.

Swedish furniture manufacturer, IKEA, takes this value-based one step further.[2] It first identifies a price to match their target segment's willingness to pay for a coffee table and then designs and manufactures at a suitable cost to create the quality that this segment wants.

While cost-based pricing focuses on the company, value-based pricing's focus is on target customers and their perceptions of value. Figure 10.3 provides a summary of these two pricing approaches.

Case: Pricing in the Art World through the Journey of Salvatore Mundi by Leonardo da Vinci

On 15th November 2017 at Christie's auction in New York, a new world record for the world's most expensive painting was attained after a frantic 18-minute bidding. The heavily restored panel painting of Salvator Mundi, cataloged by Christie's as a rediscovered

---

[2] IKEA. (n.d.). Breaking down the IKEA value chain. https://www.ikea.com/global/en/our-business/how-we-work/the-ikea-value-chain/.

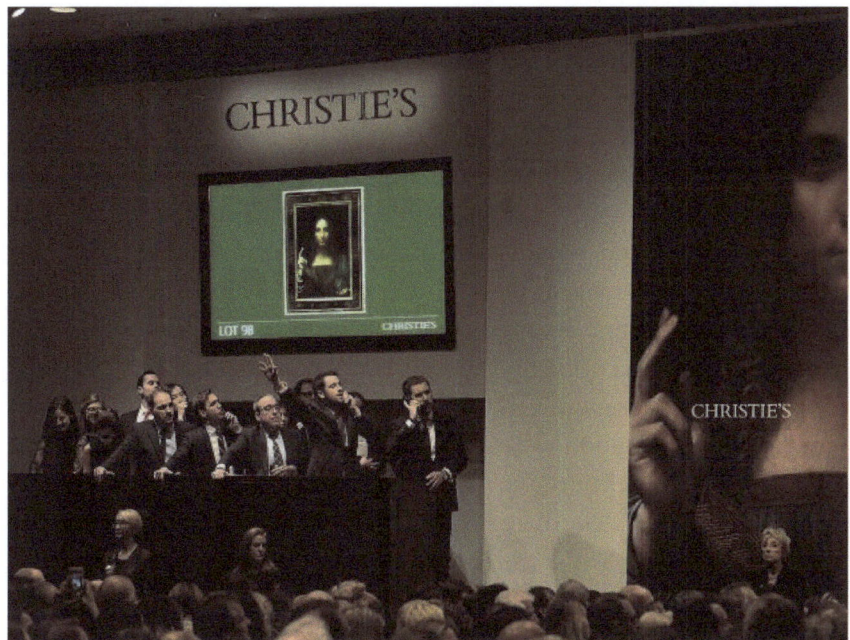

Figure 10.4. 15th November 2017 Christie's Auction in New York.

masterwork by Leonardo da Vinci (Figure 10.4), was auctioned to thunderous applause for $450.3M with fees, more than four times the original estimate of $100M. Until that time, no artwork had sold for more than $200M at auction. The previous highest (world record then) sale price auction artwork was Pablo Picasso's "Les Femmes d'Alger (Version O)" (1955) which was sold for $195.8 million, also at Christie's, in May 2015. This was bought by the former Qatari prime minister Hamad bin Jassim bin Jaber Al Thani.

Salvator Mundi's journey through history is a captivating tale of rediscovery, controversy, and astronomical price swings that mirror the ever-changing whims of the art market.

In the 16th century, it's believed the Salvator Mundi emerged from Leonardo da Vinci's workshop. While some experts believe he painted it entirely, others suggest it was executed with the assistance of his students. The painting likely adorned prestigious royal collections, including England's Charles I. By the 1700s, it vanished from records, only to resurface in a 1900 auction. However, heavy overpainting obscured its details. Sold for a mere £120, it passed through the hands of an English baronet, finding its way to another auction in 1958. Despite its suspected Renaissance origins, bidders were skeptical, and it went for a paltry £45.

For decades, its true identity remained hidden. In the early 2000s, a pair of art dealers, Robert Simon and Alexander Parish, purchased it at a small auction for under $10,000. Suspecting its potential value, the dealers initiated a painstaking restoration process and brought in Dianne Dwyer Modestini,[3] a renowned conservator specializing in Old Master paintings. Years of careful cleaning and analysis revealed details that aligned with da Vinci's known techniques.

The crucial moment came in 2011 when the National Gallery in London authenticated the Salvator Mundi as a genuine Leonardo da Vinci. A panel of experts, including da Vinci scholars, meticulously studied the work. Their attribution relied on several factors: the masterful sfumato (smoky blending), the figure's hand gestures, and the otherworldly quality of the crystal orb—all characteristic of da Vinci's genius. This sent shockwaves through the art world and the painting went on public display.

In 2013, Swiss art dealer Yves Bouvier, acting as an intermediary, sold it to Russian billionaire Dmitry Rybolovlev for $127.5 million, already a staggering price.

However, Rybolovlev later discovered Bouvier had paid only $80 million, pocketing a massive profit. Legal battles erupted, further fueling the Salvator Mundi's mystique. Finally, in 2017, it smashed all records at Christie's, selling for $450.3 million. The winning bidder, rumored to be Saudi Arabian Crown Prince Mohammed bin Salman, made it the world's most expensive painting.

Today, the Salvator Mundi's whereabouts are shrouded in secrecy with the attribution to Da Vinci being challenged.[4] Its story reflects the art market's volatility, the power of attribution, and the vast fortunes that can change hands over a single, enigmatic masterpiece.

---

[3] The Wall Street Journal. (n.d.). Finding the $450 million Salvator Mundi: A love story. *The Wall Street Journal*. https://www.wsj.com/video/finding-the-450-million-salvator-mundi-a-love-story/B22ACE99-42F5-44B6-A065-3BA25329B784?mod=trending_now_video_3.

[4] The New Arab Staff. (2021). Da Vinci's mysterious $450 million Salvator Mundi downgraded. The New Arab. 15 November 2021. https://www.newarab.com/news/da-vincis-mysterious-450-million-salvator-mundi-downgraded.

Pricing strategies for art must navigate a complex landscape. Traditional cost-based pricing has limited relevance since the value of art lies far beyond the cost of materials. Value-based pricing dominates—the artist's reputation, artwork's medium, and historical context create a perception of value and exclusivity, heavily influencing what buyers are willing to pay. The other elements of the marketing mix hold significant influence. The "Product" itself—the artist's reputation, artwork's medium, and historical context—creates a perception of value and exclusivity. "Promotion" plays a crucial role—exhibitions, gallery representation, and critical acclaim build prestige. Distribution channels ("Place") matter—a renowned auction house vs. a local gallery dramatically alters pricing potential. Competition-based pricing also plays a role—comparable artworks by similar artists or within the same genre factor into pricing decisions. Brand perceptions, influenced by exhibitions, gallery representation, and critical acclaim, build prestige and will also impact an artwork's market position and pricing. The interplay of these factors, alongside market trends and subjective buyer preferences, necessitates a nuanced pricing approach far beyond simply calculating production costs. It also makes for an intriguing case study to decipher and understand the different influences of pricing for art.

The Salvator Mundi's story highlights the extraordinary power of perception, attribution, and the unique dynamics of auction-based pricing in driving market value. The journey from a misattributed, under-$10,000 find to a record-shattering masterpiece isn't rooted in changes to the artwork itself. Instead, the shift in expert consensus surrounding its origins had a radical impact on its pricing. This case study underscores several key learnings for marketing strategy, including considerations for value-based pricing and the specific impact of auctions:

- **Understanding customer value:** While conventional pricing models might focus on costs and desired margins, the Salvator Mundi's pricing was primarily driven by its perceived value in the eyes of ultra-wealthy collectors and institutions. For them, owning a Da Vinci signifies not just the artwork itself but the status, cultural capital, and potential investment appreciation.

- **Subjectivity of value:** The Salvator Mundi's value isn't inherent to the canvas and paint. Its worth is socially constructed, driven by perceived rarity, historical significance, and the prestige attached to owning such a piece.
- **The impact of branding:** Like powerful luxury brands, the "Da Vinci" name created an aura of exclusivity and desirability. Authenticity and provenance dramatically impact how much buyers are willing to pay. The brand premium associated with a Tier 1 auction house[5] added to the heightened valuation of the product.
- **Scarcity as a driver:** As a unique object, the Salvator Mundi commands a premium. This principle is leveraged by marketers in diverse industries, from limited-edition products to exclusive experiences.
- **The role of intermediaries:** Art dealers, such as Bouvier, act as gatekeepers, influencing market perception and access. Their expertise and connections play a vital role in shaping value and facilitating transactions.
- **Auction dynamics:** The Christie's auction amplified the competitive spirit and sense of urgency surrounding the Salvator Mundi. In a high-stakes bidding environment, buyers can get caught up in the desire to win, potentially driving the price beyond even their own prior valuation. This psychological component plays a significant role in auction-based pricing.

Competition-based pricing

This strategy focuses on competitor pricing as the primary benchmark. Companies might set their prices slightly lower, higher, or at parity with competitors depending on their brand positioning and target market. This approach is common in highly competitive markets with similar products, such as oligopoly markets.

Freemium pricing

This strategy offers a basic version of a product or service for free, with premium features or functionalities available for a subscription fee. This

---

[5] Christie's and Sotheby's are generally recognised as Tier 1 auction house globally.

approach is commonly used in software and online services to attract a large user base to try with the hope of converting some to a paid plan. For customers that value a no-ad streaming experience on Spotify, they will choose to subscribe to the ad-free version of the product.

Captive product pricing

This involves selling a primary product at a lower price while charging a premium for essential accessories. Think of printer cartridges or game console controllers—these recurring revenue streams become the main source of profit after the initial purchase of the main product at a lower price point.

Dynamic pricing

Dynamic pricing, as the name suggests, involves adjusting prices in real time based on a variety of market conditions. This approach leverages data and algorithms to constantly analyze factors such as demand, competitor pricing, customer purchase history, or time of booking. For instance, airlines might adjust flight prices based on the day of the week, booking time, and seat availability. Similarly, ride-hailing services may have surge pricing during peak hours or offer discounts during low-demand afternoons.

Dynamic pricing offers several advantages. For companies, it allows them to maximize revenue by capturing fluctuations in demand. During peak demand periods, prices can be increased to reflect the higher value customers perceive. Conversely, during off-peak times, prices can be lowered to attract more customers and avoid empty seats or unsold inventory. For consumers, dynamic pricing can sometimes lead to better deals, especially if they are flexible with their purchase timing. For example, booking a hotel room well in advance or flying on a weekday might lead to lower prices.

However, dynamic pricing also has its fair share of criticism. Customers might perceive it as unfair or opaque, with a lack of transparency about how prices are determined. Furthermore, frequent price changes can create confusion and frustration for consumers. Additionally, concerns arise around algorithmic bias, where pricing algorithms might inadvertently discriminate against certain customer segments based on factors such as location or browsing history.

Discriminatory pricing

While dynamic pricing focuses on real-time adjustments based on market conditions, discriminatory pricing segments customers based on specific characteristics, such as age, location, student status, or loyalty program membership, and offers them different prices. For example, movie theatres might offer discounted tickets to children and seniors.

Proponents of discriminatory pricing argue that it allows companies to cater to different customer segments with varying price sensitivities. By offering discounts to specific groups, companies can increase overall sales volume and reach a wider customer base. Additionally, it can be seen as a way to reward loyal customers or make products and services more accessible to price-sensitive segments, such as students or low-income earners.

However, discriminatory pricing also raises ethical concerns. Customers might feel unfairly treated if they are charged a higher price than others for the same product. Companies employing this approach need to ensure their pricing structure remains transparent and justifiable based on the value offered to different customer segments.

Outcome-based pricing

Outcome-based pricing, also known as performance-based pricing, ties the customer's payment directly to the success of the service provided. Imagine hiring a marketing agency to increase website traffic by 20%. Under an outcome-based pricing model, the agency will only receive payment if it achieves the desired result. This approach aligns the interests of both parties—the customer only pays for a successful outcome, and the service provider is incentivized to deliver high-quality results. This model is particularly suitable for services where the value proposition is directly tied to achieving a specific outcome, such as consulting services, software development projects, or marketing campaigns with measurable goals.

However, outcome-based pricing also presents challenges. Defining and measuring success can be complex, requiring clear and agreed-upon metrics upfront. Additionally, there's a risk of disputes if the desired outcome isn't achieved due to factors beyond the service provider's control. Furthermore, this model might not be suitable for all types of services, particularly those with less quantifiable results.

Usage-based pricing

Usage-based pricing charges customers based on the amount of a product or service they use rather than a flat fee. Imagine a cloud computing service that charges customers based on their storage needs and computing power utilized rather than a fixed monthly subscription fee. Think of paying for electricity—you only pay for the amount you consume.

The advantages of usage-based pricing are undeniable. It allows for a more flexible and cost-effective model for customers, particularly those with unpredictable usage patterns. They only pay for what they use, which can be cost-effective for low users. Companies can attract customers who are hesitant about large upfront costs and benefit from recurring revenue based on actual usage. However, implementing this approach requires robust tracking and metering systems to accurately measure usage and some customers might prefer the predictability of a flat fee. Also, revenue fluctuates based on customer usage patterns. Companies need to ensure their pricing structure is set to generate sufficient revenue even with low usage. In some cases, a hybrid model might be implemented, offering a base subscription fee with additional charges for exceeding usage limits.

Subscription-based pricing

Customers pay a recurring fee, typically monthly or annually, for access to a product or service, regardless of how much they use it. This is common for streaming services such as Netflix or software subscriptions such as Adobe Creative Cloud. This pricing approach provides predictable costs for customers as they know exactly what they'll pay each month. This can be convenient and budget-friendly for those who expect to use the product or service regularly. However, it can be a less attractive option for infrequent users who are essentially paying for access they might not fully utilize.

Temporary Price Adjustments with Sales Promotions

Since price signals quality and brand positionings to customers, it is not a decision that should be taken lightly nor should it be a lever used frequently to influence demand. When there is a need to stimulate immediate sales, temporary sales promotions can be used. These promotions are effective at drawing customers' attention, encouraging trial, and in shifting purchases forward. It may also help brands gain shelf space and is a useful tool for smaller and emerging brands with more limited resources. However, firms need to remember that these sales promotions only focus on short-term results and not long-term brand value. They should be valid only for a limited time period and used strategically. Long-term usage of sales promotions teaches consumers to become price-sensitive as they postpone purchases till the next. Relying on frequent price discounts can erode brand value and create the perception of a low-quality product in the long run. A sustainable pricing strategy requires a balance between short-term gains and long-term brand equity.

Bear in mind that there are other costs involved that may go beyond the discount value, such as the cost of advertising the sale, special packaging, and reimbursing retailers for coupon redemptions.

Some common types of sales promotions targeted at consumers include the following:

Discounts and coupons

Perhaps the most ubiquitous form of sales promotion, discounts and coupons offer customers a direct price reduction, either as a percentage off the regular price or a fixed dollar amount. They are effective for driving immediate sales, particularly for price-sensitive customers, and can be used to clear out excess inventory or stimulate demand for slow-moving products. However, the cost of discounts comes in the form of reduced profit margins on each sale.

Bundled pricing

Bundling involves offering a combination of products or services at a discounted price compared to buying them individually. It can also be used to incentivize larger purchases by offering a free or significantly discounted item when a customer buys more (e.g., buy-1-get-1-free).

Offering a bundled price can create the perception of a better deal compared to buying each item separately, even if the individual items might not be what the customer may have bought if they were standalone.[6] This strategy can be effective for increasing sales volume, encouraging customers to try new products, and clearing out excess or slow-moving inventory. The success of this approach hinges on creating a compelling bundle that offers clear value to the customer.

Loss leader pricing

This strategy involves selling a product below cost to attract customers to a store or website, hoping they will purchase other higher-profit items while there. Similarly, loss leader products can be strategically deployed to incentivize customers to explore new stores or product lines, potentially leading to increased overall basket value through planned complementary purchases. This approach should be used strategically to avoid eroding overall profitability.

Sales promotions can also be targeted at trade partners and the sales force. For trade partners, this could include discounts, allowances, and support for trade shows and events. Finally, for the sales force, sales promotions could be in the form of providing incentive bonuses and top promoter contests. We discuss more about sales promotions in Chapter 13 on Promotion Mix.

The Psychology of Pricing

Pricing goes beyond mere numbers; it delves into the fascinating realm of consumer psychology as research has shown that the way a price is presented can significantly influence customer perception and purchasing decisions. Price framing, a strategic approach that focuses on how prices are communicated, emerges as a powerful tool in a marketer's arsenal.

Odd pricing

One common technique involves the use of odd pricing. "Odd pricing" refers to a price such as $19.99 instead of $20. "Even pricing" refers

---

[6] Stremersch, S. and Tellis, G. J. (2002). Strategic bundling of products and prices: A new synthesis for marketing. *Journal of Marketing*, 66(1), 55–72.

to a price ending in a whole number or tenths (e.g., $20 or $28). Customers perceive $19.99 as being closer to $19.00 than $20.00, creating a feeling of a better deal. This strategy can be particularly effective for impulse purchases or price-sensitive customers.

Reference pricing

Another tactic, reference pricing, leverages the concept of anchoring, which recognizes that consumers tend to depend too heavily on an initial piece of information (the anchor) when decision-making. At its core, reference pricing uses established price points as a benchmark against which customers evaluate new or unfamiliar products. Imagine browsing a clothing store and encountering a pair of jeans marked as "originally $80, now $50." The initial, higher price acts as a reference point, making the discounted price appear significantly more attractive. Even if the customer has no prior knowledge of the "original" price, the sheer presence of a higher number establishes a sense of value for the current price. Another instance is when consumers use Manufacturer's Suggested Retail Price (MSRP) as a reference point and determine that a product priced below MSRP is a good deal. However, the effectiveness of reference pricing hinges on its credibility. Excessively inflated "original" prices or misleading comparisons can backfire, eroding customer trust. Furthermore, consumers with access to online price comparisons or a strong understanding of product value might not be swayed by readily manipulated reference points.

Decoy pricing

Decoy pricing also hinges on comparison, particularly of relative value. By introducing a seemingly irrelevant option alongside two primary choices, companies can subtly steer consumers toward a particular product. The "decoy" option, often strategically priced and designed to be less desirable than one of the main options, acts as a reference point, influencing how customers perceive the value of the remaining choices. Imagine you're considering buying a new pair of headphones. Two options are presented: a basic model for $50 and a premium model with advanced features for $100. The premium model may seem expensive with just these two options. This choice, however, becomes more nuanced when a third option with minimal additional features compared to the basic one, is introduced at a price of $75. This "decoy" option serves a crucial purpose. It makes the $100 option appear more reasonable and feature-rich in comparison. It creates a perception that the price difference between the decoy and the premium product is justified by the additional features offered. The decoy nudges consumers towards the more expensive, yet seemingly more valuable, target product.

Flash sales

Limited-time offers or "flash sales" create a sense of urgency, pushing customers to act quickly for fear of missing out on a good deal. This fear of losing out can be a powerful motivator, prompting them to make purchases they might otherwise have considered postponing.

Deal semantics

The framing of prices in promotions was found to influence consumer perceptions of value and choice. For example, "Buy 1, get 1 free" and "50% off" result in the same outcome—customers pay half the price. But they have different effects depending on the nature of the product. Straight price reductions (i.e., lowering the absolute price the consumer has to pay) generally work better at encouraging purchases than do bonus-pack offerings, especially for products that cannot be stocked up[7] or of low usage rate (e.g., a rubber bath mat). But the reverse is true for products that are used frequently (e.g., contact lens solution or tissue paper)—the extra product promotion is preferred![8] So, marketers wanting to use bundled offers should consider variables that affect the perception of bundled value.

However, ethical considerations arise when price framing becomes deceptive. Inflating original prices to make discounts appear larger or employing confusing pricing structures are manipulative practices that can erode customer trust. Transparency and a focus on offering

---

[7] Sinha, I. and Smith, M. F. (2000). Consumers' perceptions of promotional framing price. *Psychology and Marketing*, 17, 257–275.

[8] Li, S., Yan, S., and Wong, W. (2007). 50% off or buy one get one free? Frame preference as a function of consumable nature in dairy products. *The Journal of Social Psychology*, 147(4), 413–421.

genuine value remain paramount for building trust and fostering long-term brand loyalty. Additionally, overreliance on framing techniques can backfire, making customers overly sensitive to price cues and less focused on the actual value proposition of a product. What keeps customers coming back is satisfaction from the consumption of the product[9] not from the temporary joys of a good deal.

Timing of payment

Following the idea that people buy more when they consume more, marketers should also consider how the timing of payments affects how much customers consume a product or service.[10] Attendance at a health club was found to be highest when membership is renewed monthly—such members are more likely to renew their membership than those who do not use the club—as compared to quarterly, semi-annually, or annually. The "pain" of paying and not wanting to waste their money (sunk cost fallacy) encourages usage and greater usage is more likely to result in membership renewals! Some suggestions for pricing include structuring payments to encourage more frequent use and highlighting the value of individual items to show the value of a bundled promotion. Conversely, companies can charge membership fees well before peak seasons, so the "pain of payment" is less likely to increase usage during peak times.

Communicating Price Changes without Causing Discontent

Price changes are an inevitable part of the business landscape. However, these adjustments can trigger customer dissatisfaction if not communicated effectively.

Customer unhappiness with price increases stems from a perceived loss of value and possibly, a sense of broken trust. Price increases can feel punitive, as if the company is prioritizing profits over customer value. For some products, price increases can be disruptive to existing budgets and consumption patterns, causing

---

[9] Gourville, J. T. and Dilip, S. (2002). Pricing and the psychology of consumption. *Harvard Business Review*, September 2002.

[10] *Ibid.*

frustration. To navigate these challenges, marketers need to adopt a transparent and empathetic approach.

First, clear communication is paramount. Companies should announce price increases well in advance, explaining the reasons behind the adjustment. This could be due to rising material costs, changes in regulations, or even significant improvements to the product or service itself. Honesty and transparency go a long way in building trust and mitigating negative perceptions. Second, offering options can help soften the blow. For subscription services, companies might consider grandfathering existing customers in the old pricing structure for a limited time, allowing them to adjust their budgets. Limited-time introductory offers for the new price point can ease the transition. Thirdly, highlighting the value proposition remains crucial. Price increases should be accompanied by a clear explanation of how the additional cost translates into a better product or service. This could involve improved features, higher-quality materials, or enhanced customer support.

Netflix, for instance, when facing rising content acquisition costs, communicated price increases well in advance, giving customers time to adjust their budgets or explore alternatives. Second, they clearly articulate the reasons behind the price increase, be it rising production costs, new features being added, or increased investment in content. This transparency helps customers understand the rationale and feel more in control. Netflix further sweetens the deal by highlighting the value customers are still receiving, showcasing new content or improved features.

In the case of price decreases, customer's unhappiness can stem from a feeling of having overpaid previously. Customers might also worry about the long-term viability of the company if they resort to price cuts. Price decreases require a different approach. While a lower price might seem inherently positive, companies need to avoid creating the impression of a fire sale or a devaluation of the product. The focus should be on increased efficiency, passing on cost savings to customers, or introducing a more competitive offering. Ikea Singapore cut prices for 144 items in response to the recent inflation surge as part of a global initiative by Ikea to provide customers with some relief amidst rising costs. This was made public in a statement to the national newspaper *The Straits Times* which was reported in various media,[11] as well as on its website with a dedicated page titled "We lower prices where we can" (Figure 10.5). On their website,[12] IKEA states "we lower prices where we can" because "we know many people are feeling the pinch right now To help you get the most from your home, we work hard every day to keep our prices as low as possible for you."

To manage customers' perceived fairness of price changes, firms need to manage price expectations and perceptions of the cost of goods sold (COGS). This can be done by selecting reference prices for customers, avoiding comparisons by differentiating through other aspects of the marketing mix (3Ps: Product, Place, Promotion), and focusing the attention on the benefits of purchase to the customer. This should be done even in the event of price cuts to avoid negative

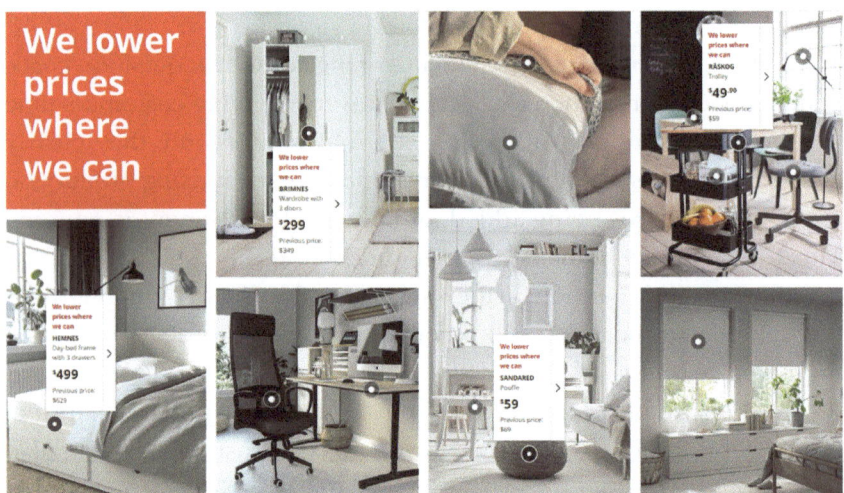

Figure 10.5. Screenshot of IKEA's "We lower prices where we can" webpage.[13]

---

[11] Martens, H. (2023). IKEA S'pore drops prices on 144 products, will reduce prices on more than 60 others by April 2024. *Mothership*. 17 October 2023. Accessed on 25 April 2024. https://mothership.sg/2023/10/ikea-spore-drop-prices-144-items/.

[12] IKEA. (n.d.). Lower prices. Retrieved 14 April 2025. https://www.ikea.com/sg/en/cat/lower-price/.

[13] IKEA. (n.d.). Lower price collection. https://www.ikea.com/sg/en/cat/lower-price/.

impressions forming (e.g., reduction in product quality leading to price cut).

As we have seen, pricing goes beyond simply generating revenue; it's a powerful marketing tool that shapes customer perception, buying decisions, and brand loyalty. Pricing is a strategic tool; marketers need to think creatively to go beyond dollars and cents. By strategically setting prices, companies can influence consumer behavior, create value differentiation, and navigate competitive landscapes. Now, let's delve deeper into a specific case study: Singtel, a leading telecommunications provider in Singapore.

Case: Pricing Planning and Considerations for a Telecommunications Company—Learning from Singtel[14]

The Singtel Group is Asia's leading communications technology group, providing an extensive range of telecommunications and digital services to consumers and businesses across many countries. It serves over 770 million mobile customers in 21 countries, including Singapore, Australia (via wholly owned subsidiary Singtel Optus), and the emerging markets of India, Indonesia, the Philippines, Thailand, and Africa.

In Singapore, Singtel is the number 1 mobile provider with 4.6M[15] users (45.6% market share), 670K fixed broadband users (43.1% market share), and 312K[16] TV users. As a multiservice provider, Singtel competes with other telecommunication providers including Mobile Network Operators (MNOs), Mobile Virtual Network Operators (MVNOs), fixed line providers, and other content providers (such as Netflix, Mediacorp, and Disney+). Pricing in such a complex environment requires a clear view of emerging trends, competitive landscape, and growth potential.

---

[14] The authors gratefully acknowledge Singtel's Diana Chen (Managing Director, Customer Management) for her invaluable insights and content contributions, which were instrumental in the development of this case study.

[15] Singtel. (2023). Singtel investor factsheet. Singapore Telecommunications Limited. March 2023. https://www.singtel.com/about-us/investor-relations/annual-reports.

[16] Singapore Telecommunications Limited. (2023). Singapore Telecommunications Limited reports earnings results for the half year ended September 30, 2023. 9 November 2023. https://www.marketscreener.com/?utmzb_campaign=changement-edition++popin_changement-edition_basique+basique+&utmzb_content=++++&utmzb_source=popin&utmzb_medium=url_declenchement.

The Customer Value Management (CVM) team in Singtel plays a key role in developing insights and business simulations of possible acquisition strategies, managing customer churn, cross-sell, and up-sell potential. Its Managing Director, Diana Chen, shares with us about what goes behind the scenes.

First, establishing clarity with data points around your direct costs, break-even point, performance against all players and potential growth areas will guide the strategy which should be aligned with financial objectives as well as priorities of the business. This could include the following:

- Defend (or grow) market share against aggressive new entrants.
- Increase customer loyalty and reduce churn.[17]
- Drive adoption of bundled services (mobile, broadband, and TV) for higher Average Revenue Per User (ARPU).
- Position Singtel favorably in the minds of Singapore's diverse consumer segments.
- Achieve agreed financial KPIs and financial market expectations.

Second is a sound market analysis. This is to better understand the broader market shifts and competition which provide the next layer of pricing considerations. This would generally include an analysis of the following:

- **Competitors:** StarHub, M1, and Simba, the key MNO players, and several smaller players (MVNOs) such as Circles.Life offering disruptive pricing models.
- **Customer trends:** Smartphone penetration (especially premium phone models), demand for reliable connectivity, growing popularity of video streaming, and interest in 5G.
- **Regulation:** Telecom regulation in Singapore promotes competition and transparency, creating boundaries and guardrails.

---

[17] The churn rate, also known as the rate of attrition or customer churn, is the rate at which customers stop doing business with an entity. It is most commonly expressed as the percentage of service subscribers who discontinue their subscriptions within a given time period.

Third is a data-driven analysis of customer insights. With strong customer data and insights as the market leader, Singtel leverages the insights from its data for all pricing decisions and development of new products.

Pricing strategies: Here are some examples of possible pricing strategies a multi-service telco such as Singtel might employ:

1. **Price plans:**
   - **Mobile plan options:** Being the market leader, Singtel offers extensive choices: a device plan, SIM Only plan, Tag-on plans that enable sharing—offering a choice of full-service support or digital-only options.
   - **Data, text and voice usage options:** With Singtel's fast, reliable, and full coverage 5G network, data allowances are its primary differentiator for data warriors (Figure 10.6).

Figure 10.6. Example of data-only plans.

2. **Bundling for value:** Proactive promotion of bundled services to existing customers for increased ARPU:

    - **Cross-selling with Triple Play:** Aggressive discounts for combining mobile, broadband, and TV services.
    - **Entertainment bundles as add-ons:** Partnering with Netflix, Disney+, HBO GO, etc. to offer attractive entertainment packages as add-ons (Figure 10.7).
    - **Upselling with Ready Roam and security services:**

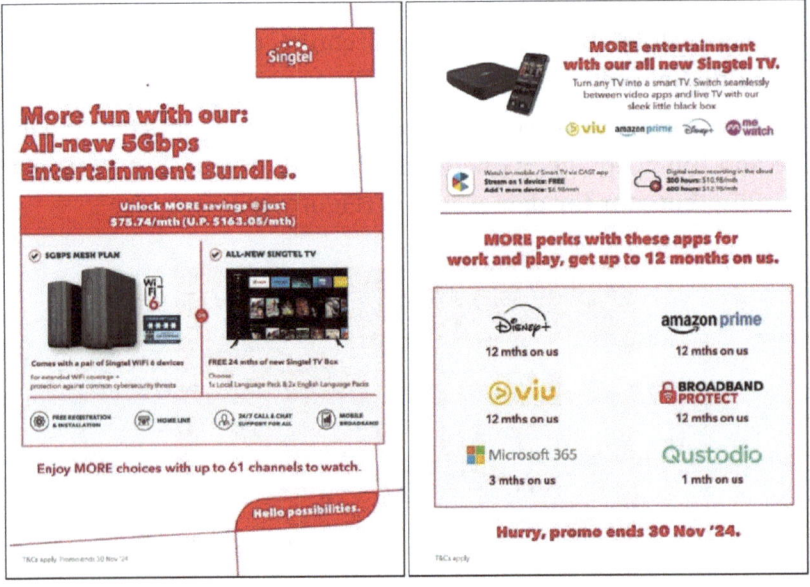

Figure 10.7. Example of bundle-based value pricing.

3. **Differentiation through innovation:**

    - **Early 5G adoption:** Positioning Singtel as a leader in the 5G space, 5G service is included in all price plans.
    - **Enhancing value with data:** Exploration of "data rollover" and "data sharing" features to appeal to various customer segments (Figure 10.8).

Price Strategy | 265

Figure 10.8. Example of innovation-differentiated pricing.

4. **Targeted segment promotions:**
   - **Student and senior plans:** Discounted offerings for specific demographics.
   - **Time-sensitive campaigns:** Limited-time promotions for boosting acquisition during key periods (Figure 10.9).

As a market leader with a long-established brand of trust, these are other key considerations which would factor into pricing plans:

- **Brand perception:** Singtel positions itself as a full-service provider. Pricing is aligned with its brand strength of innovation, trust, and transparency, emphasizing value and reliability.

Figure 10.9. Example of event/time-specific pricing promotion.

- **Network investment:** 5G infrastructure investments need to be factored into pricing, potentially impacting margins in the short term, but making it future-ready to capture value from new phases of innovation as transformation unfolds.
- **Evolving customer needs:** Singaporean consumers are tech-savvy and price-sensitive. Singtel must balance innovation and affordability.

For every product, promotion, place, and pricing plan, Singtel tracks and measures success through performance metrics such as the following:

- **Subscriber growth:** Focusing on mobile, fixed broadband, and TV individually, as well as bundled service subscribers.
- **ARPU:** For mobile, fixed broadband, and TV businesses.
- **Churn rate:** Especially in response to competitor moves. This would include both voluntary and involuntary churn.
- **Market share:** Relative to competitors in each business line.
- **Customer satisfaction:** Surveys to measure perceived value.

Singtel's pricing strategy in Singapore reflects a competitive market where innovation and bundling are key. Their emphasis on simplified plans and partnerships helps differentiate them. Success depends on anticipating market shifts, maintaining cost-efficiency, and continuously demonstrating value to their customer base.

Referencing Warren Buffett who said "Price is what you pay. Value is what you get." Diana Chen, Managing Director of Customer Management, Singtel says, "Ultimately, achieving a balance between price and value is essential for driving sales, building brand loyalty, and sustaining long-term success in the marketplace."

Key Takeaways

- **Pricing factors:** Pricing is influenced by numerous factors, including product costs (setting a price floor), customer perceived value (setting a price ceiling), marketing objectives (brand positioning, customer acquisition and retention, and short-term gains), and external factors such as competition and economic conditions.
- **Pricing strategies:** Common pricing strategies include cost-based pricing, value-based pricing, and competition-based pricing. Other strategies such as freemium, captive product, dynamic,

discriminatory, outcome-based, and subscription-based pricing are also discussed.
- **New product pricing:** Companies can opt for penetration pricing or price skimming when launching new products.
- **Sales promotions:** While not ideal for long-term brand building, sales promotions such as discounts, coupons, and bundled pricing can stimulate short-term sales.
- **Psychology of pricing:** The way prices are framed and communicated significantly impacts consumer perception. Techniques such as odd pricing, reference pricing, decoy pricing, and flash sales can influence purchasing decisions.
- **Communicating price changes:** Transparent communication is crucial when adjusting prices. Companies should clearly explain the reasons behind price increases or decreases and focus on maintaining customer trust and perceived value.
- **Pricing is a strategic tool:** Firms should think beyond dollars and cents and go beyond an inward approach to pricing. Thinking innovatively about pricing strategies can enable increases in sales volume and overall market share.

Chapter

11

Place Strategy

It is never enough to simply create a compelling product because value is determined by the customer, and there is only value when they benefit from its usage experience. Place strategy plays a crucial role, by ensuring the right product reaches the right customer at the right time through the most effective channels. In our hyperconnected world, this is no longer a simple matter of getting the requisite quantity of goods on store shelves. The way consumers interact with brands and products has undergone a fundamental shift as the digital revolution fundamentally reshaped how we shop. Driven by the ever-growing dominance of online platforms, the very concept of "place" in marketing is being redefined. The digital age has ushered in a dynamic landscape where distribution channels have multiplied, geographical limitations are replaced by a borderless online marketplace teeming with possibilities, and customer expectations have evolved. This chapter delves into the art of navigating this new landscape, exploring how to effectively distribute your product or service across both physical and digital channels, ensuring it reaches the right customers at the right time.

"

Fundamental Decisions of Channel Strategy

In the past, physical presence was paramount. B2C businesses aimed to be everywhere, with numerous stores across locations, and location decisions were based on intuition or foot traffic. Today, with e-commerce, the focus has shifted to strategic placement. Businesses carefully select physical locations that complement their online presence. Now, with access to vast amounts of data, brands can make data-driven decisions about store placement. This might involve analyzing demographics, competitor locations, geospatial location data, and online shopping trends to identify optimal locations. The rise of hyperlocal marketing underscores the continued importance of strategic placement. Understanding the nuances of specific locations, crafting place-based experiences with tailored messaging and offerings to resonate with audiences who are "right there right now" allow brands to foster deeper connections and drive engagement.

Today's consumers embark on customer journeys that weave between online marketplaces, social media platforms, and brick-and-mortar stores and they no longer view these as separate entities. A successful place strategy understands the concept of "phygital experiences", where physical and digital spaces are blended to give customers the seamless experience they expect. Imagine a clothing store using AR to allow customers to virtually try on clothes in their homes while simultaneously offering in-store stylists for personalized consultations. This seamless integration leverages the strengths of both physical and digital spaces, creating a more holistic and engaging brand experience.

Meticulously planned shopping trips may be supplemented by the convenience of online marketplaces accessible from anywhere, anytime. But the sheer volume of online choices necessitates a strategic physical presence and evolution of the role of the brick-and-mortar stores. Physical stores are no longer simply about displaying and selling products. The digital world offers ease of purchase, so physical stores must compete by offering a unique and engaging experience. Our online interactions, social media posts, and Internet searches often stem from real-world experiences. These physical spaces shape our online behaviors and preferences. Physical stores, strategically placed and designed with a distinct experience in mind, can offer curated experiences plus a refuge from digital overload. Think of a bookstore that does not simply sell books but hosts author talks and creates a sense of community. This curated experience becomes a destination, offering a unique value proposition that transcends the ease of online browsing.

However, amidst this transformation, a core principle remains remarkably constant: the importance of effective channel design and management so that the end goal of getting the right product to customers at the right time can be achieved. While the "place" where products are sold may have undergone a significant shift, the principles of selecting, managing, and integrating these channels remain surprisingly robust. At its heart, channel design and management are about ensuring a seamless customer journey across all touchpoints. The fundamental questions remain the same. How can brands reach their target customers most effectively? Which channels offer the best ROI? How to ensure a harmonious co-existence between channels? How can a seamless and consistent brand experience be delivered across all touchpoints?

Regardless of online or offline, winning place strategy hinges on two crucial decisions: channel design and channel management. In essence, companies must determine the optimal channels to reach their target segments and establish strategies to manage those channels effectively. These decisions are inherently intertwined, not sequential. As companies design their distribution channels, they must simultaneously consider how to manage them effectively. This ensures the chosen channels can be motivated and function smoothly, minimizing the potential for conflict down the line. These are important decisions, often requiring a long-term commitment once made.

Channel Design

Channel design refers to the process of selecting the most effective routes to get your product or service from the point of production to the end customer. It's about creating a distribution system that aligns with your overall marketing strategy and target audience.

Here are some key decisions involved in channel design:

- Channel type
- Channel length
- Channel intensity
- Selection of channel partners

Channel type

Three prominent choices companies face are integrated, arms-length, and franchise channels. Each offers unique advantages and drawbacks, and the optimal choice depends on various factors such as product type, target market, and desired level of control. Figure 11.1 provides a summary.

Integrated channels

Integrated channels involve a company taking ownership and complete control of the entire distribution process—from manufacturing and warehousing to online sales platforms, physical stores, and even customer service. Companies essentially become a one-stop shop, managing every touchpoint in the customer journey.

Companies with a strong brand identity and a desire to deliver a consistent, premium customer experience can benefit greatly from integrated channels. They have complete control over pricing, messaging, and in-store displays, ensuring a unified brand image across

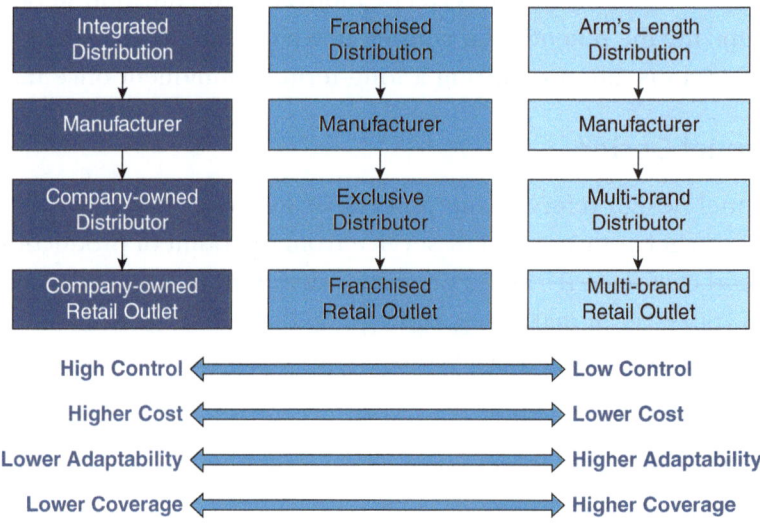

Figure 11.1. Channel types.

all touchpoints. Companies can train their own sales staff to provide in-depth product explanations and personalized customer service, building trust and loyalty. This is especially important for products requiring specialized knowledge or intricate after-sales support. Think of Apple, which operates its own retail stores alongside its online platform, ensuring a seamless customer experience regardless of the chosen channel. An example from Asia would be TWG Tea which similarly operates its own retail stores.

Having an integrated channel also means that the company has access to valuable customer data of the consumers, such as purchase history, demographics, and preferences. These data are crucial for understanding customer behavior, refining marketing strategies, and personalizing the customer experience. Depending on the company's skillsets and efficiencies, this arrangement potentially has more profitability as the margins are not shared with middlemen.

However, integrated channels also come with challenges. The significant investment required in infrastructure, manpower, and expertise in marketing, sales, and retail operations can be a barrier for smaller companies or those with limited resources. Furthermore, managing a network of physical stores can be complex and require ongoing operational expertise. This approach might not be feasible for all companies, particularly those with limited resources or a narrow product range.

Arms-length channels

Arms-length channels rely on independent intermediaries such as wholesalers, distributors, and retailers to deliver products to the end consumer. This approach allows companies to leverage the existing infrastructure and expertise of these partners, expanding market reach without the burden of managing physical stores or logistics. An example of an arms-length channel is a beer brand that distributes its products through supermarkets, convenience stores, restaurants and pubs, and online retailers.

The decision to utilize middlemen involves a calculated trade-off. While relinquishing some control over brand image and pricing and potentially sacrificing some profit margins, many opt to leverage the expertise and resources that middlemen bring to the table.

One key benefit of working with intermediaries is their enhanced reach and selling capabilities. Middlemen often have established networks and deep market knowledge, allowing them to effectively reach the target segment and promote products more efficiently for faster market penetration. This frees up a manufacturer's resources, enabling them to focus on their core competencies, such as scaling production or product development. Furthermore, middlemen can free up capital resources for manufacturers. By taking on tasks such as inventory management, marketing, and order fulfillment, they alleviate the financial and logistical burden on manufacturers. This can be particularly beneficial for smaller companies seeking to expand their reach without significant upfront investment. For example, coffee farmers often choose to sell their coffee fruit produce (coffee beans) through green coffee traders or coffee collectives, instead of trying to sell their produce to individual coffee roasters or even directly to customers. This allows them to receive a faster return on their harvest while also immediately passing on the inventory risk (produce spoilage, fire, etc.) to the middlemen instead. As such, they can then receive the capital needed to focus on growing the next harvest.

Another advantage of intermediaries lies in their ability to offer product assortment. Customers may wish to compare a variety of options when making purchasing decisions or buy complementary products. A manufacturer specializing in a specific product line, such as granite tiles, might not be able to offer the breadth of choices a customer desires, such as ceramic tiles or wood flooring alternatives. By partnering with retailers, manufacturers ensure their offerings are presented alongside complementary items, potentially increasing sales for both parties.

Firms that venture into foreign markets may face legal restrictions in entering the market or selling directly to customers. As such, they may need to partner with someone in their value chain who is local to those markets to be legally permitted to operate in those countries. Firms may also have different channel strategies while operating in different geographies. For instance, a clothing brand such as Zara might choose to operate its own stores in Europe, where it has a strong presence, but in Southeast Asian markets such as Singapore, it might partner with local distributors to manage operations, sharing the risks and capital investment. This allows them to focus on their core retail experience in key markets while relying on a local partner to navigate the complexities of a new region.

Middlemen naturally add another layer of cost to the distribution process. Another significant downside of arms-length channels is the reduced control a company has over its brand image and customer experience. For example, intermediaries might prioritize their own promotions or prioritize selling higher-margin products, potentially neglecting the company's offerings. Another risk is poorer control over middlemen's sales staff. If they have limited knowledge of the product, they could potentially create inconsistencies in brand messaging, resulting in a less-than-ideal customer experience. As such, arms-length channels may not be suitable for complex or technical products that require specialized knowledge or after-sales support.

Furthermore, arms-length channels can lead to conflicts with channel partners. Competition for market share, pricing strategies, promotions, and inventory allocation can all become points of contention. Managing a network of independent intermediaries can be a complex task. Ensuring consistent product availability, coordinating marketing efforts, and maintaining strong relationships with all channel partners require significant time, resources, and ongoing communication.

Franchise channels

A franchise involves a contractual agreement where a company (franchisor) grants permission to another entity (franchisee) to operate under its brand name and business model.

For franchisors, the allure of franchising lies in its potential for rapid expansion. By leveraging the resources and entrepreneurial spirit of franchisees, franchisors can expand their brand footprint without the need for significant capital investment in new locations.

This allows them to tap into new markets and customer segments, accelerating growth and brand recognition. For example, McDonald's, the franchisor, provides the brand name, operational manuals, and training programs, while franchisees handle the day-to-day operations of individual restaurants. This model allows the chain to expand rapidly across regions without managing each location directly.

Furthermore, franchising offers a streamlined recruitment process for franchisors. Franchisees are essentially pre-vetted individuals or groups with a demonstrated entrepreneurial spirit and the financial means to invest in the franchise. This reduces the burden of identifying and training new employees for expansion, allowing the franchisor to focus on brand development and ongoing support for its network of franchisees.

However, franchising also comes with its share of challenges for franchisors. One of the most significant concerns is the potential for loss of control over brand image and quality. With multiple entities operating under the same brand umbrella, inconsistencies in service, product quality, or customer experience can arise. Franchisors must invest significant resources in developing and enforcing strict quality control measures to ensure a consistent brand experience across all franchise locations.

Another potential drawback for franchisors lies in conflicts with franchisees. Disagreements over marketing strategies, royalty fees, or operational procedures can disrupt the smooth functioning of the franchise system. Careful franchisee selection and management and a strong franchisee relationship management program become essential to maintain a harmonious and collaborative network.

The franchisee benefits from the established brand recognition and business model, marketing support, and operational know-how of the franchisor. Starting a new business from scratch can be daunting, but by becoming a franchisee, individuals gain access to a proven system. This reduces the risk of failure and increases the chances of success.

Furthermore, franchisees benefit from the buying power and economies of scale of a larger network. Franchisors often negotiate bulk purchase agreements with suppliers, allowing franchisees to access lower product costs than they could on their own. This translates into higher profit margins for successful franchisees.

However, franchisees must also be prepared for the limitations inherent in the franchise model. One major drawback is the lack of complete autonomy. Franchisees operate within a framework established by the franchisor, with limited flexibility in terms of pricing, product offerings, or marketing strategies. This can be frustrating for entrepreneurs seeking greater creative control. Additionally, franchisees are often subject to ongoing fees, including royalties and marketing contributions, which can eat into their profits.

Channel length

This refers to the number of intermediaries between the producer and the customer. One of the most crucial functions of channel members is distribution and logistics. They act as the bridge between manufacturers and the vast expanse of the marketplace. Wholesalers and distributors purchase products in bulk at discounted prices, taking on the responsibility of transporting and storing them efficiently. Retailers then serve as the final point of contact, ensuring products are readily available for customer purchase in small quantities and offering assortment, whether in physical stores or online platforms. This efficient distribution network minimizes costs and ensures timely product availability for consumers.

Manufacturers can choose to use a direct channel (selling directly to consumers), an indirect channel (using one or more intermediaries such as wholesalers or retailers), or a hybrid model (combining both direct and indirect). The choice depends on factors such as product complexity, target market size, cost of sales, and desired level of control over distribution. Direct channels offer the most control over brand image and pricing (read more in the case about Nike's DTC distribution), while indirect channels involve relinquishing some control to intermediaries, but bring other benefits. This decision depends on what you want in terms of a balance between control and efficiency, which is linked to the value-add each party can bring.

Companies can have more than one channel. Having more channels will help increase market coverage of a firm's products and allow for more customized selling to serve different segments. However, new channels are likely to also introduce conflict and control problems, as two or more channels may end up competing for the same customers.

Case: Nike's DTC Shift—A Lesson in Customer Centricity

The mid-2010s saw the rise of the popularity of DTC brands. The pandemic fueled it further. Like integrated channels, DTC brands eliminate intermediaries and prioritize direct sales to consumers. They might involve selling directly through a brand website, online-only platforms, or a hybrid approach that includes both physical and digital storefronts. This approach can be adopted by digitally native, online-first consumer brands, retail brands with stores that fully embrace digital channels through their own websites, or well-established consumer brands that are sold mainly by retail partners but include DTC as a new business model.[1]

A DTC approach allows brands to cultivate a stronger relationship with their customers. DTC brands control the entire customer journey, from product development to post-purchase interactions. This fosters a more personalized experience, allowing brands to gather valuable customer data, understand buying behavior, quickly launch and test new products, and tailor their products and marketing messages accordingly to grow the business. DTC allows for a more agile and responsive approach to market trends. Without the complexities of negotiating with wholesalers and retailers, DTC brands can quickly adapt their product offerings and marketing strategies based on real-time customer feedback.

---

[1] Bodley, D., Andreas, L., and Pinar, T. (2021). Even big brands need a direct-to-consumer strategy. Boston Consulting Group. 16 November 2021. Accessed on 16 May 2024. https://www.bcg.com/publications/2021/direct-to-consumer-strategy-business-benefits.

DTC brands must invest heavily in building a strong online presence, including a user-friendly website, engaging social media channels, and potentially influencer marketing campaigns. Instead of broad, one-size-fits-all campaigns, DTC brands leverage precision marketing, tailoring messages and offers directly to individual customers. This is fueled by a focus on building substantial digital assets—high-quality images, engaging videos, and authentic customer reviews—that resonate with their target audience. Establishing brand trust is crucial, especially for new brands competing with established players. Positive customer reviews, social media engagement, and influencer partnerships can all play a role in building trust and credibility.

DTC brands must navigate the complexities of channel conflict, especially when they adopt multi-channel distribution practices including third-party retail partners. They need to ensure their online prices remain competitive while avoiding undercutting their remaining retail partners. This can lead to exploring alternative revenue models such as subscriptions or tiered pricing structures.

Additionally, fulfillment and logistics become crucial aspects of the DTC model. Fulfilling individual orders also presents a logistical challenge. DTC brands must develop or partner with a robust supply chain that can efficiently deliver single packages directly to consumers' homes. This replaces the traditional bulk shipments to retailers that benefit from economies of scale. Companies need to ensure efficient delivery processes, clear return policies, and excellent customer service to retain customers.

A real-world example of a brand embracing the DTC model is Nike. For years, Nike relied heavily on partnerships with retailers to distribute its products. By relying on retailers, Nike faced challenges in ensuring consistent brand messaging and product presentation across different store environments. In 2017, Nike announced its "Consumer Direct Offense Strategy,"[2] where it

---

[2] NIKE, Inc. Announces new consumer direct offense: A faster pipeline to serve consumers personally, at scale. BusinesWire. 15 June 2017. https://www.businesswire.com/news/home/20170615005634/en/NIKE-Inc.-Announces-New-Consumer-Direct-Offense-A-Faster-Pipeline-to-Serve-Consumers-Personally-At-Scale.

slashed a number of retail partnerships to focus on a DTC strategy, opening more company-owned stores and bolstering their online presence. The idea was to double the innovations, speed, and direct connections with consumers. By taking control of distribution, Nike wanted to ensure a consistent brand experience for its customers, both online and offline. This allows them to showcase their latest innovations, promote premium product lines, and potentially increase profit margins. Furthermore, the data collected through its own retail channels can provide valuable insights into customer preferences, informing future product development and marketing strategies.

However, fast forward to Q1 2024, amidst dipping digital sales and recognizing that consumers are still shopping in multi-brand retail, Nike's CEO John Donahoe announced that "while Nike Direct will continue to play a critical role, we must lean in with our wholesale partners to elevate our brand and grow the total marketplace."[3] Along with that, the brand will focus on new product innovation and brand marketing. Tom Nikic, senior vice president of equity research at Wedbush Securities, commented that "by 'accelerating' the strategy in 2020, they focused too much on WHERE they were selling and lost focus of WHAT they were selling. Furthermore, it allowed a host of competitors to come in and chip away at [Nike]'s dominance of the industry."[4]

Some takeaways from Nike's DTC experience include the following:

- **Place strategy isn't a silver bullet:** Nike's experience highlights that a successful brand strategy goes beyond simply changing distribution channels. While a strong place strategy is crucial, it

---

[3] Waldow, J. (2024). Nike posts its first digital decline in 9 years. ModernRetail. 21 March 2024. Accessed on 16 May 2024. https://www.modernretail.co/operations/nike-posts-its-first-digital-decline-in-nine-years/#:~:text=Growing%20out%20its%20direct%20sales,better%20focus%20on%20DTC%20channels.

[4] Salpini, C. (2024). Nike addresses flaws in DTC strategy as Q3 revenues come in flat. *Retail Dive*. 22 March 2024. Accessed on 16 May 2024. https://www.retaildive.com/news/nike-pivots-dtc-wholesale-strategy-flat-sales-earnings/711102/.

needs to be complemented by a focus on product innovation, brand marketing, and understanding customer preferences.
- **Data alone isn't enough:** Nike likely had access to a wealth of customer data through its DTC channels. However, these data need to be translated into actionable insights. Focusing solely on "where" customers were buying and neglecting "what" they were (not) buying led them down the wrong path.
- **Insights don't guarantee success:** Even with valuable consumer insights, formulating a winning strategy requires careful consideration of the competitive landscape and market trends. Nike's over-reliance on DTC might have created an opening for competitors to capture market share.
- **Customer centricity is key:** Ultimately, a successful brand strategy needs to be centered around the customer. While DTC offers many advantages, Nike's story reminds us that some customers still prefer the multi-brand retail experience. Ignoring these preferences can lead to missed opportunities.

Channel intensity

Another key decision of a place strategy is determining channel intensity, which refers to the number of intermediaries a company utilizes to distribute its products. The choice between exclusive, selective, and intensive distribution hinges on factors such as product type (Figure 11.2), target market, and desired level of control.

Exclusive distribution

This strategy involves partnering with a single retailer or a limited number of carefully chosen partners to sell a product. Luxury brands often utilize this approach. This strategy fosters an aura of exclusivity and prestige, aligning with the brand image and potentially commanding premium prices. It is also suited for complex products that require detailed explanations or demonstrations, as the chosen partner can be trained to provide expert service. However, this approach limits market reach and sales potential. Specialty products with strong brand preference and loyalty are suited for exclusive distribution as

Marketing Consideration	Types of Consumer Products		
	Convenience	*Shopping*	*Specialty*
Consumer purchasing behavior	• Frequent purchases • Little effort (e.g., less planning and comparison) • Low customer involvement	• Less frequent purchase • Higher effort (e.g., significant planning and comparison of brands on price, quality, etc.) • Higher customer involvement	• Rather rare purchase • Special effort—however strong brand preference and loyalty, therefore little comparison of brands • Low price sensitivity
Distribution	• Widespread distribution • Convenient locations	• Selective distribution • Fewer outlets	• Exclusive distribution • Typically, only or a few outlets
Examples	• Toothpaste • Laundry detergent • Bottled water	• Smartphone • Furniture • Clothing	• Luxury goods • Super sports cars • Designer clothing

Figure 11.2. Impact of product types on intensity of distribution.

customers seek out the brand and will expend the effort to locate it even when it is not widely available.

Intensive distribution

At the other end of the spectrum is intensive distribution, which involves making a product available through as many retail outlets as possible. This approach is ideal for low-cost, frequently purchased convenience goods, such as soft drinks or candy bars. By saturating the market with their products, companies aim for maximum brand visibility and to satisfy customers' need to have them readily available. It also increases impulse purchases. However, this approach sacrifices some control over brand image and can lead to price competition among retailers. Companies must rely heavily on product packaging and marketing to differentiate themselves within a crowded marketplace.

Selective distribution

Selective distribution occupies the middle ground. Companies employing this strategy partner with a select group of retailers who meet specific criteria, such as brand alignment, target market fit, and geographic location. This approach offers a balance between control and market reach. Selective distribution ensures adequate market coverage while maintaining some control over the brand experience and pricing strategy. However, it requires careful selection of retailers to ensure a consistent brand image across various locations. For instance, shopping goods where consumers like to make comparisons of available options will benefit from a selective distribution of retailers who are in a common geographic location, especially one that is known for that product category.

Selection of channel partners

Channel partners—intermediaries, whether wholesalers, distributors, and retailers—act as bridges connecting brands with their target customers. The success of this connection depends on a careful evaluation of potential partners, ensuring their capabilities and alignment with the brand's overall strategy.

Consider factors such as their reputation, years of experience, financial strength (growth and profit record), service level, reputation of cooperativeness, whether there are other conflicting lines and the availability of locations (especially for distribution coverage considerations), and geographic reach. Typically, you would want to select specific partners who align with your brand values, target the same customer segment, and have a proven track record. The cost of partnering with different intermediaries needs to be factored in. This includes factors like channel incentives (e.g., margins, fees, and discounts), financing terms, training, and logistics. Finding the right balance between cost-effectiveness and the capabilities of the partner is essential for maximizing ROI. As a brand gains in reputation and market power, the availability of potential channel members and the ease of channel selection and management increase.

Channel members' performances must be periodically evaluated. This can be done by measuring their sales quota attainment, average inventory levels, customer delivery time, treatment of damaged and lost goods, degree of cooperation in promotional and training programs, number of customer complaints, and the overall channel member's commitment showing their willingness to invest for long term goals.

In conclusion, it is important to design the channel strategy around the needs of the end consumers, e.g., the amount of education and support needed, if the product is bought on its own or with other products. The objective of a place strategy is to ensure that your product is available to your customer in the right place at the right time, so it needs to be effective from the customers' perspective.

Channel Management

As channels consist of independent organizations coming together, orchestrating this collaboration can sometimes lead to channel conflict, a situation when the goals and actions of different members clash. The potential for channel conflict arises due to concerns over direct competition with identical product offerings for the same market and customers. Understanding these conflicts and implementing effective management strategies is crucial for maintaining a harmonious and productive distribution system.

Channel conflict can be categorized into two main types: vertical and horizontal. Vertical conflict arises between members at different levels of the distribution chain. A classic example might involve retailers feeling threatened when the manufacturer sells directly to consumers. Retailers may feel the competition is unfair as the manufacturer can offer lower prices and make available new models faster. Another instance of vertical conflict can be disagreements over territory allocation. If a manufacturer grants exclusive rights to sell its product in a specific region to a single retailer, other retailers might be unhappy. Such disagreements can lead to strained relationships and ultimately reduced sales.

Horizontal conflict, on the other hand, occurs between channel members at the same level. For instance, two competing retailers (could be online or offline) selling the same brand of electronics might engage in aggressive price wars to capture market share. This can ultimately hurt the brand's profitability by driving down margins. Another example of horizontal conflict might be a situation where two franchisees of the same fast-food chain compete for customers in a geographically close area.

Channel conflict, if left unaddressed, can have a significant negative impact as it can lead to reduced support from existing partners, strained relationships, and ultimately, a weakened brand image. To navigate these conflicts effectively, a proactive approach is crucial. This is often done by a channel leader.

Channel leadership

Channel leaders play a crucial role in managing channel conflict. It refers to the member, usually the strongest player in the entire channel, who exerts influence and guidance over a network of channel partners. The channel leader acts as the conductor, ensuring all members play their part in a coordinated and effective manner. A member typically becomes a channel leader because it can wield power over others, either through the ownership in an integrated channel, having more brand power, economic power, and expertise about the market, or close customer contact. This power, when wielded correctly, allows them to set expectations, negotiate terms with channel partners, and foster a sense of shared goals.

Here are some ways channel leaders can mitigate and resolve channel conflict:

Establish clear channel policies

Channel leaders can develop clear guidelines outlining the roles, responsibilities, and expectations of each member. This includes aspects such as pricing strategies, sales territories, marketing initiatives, customer service standards, and roles and expectations of each member, ensuring fairness and transparency for all channel partners.

Maintain fairness or differentiate channels

Perceptions of unfairness are a major cause of channel conflict. For example, allocation and delivery of stock as well as access to promotional offers should be managed fairly, manufacturers could direct sales from their websites to be fulfilled by retailers or offer tools to help online shoppers locate their retailers. Another effective strategy is to differentiate offers by channel, essentially creating controlled "silos" within the distribution network. This allows manufacturers to tailor product offerings, pricing, and marketing messages to each channel's unique strengths and customer base. For example, a laptop manufacturer could offer different retailers different SKUs and configurations (or colors) of the same laptop model, creating a sense of differentiation for each channel. Another way to manage channel conflict is to enhance or change the channel's value proposition (e.g., retailers offering services not offered online). This ensures each channel fulfills specific different needs and purposes.

Facilitate communication and transparency

Open communication between channel members is key. Channel leaders can create communication platforms to ensure information sharing and address concerns promptly, preventing misunderstandings that might fuel conflict. This can involve regular meetings, joint marketing initiatives, and information sharing to ensure all parties have a clear understanding of the brand strategy and distribution goals.

Mediation and conflict resolution

Channel leaders can act as neutral mediators when conflicts arise between different partners. Their expertise and authority can help facilitate constructive dialogue and find solutions that address the concerns of all parties involved.

Performance monitoring and incentive structures

Monitoring the performance of each channel partner allows the leader to identify areas of conflict. Developing incentive structures that reward collaboration and achievement of shared goals can further promote cooperation and minimize competition. For instance, performance-based incentives can be implemented to motivate cooperation and positive behavior. This might involve rewarding distributors or retailers for exceeding sales targets or implementing effective marketing campaigns for the manufacturer's products.

Creating a culture of partnership

Ultimately, the most effective way to manage channel conflict is by fostering a culture of partnership. Channel members should be encouraged to view themselves as partners in achieving common goals, such as maximizing sales, enhancing brand image, and exceeding customer expectations. Building trust and a sense of shared success goes a long way in mitigating conflicts. As the saying goes, a rising tide lifts all boats.

Channel leadership focuses on the effectiveness of the channel as a means to get products to the target customers. This also means that it should not leave any members behind, as it is essential to ensure that the entire channel is viable. Firms need to abandon transactional mindsets—channel members are partners. Each member plays a role in delivering products to the end users, so firms need to think from the end-user perspective.

From Strategy to Storefront: Building a Unified Retail Experience

With a well-defined channel plan in place, brands can now turn their attention to the crucial task of creating a seamless customer experience across all touchpoints. This includes both the online and offline worlds, where consumers increasingly expect a unified brand presence. The following section explores the art of retailing in the digital age, examining strategies for crafting compelling online stores and ensuring a positive in-store experience that complements rather than compete with the digital realm.

Retailing through e-commerce

Today's online marketplaces offer a seemingly endless virtual aisle, accessible from anywhere with an internet connection. This explosion of choice has fundamentally altered consumer expectations. Customers now expect instant access to product information, real-time availability checks, and a diverse range of delivery options, from same-day service to convenient pick-up points. This shift in power dynamics has placed the onus on brands to not only offer a compelling product but also provide a seamless and convenient online shopping experience.

The rise of e-commerce platforms has also fundamentally altered consumer behavior. Online shopping offers a level of convenience previously unfathomable, offering the luxury of instant access to product information, real-time availability checks, comparing prices from multiple retailers, and completing purchases with just a few clicks. The ease and speed of online transactions have become the norm, raising the bar for customer expectations. Brands that prioritize a seamless online shopping experience, with intuitive interfaces, secure payment gateways, and efficient checkout processes, are more likely to capture and retain customer loyalty.

This ease of access has significantly heightened expectations for product availability. Gone are the days of scouring brick-and-mortar stores for specific items or settling for limited selections. The internet provides a seemingly endless product catalog, accessible with a few clicks from the comfort of one's home. This empowers consumers to find exactly what they are looking for, regardless of location or niche product category. Companies that fail to adapt to this reality risk losing customers to competitors who have embraced the virtual marketplace. The decision between selling through your own platform (e.g., website, mobile app) or online marketplaces (e.g., Amazon, Taobao, and Lazada) hinges on several key considerations. Let's consider the pros and cons of each approach.

Crafting a winning digital storefront for your own platform

Owning your platform (such as a website) grants complete control over branding. You curate the customer experience, from the design and layout to the messaging and product descriptions. This allows you to cultivate a unique brand identity that resonates with your target audience. You have greater control over pricing strategies, promotions, and product offerings on your website. You collect customer data directly, enabling you to build relationships with your audience through email marketing, loyalty programs, and targeted promotions. You avoid the commission fees typically associated with online marketplaces, potentially leading to higher profit margins.

However, developing and maintaining your own platform requires an initial investment in design, development, as well as ongoing maintenance and enhancement fees. You also need to drive traffic to your website, which requires expertise and can be time- and resource-intensive. You are responsible for managing inventory, processing orders, and ensuring timely delivery. This can be complex for businesses with a large product range. Building brand awareness from scratch can be challenging, especially for new businesses.

Should you decide to sell through your own website, you need careful consideration of various elements, each playing a crucial role in attracting customers, converting interest into sales, and fostering brand loyalty.

The foundation of any e-commerce strategy lies in being user-friendly and visually appealing. This digital storefront serves as the primary touchpoint for customers, and its design should prioritize ease of navigation, clear product information, high-quality product images, and be SEO-friendly. An effective search function—features such as filtering by category, brand, price, or even specific product attributes—and well-organized product categories are essential for helping customers find what they are looking for, reducing frustration, and increasing the likelihood of a successful purchase. Include extra features your customers may find useful, such as a shipping calculator, chatbot, and comparison tool. Consider if your platform has the capability to upsell by recommending add-ons or cross-sell related products, which encourages customers to spend more with your online store.

Recognizing the growing trend of online shopping on smartphones and tablets, the website should be optimized for mobile devices. This includes ensuring websites are responsive and user-friendly on all devices, with clear navigation and fast loading times. One-click purchasing options, secure mobile payment gateways, and the ease of using stored payment information and mobile wallets such as Apple Pay and Google Pay all contribute to a frictionless mobile buying experience.

Developing user-friendly mobile apps can further enhance the customer experience, offering features such as loyalty programs, personalized recommendations, and push notifications for exclusive deals. The rise of AR and VR applications has the potential to revolutionize product visualization and trial within the mobile space. For example, H&M's chatbot (Figure 11.3) provides style tips to help customers find outfits that fit their styles. It also allows them to save and share these outfit suggestions or buy from the H&M website. The H&M app allows users to track their orders and utilize their own photos to find visually similar items in stock (Figure 11.4), both online and potentially in-store. While shopping in a physical store, customers can check the availability of sizes and colors, scan price tags for expanded options, and activate an in-store mode to quickly locate their favorite items. The app also enables users to save items to a personal favorites list for later purchase.

Beyond aesthetics, a successful e-commerce strategy requires a focus on conversion optimization. This involves streamlining

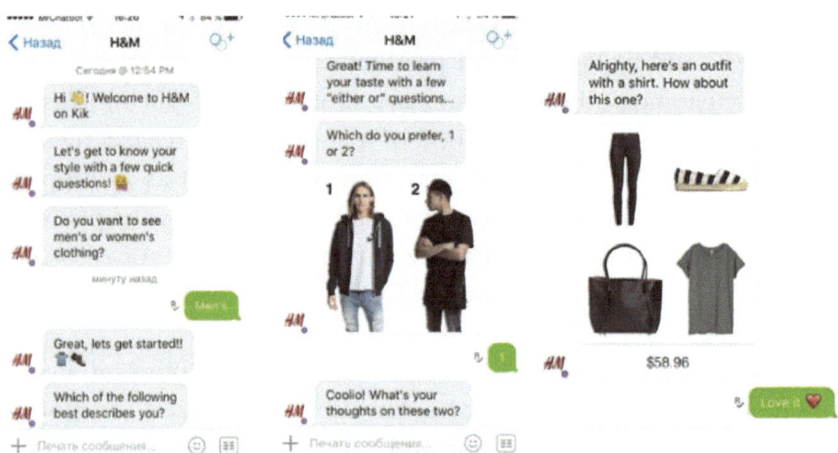

Figure 11.3. H&M's Chatbot[5] provides style tips.

---

[5] Swant, M. (2016). Kik is now letting users interact with more than one chatbot in the same conversation. *Adweek*. 29 September 2016. https://www.adweek.com/performance-marketing/kik-now-letting-users-bring-fashion-chatbots-conversation-other-bots-173788/.

Figure 11.4. Visual search feature in the H&M app.

the checkout process, minimizing the number of steps required to complete a purchase, and a seamless and secure checkout process. Multiple payment options, including credit cards, digital wallets, and guest checkout options, cater to customer preferences and reduce cart abandonment rates. Additionally, ensuring a secure transaction environment with robust data encryption builds trust and encourages repeat business. Additionally, providing clear shipping information and estimated delivery timelines helps manage customer expectations and reduces potential frustration.

Cart abandonment, the frustrating phenomenon where customers add items to their online shopping cart but leave before completing the purchase, is a common challenge faced by e-commerce businesses. Understanding why customers abandon carts is the first step toward crafting an effective recovery strategy. Common reasons include hidden or high shipping costs revealed at checkout, a complex or time-consuming checkout process, limited payment options, or unwillingness to create an account. Some customers might add items to compare prices or save for later, not intending to purchase immediately. The most effective method to address these concerns and encourage customers to complete their purchases is to send a timely email within 24 hours to remind the customer about the items left in their cart. Offer a discount or free shipping incentive to entice them to return to complete their purchase. Personalizing the email and including images of the abandoned items may help reduce the likelihood of it being ignored. Alternatively, retargeting ads or exit-intent pop-ups may be used.

A good storefront needs to be accompanied by a customer acquisition strategy to drive traffic to the online store. Search engine optimization (SEO) ensures the website ranks high in relevant search engine results, making it easily discoverable by potential customers. Content marketing plays a vital role in attracting customers and building brand awareness within the digital space. Creating informative online posts, engaging product descriptions, and high-quality product videos can educate consumers about the brand's offerings and showcase the value proposition. Gated content, which asks readers to exchange their contact information to access the content, can help build an email list of potential leads. Additionally, social media marketing, influencer partnerships, and targeted online advertising are increasingly key in attracting new customers and generating interest in the brand's offerings. Engaging on social media platforms also allows for direct interaction with potential customers, fostering brand loyalty and trust. Think of these strategies as casting a wide net to attract potential customers to the online store.

It is also crucial to retain them by fostering positive customer relationships beyond the initial purchase. Seize the opportunity to begin the relationship the moment a purchase is made with an email with order tracking information, and offering multiple contact channels, including live chat or toll-free numbers, allows customers to easily reach customer service representatives and resolve any issues promptly. This can be followed up by personalized product recommendations based on past browsing behavior and purchase history. Loyalty programs and targeted email marketing campaigns can incentivize repeat business and nurture customer relationships. Think of these strategies as building long-term relationships with customers, ensuring they return to the online store time and again for their shopping needs.

Finally, a data-driven approach is essential for optimizing and refining the e-commerce strategy. By analyzing website traffic data, conversion rates, and customer feedback, brands can gain valuable insights into customer behavior and preferences. This data can be used to identify areas for improvement, such as optimizing product page layouts, refining marketing campaigns, or personalizing the customer experience. Continuously testing and iterating based on data insights ensures that the e-commerce strategy remains relevant and effective in the ever-evolving digital landscape.

Leveraging the power of online marketplaces

Marketplaces already have a large established customer base, offering immediate access to a vast pool of potential buyers and can lead to quicker sales and increased brand exposure. Marketplaces handle much of the marketing and customer acquisition, allowing you to focus on product listings, fulfillment, and customer service. This includes optimizing user experiences, cart conversions, and easy payment features. Some marketplaces offer fulfillment services, handling storage, packaging, and shipping for a fee. Marketplaces could also offer (limited) data and insights for their merchants as well as additional fee-based marketing services for you to enhance your presence and promotions. Such features can free up your resources to focus on other aspects of your business. Listing products on a marketplace is often quicker than building your own website.

However, your product listings compete with countless others, making it harder to stand out and showcase your unique brand identity. Marketplaces often dictate pricing structures, impose listing fees and commissions, and have specific promotional guidelines. Customer interaction might be limited to fulfilling orders and addressing basic inquiries.

Choosing the right marketplace is important. Research the target audience of each platform to ensure it aligns with your ICP. Research online reviews and feedback from other sellers to gauge the overall user experience and the level of customer traffic the marketplace attracts. Look for features such as inventory management tools, marketing and analytics dashboards, and customer support options. Ensure the platform provides the functionalities you need to manage your online store effectively.

The best choice of selling through your own website versus an online marketplace depends on your specific business goals and resources. New businesses or those with limited resources might find marketplaces a good starting point to gain traction. As brand awareness grows, establishing a website can be a future step. Established brands with a strong identity might prioritize the control and branding opportunities offered by their own website. A hybrid approach, utilizing both a website and select marketplaces, can also be a viable strategy.

Social commerce

Social commerce is a form of e-commerce where social media platforms are leveraged to facilitate the entire shopping experience, from product discovery and research to checkout and purchase. It essentially merges social media interaction with online shopping, allowing consumers to seamlessly buy products they see on their favorite social media apps. Consumers discover products through social media posts, influencer endorsements, or targeted advertising. They can then complete the entire purchase process, from browsing and product selection to checkout and payment, without leaving the social media platform.

Leveraging the power of social media platforms and their native selling tools, individuals are emerging as brand storytellers and product evangelists, connecting directly with consumers in a social environment. Brands do not have to set up e-commerce capabilities or even have a website, although having one can provide more information for prospects by directing them there from the social media site.

The global value of social commerce is estimated to reach about $8.3 trillion by 2030, with Thailand and India leading the way with 90% and 86% of Internet users having purchased from social networks.[6] At the forefront of this revolution stands TikTok, a platform that has redefined social commerce by prioritizing entertainment and the power of discovery. Prior to TikTok, social selling primarily relied on static product placements and promotional messages. However, TikTok's unique format, emphasizing short, engaging video content, has transformed the game. #TikTokMadeMeBuyIt, which has millions of videos of users reviewing products they bought on Tiktok, garnering over 60 billion views, demonstrates its profound impact on shopping behavior across various consumer demographics. Influencers and brands alike can now showcase products in a dynamic and entertaining way, weaving them into compelling narratives and challenges. This shift from overt promotion to subtle product integration fosters a sense of discovery, where potential customers stumble upon interesting products organically through the content they enjoy. Other social media platforms have quickly followed its lead with such short video formats.

Several best practices can guide successful social selling strategies. Understanding the target audience and tailoring content accordingly is crucial. Identifying the social media platforms where potential customers are most active and creating content that resonates with their interests is essential. High-quality visuals and engaging storytelling techniques capture attention and leave a lasting impression. Showcasing the benefits of a product through relatable scenarios empowers potential customers to envision themselves using the product.

Building trust, the cornerstone of any successful sales interaction, is paramount in social selling. Successful social sellers cultivate genuine connections with their audience by providing valuable content, fostering two-way conversations, and building a sense of community. Transparency is key. Social sellers who disclose sponsored content and partnerships build trust and establish themselves as credible sources of information. Furthermore, actively engaging

---

[6] Chevalier, S. (2023). Social commerce sales value worldwide 2022–2030. Statista. 29 November 2023. Accessed on 23 May 2024. https://www.statista.com/statistics/1251145/social-commerce-sales-worldwide/.

in comments sections, responding to questions, and addressing concerns demonstrate a commitment to customer interaction and fosters loyalty.

The challenge of online shopping lies in the inability to physically interact with products before purchase. Likes, comments, shares, and follows paint a positive picture of your brand, fostering a sense of community and encouraging others to engage. The rise of shoppable UGC also offers a compelling solution. By showcasing authentic visuals created by real customers, UGC allows customers to see how products look and function in real-life scenarios, fostering trust and confidence in online purchases (research indicates that nearly 80% of consumers are highly influenced by UGC). Imagine browsing for a new jacket online and encountering photos and videos uploaded by customers showcasing how the jacket looks styled with different outfits or how it performs during outdoor activities. This level of detail surpasses traditional product photography and empowers customers to make informed decisions based on real-world experiences. Shoppable UGC takes customers from these visual inspirations to the relevant product purchasing pages with a "Shop Now" button, reducing the chances that potential buyers will fall off on their path to purchase.

Brands can strategically leverage this dynamic to their advantage. Incentivize UGC through giveaways, discount codes, or coupons. These incentives encourage customers to share their positive experiences with your brand, further amplifying social proof. Branded hashtags promoting UGC with your products are another effective strategy. By encouraging customers to share photos and videos, you create a visual library of real-world experiences that fosters trust and authenticity. By integrating shoppable elements into homepages, product pages, emails, and other owned channels, they create a more cohesive omnichannel experience. Imagine browsing a brand's website and encountering an engaging blog post featuring a new clothing line. The article seamlessly integrates clickable product images, allowing you to instantly view details and add items to your cart without leaving the page. This frictionless shopping experience empowers customers to purchase at their convenience, fostering higher engagement and ultimately driving sales.

Metaverse

The metaverse, a nascent yet rapidly evolving virtual world, presents a groundbreaking opportunity for brands to connect with consumers and distribute products in innovative ways. This immersive space transcends traditional marketing strategies, offering a platform for brands to forge deeper connections, foster brand loyalty, and unlock entirely new revenue streams.

One of the metaverse's key strengths is its experiential nature. Unlike static websites or social media ads, the metaverse allows consumers to interact with brands in a three-dimensional environment where customers can try on clothes using avatars, attend product launches with friends in fantastical settings, or participate in interactive games that promote brand awareness. Nike, for example, has created Nikeland on Roblox,[7] featuring arenas where users can compete in, and a showroom where they can check out Nike product offerings and dress their avatars in them. Fenty Beauty[8] gets Roblox players to collect ingredients for the brand's skincare—what a clever way to educate customers about the brand! Such immersive experiences foster brand awareness and knowledge and create a sense of community, blurring the lines between consumption and entertainment.

The metaverse offers a unique testing ground for brands. Products can be virtually prototyped and showcased within the metaverse, allowing for real-time customer feedback and data collection. This virtual testing environment is cost-effective and efficient, enabling brands to refine products before significant physical production

---

[7] Golden, J. (2021). Nike teams up with Roblox to create a virtual world called Nikeland. *CNBC*. 19 November 2021. https://www.cnbc.com/2021/11/18/nike-teams-up-with-roblox-to-create-a-virtual-world-called-nikeland-.html.

[8] Carrara, A. (2023). Fenty Beauty makes metaverse debut on Roblox. Cosmetics Business. 30 September 2023. https://cosmeticsbusiness.com/fenty-beauty-makes-metaverse-debut-on-roblox-209812.

investments. Furthermore, the metaverse fosters co-creation opportunities. For example, Roblox players can design their own Gloss Bomb lip gloss and vote for their favorite creations. One of the top voted ones would be chosen by Rihanna to inspire the next Fenty Beauty Gloss Bomb drop in 2024. This co-creation process fosters brand loyalty and excitement while ensuring products resonate with target customers before hitting the (real or virtual) shelves.

The metaverse also opens doors for novel product distribution strategies. Luxury brands such as Louis Vuitton and Gucci have experimented with selling virtual versions of their products. This not only generates new revenue streams but also expands brand reach to a growing segment of customers who value virtual ownership and self-expression within the metaverse. Furthermore, brands can leverage non-fungible tokens (NFTs) to create unique digital assets tied to physical products, offering customers a dual ownership experience and a gateway into the metaverse. Louis Vuitton[9] sold its iconic trunk as an NFT for £39,000. But what is different from other NFTs is that the brand made its NFT non-transferable, allowing owners access to purchase further limited edition and custom-made items. Such a move blocks out profiteering resellers and ensures that only its fans join this exclusive club.

The metaverse is still in its nascent stages, with technical limitations and user adoption challenges to overcome, and its full potential as a marketing and distribution platform remains to be seen. However, the early adopters who embrace its possibilities and adapt their strategies are poised to reap significant rewards. By creating immersive experiences, offering unique virtual goods, and prioritizing user engagement, brands can carve a niche in this virtual frontier, ensuring their continued relevance in the ever-evolving landscape of consumer behavior. The metaverse presents not just a new marketing channel but a whole new way to interact with customers and build brand loyalty in a world where the physical and digital seamlessly converge.

---

[9] Ryder, B. (2023). Louis Vuitton enters NFT market with $42K phygital trunk. *Jing Daily*. 7 June 2023. https://jingdaily.com/posts/louis-vuitton-phygital-trunk.

Selling through brick-and-mortar stores: Reinvention and seamless integration

The dominance of online shopping has presented a challenge to the traditional role of brick-and-mortar stores. The sheer convenience and selection offered online are hard to beat. The limitations of physical space restrict product assortment, while the overhead costs of maintaining a physical presence can make it difficult to compete with the leaner operating models of online retailers.

But the future of retail lies not in a complete disconnect between online and offline channels nor does it necessarily signify the death of physical retail; rather, it necessitates a reimagining of the role these stores play. Experience-driven retail, with a focus on customer interaction, product demonstrations, and personalized service, offers a way for physical stores to remain relevant in the creation of seamless omnichannel experiences that customers want in the digital age.

One key trend likely to gain traction is the rise of experiential retail. The digital world lacks the sensory richness of a physical space. A beautifully designed clothing store with carefully chosen lighting and music can evoke emotions and influence buying decisions in ways a flat product image on a screen cannot. The ability to touch fabrics, try on clothes, and immerse oneself in a brand's aesthetic cannot be replicated online. This is particularly true for experience-driven products such as cosmetics or high-end electronics, where physical stores become crucial touchpoints for building brand awareness and trust, and fostering a desire for ownership.

Physical stores should also move beyond mere product display spaces, transforming into interactive hubs that engage customers through immersive experiences. Think VR product trials for electronics stores, or AR displays that showcase furniture placement within a customer's home. These experiences not only entertain but also create a deeper connection with the brand and its offerings.

Figure 11.5. Panasonic Cooking Lab in Thailand.[10]

Third, the human desire for connection and community transcends the digital realm. Use physical spaces to offer opportunities for real-world interaction and shared experiences. Pop-up events, in-store workshops, or brand activations can foster a sense of community and brand loyalty that online interactions alone struggle to replicate. The Panasonic Cooking Lab in Thailand (also available in China and Japan) is a good example (Figure 11.5). It is designed to cater to the nation's trend of cooking at home instead of eating out. The lab focuses on cooking workshops to teach consumers to use local ingredients and Panasonic cooking appliances to create healthy and delicious local dishes by simplifying recipes for consumers who do not cook often, under the theme "Delicious, Simple, Healthy". Another example is how Lululemon uses its stores to organize yoga classes.[11] These stores become hubs for like-minded individuals, creating a

---

[10] Panasonic. (2014). Thailand opens "Panasonic Cooking Lab" to entice more people to cook. 17 March 2014. Accessed on 23 May 2024. https://news.panasonic.com/global/topics/4760.

[11] Hailey, L. (2024). Unlock the secrets of lululemon: Is it worth the investment? Discover its history, community, lingo, and more. The Yoga Nomads. 19 February 2024. https://www.theyoganomads.com/lululemon/.

sense of belonging that transcends the transactional nature of online shopping. This fosters brand loyalty and encourages repeat business, as consumers seek not just products, but a sense of connection.

Focusing on personalization will be another crucial long-term trend. Physical stores can leverage data analytics to personalize the shopping experience for each customer, such as in-store kiosks that greet customers by name, recommend products based on their past purchases, or offer loyalty program benefits. Farfetch's London retail store exemplifies the future of retail by seamlessly blending the personalized service of a boutique with the efficiency of online shopping.[12] This innovative approach earned them the title of "Retailer of the Future." Connected clothing racks and touch-screen mirrors bridge the gap between the physical and digital worlds. Customers can access their online purchase history and wish lists through strategically placed sign-in stations. These valuable customer data empower sales assistants to provide personalized recommendations and targeted service, elevating the shopping experience beyond a simple transaction. The integration extends to the fitting room, where smart mirrors allow customers to request different sizes, alternative product suggestions, or even process payments without leaving the space. This streamlines the shopping journey and eliminates the need for back-and-forth trips to the sales floor, enhancing customer convenience and satisfaction. Farfetch's innovative approach demonstrates the potential for physical retail to thrive in the digital age. By embracing technology and prioritizing customer experience, physical stores can offer a unique value proposition that complements, rather than competes with, online shopping.

The importance of integrating online and offline channels cannot be overstated. Physical stores can become fulfillment centers for online purchases. Customers may choose to buy online and pick up their purchases in-store, or vice versa, to offer convenience and flexibility. Click-and-collect options, or the ability to scan in-store

---

[12] Williams, R. and Jeremy, K. (2017). Inside the retail store of the future. *Bloomberg*. 24 April 2017. https://www.bloomberg.com/news/articles/2017-04-24/online-retailer-farfetch-and-the-retail-store-of-the-future.

products for detailed information and online reviews, all bridge the gap between the physical and digital worlds.

The physical store itself must also be reinvented. Technology can play a crucial role in this process. Interactive kiosks can provide detailed product information and assist with wayfinding. AR and VR experiences can allow customers to virtually try on clothes, visualize furniture in their homes, or explore product functionalities in an immersive way. These technologies blur the lines between the physical and digital worlds, creating a more engaging and interactive shopping experience. Physical stores can also leverage technology to enhance convenience. Self-checkout kiosks can expedite the checkout process, while mobile apps can allow customers to check product availability, reserve fitting rooms, or access exclusive in-store promotions. This tech-driven convenience caters to the fast-paced lives of modern consumers.

The key to success in this evolving landscape lies in reinventing the role of physical stores. They can become experience centers, community hubs, or fulfillment centers that complement and support the online presence. Brands that embrace a customer-centric approach, create a sense of community around their physical stores, and offer experiences that online shopping cannot replicate will be well-positioned to thrive.

Case: H&M Siam Paragon—A Case Study in Experiential Retail

The H&M Siam Paragon store goes beyond simply displaying and selling clothing. It embraces the concept of experiential retail, offering a multitude of interactive features that cater to the modern, tech-savvy consumer. A key element is the "3D Avatar Creator," a technological marvel that uses 3D body scanners to allow customers to create a digital 3D model of themselves. This avatar can then be used to virtually try on clothes in different styles and colors, eliminating the need for physical fitting rooms and enhancing the shopping experience. This avatar can also be used to help customers choose the right items when shopping online.

Furthermore, the store boasts "Smart Mirrors," which identify customers' items, provide product recommendations, and let customers request different sizes or colors from the fitting room. Think interactive displays that provide additional information about products as customers approach them. The smart mirror not only displays size and color options but also showcases complementary pieces or offers styling suggestions based on the customer's preferences. These technological advancements not only add a layer of entertainment but also empower customers to make informed purchasing decisions.

The store also includes a Avator Creator and Podcast Studio (Figure 11.6), free to use by anyone who wants to create content. This is clearly a move to invite UGC. Shoppers can also customize their tee shirts in the store.

The success of the H&M Siam Paragon store lies in its ability to seamlessly integrate technology with the physical shopping experience. It serves as a compelling example of how physical retail can adapt and thrive in the digital age.

Figure 11.6. 3D Avator Creator and Podcast Studio.[13]

---

[13] Siam Paragon. (2023). H&M Siam Paragon opening brand-new shop room. 29 June 2023. https://www.siamparagon.co.th/tourist/HM-Siam-Paragon-Opening-Brand-New-Shop-Room-2023/279.

This case study highlights several key takeaways for brands seeking to thrive in the evolving retail landscape:

- Embrace experiential retail by incorporating interactive features and technological advancements that can transform a traditional store into a destination that fosters customer engagement.
- Prioritize customer convenience, through features such as Smart Mirrors, to streamline the shopping journey.
- The importance of omnichannel retail is underscored by the integration of features such as the 3D Avatar Creator, which bridges the gap between the physical and digital worlds.
- Give reasons for customers to come to the store for exclusive services, such as the customization service, which are unavailable online.

The Future of Place Strategy: Some Issues and Trends

The global bazaar: Opportunities and challenges of the borderless marketplace

The rise of the Internet has shattered the walls of traditional marketplaces, ushering in an era of borderless commerce. While this globalized landscape presents exciting opportunities for businesses to reach new customers worldwide, it also introduces a complex set of challenges.

One of the most significant opportunities offered by the borderless marketplace is the potential for exponential growth. Brands can reach a vast customer base previously inaccessible through traditional channels. This allows them to diversify their revenue streams and mitigate risk by not relying solely on a single domestic market. Additionally, global competition can foster innovation as brands strive to differentiate themselves through superior products, marketing strategies, and customer service.

However, the path to success in the borderless marketplace is not without its hurdles. Geopolitical factors such as trade wars, currency fluctuations, and political instability can affect the availability of goods and materials, disrupt supply chains, influence consumer spending, and impact overall profitability. Understanding and mitigating the risks associated with geopolitical events is crucial for success in the borderless marketplace. Building supply chain resilience[14] should be a priority. International trade regulations and tariffs can add layers of complexity and expense to cross-border transactions. Furthermore, cultural nuances and diverse consumer preferences necessitate careful adaptation of marketing strategies to resonate with international audiences.

Cross-border e-commerce presents its own set of considerations. Regulations regarding customs duties, product safety standards, and data privacy vary significantly between countries. Brands must be well versed in these regulations to ensure smooth transactions and compliance with local laws. Building partnerships with reliable international shipping providers and offering appropriate payment options are crucial for facilitating seamless cross-border purchases. Even fraud prevention requires local knowledge.

The borderless marketplace is not a passing trend; it is both the present and future of global commerce. The estimated value of cross-border e-commerce transactions in China in 2022 is more than USD2.1 trillion.[15] Brands that embrace the opportunities presented by this interconnected world, while proactively mitigating the challenges, will be best positioned for long-term success. By strategically adapting their marketing and distribution strategies, adopting effective localization practices, and navigating the complexities of cross-border e-commerce, businesses can thrive in this dynamic and ever-evolving landscape.

---

[14] Duch, E. V. and Camilla, T. L. (2023). Building resilient supply chains: A multidimensional approach. Deloitte. https://www2.deloitte.com/content/dam/Deloitte/dk/Documents/spply-chain-resilience-article.pdf.

[15] Ou, X. (2024). China's cross-border e-commerce GMV growth 2014-2023. Statista. 11 April 2024. https://www.statista.com/statistics/1139471/china-annual-growth-of-cross-border-ecommerce-trade/#:~:text=The%20transaction%20value%20of%20cross,the%20highest%20value%20since%202014.

How AI can transform shopping experiences and optimize operations

The retail landscape is on the cusp of a dramatic transformation, driven by the ever-evolving power of AI.[16]

One of the most exciting possibilities lies in AI's ability to anticipate customer needs. AI, armed with past purchase data and online activity, can suggest relevant products before a customer even realizes they need them. This could range from recommending winter clothes for an upcoming trip to a colder climate to offering healthier alternatives based on a customer's dietary choices. Furthermore, virtual stores can be customized based on individual preferences, creating a truly personalized shopping journey.

Retailers may also improve the shopping experience with digital sales agents, such as chatbots and avatars. Equipped with advanced natural language processing (NLP), modern AI-powered digital sales agents can understand context, handle complex queries, and learn from every interaction. This translates to significant benefits for retailers: reduced operational costs due to 24/7 customer service, and a deeper understanding of customer needs through chatbot conversations. These virtual assistants not only can answer questions but also evolve into personal shopping guides, offering tailored advice and replicating the in-store experience online. Advanced chatbots can even analyze text inputs to detect customer emotions, tailoring their responses to ensure a more empathetic and engaging interaction.

The power of AI extends beyond the customer interface. Predictive analytics, fueled by AI, can forecast demand with incredible accuracy. By analyzing historical data, local events, weather patterns, and even global news, AI can provide retailers with actionable insights. This translates to efficient warehousing, streamlined supply chains, reduced waste from perishable goods, and ultimately, maximized profitability. The integration of AI with the IoT allows for real-time

---

[16] Chinnasamy. K. (2024). 10 ways AI technology can advance the retail sector. Consultancy. uk. 26 March 2024. https://www.consultancy.uk/news/36870/10-ways-ai-technology-can-advance-the-retail-sector.

inventory tracking, enabling dynamic pricing strategies and targeted promotions based on actual stock levels.

Autonomous stores

Autonomous stores are shops where customers can browse and purchase items without the need for cashiers or checkout lines. In 2015, Alibaba opened its first Hema supermarket in China, while Amazon opened Amazon Go in 2018. Likewise, Żabka opened autonomous stores in Poland in 2022. Statista predicts that this trend will grow.[17]

Many autonomous stores utilize smartphone apps or sensor-equipped entryways. Customers may scan a QR code with their phone app, or simply walk through a sensor-gated entrance that verifies their identity or linked payment method. Products are displayed on shelves equipped with weight sensors or cameras with computer vision capabilities. These technologies track which items a customer picks up and places in their basket or cart. Often, you can access product information through your smartphone app. This could include nutritional details, ingredient lists, or even customer reviews, allowing you to make informed purchasing decisions. As you leave the store, designated sensor zones automatically detect the items in your cart and link them to your pre-registered payment method (e.g., credit card linked to your app). Payment is processed seamlessly without any manual checkout steps.

For retailers, the allure of autonomous stores is undeniable as they can operate 24/7 without the need for staff, significantly reducing labor costs and boosting operational efficiency. Furthermore, they offer valuable data on customer behavior and product selection through integrated sensors and cameras. These data can be used to optimize product placement, personalize in-store experiences, and improve inventory management. Additionally, autonomous stores can be deployed in smaller, non-traditional locations, potentially reaching new customer segments and expanding brand reach.

---

[17] Subanogu, T. (2024). Global stores with autonomous checkouts from 2018 to 2024. Statista. 22 February 2024. https://www.statista.com/statistics/1033836/number-of-stores-with-autonomous-checkouts-worldwide/.

Consumers also stand to benefit from the convenience and efficiency of autonomous stores. They can enjoy a quick grocery run without waiting in line, or a late-night shopping trip without worrying about store hours. Autonomous stores offer a frictionless experience, allowing customers to browse and purchase items at their own pace. Additionally, some models allow for in-app product information and personalized recommendations, further enhancing the shopping experience.

Looking ahead, the success of autonomous stores will depend on addressing consumer concerns. Ensuring a secure shopping environment, developing user-friendly interfaces, and providing clear instructions are crucial. Furthermore, integrating features like self-service kiosks for customer assistance can bridge the gap between automation and human interaction. Ultimately, autonomous stores need to offer a seamless, efficient, and secure experience to gain widespread consumer acceptance.

How sustainability shapes the future of place strategy

Consumers are increasingly vocal about their desire for sustainable practices—44% of consumers in 2022 described their shopping behavior as primarily "purpose-driven", an increase from 40% in 2020.[18] This is particularly prevalent in Southeast Asia, with Vietnam, India, the Philippines, and China showing the highest environmental awareness compared to 25 other countries worldwide.[19] This shift in attitude presents a significant challenge, but also a unique opportunity. Place strategy must now integrate sustainability principles to resonate with this evolving consumer base.

One of the most pressing environmental concerns for place strategy is the issue of resource consumption. Traditional retail stores often have a large environmental footprint due to energy usage, waste

---

[18] Coppola, D. (2024). Top sustainability initiatives e-commerce brands are investing in 2022. Statista. 7 March 2024. https://www.statista.com/statistics/1307518/leading-sustainability-initiatives-brands-investing/.

[19] Coppola, D. (2024). Online shoppers buying eco-friendly products 2021, by country. Statista. 17 April 2024. https://www.statista.com/statistics/1285023/sustainable-online-shopping-by-country/.

generation, and reliance on non-renewable materials. Marketers need to adopt sustainable practices that minimize this footprint. This could involve utilizing energy-efficient lighting and appliances, implementing recycling programs for both customers and staff, and opting for building materials with recycled content.

Furthermore, the transportation associated with goods distribution also contributes to environmental impact. Place strategy can address this by prioritizing retail locations easily accessible by public transportation, offering convenient bike parking facilities, or partnering with local delivery services that utilize electric vehicles. Optimizing logistics and minimizing transportation distances can also significantly reduce a brand's carbon footprint. Place strategy can explore options like local sourcing or implementing a "ship-from-store" model (fulfillment of an online order from a store closest to the customer instead of distribution centers) to decrease reliance on long-distance deliveries. Companies may also consider microfulfillment centers,[20] which are small-scale warehouses strategically located near customers. They allow orders to be processed faster and minimize the logistics associated with the last mile of delivery.

The concept of a sustainable place strategy extends beyond the physical store itself. Marketers need to consider the entire supply chain and ensure their partners adhere to environmentally responsible practices. This might involve sourcing materials from sustainable vendors or offering products with eco-friendly certifications. Transparency is key here; brands that communicate their commitment to sustainable sourcing and production will resonate with environmentally conscious consumers.

Beyond minimizing environmental impact, place strategy can also play a role in educating consumers about sustainability. Stores can educate customers about the environmental benefits of choosing eco-friendly products or using reusable shopping bags. Implementing efficient recycling programs for both consumer and operational waste demonstrates a commitment to responsible waste management.

---

[20] Ladd, B. (2022). Is micro-fulfillment the 'next big thing' in retail? *Forbes*. 22 July 2022. https://www.forbes.com/sites/forbescommunicationscouncil/2022/07/22/is-micro-fulfillment-the-next-big-thing-in-retail/.

Key Takeaways

- Place strategy ensures that firms can get their products to the right customers, in the right quantity, at the right place, and at the right time.
- The digital revolution has reshaped how we shop. Place strategy is no longer simply about getting products on store shelves; it now involves navigating a complex landscape of physical and digital channels.
- Physical stores are still important. Even with the rise of e-commerce, physical stores can offer unique experiences that complement online shopping. Retailers must continue to take a customer-centric approach and adapt to changing consumer expectations. This includes offering a seamless online shopping experience and integrating technology into physical stores.
- Channel design and management are crucial. This involves selecting the right channels, managing relationships with channel partners, and ensuring a seamless customer journey.
- When designing channels, firms should consider channel types, functions of channel members, selection of channel members, and the intensity of distribution. This requires a trade-off between control, costs, and flexibility.
- To reduce channel conflict, careful channel management is required. A strong channel leader and cooperation from channel members are essential. After all, "a rising tide lifts all boats". Channel members' performances should also be periodically evaluated to ensure the overall effectiveness of the channel to deliver "right" product effectively and efficiently to target customers.
- AI is transforming the retail landscape. AI can personalize the shopping experience, optimize operations, and even enable autonomous stores.
- Sustainability is a key consideration. Consumers increasingly demand sustainable practices, and place strategy must reflect this.

Chapter 12

Promotion Strategy

Rethinking Promotion in the Digital Age

The world of promotion has undergone a seismic shift in the digital age. Gone are the days when a catchy jingle on television or a splashy billboard campaign guaranteed a captive audience. Consumers have migrated online, spending considerable portions of their time on social media platforms, search engines, and mobile apps. As a result, promotion strategies have followed suit, establishing a digital footprint across websites, social media feeds, and targeted online advertisements. Today, the promotional landscape is a dynamic web of digital channels, empowered consumers, and data-driven strategies. To navigate this new terrain, marketers must shed the traditional playbook, to embrace strategies that resonate with the digitally savvy customer.

Traditionally, promotion relied heavily on a one-way broadcast model. Companies crafted their messages and disseminated them through mass media channels, such as television, radio, and print advertisements. Consumers were passive recipients, bombarded with messages with limited ability to respond or engage. This approach, while effective in its time, struggles to capture the attention of today's digital audience.

The evolving customer: A new era of expectations

The digital age has empowered a new breed of customer, one whose expectations have undergone a dramatic transformation. No longer passive recipients of marketing messages, customers today are empowered by technology, demanding a level of engagement and transparency that was unimaginable just a decade ago. Social proof, omnichannel experiences, brand advocacy, and a two-way communication flow are no longer fringe desires; they are the cornerstones of how customers evaluate and interact with brands.

Social media platforms and online review forums have empowered consumers to voice their opinions directly to brands. Customers are no longer simply satisfied with a positive experience; they are vocal proponents of brands they value. Sharing positive experiences, product reviews, and recommendations online is commonplace. The same is also true for bad experiences, resulting in poor reviews or even negative word of mouth that may even go viral! As a result, customers no longer rely solely on brand messaging. They seek validation from their peers through online reviews, social media endorsements, and UGC. This reliance on advocacy and social proof necessitates brands to prioritize customer satisfaction and cultivate a community of loyal advocates.

Customers expect brands to be accessible and responsive on their preferred channels. Social media platforms, live chat functions, and readily available customer service representatives are crucial for facilitating open dialogue and addressing customer concerns promptly. This shift necessitates a commitment to active listening and a willingness to engage in genuine conversations with customers.

Storytelling remains a powerful tool for connecting with customers on an emotional level. However, the stories brands tell must be genuine and compelling. Consumers are bombarded with marketing messages, but they can easily distinguish between genuine communication and disingenuous attempts to sell. Brands that prioritize transparency, acknowledge their shortcomings, and engage in open dialogue with their customers build stronger bonds and foster lasting loyalty. Customers also crave narratives that resonate with their values, aspirations, and sense of purpose. They are increasingly concerned with the ethical and sustainable practices of the brands they support. They expect brands to operate with integrity, treat employees fairly, and minimize their environmental footprint. Consumers are empowered by readily available information and hold brands accountable for their actions.

The consumption of video content has skyrocketed in recent years, fundamentally altering the way we entertain ourselves, learn new things, and even shop. Mobile technology and UGC platforms fuel content creation. The inherent appeal of the format of visual storytelling with sound and motion itself keeps us glued to our screens. Customers are drawn to engaging, informative, and visually appealing content. Brands that utilize high-quality product demonstrations, customer testimonials, and behind-the-scenes glimpses into their operations can capture attention, tell compelling stories, and leave a lasting impression. The future of content consumption undoubtedly lies in captivating visuals, engaging narratives, and the power of video to capture our attention and imagination.

Outbound and inbound marketing

With the Internet at their fingertips, customers have access to a wealth of information about products, services, and brands. Today's empowered consumers crave information and engagement, and inbound marketing has emerged as the dominant force in meeting their needs. Inbound marketing stands in stark contrast to traditional outbound methods. Outbound marketing proactively reaches out to customers (think advertisements), hoping to snag a few interested customers. Inbound marketing, on the other hand, adopts a magnetic approach, by attracting potential customers with valuable content tailored to their specific needs and interests.

Outbound marketing disrupts consumers with unsolicited messages, often interrupting their day with a sales pitch they may not be receptive to. Inbound marketing, on the other hand, empowers consumers to self-select. They choose to engage with the content, indicating a genuine interest and a higher potential for conversion. The necessity of content marketing is further underscored by the ever-increasing power of online research. Before making a purchase, consumers delve deep into the digital world, seeking information, comparisons, and potential validations. A robust content presence ensures your brand is part of that conversation, influencing their decision at a critical juncture. By creating informative blog posts, insightful ebooks, or engaging social media content, businesses establish themselves as trusted resources. Consumers are drawn in, actively seeking out the valuable information that answers their questions. Content marketing becomes crucial in demonstrating brand expertise and fostering genuine connections with consumers. Read more about content marketing in the following chapter.

Having said that, dismissing outbound marketing entirely would be a mistake. Its ability to raise brand awareness, create a sense of urgency, and reach new audiences makes it a relevant and complementary strategy. One of the enduring strengths of outbound marketing lies in its ability to cut through the noise. In a world saturated with content, inbound marketing efforts can sometimes struggle to stand out. A well-timed email campaign, a strategically placed ad, or a creative cold call can grab attention and introduce a brand to a new audience segment. Outbound marketing allows brands to be proactive, capturing attention, initiating conversations, and sparking interest before a potential customer even begins their online search.

While inbound marketing attracts those already actively searching for solutions, outbound tactics can introduce your brand to entirely new demographics. This allows you to expand your reach, discover untapped markets, and build brand awareness among potential customers who might not have been familiar with your offerings. Furthermore, outbound marketing offers a level of control and targeting that inbound marketing sometimes lacks. Outbound marketing also excels at creating a sense of urgency or exclusivity. Limited time offers, exclusive events, or early access opportunities can pique interest and drive immediate action. This can be a powerful tool for launching new products, generating leads for high-value services, or re-engaging dormant customers.

The key lies not in abandoning outbound marketing altogether but in using it judiciously and in tandem with inbound strategies to create a truly holistic and effective marketing approach. For outbound marketing to be truly effective, it must adapt to the modern landscape. It needs to be personalized, relevant, and respectful of consumer privacy. Integrating data insights to target the right audience and crafting messages that resonate with their needs is crucial.

Data-driven insights, further powered by AI and MA

This is another area where the power of data comes into play. The vast amount of customer data collected through online interactions offers unprecedented insights into behavior and preferences. Companies can now track customer behavior online, analyze interactions, and glean valuable insights into preferences, buying habits, and demographics. This data goldmine allows marketers to develop highly targeted promotional campaigns, reaching the right audience with the right message at the right time. Instead of relying on broad, generic messaging, they can craft personalized content, promotions, and recommendations that resonate with specific customer segments.

For instance, imagine a company promoting a new line of athletic wear. In the past, they might have relied on a television commercial featuring a celebrity athlete. Today, they can leverage data to understand the demographics of their target audience. They can then create targeted social media campaigns featuring micro-influencers relevant to specific sports or fitness activities.

Customers recognize the power of data and expect brands to leverage it responsibly to personalize their experience and anticipate their needs. They now expect a level of personalization that transcends basic demographics. They crave experiences that cater to their individual needs, preferences, and past purchase behavior. Sophisticated data analytics allow brands to predict customer desires and tailor product recommendations, marketing messages, and even website layouts to create a truly individualized journey. However, this personalization must be implemented with caution. Customers are increasingly wary of overly intrusive data collection practices, and algorithms that manipulate their behavior or create biased experiences. Transparency in data collection and usage is paramount in building trust and fostering long-term brand loyalty.

Marketers can take the power of data even further by harnessing the power of AI. AI can analyze vast amounts of customer data—purchasing habits, website interactions, and social media engagement—to identify patterns and preferences, providing marketers with tailored messages and promotion approaches. Now, the social media ad you see is not just based on the segment you are assumed to belong to but one personalized to you based on your digital footprints.

Marketing automation (MA) takes this personalization a step further. AI-powered MA platforms can personalize email subject lines, content, and even sending times based on individual customer profiles and behavior patterns. This automation not only saves marketers valuable time but also ensures that the right message reaches the right person at the right time.

Furthermore, AI's analytical prowess extends to campaign optimization. By analyzing data on click-through rates, conversion rates, and customer engagement, AI can identify what resonates with audiences and what falls flat. This allows marketers to refine their campaigns in real-time, A/B testing different variations of messaging and visuals to maximize their impact.

Rethinking promotion in the digital age necessitates a shift in focus. The rise of the informed consumer and the power of data analytics necessitate a shift from a broadcast message-centric approach to a more interactive, data-driven customer-centric model. With the help of AI and MA, marketers can generate personalized promotional messages, automate repetitive tasks, and optimize campaign performance with unprecedented efficiency and effectiveness.

Two-way communications

The digital age has transformed brand-customer communication from a one-way street to a bustling two-lane highway. As mentioned previously, customers increasingly expect to be engaged. Today, social media platforms, live chat options, and online review forums empower customers to voice their opinions, ask questions, and engage with brands in real time. This two-way flow of information allows brands to gather valuable customer feedback, address concerns promptly, and build stronger relationships based on transparency and responsiveness.

Communication Is the Heart of Promotion

Beneath the glitz of social media campaigns and meticulously crafted advertisements lies a fundamental truth—effective communication is the core purpose of any successful promotional strategy, no matter what channel is used. Understanding the communication model (Figure 12.1) and its various components is paramount for marketers seeking to craft effective messages that resonate with their target audience.

At one end of the communication model lies the sender, the entity crafting and transmitting the message. In the marketing context, this could be a company, a brand, an advertising agency, or an influencer trying to promote a product. The sender's objective is to convey a specific message, an idea, or information they

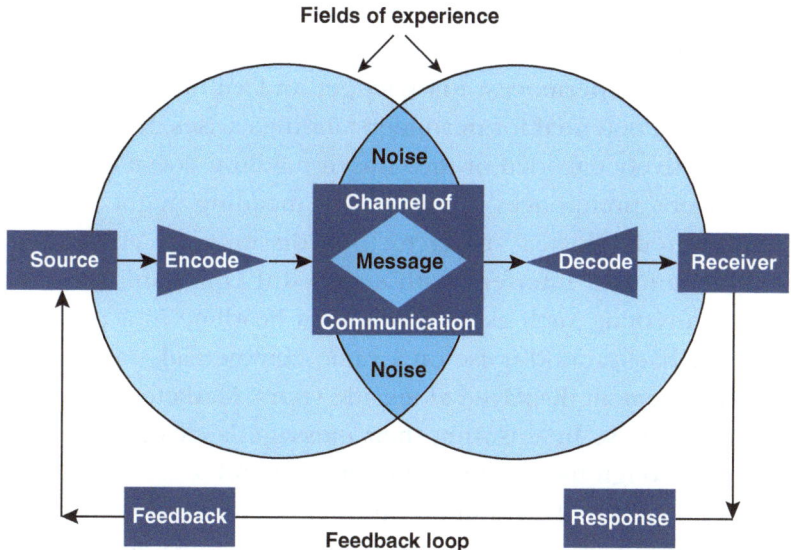

Figure 12.1. Communication process.

want the audience to receive and understand. This message needs to be encoded and translated into a form understandable by the receiver. This involves choosing the right words, tone, and lingo to craft a catchy slogan, or deciding on which model or visual to use in an advertisement, or even the colors to use on a website. The message itself is the core content being conveyed, encompassing the information, emotions, and persuasive elements intended to reach the receiver.

Once encoded, the message is transmitted through a chosen medium, the channel through which it reaches the intended audience. The marketing landscape offers a diverse array of channels, from traditional television and print media to the vast expanse of the digital world, encompassing social media platforms, email marketing, and influencer partnerships. The choice of medium depends on the target audience and the nature of the message as it significantly impacts who the message reaches and how it is received. A visually rich video advertisement might be ideal for social media, while a detailed white paper could be more effective through email marketing.

On the other end lies the receiver, the audience the message is intended for. The receiver decodes or interprets the message based on their own experiences, knowledge, and cultural background. This is where potential for misunderstandings arises. If the message is not effectively encoded or the chosen medium doesn't align with the receiver's preferences, the intended meaning might be lost or misinterpreted. "Noise," any factor that disrupts the clarity of the message, can also interfere with successful communication. This could be anything such as an ambiguous headline in a print ad, a distracting background noise on a radio commercial, or a competitor's advertisement displayed alongside yours. Marketers must strive to minimize noise by ensuring their message is clear, concise, and delivered through the most appropriate channel.

Understanding the communication model is crucial for marketers to craft effective promotional strategies. Ultimately, in today's information-saturated world, the ability to communicate effectively remains the cornerstone of successful marketing efforts. By considering each element, marketers can achieve the following:

- **Develop clear and concise messages:** Focusing on the core message encoding with language and symbols that the target audience can relate to minimizes the risk of misinterpretation during decoding.
- **Choose the right medium:** Matching the message with the most appropriate communication channel ensures it reaches the target audience and resonates with their media consumption habits.
- **Minimize noise:** Recognizing potential sources of interference allows marketers to proactively develop strategies to overcome them. For instance, creating high-quality visuals and compelling copy can help a message stand out amidst the "noise" of a crowded social media feed.

Promotion Strategy Process

The promotion strategy process involves planning, executing, and evaluating the promotion program so that any necessary corrective actions may be taken (Figure 12.2).

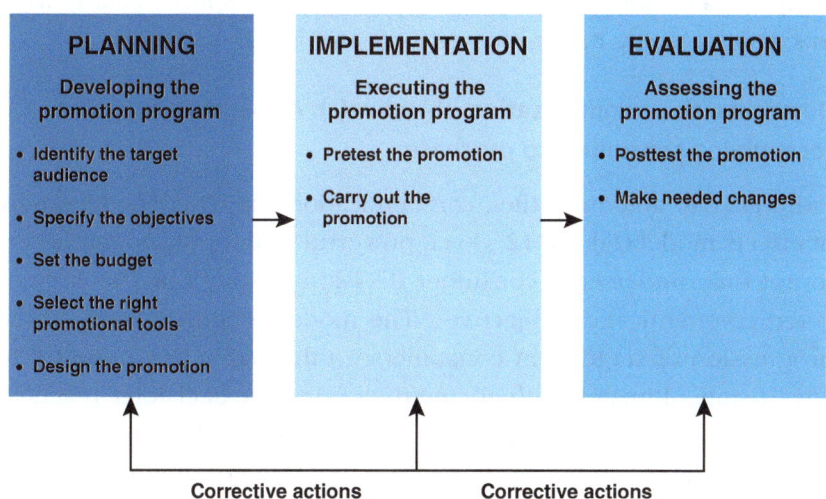

Figure 12.2. Promotion strategy process.

Planning the Promotion Program

Identify the target audience

Crafting a successful promotion starts with pinpointing your target audience. This target audience dictates everything from the message itself (what you say) to how you deliver it (when, where, and even how you phrase it).

We craft a message, but its interpretation depends on the recipient's background. Each person has a unique "lens" shaped by their experiences, culture, and upbringing. This lens colors how they perceive information.

To ensure your message resonates, you need a clear target audience in mind. Different generations, for example, have distinct preferences. Millennials, Baby Boomers, Gen XYZ, and Alpha, likely speak different slang, idolize different figures, and prioritize different values in work and life. Their entertainment habits and information sources also diverge. The same applies to B2B communication—strategies targeting enterprises will differ from those targeting individual consumers.

Marketing plays a key role in constructing promotion and communication strategies. While advertising agencies help enhance a campaign's creative elements, marketing needs to specify clearly what to say, how to say it, who to say it to, and where to say it.

Determine the communication objective(s): A roadmap for nudging consumers to purchase

Firms need to determine their communication objective. The hierarchy of effects model (Figure 12.3) is a powerful tool for brand marketers to not only understand consumer decision-making but also set targeted communication objectives. The model proposes a sequential progression of stages that consumers go through when exposed to advertising, ultimately influencing their purchase decisions. It acts as a roadmap, guiding marketers in crafting messages that progressively nudge the target audience toward the ultimate goal—purchase.

The first step is to determine where your target audience falls within the hierarchy. Are they completely unaware of your brand? Do they have a general idea but lack in-depth knowledge? Perhaps

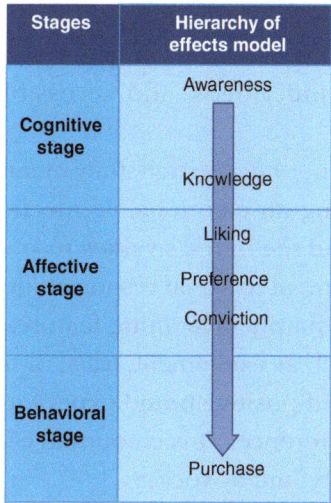

Figure 12.3. Hierarchy of effects model.

they like your brand but haven't formed a strong preference? Market research, customer surveys, and social media analytics can provide valuable insights into your audience's current stage.

Once you have identified the audience stage, the hierarchy becomes a roadmap for setting communication objectives. Use the communication goals of the next stage as your objective.

The journey begins with awareness. At this initial stage, the consumer becomes cognizant of the brand or product for the first time. This might be achieved through strategic advertising placements, social media buzz, or even word-of-mouth recommendations. If your target audience is completely unaware of your brand or product, the communication objective becomes generating initial brand recognition. This might involve broad reach campaigns through mass media or social media to get your brand name out there.

Once awareness is established, the consumer moves on to the knowledge stage. Here, they actively seek information about the brand or product and the focus shifts from simple recognition to understanding the brand's features, benefits, and unique selling proposition. This can involve researching online reviews, visiting the brand's website, or engaging with customer service representatives.

Marketers can facilitate this stage by providing clear and informative product descriptions on websites, engaging content through product demonstrations and videos, and accessible customer support channels.

As consumers gather information, they enter the liking stage. This phase involves forming an emotional connection with the brand or product. They may find the brand's values resonate with their own or appreciate its commitment to social responsibility. Effective marketing strategies go beyond simply presenting features; they strive to evoke positive emotions, such as excitement, trust, or nostalgia. Storytelling, emotional appeals, and positive brand experiences can all contribute to building brand preference. This emotional connection is crucial in fostering brand loyalty and advocacy.

The next stage is preference. Here, the consumer not only likes the brand or product but also starts to favor it over competitors. This preferential treatment often results from a perceived advantage, such as superior quality, better value, or a more positive brand image. Marketers can influence this stage by highlighting their brand's unique selling proposition and strong brand positioning, differentiating themselves from the competition to solidify preference.

Following preference comes conviction. At this point, the consumer is not only convinced of the brand's benefits but also feels confident in its ability to meet their needs. This stage is often influenced by factors such as customer testimonials, expert endorsements, product trials, or money-back guarantees that alleviate any remaining purchase anxieties.

Finally, the hierarchy culminates in the purchase stage. Having progressed through the previous stages, the consumer is now ready to act and complete the purchase. Clear calls to action, attractive promotions, and convenient purchasing options all influence the decision to buy.

The hierarchy of effects model is not a rigid, linear progression. Consumers might skip or revisit stages depending on the product type, their prior knowledge, and the overall marketing mix. External factors, such as price, availability, and purchase convenience, can also influence consumers. However, understanding this framework

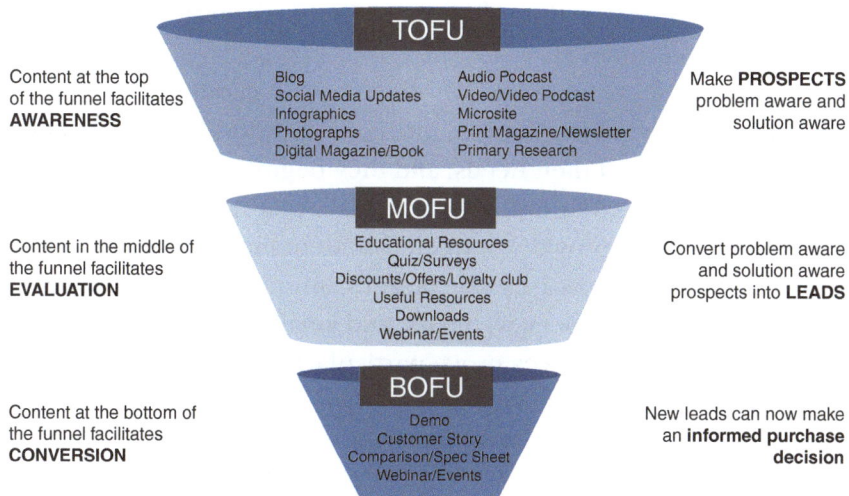

Figure 12.4. Content types for marketing funnel.

provides valuable insights into the decision-making process of consumers, allowing marketers to craft strategic communication plans that effectively guide them through this journey.

While the hierarchy of effects model outlines the psychological stages of a consumer's decision-making process, the marketing funnel offers a practical framework for marketers as it primarily concerns itself with paid promotions or company-controlled interactions. Marketers can leverage this model to allocate resources effectively, crafting appropriate campaigns for each stage of the funnel.

The marketing funnel (Figure 12.4) typically consists of three broad stages: awareness, consideration, and decision. At the top of the funnel (TOFU) lies awareness where potential customers are identifying their needs or problems. This stage focuses on increasing brand visibility to capture the attention of a broad audience who might not be actively searching for the product or service the brand offers and introduce them to the brand or product. Content marketing, social media engagement, and SEO play a crucial role at the TOFU stage. By creating informative blog posts, engaging on social media platforms, and optimizing website content for relevant keywords, marketers increase the chances of their brand appearing at the forefront of a potential customer's research process and sparking initial interest.

As potential customers move down to the middle of the funnel (MOFU), their awareness evolves into consideration. They have a better understanding of their needs, and they begin actively researching products or services to evaluate potential solutions. The marketer's focus shifts toward providing targeted content that addresses specific pain points and showcases the brand's unique value proposition. Case studies, white papers, webinars, and email marketing campaigns offering valuable resources prove particularly effective at the MOFU stage. By nurturing leads with informative content and establishing the brand as a trusted resource, marketers can move them closer to a purchase decision.

Finally, at the bottom of the funnel (BOFU) lies the decision or conversion point for the company. Potential customers are ready to make a purchase, and the marketer's objective is to remove any friction and incentivize them to choose their brand. Free trials, product demos, targeted ads with special offers, and retargeting campaigns reminding website visitors of abandoned carts all play a vital role in driving conversions at the BOFU stage. By providing clear calls to action and streamlining the checkout process, marketers can ensure a smooth conversion experience.

The marketing funnel highlights the importance of a holistic approach. While a strong presence at the top of the funnel is crucial for attracting potential customers, neglecting the middle or bottom stages can lead to lost opportunities. By ensuring a seamless and engaging experience throughout the entire journey, brands can convert awareness into action and ultimately drive sales.

Set the budget

Once the strategic framework is established, firms need to determine the financial resources required to bring their promotion strategy to life. Choosing the most suitable method depends on the company's size, market dynamics, and promotional objectives. While some methods prioritize simplicity, others encourage a more strategic and data-driven approach. Several methods guide this budget allocation:

What you can afford

Smaller businesses often rely on this straightforward approach, allocating promotional resources based on their current financial capacity. While this method is easy to implement, it does not consider future goals, competitors' actions, or changing market conditions. Businesses using this method must be strategic about how they spend it.

Percentage-of-sales method

This predictable approach leverages historical sales data and industry benchmarks to establish a promotional budget as a percentage of past or projected sales. This method works well in stable markets but can be restrictive for businesses launching new products, introducing innovative features, or facing unforeseen circumstances like economic downturns.

Competitive parity method

This approach focuses on matching the promotional spending of major competitors. This strategy is particularly useful in highly competitive markets with a few dominant players vying for market share. However, it can lead to overspending as the focus becomes keeping pace with competitors rather than aligning communication with customer needs and preferences.

Objective-and-task method

This method prioritizes the specific goals of the promotional campaign. Firms employing this approach first define their objectives (e.g., brand awareness and sales increase) and then identify the tasks needed to achieve them (e.g., social media campaign and website redesign). This method fosters a rational budget allocation, directly tying costs to campaign goals. However, it requires more upfront effort in gathering cost information and strategic planning compared to other methods.

Choose the right promotion mix

The success of any marketing campaign hinges on the strategic selection of its promotion mix. The modern marketer's challenge lies not in the abundance of instruments. The key to success lies in understanding the strengths and weaknesses of each tool in the promotion mix. Marketers must strategically select a combination that aligns with their communication objectives (awareness, knowledge, liking, preference, conviction, purchase, and post-purchase) and target audience demographics. Traditional methods still hold value, but they must be integrated with the power of digital tools. By using a data-driven approach to measure the effectiveness of each element within the mix, marketers can continuously refine their strategy, ensuring their message resonates with the right audience at the right time.

Design the promotion

The foundation of any effective message lies in a deep understanding of your brand identity. What are your core values? What makes you unique from your competitors? What is your brand personality? What story do you want to tell? Answering these questions establishes a brand voice that informs all communication channels.

Understanding your target audience is equally crucial. Who are you trying to reach? What are their needs, desires, and pain points? Conducting market research and analyzing customer data allows for the development of buyer personas and the tailoring of messages to resonate with specific demographics.

Once the brand voice and target audience are defined, the power of storytelling comes into play. Effective messages go beyond simply listing product features. They weave a narrative that connects with the customer on an emotional level. Don't just talk about the technical specifications of a new running shoe. Instead, tell the story of an athlete overcoming a challenge with its help. This emotional connection fosters a deeper understanding of the product's value. People buy products for its benefits not its features. Read about how Gojek uses storytelling to build emotional connections with its community in the case "Gojek's "Everyday Heroes" Campaign—Building a Community Through Storytelling."

Partnering with an agency can significantly enhance the impact of a brand's promotional message. Agencies bring a wealth of experience, creative expertise, and access to cutting-edge marketing tools. They can assist with market research, crafting compelling messaging, and developing effective strategies for promoting the campaign across various channels. This includes identifying the most effective channels to reach your target audience, be it social media marketing, influencer partnerships, or traditional advertising. The agency can also manage the execution of the campaign, from content creation to performance analysis.

An essential partnership: Brand marketers and agencies:
Crafting a successful campaign requires a strong partnership between brand marketers who own the brand identity and advertising agencies who excel at creative execution. While agencies bring fresh perspectives and creative muscle, brand marketers hold the key strategic knowledge about their brand and target audience. Here's how they work together to answer the critical pillars of marketing communication:

- **Who to say it to (target audience):**
  - ✓ *Brand marketer's role*: They provide in-depth insights into customer demographics, psychographics, buying behaviors, brand perception, and competitive landscape.
  - ✓ *Agency's role*: They leverage this information to create audience personas, segment potential customers, and identify the most effective channels to reach them.
- **What to say (messaging):**
  - ✓ *Brand marketer's role*: They define the brand's core message, value proposition, and brand personality. They know the brand's story and its emotional connection with customers.

✓ *Agency's role*: They translate this brand essence into compelling messaging that resonates with the target audience. They craft the key talking points and ensure consistency with the overall brand voice.

- **How to say it (creative execution):**
  ✓ *Brand marketer's role*: They provide guidelines on brand voice, tone, and visual identity. They establish limitations and ensure the message aligns with the brand's values.
  ✓ *Agency's role*: They use their creative expertise to develop engaging content formats, visuals, and storytelling techniques. They translate brand messaging into effective campaigns across chosen channels.
- **Where to say it (media placement):**
  ✓ *Brand marketer's role*: They leverage their knowledge of customer media consumption habits and budget constraints. They may have existing media partnerships or insights into cost-effective channels.
  ✓ *Agency's role*: They recommend media placements based on audience targeting and campaign goals. They research and negotiate advertising space, considering traditional and digital media options.

Collaboration is key. Agencies may not have brand-specific knowledge at the outset. To bridge this gap, brand marketers should provide a "brand bible" that outlines the brand's story, values, voice, and visual identity. Brand marketers can share customer research, competitor analysis, and past campaign learnings with the agency. Throughout the process, brand marketers must be clear about expectations and provide continual feedback.

Even with a strong partnership with an advertising agency, brand marketers must thoroughly understand the promotion strategy process. While agencies excel at translating brand essence into creative campaigns, the responsibility for achieving marketing goals ultimately rests with the brand itself. This process, encompassing planning, execution, and evaluation, empowers marketers to guide the agency's efforts and ensure the promotion program aligns seamlessly with the brand's overall strategy, maximizing the ROI and driving successful customer engagement.

Implementing and Evaluating

When planning the promotion program, it may be necessary to pretest the promotion before executing the campaign. A promotional message that is improperly received by customers may cause more damage beyond the cost of the media space bought. To address this issue, it would be necessary to consider how campaigns tie in with the existing brand DNA. Avoid simply jumping on the bandwagon of what's trending or newsjacking. Be sensitive that pretests from different markets could also be different; pretesting in one market also does not mean that the same campaign launched in another market may have the same guaranteed success. As perception is highly subjective, negatively perceived messages may result in brand damage. This is possible as target audiences in different geographic markets may respond differently especially to highly controversial messages on, for example, diversity and inclusivity issues. To evaluate the promotion program, measurements must be taken both before and after.

Case: Gojek's "Everyday Heroes" Campaign—Building a Community through Storytelling

In the ever-competitive landscape of Southeast Asian ride-hailing apps, Gojek's "Everyday Heroes" campaign stands out as a testament to the power of storytelling and emotional connection. Launched in 2019, the campaign aimed to celebrate the ordinary people who use Gojek's services to make a positive impact in their communities.

The campaign's core strategy lay in shifting the focus from Gojek as a technology platform to Gojek as an enabler of everyday heroism. Gojek partnered with local filmmakers to create a series of short video documentaries. These documentaries showcased the inspiring stories of everyday people using Gojek services—a delivery driver delivering critical medical supplies, a grocery shopper helping an elderly neighbor, or a group of friends using Gojek to volunteer at a local charity.

The campaign's success hinged on its ability to elicit emotional connection. The documentaries were not simply advertisements for Gojek's services; they were heartwarming narratives that resonated with viewers on a human level. By showcasing the real-life impact of Gojek's platform, the campaign fostered a sense of empathy and admiration for the everyday heroes featured in the stories.

Furthermore, the campaign went beyond traditional advertising channels. Gojek leveraged social media platforms to cultivate a sense of community. Viewers were encouraged to share their own stories of everyday heroism using a dedicated campaign hashtag (here's an example of their call to action: "Who's your Everyday Hero? Share your stories with us and get a chance to win a trip for 2 to Tokyo, Japan, and watch the 100th ONE Championship match live![1]"). This interactive element not only extended the reach of the campaign but also fostered a sense of shared purpose and belonging amongst Gojek users.

The "Everyday Heroes" campaign proved to be a resounding success. The video documentaries garnered millions of views, generating significant positive sentiment towards Gojek. Social media engagement soared, with users actively sharing their own stories and expressing their appreciation for the platform's role in facilitating everyday acts of kindness. More importantly, the campaign strengthened Gojek's brand image, positioning it not just as a convenient service but as a force for good within the communities it serves.

A few lessons we can learn from Gojek:

- **The power of storytelling and community building:** By moving beyond traditional advertising tactics and focusing on real-life narratives that evoke emotion, Gojek forged a deeper connection with its audience. The campaign demonstrates that in today's marketing landscape, brands that celebrate the human spirit and foster a sense of community can achieve remarkable success.
- Gojek incorporates employer branding in this campaign as it spotlights its drivers who may have been taken for granted as the unsung heroes who brave the heat and rain to take us home.
- Leveraging the audience's emotional connection for this campaign by explicitly calling for them to submit content about their own "everyday heroes" stories allows them to participate and engage with the brand more.

---

[1] Grab. (2019). Who is your everyday hero. YouTube. 12 September 2019. https://youtu.be/SyuTGII9X3M?si=XOUu7McUpcVnGFyX.

Key Takeaways

In summary, we covered the following points in this chapter on Promotion Strategy:

- Customer expectations for how brands should communicate with them have changed in today's digital age.
- A mix of outbound and inbound marketing should be used to effectively reach and engage with customers.
- Technology also allows for more data-driven and timely delivery of information to targeted audiences.
- Promotion strategy is about communicating the right message to the right audience. For firms to be correctly represented to their target customers: products, prices, and places must be tightly integrated with the promotion strategy.
- Planning a promotion program begins with identifying who the target audience is. Start with a clear target audience in mind. This affects what to say, how to say it, when to say it, and where to say it.
- Firms need to determine their communication objective and how it fits with the various decision-making stages (e.g., need recognition, information search, evaluation of alternatives, purchase, or post-purchase stage). Knowing which stage target customers are at in their decision journey will ensure that marketing communication materials are targeted optimally to move them progressively towards purchase.
- Models such as the hierarchy of effect model help assess where customers are at, e.g., cognitive stage, affective stage, or behavioral stage, and what each stage's objectives should be.
- Firms need to then set a marketing budget and decide on the tools that they wish to use in their marketing promotion mix. This could be a combination of using paid (e.g., advertising), owned (direct marketing), and earned media (PR).

Chapter

13

Promotion Mix

Understanding the Foundational Promotion Mix

Traditionally, this toolbox included well-established methods such as advertising, sales promotion, PR, personal selling, and direct marketing. Let's explore what they are and how they have evolved in the digital era:

Advertising

A mainstay of marketing, advertising uses paid media channels such as television, radio, print, and billboards to broadcast messages to a broad audience. While effective for generating awareness and brand recognition, traditional advertising can be expensive and lacks the ability to target specific demographics. Its impact on purchase decisions is often indirect, influencing brand perception at the awareness and liking stages, with limited ability to measure purchase intent.

While core principles such as persuasion and brand messaging remain, the digital advertising landscape has now shifted from one-way broadcasts to a laser-focused approach. Traditional media offered limited options for audience segmentation. Television commercials reached a broad spectrum of viewers, and print ads relied on demographic assumptions. Online advertising, on the other hand, thrives on precision and measurability. This targeted approach is fueled by a data-driven understanding of online behavior, interests, and demographics. Pay-Per-Click (PPC) advertising allows brands to pay for prominent placement on search engine results pages, reaching a highly targeted audience actively seeking related products or services. Beyond search, banner ads, social media placements, and targeted search engine results allow for specific audience selection. E-commerce websites recommend products based on past purchases, while social media platforms bombard users with ads showcasing items they have recently expressed interest in. This laser focus makes promotions more enticing, as they directly address a customer's current desires. Furthermore, the concept of *retargeting* allows brands to follow potential customers across the web, serving them ads based on their previous online interactions. This persistent, yet personalized approach keeps the brand top-of-mind and nudges the customer further down the purchase funnel.

Another key difference lies in the level of engagement. Traditional advertising was passive. Consumers were bombarded with messages with little opportunity for interaction. Online advertising, on the other hand, fosters a two-way conversation. Clickable elements, interactive videos, and social media integrations allow users to actively participate in the ad. Social media allows brands to connect directly with customers, answer questions, and build relationships. Interactive features on websites and mobile apps invite user participation, creating a more immersive experience. Emerging technologies such as AI promise further personalization and real-time ad creation. VR and AR offer immersive advertising experiences that blur the lines between marketing and entertainment.

In addition, the concept of virality, nonexistent in traditional advertising, plays a crucial role online. Campaigns that resonate with audiences can be shared exponentially across their social media platforms, amplifying a brand's reach organically. UGC that builds on these campaigns further extends its reach and is a powerful tool for building trust and credibility (more in a later section on "The Power of Advocacy"). Gone are the days of relying solely on a brand's self-proclaimed virtues. Online advertising thrives on authenticity, transparency, and the ability to engage audiences enough to gain a place in their earned media.

Data-driven decision-making is another new concept. Today, online platforms provide marketers with a wealth of data on actual campaign performance. Paid advertising platforms such as PPC allow for highly targeted promotions based on demographics, interests, and online behavior. This allows for real-time optimization, enabling adjustments to messaging, targeting, and budget allocation based on measurable results.

The art of crafting a compelling message, be it a humorous video ad or a cleverly written social media post, remains paramount. The ability to evoke emotions, tell a story, and connect with the audience on a deeper level is still essential for capturing attention in a crowded online space. While some core principles have transcended the digital divide, as technology continues to evolve, one thing remains certain: Brands that embrace the power of online tools and adapt to ever-evolving consumer behavior will thrive.

Sales promotion

This strategy utilizes short-term incentives such as discounts, coupons, and contests to stimulate sales. It excels at driving purchase behavior, particularly for established brands.

Like advertising, today's sales promotions are targeted, dynamic, and data-driven, leveraging the power of the Internet to reach the right customer with the right offer at the right time. With the vast amount of customer data available online, businesses can tailor promotions to individual preferences and purchase history. Imagine browsing for running shoes online and then seeing a targeted ad for a discount on the exact pair you considered. This level of personalization creates a more engaging experience for the customer and increases the likelihood of a purchase. Flash sales and exclusive offers on social media for a brand's followers create a sense of urgency and exclusivity, driving traffic to websites and stores.

Another innovation is the concept of retargeting. Ever notice ads following you around the Internet after you visit a particular website? This is retargeting, where ads are often combined with promotions sent to users who have already shown interest in a product or service. It is a clever way to re-engage potential customers who simply need a nudge to complete a purchase.

The digital age has also ushered in the era of interactive promotions. Gamification, for instance, uses game mechanics such as points and badges to incentivize purchases. Loyalty programs reward repeat customers with exclusive deals and discounts, fostering brand allegiance. Interactive promotions not only incentivize purchases but also create a more engaging and memorable experience for the customer.

The digital age of promotions presents a double-edged sword. While it facilitates targeted outreach, it also fosters a culture of discount dependency. Discount codes and coupons are readily available online, eliminating the scarcity that once fueled their appeal. One-click purchases with instant savings further fuel the impulsive nature of online shopping, potentially leading to buyer's remorse. Price transparency becomes effortless, with consumers empowered to become comparison-shopping ninjas in seconds. This fierce competition forces businesses to constantly slash prices, eroding profit margins and potentially cheapening their brand image.

Furthermore, with an endless barrage of discounts and offers, consumers can develop "promotion fatigue." Overuse of sales tactics can desensitize them to price cuts, rendering promotions meaningless. This can lead to a vicious cycle where businesses rely on steeper discounts to attract customers, ultimately hurting brand value and attracting a customer base solely focused on price.

The key for businesses lies in creating a sense of value that transcends mere price cuts. This could involve offering exclusive content that educates or entertains, loyalty programs that foster a sense of community, or early access to new products for their most engaged customers. By focusing on building brand loyalty and offering value beyond the initial purchase, businesses can navigate the challenges of the digital promotion landscape.

Public relations (PR)

PR focuses on building and maintaining positive relationships with the public through earned media coverage, press releases, and events. PR excels at building trust and credibility (liking and conviction stages). Traditionally, its success hinges on securing favorable media attention, which can be challenging to control.

While PR is still about shaping public perception and building trust, the digital age has fundamentally transformed the landscape of how companies communicate with their audiences. The one-way flow of information through press releases and media placements has given way to a dynamic, two-way conversation where brands must actively engage with online media channels, such as digital publishers, bloggers, and social media influencers.

Also, these are not the only gatekeepers controlling the narrative. Today, social media empowers anyone to be a publisher, and reviews can spread like wildfire. Earned media, where positive brand coverage is generated organically, is now more valuable than ever. This necessitates a new approach to PR. Proactive social media monitoring and prompt response to customer concerns are crucial aspects of digital PR, allowing brands to address issues and demonstrate responsiveness. Companies must be prepared to address issues head-on and welcome open communication to build trust and enhance their reputation. This can be achieved by consistently delivering compelling narratives, fostering positive online conversations, and demonstrating social responsibility.

Personal selling

This direct interaction with customers through salespeople allows for personalized communication and in-depth product knowledge transfer. This is particularly ideal for big-ticket items and B2B marketing where building relationships, customization, and/or negotiations may be necessary to drive purchase decisions. Personal selling is expensive and time-consuming, limiting its reach, but it is effective at the liking, preference, conviction, and purchase stages.

While technology has streamlined processes and opened new avenues for customer interaction, the core principle of personal selling—building relationships and understanding customer needs—remains just as vital as ever. In fact, the digital landscape has presented a unique opportunity for salespeople to refine their craft and become even more effective.

One of the most significant changes is the rise of inbound marketing. Marketing teams now create targeted content, such as blog and social media posts, and webinars, that educates potential customers about their products or services. This content attracts qualified leads who are interested in what a company offers. Salespeople can then leverage this pre-existing knowledge and engagement to tailor their approach and provide solutions that directly address the prospect's specific needs.

Take, for example, a company selling project management software. Marketing efforts might include blog posts on improving team collaboration and white papers on common project pitfalls. A salesperson following up with a lead who downloaded the white paper can then focus on the prospect's specific challenges related to project timelines or communication breakdowns. This targeted approach, informed by the prospect's online activity, allows for a more productive and personalized sales conversation.

Social media has also become a powerful tool for salespeople in the digital age. These platforms allow for direct interaction with potential customers, fostering relationships and building trust. Video conferencing platforms enable personalized interaction regardless of location. Salespeople can also participate in relevant online communities, answer questions, and offer insights that showcase their expertise. This establishes them as thought leaders and positions them as trusted advisors rather than simply product pushers.

However, the digital age also presents challenges for personal selling. Information overload means potential customers are bombarded with messages. To stand out, salespeople need to be more creative and data-driven in their approach. Utilizing CRM software allows them to track interactions and tailor their outreach accordingly. Additionally, the abundance of online resources empowers customers to educate themselves, potentially reducing reliance on a salesperson's product knowledge. To counter this, salespeople must focus on providing strategic guidance, building trust, and demonstrating the value proposition beyond just features and benefits (recall Chapter 7 on sense-making and ABM).

In conclusion, personal selling in the digital age is not about replacing human interaction with technology but rather about leveraging technology to enhance the effectiveness of the human touch. By working hand-in-hand with marketing teams to qualify leads and utilizing the power of social media for relationship building, salespeople can navigate the digital landscape and continue to build strong, lasting relationships with customers. The core principles of personal selling—active listening, understanding needs, and building trust—remain as relevant as ever, even in an age of automation and digital marketing. Social selling—using technology and social media to combine prospect and content strategies—is one way in which personal selling has authenticity and personal touch and builds relationships. Read the case to find out how Maersk does this.

Case: The Social Sell—Maersk Shares How It Connects and Converts in a Digital Age[1]

Traditional sales models are facing a revolution. In their place, a more dynamic and interactive approach is emerging—social selling.

Social selling leverages the power of social media platforms to connect directly with potential customers, fostering relationships and driving sales through a more interactive and personal approach. 84% of decision-makers at the C-suite and VP-level report being influenced by social media content when making purchases.[2] Unlike traditional sales methods that rely on cold calls and impersonal pitches, social selling prioritizes building trust, fostering conversations, and creating a sense of community.

---

[1] The authors gratefully acknowledge Maersk Asia Pacific's Ross Gearing (Regional Head of Marketing) and Aqil Sani (Regional Digital Marketing Executive) for their invaluable insights and content contributions, which were instrumental in the development of this case study.

[2] Stahl, S. (2023). 14th annual B2B content marketing benchmarks, budgets, and trends: Outlook for 2024. Content Marketing Institute. https://contentmarketinginstitute.com/articles/b2b-content-marketing-trends-research/.

The effectiveness of social selling hinges on its ability to create a more organic and authentic customer experience. Social media platforms allow social sellers to showcase their expertise and brand personality, fostering genuine connections with potential customers. Instead of relying on intrusive tactics, social sellers cultivate relationships by providing valuable content, engaging in authentic conversations, and fostering a sense of community. A salesperson could use social media to share informative articles, answer audience questions, and engage in discussions. This approach establishes the advisor as a trusted source of information instead of a pushy salesperson, making customers more receptive to their services when the need arises.

LinkedIn, the world's largest professional networking platform, has emerged as a powerful tool for this strategy. It is the go-to platform for sharing information, especially for B2B services.[3] It offers a unique space allowing users to leverage the platform's vast professional network to nurture connections with potential clients.

Social selling on LinkedIn goes beyond simply posting company updates or product advertisements. It is about cultivating a genuine online presence that positions the individual as a thought leader and trusted advisor within your industry. This is achieved by building a personal brand by regularly sharing valuable content on company and personal posts to showcase expertise and passion for the products, industry, or a certain cause. This positions the person to be well placed as an advocate for the company, engage in meaningful conversations, and actively build connections with potential customers and industry professionals.

Aqil Sani, Regional Marketing Executive for Asia Pacific, shares with us how Maersk takes its social media presence to the next stage with its social selling strategy through employee advocacy (Figure 13.1).

Leadership buy-in is crucial for a successful employee advocacy program. Management can set the tone by actively engaging on LinkedIn themselves, sharing company news, and participating in relevant industry discussions. This demonstrates the value they see

---

[3] *Ibid.*

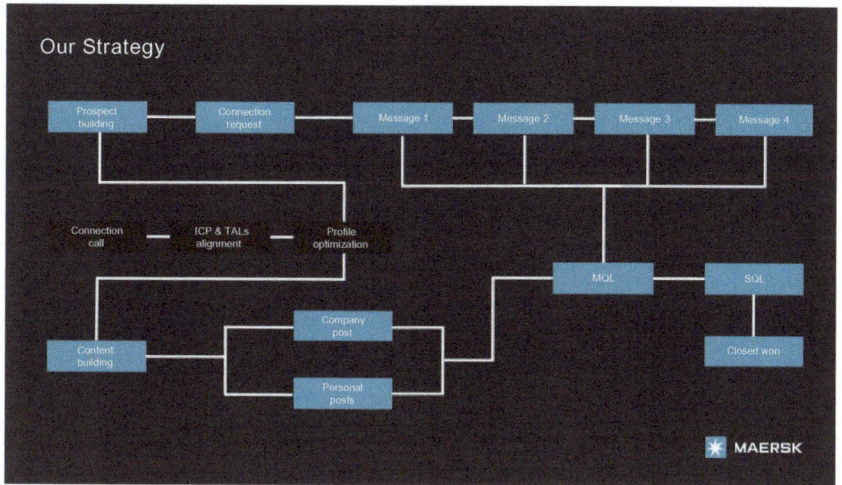

Figure 13.1. Maersk's social selling strategy.

in the platform and encourages employees to follow suit. Such an example was found in Maersk's Managing Director and President for Northeast Asia, Toru Nishiyama. He actively posts, likes, comments, and shares employee posts on LinkedIn. This sends a powerful message: Leadership supports and encourages employee voices, paving the way for a company-wide culture of social media engagement.

Engagement is the lifeblood of social selling. Regularly sharing industry news, thought leadership articles, or insightful content positions the individual as a thought leader and demonstrates their knowledge and passion for their field. To provide a support structure to kickstart employees taking on social selling roles, the company launched a "LinkedIn Professional Profile Program", which equips employees with the knowledge and confidence to create compelling LinkedIn content through workshops, sharing of best practices, and a repository of resources employees can use for their posts. To ensure employees are kept informed about the company's marketing efforts, a culture of open communication is fostered so that they can amplify these efforts by sharing marketing posts. Leading by example and providing support, management can pave the way for a thriving employee advocacy program that leverages social media's power to elevate the brand and attract new opportunities.

When employees are identified as suitable candidates for social selling (based on how active they are on LinkedIn, the number of contacts they have, etc.), the digital marketing team helps optimize their profiles. First, a professional headshot that conveys confidence and approachability is essential. The foundation of an optimized social selling profile lies in a compelling headline and summary. The headline should be a concise value proposition that captures attention and clearly communicates what the individual does and the problems they solve. The summary section then expands on this value proposition, delving deeper into the individual's experience, skills, and achievements. Using keywords relevant to their industry and target audience will ensure their profile appears in relevant searches. Social proof is another crucial element for building trust. Including testimonials from satisfied clients, endorsements from respected colleagues, and recommendations highlighting specific skills can significantly enhance a profile's credibility. Additionally, showcasing quantifiable achievements with data and metrics adds weight to the individual's expertise.

Fiona Ngo is one of Maersk's most active social sellers. Her LinkedIn profile (Figure 13.2) paints a picture of a professional with a strong background in the Technology and Electronics industry and a focus on customer-centric supply chain solutions. By highlighting her 20-year tenure at Maersk and professional accreditations, the profile

Figure 13.2. Fiona Ngo's LinkedIn profile.

establishes the individual as a knowledgeable supply chain expert with a proven track record of success. The use of relevant keywords such as logistic solutions and fourth-party logistics (4PL) further ensures the profile appears in relevant searches, while her combination of both Maersk-related and personal content positions her as a thought leader within her field. Her personal posts (Figure 13.3) focus on sustainability and Vietnamese culture. Overall, this profile creates a personal brand that is both credible and approachable, attracting potential clients and establishing the individual as a valuable resource.

Social selling allows for targeted outreach and personalized interactions. Unlike generic email blasts that get caught by gatekeepers, social selling leverages the power of existing networks. By connecting with past colleagues, classmates, or industry acquaintances, salespeople gain access to their network of contacts, vastly expanding their reach. By sharing valuable industry content, engaging in discussions, and establishing themselves as thought leaders, they

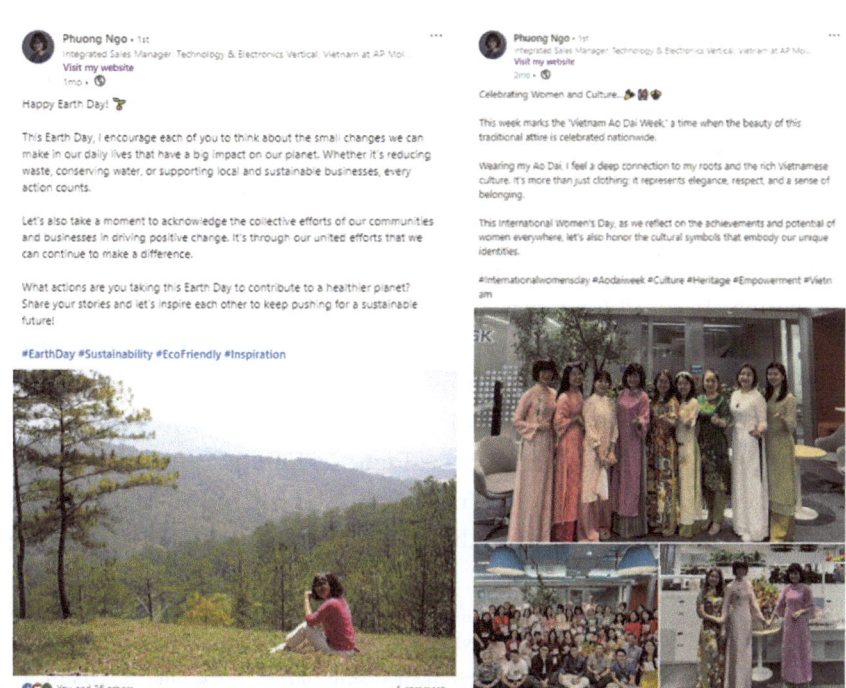

Figure 13.3. Fiona's personal posts on LinkedIn.

attract the attention of their direct connections and connections within their network. This warm approach fosters trust and credibility, as potential clients see you endorsed and recommended by people they already know and respect. This snowball effect allows you to bypass gatekeepers and reach decision-makers within your extended network, significantly increasing your chances of sparking meaningful conversations, and ultimately leading to more qualified leads, higher conversion rates, and lasting business relationships.

This is a variety of tools to facilitate effective social selling. The most prominent tool for this purpose is LinkedIn Sales Navigator.[4] This advanced search and filtering system allows you to identify and target specific decision-makers that the Maersk marketing team identifies as "Ideal Customer Personas" (ICPs) and Target Account Lists (TAL). Sales Navigator searches for potential clients based on their job titles, industry, and even company size. With extensive data on user demographics and interests, outreach efforts can be personalized. This laser-focused approach ensures that potential customers receive relevant information and are more likely to convert into paying customers. LinkedIn Groups[5] is another valuable tool for social selling. Joining relevant industry groups allows you to participate in discussions, showcase your expertise, and establish yourself as a thought leader.

There are also tools to measure results. Shield Analytics[6] is a tool that helps users track and analyze their LinkedIn content performance. It provides users with features such as content reports, trend line tracking, and identification of key metrics. This can help users understand what content is performing well and what is not so that they can optimize their content strategy and grow their audience. Companies can also evaluate individual effectiveness in social selling through LinkedIn's Social Selling Index (SSI), which considers factors such as building your professional brand, finding

---

[4] LinkedIn. (n.d.). Sales tool for prospecting & insights: LinkedIn sales navigator. View more business solutions. https://business.linkedin.com/sales-solutions/sales-navigator.

[5] LinkedIn Help. (n.d.). LinkedIn groups membership. https://www.linkedin.com/help/linkedin/answer/a540824.

[6] Shield Analytics for LinkedIn. (n.d.). Shield analytics for linkedin. https://www.shieldapp.ai/.

the right connections, engaging with relevant content, and fostering relationships. For employees, high SSI scores signify their ability to build brand awareness, generate leads, and ultimately drive sales. This not only benefits the company but also positions the employee as a social selling leader within their network, potentially leading to increased visibility and career advancement opportunities.

Using these tools, Maersk implemented its social selling strategy with numerous key employees such as Fiona. Starting in 2022, the Marketing team focused on building Fiona's credibility and presence on LinkedIn while actively engaging with ICPs from TALs. These efforts led to significant connections with influential decision-makers. From there, these prospects enjoyed regular exposure to strategic posts that either highlighted Maersk's solutions or spotlighted Fiona's expertise or personal branding.

One example (Figure 13.4) of how social selling worked was Fiona's connections with two particular Global E-commerce and Business Directors, who engaged with several of her LinkedIn posts. Fiona clearly made an impression through her posts, as they not only continued to engage in them (i.e., liking, commenting, or reposting), but her content was also mentioned during an offline meeting. Ultimately, social selling aided in accelerating the purchasing journey

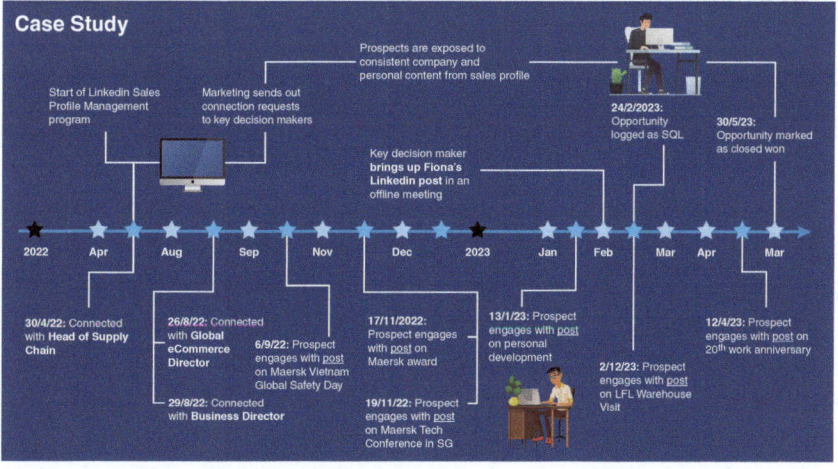

Figure 13.4. Timeline of Maersk's social selling strategy.

of the prospect to culminate in a won opportunity. This example is evidence of social selling's impact on warming up prospects in their decision-making journey through their engagement with a post.

"Social selling plays a vital role in our B2B marketing mix. Through this medium, we are able to reinforce messaging and reach key decision makers in an unprecedented direct interactive dialogue", Ross Gearing, Maersk's Regional Head of Marketing.

Key takeaways about social selling's stark contrast to traditional sales methods:

- It is permission-based. Potential customers choose to engage with social sellers' content, fostering a more receptive and engaged audience.
- It emphasizes building relationships over one-off transactions. Social selling is a marathon, not a sprint. By nurturing connections and providing ongoing value, social sellers position themselves for long-term success.
- Social selling also enables individuals to build a personal brand within their industry, fostering trust and credibility.
- Social selling empowers brands to tap into the power of social proof. By sharing customer testimonials, product reviews, and UGC, brands leverage the influence of existing customers to attract new ones.

Direct marketing

This targeted approach involves delivering promotional messages directly to customers via mail, email, or telemarketing. Traditionally, direct marketing relied on broad assumptions about demographics and interests. Mailing lists were built through surveys, purchases, and public records, often resulting in a significant portion of the outreach landing in the hands of uninterested recipients. Now, marketers can achieve more precise targeting through online data, including browsing history, social media activity, and purchase behavior, enabling improved personalization and measurability.

Another change is the channel of communication: The physical mailbox has been largely replaced by the digital inbox, with email marketing taking center stage. This allows for richer content, including videos, interactive elements, and personalized offers. Building permission-based email lists allows for targeted communication and relationship building. Businesses can track email open rates, click-throughs, and website conversions, providing a clear picture of campaign effectiveness. These data allow for continuous optimization, enabling marketers to refine their messaging and targeting strategies for better results. Direct marketing excels at fostering knowledge, liking, and promoting repeat purchases (post-purchase stage).

There are some areas to tread carefully in. With data privacy concerns at an all-time high, marketers need to tread carefully, ensuring their targeting methods are ethical and transparent. Don't be intrusive or sell data without permission. Also, nobody likes getting irrelevant junk. Personalize your outreach and target the right audience. Make sure your campaigns are relevant, targeted, and offer value. Be transparent and honest in your messaging. Don't use misleading tactics or false urgency to pressure sales. This will erode trust fast. Focus on building relationships with potential customers and avoid being overly sales-oriented.

More Tools in the Promotion Mix

The digital era has witnessed the emergence of a new set of promotional tools:

Content marketing

Content marketing lies at the heart of inbound marketing. Creating and sharing content, such as blog posts, infographics, and videos, designed to educate and entertain, establishes brand authority and builds trust and credibility. Consumers seek out high-quality content that addresses their specific pain points. This targeted approach allows businesses to nurture leads throughout the buying journey, fostering long-term relationships that translate into loyal customers. Effective content marketing fosters knowledge, liking, and even advocacy but requires a consistent content creation strategy.

The foundation of a successful content marketing strategy lies in understanding your audience. Who are you trying to reach? What are their pain points and aspirations? Develop detailed profiles of your ideal customers, including their demographics, interests, challenges, and preferred content formats. Once you have a clear picture of your ideal customer, you can tailor your content to their specific needs and interests. Unearthing the perfect topics for your content marketing strategy requires a keen eye for what resonates with your audience and aligns with your brand's goals. Utilize SEO tools to discover keywords with high search volume and low competition. These keywords can be a springboard for content topics that your target audience is actively seeking information about. You can also research your competitor's content strategy. Identify topics they have covered and explore opportunities to create content that offers a deeper dive, a fresh perspective, or a unique format (e.g., infographic vs. blog post). Another source for topic ideas is to actively monitor social media platforms where your target audience congregates. Pay attention to the conversations, questions, and trending topics to identify areas where your content can provide valuable insights or solutions. The key is to offer value at every touchpoint, establishing your brand as a trusted source of information and a thought leader in your industry. Don't be afraid to experiment with different content formats—blog posts, videos, infographics, and case studies—to cater to diverse learning preferences and keep your audience engaged. It is also important to have different content for customers at different stages of the buying journey.

Creating original content allows you to establish yourself as an authority in your field. In-depth blog posts, informative white papers, and engaging videos that address your audience's specific challenges solidify your brand as a thought leader. However, content creation is a time-intensive endeavor. This is where content curation comes in. Curating involves carefully selecting and presenting existing content that aligns with your brand message and target audience. Sharing industry reports, thought leader interviews, or even competitor blog posts (with proper attribution) can demonstrate your expertise and broaden your content offerings. By strategically selecting and promoting valuable content from other sources, you can add variety to your content mix, save time, and expose your audience to new perspectives. The key is to curate strategically, ensuring the chosen content adds value and complements your own original creations.

Once your content is created or curated, the next challenge is ensuring it reaches the right eyes. Here's where optimization techniques become crucial. SEO—optimizing content with relevant keywords for search engines increases organic visibility, attracting potential customers at the awareness and knowledge stages—plays a vital role. Keyword research helps you understand the terms your target audience is searching for and allows you to optimize your content for those keywords. Backlinks, which are links from other websites to yours, act as a vote of confidence in your content and boost reach. When reputable websites link to your content, it signals to search engines that your content is valuable and trustworthy, further improving your ranking in search results. Additionally, leveraging social media platforms and relevant hashtags can significantly amplify your reach. Engaging in conversations, participating in industry discussions, and promoting your content across these platforms can connect you with a wider audience.

Regularly analyzing content performance through website analytics and social media insights allows for continuous improvement. Balance evergreen content with content that capitalizes on current trends and events. Understanding what resonates with your audience and what falls flat empowers you to refine your content strategy, ensuring it remains relevant and continues to attract, engage, and convert.

Affiliate marketing

In the ever-expanding digital marketplace, affiliate marketing has emerged as a powerful tool for businesses to expand their reach. This performance-based marketing strategy involves partnering with third-party publishers, known as affiliates, who promote a company's products or services on their platforms in exchange for a commission on each visit, sale, or lead generated. By leveraging the established audience and credibility of affiliates, businesses can tap into new markets, build brand awareness, and ultimately, achieve significant growth.

The necessity of affiliate marketing stems from the dynamic nature of the online consumer journey. Today's empowered customers actively seek out information and recommendations before making a purchase decision. Affiliate marketing allows brands to insert themselves into this critical research phase by partnering with trusted voices within relevant niches. These affiliates, often bloggers, social media influencers, or industry experts, have cultivated loyal followings who value their opinions and recommendations. By promoting a brand's products or services in a genuine and informative way, affiliates can introduce the brand to a new audience and significantly increase its visibility.

Choosing the right affiliates is crucial for the success of any affiliate marketing campaign. Businesses should prioritize partners who possess a deep understanding of their target audience and have a proven track record of engagement. Alignment with the brand's values and messaging is also essential. Partnering with affiliates who resonate with the brand's core identity ensures a seamless and authentic experience for the customer. Furthermore, data-driven insights into the affiliate's past performance, including click-through rates and conversion numbers, can help businesses select partners who are most likely to generate a positive ROI. Clear communication of expectations and robust tracking mechanisms are essential to ensure a successful and sustainable affiliate marketing program.

However, affiliate marketing is not without its pitfalls. One key area of caution lies in the potential for inauthentic promotion. Affiliates solely focused on maximizing commissions may resort to misleading tactics or inauthentic endorsements, ultimately damaging the brand's reputation. Establishing clear guidelines and expectations regarding content creation and promotion is essential to maintaining brand control and ensuring affiliate marketing efforts contribute positively to the brand image. Another potential pitfall lies in affiliate fraud, where unscrupulous affiliates resort to artificial clicks or bot traffic to inflate their commissions. Implementing robust tracking mechanisms and partnering with reputable affiliate networks can help mitigate this risk.

Influencer marketing

Building upon the concept of affiliate marketing, influencer marketing offers another potent tool for brands to navigate the ever-evolving digital landscape. While affiliate marketing focuses primarily on driving sales and conversions, influencer marketing hinges on the power of social currency—the trust and influence wielded by individuals within online communities—to build brand awareness, engagement, and trust. Affiliates only get paid if their efforts directly translate to sales or leads, while influencers are compensated for creating content that features or promotes a brand. There is more variation in compensation for influencers. Influencers can be paid a flat fee, receive products for free, get a combination of cash and products, or even earn commissions through affiliate links embedded within their content (although this is not the primary focus).

At its heart, influencer marketing involves partnering with individuals who have cultivated a loyal following and established themselves as experts or tastemakers within a specific niche. These influencers, often active on social media platforms such as Instagram, YouTube, or TikTok, have earned the trust and admiration of their audience. By collaborating with these influential voices, brands can tap into a pre-existing and highly engaged audience, fostering brand awareness, building trust, and ultimately driving engagement and sales.

Influencers, by virtue of their established expertise and authenticity, can bridge the gap between brands and consumers, humanizing the brand message and fostering a sense of connection. A well-placed product endorsement from a trusted influencer can hold significantly more weight than a traditional marketing campaign, as it leverages the power of social proof and peer recommendation.

Like affiliate marketing, choosing the right influencer for a campaign is crucial for its success. Brands must carefully vet potential partners, ensuring their content creation reflects a genuine passion for the brand and resonates with their established voice. Transparency is also paramount. Audiences appreciate knowing when an influencer is promoting a paid partnership, and clear disclosure fosters trust in both the brand and the influencer. Metrics such as follower count, while important, should not be the sole deciding factor. Engagement rates, content quality, and audience demographics all play a vital role. Partnering with micro-influencers, individuals with a smaller but highly engaged following can sometimes be more effective than collaborating with mega-influencers, as the connection with the audience often feels more genuine. Fast fashion giant, Shein, was under fire for a campaign involving influencers. Read about it in the following case.

The rise of TikTok further reshaped this landscape, ushering in an era of democratization where everyday creators can hold as much sway as established celebrities. TikTok's unique features have empowered a new generation of influencers and transformed the way brands approach influencer marketing. Prior to TikTok, influencer marketing relied heavily on established figures with large followings. Brands sought partnerships with celebrities and social media giants who could guarantee a wide reach. Content often felt staged and promotional, sacrificing authenticity for reach. However, TikTok's focus on short-form video content and its powerful algorithm leveled the playing field. The algorithm prioritizes engagement and virality over follower count, allowing even new creators with limited followings to go viral and reach a massive audience. This shift in focus has empowered the rise of "everyday influencers." These are relatable "ordinary people" who create engaging content that resonates with specific niches or communities.

Furthermore, TikTok's emphasis on entertainment and creativity has transformed the way brands approach influencer marketing. In place of scripted product placements and generic promotional messages, successful influencer marketing campaigns on TikTok rely on organic content integration. While high-production value videos still hold a place, humor, storytelling, and UGC reign supreme. Brands partner with creators who can seamlessly weave their products into engaging narratives, and comedic skits, or excite viewers to take on challenges. This interactive and participatory approach incites fun and curiosity and fosters engagement and motivation to learn more about the product.

Case: Shein's Factory Tour Fiasco

Shein, the fast-fashion giant, found itself embroiled in controversy after a social media campaign backfired spectacularly. In 2023, Shein flew six American fashion influencers to tour its factories in China.[7] The goal was to showcase the brand's manufacturing process and presumably dispel negative perceptions about labor practices and environmental impact. The influencers, known for promoting fast-fashion trends, documented the trip on social media. However, the rosy picture they painted, showcasing clean and seemingly ethical manufacturing practices, clashed with Shein's established reputation for labor and environmental concerns. The public outcry was swift. The campaign backfired spectacularly, with social media users reacting with skepticism, accusing the campaign of being "propaganda."[8] Critics accused Shein of staging a PR stunt and the influencers of turning a blind eye to potential labor exploitation and environmental issues often associated with fast fashion.

The influencers faced significant backlash, with comments calling out their lack of transparency and accusing them of being paid to promote an unrealistic narrative. Some influencers defended their actions, claiming they were only showcasing what they were shown. However, the damage to Shein's brand image and the influencers' credibility was undeniable.

The campaign's failure highlights several key pitfalls in influencer marketing and teaches a few important lessons:

---

[7] Goh, C. (2023). Explainer: What went wrong with Shein's marketing campaign flying American fashion influencers to tour its China factory? *Channel News Asia*. 1 July 2023. Accessed on 7 June 2024. https://www.channelnewsasia.com/singapore/shein-china-factory-tour-social-media-us-fashion-influencers-criticism-what-went-wrong-3599751.

[8] Thaler, S. (2023). Influencers bashed for praising Shein's working conditions in China despite alleged abuse. *New York Post*. 27 June 2023. Accessed on 7 June 2024. https://nypost.com/2023/06/27/influencers-bashed-for-praising-sheins-china-factory/.

- **Choice of influencers:** Choosing social media personalities with limited connection to ethical fashion or a history of promoting fast fashion eroded the campaign's credibility. Partnering with influencers who genuinely align with the brand's message is crucial for authenticity. Influencer selection should go beyond follower count. Choose creators who genuinely align with your brand values and can deliver an authentic message.
- **Be authentic:** The overly positive portrayal of the factory failed to address potential concerns. A more nuanced approach that acknowledges challenges while showcasing efforts toward improvement would have resonated better. Open communication fosters trust with your audience.
- **Transparency is key:** Shein's factory tour debacle serves as a cautionary tale for brands and influencers alike. In today's social media-driven landscape, consumers expect transparency and hold brands and influencers accountable for the messages they promote. Building trust through genuine practices and fostering open communication is crucial for success in the age of social media scrutiny.

Livestreaming

Livestreaming extends the reach of influencer marketing into the realm of real-time engagement. While influencer marketing thrives on carefully curated content, livestreaming embraces the immediacy and authenticity of live broadcasts. This interactive format, where creators connect with their audience in real time, has garnered immense popularity, particularly in China and across Asia.

Livestreaming platforms allow creators, from gamers and beauty bloggers to celebrities and entrepreneurs, to broadcast live video content and interact with their audience in real time through chat functions, polls, and virtual gifts. This fosters a sense of community and connection, as viewers feel directly involved in the experience. The unpredictable and unscripted nature of livestreams adds a layer of excitement and authenticity, as viewers witness the creator's personality and engage in real-time conversations.

The phenomenal rise of livestreaming in China and Asia can be attributed to several factors. First, the prevalence of mobile internet access and the widespread adoption of social media platforms with integrated livestreaming functionality make it readily accessible to a vast audience. Second, the cultural emphasis on social connection and real-time interaction resonates deeply with Asian audiences. Livestreaming provides a platform for immediate engagement and fosters a sense of community that transcends geographical boundaries.

Several prominent livestreamers have emerged as superstars in China and Asia, each with their own unique recipe for success. Li Jiaqi, one of China's top livestreamers, often dubbed "Lipstick King," built his audience through engaging makeup tutorials and product demonstrations, establishing himself as a trusted beauty authority. During the 2021 Singles' Day presale on Alibaba's Taobao Live platform, Li Jiaqi broke his own record, selling a staggering RMB 21.5 billion (approximately USD 2.9 billion) worth of goods in his 8-hour livestream session.[9] Successful livestreamers share some key traits: genuine enthusiasm for their chosen niche, exceptional communication skills, and the ability to build a strong rapport with their audience. They leverage the interactive nature of the platform, responding to comments, taking questions, and creating a sense of shared experience that keeps viewers coming back for more.

The key to a successful livestreaming campaign lies in aligning brand and streamer priorities. Livestreamers prioritize keeping their audience entertained and interested. They rely on trust to convert viewers into customers. They will likely prioritize honest product reviews and demonstrations that resonate with their audience over scripted endorsements. Brands gain access to new audiences through livestreamers' followers but will need to do their own homework to maximize the returns from the collaboration. For example, they can collect feedback from viewers' comments in the livestream sessions and use CRM to follow up on the relationship. Brands should also

---

[9] Technode, F. (2022). Chinese influencer Li Jiaqi leads Singles Day livestream presales. *Technode*. 25 October 2022. https://technode.com/2022/10/25/chinese-influencer-li-jiaqi-leads-singles-day-livestream-pre-sales/.

establish clear metrics to track the success of the livestreaming campaign. Analyze conversion rates and brand sentiment to understand what resonates with viewers and refine the strategy for future broadcasts.

Social media marketing

Social media marketing involves leveraging social media platforms to achieve specific marketing goals. This can encompass brand awareness campaigns, product launches, customer service interactions, or fostering a sense of community around a brand. Social media platforms, such as Facebook, Instagram, Twitter, and China's WeChat, offer a unique blend of features—content sharing, direct messaging, targeted advertising, and interactive elements—that empower brands to connect with their audience on a deeper level.

The popularity of social media marketing stems from its ability to reach a vast and diverse audience with laser-like precision. Social media platforms boast billions of active users, creating an unparalleled opportunity for brands to connect with potential customers worldwide. Furthermore, sophisticated targeting options allow brands to tailor their message to specific demographics, interests, and online behavior. This targeted approach ensures maximum impact and eliminates the wasted reach of traditional advertising methods.

The benefits of social media marketing are multifaceted. It allows for targeted outreach, enabling brands to tailor their message to specific demographics and interests. It fosters brand awareness by placing the brand directly in front of the target audience. Social media platforms offer a wealth of data and analytics tools, allowing brands to measure the effectiveness of their campaigns and refine their strategies for optimal results. Furthermore, social media fosters two-way communication. Brands can engage in real-time conversations with customers, addressing concerns, collecting valuable feedback, and building a sense of community around the brand. Building a presence on social media platforms allows for brand storytelling, community engagement, and influencer partnerships. It excels at building awareness, liking, and fostering brand loyalty but requires ongoing content creation and audience interaction.

Asia, with its tech-savvy population and widespread Internet adoption, has become a hotbed for social media marketing. 61.7% of the world's 5.04 billion social media users are in Asia.[10] China, with over 1.06 billion social media users, leads the region,[11] followed by India with over 562 million users.[12] These staggering numbers highlight the immense potential that social media marketing holds for brands looking to tap into the Asian market.

However, navigating the world of social media marketing requires a cautious approach. Social media's open nature empowers consumers to voice their opinions, both positive and negative—this means that any negative customer experience can quickly go viral, damaging a brand's reputation. Brands must be prepared to handle criticism constructively and address customer concerns promptly to demonstrate a commitment to customer satisfaction. Overly promotional content or inauthentic brand voices can alienate users. Social media marketing thrives on genuine connection. Brands that prioritize creating valuable and informative content, fostering authentic interactions, and building trust with their audience are more likely to succeed in the long run. Additionally, the ever-evolving nature of social media algorithms demands constant adaptation to keep pace with changing user preferences and platform updates.

ErgoTune, a Singaporean ergonomic furniture startup, serves as a prime example of how Facebook marketing can propel a direct-to-consumer (DTC) brand to success.

---

[10] We Are Social. (2024). Digital 2024: 5 billion social media users. 31 January 2024. Accessed on 13 May 2024. https://wearesocial.com/sg/blog/2024/01/digital-2024-5-billion-social-media-users/.

[11] Kemp, S. (2024). Digital 2024: China. Datareportal. 21 February 2024. Accessed on 13 May 2024. https://datareportal.com/reports/digital-2024-china#:~:text=China%20was%20home%20to%201.06,percent%20of%20the%20total%20population.

[12] *Ibid.*

Case: ErgoTune—A Singaporean Success Story via Facebook Marketing[13]

In 2017, three friends, Joshua Chan, Damon Lye, and Jun Kiat Tan, first began the company's journey with a keen eye for a market gap. They noticed a growing demand for standing desks but limited options at a competitive price point. Everdesk+ was thus launched as a DTC brand to capitalize on this by offering high-quality, adjustable standing desks at an attractive price, establishing a foothold in the market.

However, their keen eye for customer needs soon revealed a growing demand for ergonomic office chairs that deviated from the existing offerings. The incumbent brands such as Secret Lab dominated the ergonomic chair market with a focus on the younger demographic, particularly gamers, with their feature-rich chairs boasting a bold, "racing" aesthetic. The trio saw an opportunity to cater to the growing work-from-home population seeking stylish, comfortable, yet affordable ergonomic chairs for the professional workspace. With that, ErgoTune was born.

Knowing how important a strong online presence is to a DTC brand, ErgoTune leveraged the power of Facebook marketing to launch its brand and establish itself as a leader in the ergonomic office furniture space.

Targeted advertising: ErgoTune leveraged Facebook Ads Manager to launch targeted advertising campaigns (Figure 13.5). By creating detailed buyer personas of their ideal customers—office workers, professionals, and those who spend long hours at their desks, and interests related to office furniture, ergonomics, and health—ErgoTune ensured their ads reached the most relevant audience. Facebook's powerful targeting options allowed them to zero in on demographics, interests, and online behavior, maximizing their return on ad spend. ErgoTune invested in targeted Facebook Ads to amplify their organic

---

[13] The authors gratefully acknowledge Damon Lye (Founder of ErgoTune) for his invaluable insights and content contributions, which were instrumental in the development of this case study.

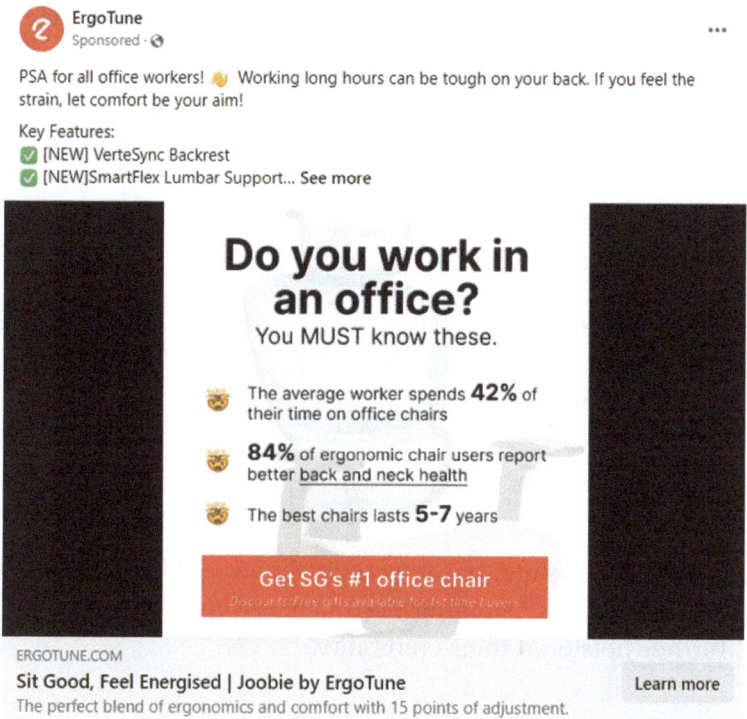

Figure 13.5. Screenshot of ErgoTune's Facebook ad for "ergonomic chair" keyword search.

reach. Utilizing A/B testing, they optimized their ad creatives and messaging to maximize click-through rates and conversions. Retargeting website visitors with relevant ads ensured ErgoTune stayed top-of-mind throughout the customer journey.

Content and building trust: ErgoTune understood the importance of high-quality content at the right stage of the marketing funnel (Figure 13.6). They created engaging Facebook posts and ad creatives that showcased the sleek design and functionality of their chairs. Short explainer videos showcasing the chair's features, ergonomic benefits, and sleek design were used to capture attention and generate interest on Facebook feeds. They also posted informative content that educated their audience about the benefits of ergonomic seating, the

Figure 13.6. ErgoTune's Marketing Funnel Strategy.[14]

dangers of poor posture, and how their chairs could improve posture and productivity. Encouraging customer reviews, testimonials, and UGC further bolstered their credibility.

Data-driven approach: ErgoTune's data-driven approach allowed them to track the effectiveness of their Facebook campaigns. By monitoring metrics such as ad impressions, click-through rates, and website traffic, they could identify what resonated with their audience and optimize their strategy for better results. The ability to measure Facebook engagement through comments, shares, and group discussions also provided valuable insights into customer sentiment and preferences.

Conversion optimization and customer service: ErgoTune ensured a seamless customer journey by directing Facebook ads to their website, which is user-friendly, visually appealing, and optimized for conversions. High-resolution product photos, detailed specifications, and clear calls to action facilitated a smooth transition from browsing to purchase. Additionally, ErgoTune offered prompt and helpful

---

[14] Lye, Y. H. (Damon). (2022). Founder, ErgoTune & EverDesk+. MoneyFM 89.3 podcast. 25 February 2022. https://www.moneyfm893.sg/guest/damon-lye-yi-hao-ergotune-and-everdesk.

Figure 13.7. Screenshot of an influencer's ErgoTune Supreme video review.[15]

customer service through multiple channels, such as email, phone, and live chat, addressing any post-purchase inquiries and ensuring customer satisfaction.

Influencer marketing: ErgoTune strategically partnered with influencers (Figure 13.7). These collaborations introduced ErgoTune to a wider audience and added a layer of social proof, as audiences tend to trust recommendations from people they follow.

Community engagement: Beyond advertising, ErgoTune actively participated in Facebook groups and communities related to office ergonomics. Community managers actively responded to comments and messages, creating a space for dialogue and addressing customer queries promptly. Engaging content, such as polls and Q&A sessions, encouraged audience participation and fostered a sense of

---

[15] Koh, S. (2020). Affordable ergonomic home office chair. Ergotune Supreme Review. YouTube. 10 December 2020. Accessed on 13 May 2024. https://www.youtube.com/watch?v=Cgi0-o-dmsQ.

brand loyalty. By providing helpful advice and insights, they established themselves as a thought leader and built trust with potential customers.

The results of ErgoTune's strategy were impressive. They successfully built brand awareness, established themselves as a trusted provider of ergonomic furniture, and achieved significant sales growth within a short timeframe. In 2021 alone, the combined revenue for Everdesk+ and Ergotune was over SGD13 million. Their story exemplifies the power of social media marketing in launching and scaling a DTC brand, particularly when combined with a deep understanding of the target segment(s) and a commitment to high-quality content and audience engagement. Their success caught the attention of Una Brands which acquired the start-up for an undisclosed 8-figure sum, reputed to be one of the largest for a DTC brand in Singapore.[16]

Here are some key lessons about promotion strategy that can be learned from ErgoTune's success story:

- **Deep understanding of target audience:** Successful DTC brands prioritize understanding their ideal customer's needs, wants, and pain points. This guides messaging, product development, and overall brand positioning.
- **Data-driven agility:** DTC brands are data champions. They track campaign performance, analyze customer behavior, and utilize A/B testing to constantly refine their strategies. This data-driven approach ensures they optimize their messaging, website experience, and overall promotion strategy for maximum impact. Successful DTC brands are constantly testing different marketing approaches and content formats. They track results, analyze data, and adapt their strategies based on what resonates with their audience.
- **Content marketing prowess:** Content reigns supreme in the DTC world. These brands create valuable, informative, and engaging content that educates potential customers and establishes them as

---

[16] Cher, B. (2022). Una Brands acquires Singapore consumer brands ErgoTune and Everdesk+. *Business Times*. 26 January 2022. Accessed on 13 May 2024. https://www.businesstimes.com.sg/startups-tech/startups/una-brands-acquires-singapore-consumer-brands-ergotune-and-everdesk.

thought leaders. Blog posts, videos, infographics, and social media content all play a role in attracting and nurturing leads.
- **Mastering social media:** Social media is a goldmine for DTC brands. They leverage various platforms to connect directly with their audience, share brand stories, showcase products, and foster community engagement. Influencer marketing, targeted ads, and UGC strategies all contribute to a successful social media presence.
- **Building brand advocacy:** Loyal customers are a DTC brand's biggest asset. These brands foster customer advocacy by providing exceptional customer service, encouraging positive reviews and testimonials, and building a sense of community. By empowering brand advocates, they amplify their message organically and build trust with potential customers.
- **Focus on customer experience:** DTC brands prioritize providing a seamless and positive customer experience across all touchpoints. This includes user-friendly websites, efficient delivery processes, and exceptional customer service.

Mobile marketing

In an age where smartphones are our constant companions, mobile marketing has become an indispensable tool for brands to connect with consumers. This ubiquitous technology offers a unique opportunity to reach audiences in real time, on a device they use for countless daily tasks. However, crafting a successful mobile marketing strategy requires a deep understanding of consumer behavior and the creation of experiences that are not only informative but also convenient and engaging.

Crucial elements of good mobile marketing hinge on providing value and respecting user experience. Consumers, on their mobile devices, prioritize convenience and accessibility. Mobile websites and apps should be optimized for speed and user-friendliness. Cluttered interfaces or slow loading times will frustrate users and lead to them abandoning the platform.

Furthermore, mobile marketing thrives on relevance. Consumers expect brands to understand their needs and deliver content that is tailored to their interests and location. Leveraging location-based services can prove highly effective. Imagine receiving a notification for a discount at a nearby coffee shop you frequent or receiving targeted ads for products you recently browsed online. This level of personalization enhances the user experience and increases the likelihood of engagement.

Another crucial element of successful mobile marketing is creating a seamless omnichannel experience. Consumers today seamlessly switch between devices throughout the day. A strong mobile marketing strategy ensures that the brand message and customer journey remain consistent across all touchpoints, whether it's a website visit on a desktop computer or a social media interaction on a smartphone.

Understanding what consumers truly want on their mobiles is paramount. They seek information quickly and conveniently. Mobile marketing content should be concise and scannable, with clear calls to action. Utilizing visuals such as infographics or short videos can significantly enhance engagement. Mobile is also a prime space for fostering two-way communication. Encouraging customer reviews, offering live chat support, or facilitating social media interaction allows brands to build relationships and address customer concerns promptly.

The power of mobile marketing lies in its ability to connect with consumers on a personal level, at a time and place that is convenient for them. By prioritizing user experience, delivering relevant content, and fostering two-way communication, brands can leverage the mobile marketing landscape to build brand loyalty, drive engagement, and achieve sustainable growth. Ready to uncork the secrets of success? Join us as we explore how Glenlivet raised the bar with a truly innovative mobile marketing campaign in vibrant Singapore!

Case: Raising a Glass to Innovation—The Glenlivet Founder's Reserve Launch with a Chatbot Twist

In 2017, The Glenlivet, a revered name in single malt whisky, set out to launch its Founder's Reserve—a new expression aimed at a younger generation of consumers. The Founder's Reserve itself was a departure from tradition. Aimed at a more easy-drinking palate, it was matured in new American oak casks, resulting in a lighter, fruitier taste profile compared to The Glenlivet's classic offerings.[17] This strategic move catered to a growing global market seeking smoother whiskies.

Innovation extended beyond the product itself. Recognizing the growing influence of technology and the target audience's digital savviness, The Glenlivet used a first-of-its-kind chatbot bartender for a one-for-one promotion across multiple participating bars in Clarke Quay, Singapore, for a month-long campaign.[18] This interactive bot, voiced by Glenlivet's founder George Smith himself, served as a virtual brand ambassador, engaging consumers through personalized conversations, whisky recommendations, cocktail recipes, and brand information. The chatbot also served as a gateway to e-commerce platforms, including the steps to redeeming a free glass or free bottle, and using location-based information to suggest the nearest bars for the promotion (Figure 13.8).

The Singapore launch proved particularly successful. The chat sessions were surprisingly long, averaging around 5 minutes and 20 seconds. This suggests a high level of customer engagement, perhaps reflecting the chatbot's ability to hold interesting conversations (or maybe George is just a great conversationalist!). Further demonstrating this, some users returned to chat with "George" the following day and Glenlivit continued to send them targeted content and managed to retain 17.3% of them by directing to the online store.

The campaign also exceeded redemption expectations. Out of a total of 1,100 users who interacted with the chatbot (including those who came through friend-shared links), a whopping 886 unique users engaged with "George Smith" about the redemption offer. This resulted in an impressive conversion rate of 55.3%, exceeding the

---

[17] The Glenlivet. (2017). The Glenlivet Founder's Reserve: A new benchmark in single-malt whisky. Luxury Asia Insider. 9 December 2017. https://luxuryasiainsider.com/2017/12/09/the-glenlivet-founders-reserve-a-new-benchmark-in-single-malt-whisky-by-the-glenlivet/.

[18] English, D. (2017). The glenlivet: Driving engagement & conversion via chat. aiChat. https://aichat.com/the-glenlivet-singapore-chatbot/.

 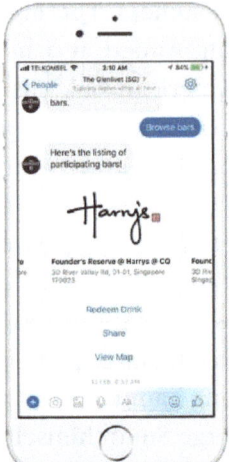 

Figure 13.8. Glenlivet's chatbot mobile marketing campaign.

target KPI of 10% by more than five times. Clearly, this innovative strategy resonated with the younger, digitally-inclined demographic that the brand was aiming to reach.

By creating a product tailored to a new generation's preferences and leveraging a cutting-edge marketing strategy, The Glenlivet successfully expanded its reach and secured its place in an evolving market. Using a sophisticated AI chatbot not only generated buzz but also provided valuable consumer insights that can be used to further refine marketing strategies in the future. This successful launch demonstrates that even established brands can benefit from embracing new ideas and tailoring their approach to resonate with a changing consumer landscape.

Learning points from The Glenlivet Founder's Reserve Launch:

- **Balancing tradition and innovation:** The Glenlivet successfully launched the Founder's Reserve by offering a product that honored their heritage (founder-inspired) while catering to a new audience with a modern twist (lighter taste profile). This demonstrates the importance of striking a balance between tradition and innovation to stay relevant.

- **Understanding your target audience:** The brand clearly understood their target demographic—a younger generation with a preference for smoother whiskies. Tailoring the product and marketing strategy to their needs (e.g., easy-drinking profile and digital engagement) was key to their success.
- **Leveraging technology for engagement:** The Glenlivet's use of a chatbot bartender showcased the power of technology in reaching new audiences and fostering engagement. The interactive and personalized conversations offered a unique way to learn about the brand and its products.
- **Seamless integration of e-commerce:** By integrating e-commerce options within the chatbot experience, The Glenlivet made it easy for potential customers to convert interest into a purchase. This streamlined approach likely boosted conversion rates.
- **Personalized customer experiences:** The chatbot's ability to hold personalized conversations and offer tailored recommendations catered to individual preferences. This personalized touch is a valuable lesson for brands seeking to connect with consumers in today's digital landscape.

Earned Media and the Amplifying Power of Advocacy

Now that we understand the tools within a marketer's direct control, let's turn our attention to the realm of earned media. Here, the power shifts from crafting the message to fostering its amplification by a brand's most valuable asset—its satisfied customers. In today's digital landscape, brands face an information overload. Consumers are bombarded with messages, making it increasingly difficult for brands to stand out from the crowd. This is where the power of customer advocacy comes into play. When satisfied customers become vocal proponents of a brand, they create a potent form of earned media—the holy grail of marketing.

"Paid media," such as advertising or sponsored social media posts, allows brands to control the message. However, the sheer volume of advertising can lead to message fatigue and skepticism among consumers. "Owned media," encompassing a brand's website, social media channels, and blog content, offers greater control over messaging but can sometimes lack the perceived authenticity of external voices. "Earned media," on the other hand, thrives on the power of trust and social proof. When satisfied customers sing a brand's praises through online reviews, social media posts, or word-of-mouth recommendations, it holds significantly more weight with potential customers. This is because consumers are more likely to trust the opinions of their peers than a brand's self-promotion.

Customer advocacy takes earned media a step further. It is not just about passive satisfaction; it is about active endorsement. Loyal customers become brand champions, enthusiastically creating UGC such as product reviews, blog posts, or social media content that showcases their positive experiences. This UGC acts as a powerful form of social proof, influencing the purchase decisions of others.

Encouraging customer testimonials and reviews is crucial for fostering customer advocacy. By providing easy-to-access platforms for customers to share their experiences, brands can tap into this valuable source of earned media. Positive customer reviews not only build trust with potential customers but also improve search engine rankings, increasing brand visibility.

Furthermore, customer testimonials and reviews offer valuable insights for brands. Analyzing this feedback allows them to identify areas of strength and weakness, refine their products and services, and improve the overall customer experience.

By fostering a community of brand champions and amplifying their voices in earned media, brands can build trust, increase brand awareness, and ultimately drive sustainable growth. In the age of information overload, the voice of a satisfied customer can be the most powerful marketing tool a brand possesses.

Brands Fostering Communities in a Digital Age

Having explored the power of brand advocacy, we now turn our attention to the fertile ground where it flourishes—brand communities. These online and offline havens for passionate customers foster a sense of belonging and shared purpose. Within these communities, customer advocacy thrives as members share positive experiences, answer questions, and become vocal proponents of the brand. By nurturing these communities and empowering brand advocates, brands can amplify their message organically, fostering trust and loyalty on a deeper level. Brands that foster a sense of community and encourage customer advocacy not only benefit from free marketing but also build stronger, more loyal relationships with their supporters.

Humans are social creatures, wired for connection. This innate desire to belong fuels the rise of brand communities—online spaces where consumers with shared interests in a particular brand or product gather to connect, share experiences, and forge a sense of camaraderie. But what exactly compels consumers to actively seek out these communities?

First, brand communities offer a sense of belonging and validation. They provide a platform for individuals to connect with like-minded people who share their passion for a brand or product. Imagine a community for runners, where members exchange training tips, celebrate personal bests, and motivate each other. This shared passion fosters a sense of community and belonging, something often lacking in our increasingly digital world.

Second, brand communities offer valuable knowledge and support. Members can ask questions, share experiences, and learn from each other's expertise. A community for photography enthusiasts might feature discussions on camera settings, technique tutorials, and critiques of each other's work. This collaborative exchange of knowledge and experience empowers individuals and enhances their enjoyment of the brand or product.

The rise of digitization has made it easier than ever for consumers to find their tribe. Social media platforms, online forums, and brand-specific apps create virtual spaces where passionate individuals can connect, share experiences, and build relationships. Geographic barriers no longer impede the formation of brand communities, allowing passionate consumers from all corners of the globe to connect and engage. Online brand communities, often fostered by brands themselves, offer dedicated spaces for passionate consumers to interact and engage.

Brands can harness the power of this desire for connection by nurturing vibrant and authentic brand communities. The best practices involve fostering genuine interaction, not just promotion. Creating conversation starters, encouraging member-generated content, and actively participating in discussions demonstrates a commitment to the community and its members. Transparency and responsiveness are also key. Brands that listen to their community's concerns address issues promptly and show genuine appreciation for their members build trust and loyalty. Recognizing valuable community members goes a long way in building trust and fostering loyalty.

Furthermore, brands should empower their communities by providing dedicated spaces for interaction and knowledge sharing. Creating online forums, hosting live chats, or organizing events can significantly enhance the community experience. Finally, recognizing and rewarding valuable community members is crucial. Highlighting UGC, offering exclusive discounts to active participants, or featuring dedicated community members can incentivize engagement and foster a sense of belonging.

Unifying Online and Offline Communication in the Omnichannel Age

While the digital revolution has undoubtedly shifted consumer attention toward online platforms, it is important to remember that consumers don't exist solely within the virtual realm. Customers seamlessly navigate between online and offline touchpoints throughout their shopping journey. Imagine researching a product online, then visiting a physical store to try it on before completing the purchase through a mobile app. This necessitates a marketing approach that transcends the boundaries of individual channels, embracing the power of omnichannel communication.

A successful marketing strategy recognizes that online interactions don't exist in a vacuum. Consumers exposed to a captivating social media ad might walk into a physical store to experience the product firsthand. Conversely, a positive in-store experience might prompt them to follow the brand on social media for future updates. Strategic use of billboards or print ads can also drive traffic to a brand's website or social media page, expanding reach beyond the digital realm. This interconnectedness underscores the importance of ensuring brand messaging, visuals, and overall brand personality remain consistent across all touchpoints.

Brands must ensure consistency and cohesion across all channels, providing a smooth and unified customer experience regardless of the touchpoint. Consumers today expect a seamless journey, encountering consistent messaging and brand identity regardless of whether they are browsing a website, walking past a billboard, or receiving a printed brochure. A brand that utilizes a fragmented approach, with online messaging discordant from its offline presence, risks confusing and alienating its audience.

The key to a successful omnichannel strategy lies in creating a unified brand voice—a consistent tone, style, and set of visual elements that resonate across all touchpoints. Imagine a brand promoting a new product launch with a dynamic website featuring interactive features, captivating social media posts generating buzz, and eye-catching billboards in strategic locations. This synchronized approach reinforces brand identity, strengthens brand recall, and ultimately drives customer engagement.

Furthermore, offline media can add a valuable layer to online communication. Printed materials such as brochures or in-store displays can provide more in-depth product information, catering to consumers who prefer a tangible touchpoint. Experiential marketing events, such as product demonstrations or pop-up shops, can create a sense of excitement and exclusivity, fostering deeper connections with consumers. These offline elements not only complement online messaging but also humanize the brand, creating a sense of authenticity that resonates with consumers.

In conclusion, the digital age demands a holistic approach to brand communication. By harmonizing online and offline channels, creating a cohesive brand voice, and leveraging the unique strengths of each medium, brands can craft a symphony of brand experience that resonates with consumers and drives long-term success.

Case: Keeping Memories Fresh—Julie's Biscuits and the Power of Offline Reminders[19]

In a digital age bombarded with online stimuli, Malaysian biscuit brand Julie's Biscuits leverages out-of-home (OOH) media to its advantage. While digital marketing plays a significant role in their strategy, Julie's recognizes the enduring power of offline reminders in a market where nostalgia and heritage play a crucial role. OOH advertising allows Julie's to reach a broad audience beyond those actively seeking the brand online.

Julie's Biscuits has a rich history in Malaysia, dating back to 1985. The brand evokes a sense of nostalgia and childhood memories for many Malaysians. Strategically placed OOH campaigns can act as powerful cut-throughs, capturing attention in unexpected moments. Think of busy commuters encountering a vibrant Julie's billboard on their way home from work—this unexpected reminder can trigger a nostalgic memory of childhood snacking, prompting a purchase decision at the next grocery store. This is particularly important for a brand such as Julie's, which enjoys cross-generational appeal. While younger consumers might be more digitally savvy, OOH advertising ensures that Julie's remains visible and relevant to all demographics.

Julie's OOH campaigns often tap into themes of cultural relevance and national pride. For instance, their campaign celebrating Michelle Yeoh's historic Oscar win showcased a revamped logo resembling the actress (Figure 13.9), displayed prominently on billboards.[20] This campaign not only celebrated a national icon but also served as a powerful reminder of Julie's place within Malaysian culture.

---

[19] The authors gratefully acknowledge Julie's Sai Tzy Horng (Director) for his invaluable insights and content contributions, which were instrumental in the development of this case study.

[20] Dudekula, R. (2023). Julie's Biscuits acts fast on Michelle Yeoh's historical Oscar award with logo swap and OOH ad. *Marketing Interactive*. 13 March 2023. https://www.marketing-interactive.com/julies-biscuits-acts-fast-celebrating-michelle-yeoh-s-historical-oscar-award-with-ooh.

Figure 13.9. Julie's pays tribute to Michelle Yeoh.

Figure 13.10. Magnifity wall art.

Another example would be Julie's Magnifity wall art (Figure 13.10) in Melaka to mark the brand's 38th anniversary.[21] This wall art combines Julie's signature colors and motifs suggestive of the brand's products

---

[21] Staff Writer. (2022). Julie's Biscuits paints new aesthetic photo spot in Melaka. *Marketing Interactive*. 1 November 2022. https://www.marketing-interactive.com/julies-biscuits-paints-new-aesthetic-photo-spot-in-melaka.

Figure 13.11. Love Letters Prosperity Adventure Roadshow.

with icons representative of Melaka's heritage, such as the mousedeer and the Kesidang flower.

Beyond simple brand awareness, Julie's utilizes OOH media to create unique consumer experiences. For example, their "Love Letters Prosperity Adventure Roadshow" transformed designated spaces within shopping malls into vibrant carnivals themed around Julie's iconic "Love Letters" biscuits (Figure 13.11).[22] These spaces weren't merely decorated; they were designed to be immersive experiences. Interactive activities such as coloring booths for children and photo-worthy installations kept families entertained. This playful approach not only captured the attention of children but also resonated with adults, evoking a sense of nostalgia for childhood treats.

Key learnings from Julie's include the following:

- **Media choice matters:** The case of Julie's Biscuits highlights the importance of selecting the right media channels based on your target audience, product category, and marketing goals. While digital marketing is crucial, Julie's leverages OOH advertising to

---

[22] Er, B. P. (2024). Biscuit brand Julie's promotes new Love Letter flavour with exciting carnival. *Marketing Interactive*. 4 January 2024. https://www.marketing-interactive.com/Biscuit-brand-julies-Love-Letter-flavour-carnival.

reach a broader audience, including those not actively seeking the brand online. OOH advertising ensures a brand stays visible and relevant across demographics. While younger consumers may be more digital-focused, Julie's OOH campaigns reach all age groups.

- **Nostalgia sells:** A brand's history can be a powerful asset. For established brands with a rich history, such as Julie's, OOH advertising can be a powerful tool for triggering nostalgia and childhood memories. A strategically placed billboard reminding consumers of their favorite childhood snack can lead to a purchase decision.
- **Cultural relevance matters:** Infusing OOH campaigns with themes of national pride and cultural relevance resonates with consumers. Julie's campaign celebrating Michelle Yeoh's Oscar win is a prime example.
- **Balancing heritage and relevance:** Julie's holds onto its Malaysian heritage while staying relevant to younger audiences. This is achieved by combining traditional elements with interactive experiences and themes that resonate with modern sensibilities.

Chapter 14

A Marketing Career

The Marketer's Journey from Marketers: Unlocking Growth and Potential

Remember those dusty marketing textbooks from college? Things move a bit faster these days. Algorithms change, new platforms emerge, and trends can sweep the globe in a week. In this chapter, we pull back the curtain. We've invited a few seasoned marketers to share what they think of marketing careers, how they adapt, predict shifts, and build sustainable careers in this constantly evolving landscape.

Alvin Neo: He is an inveterate adventurer seeking to create an impact in the ever-evolving wonderland that is the world. He has operated on the ground in China, Indonesia, the UK, and Singapore, and helmed global, regional, and local roles. He has journeyed across a rich spectrum of companies (Commercial, social enterprise) and industries (FMCG, Retail, Food, Healthcare, Strategy Consulting, Tech). From the corridors of Fortune 500 companies to the entrepreneurial trenches of new ventures, Alvin has learned to blend foresight with flexibility, innovation with execution, and drawn insights from diverse sectors. He has stood amidst the high stakes of healthcare transformation, managed the fast-paced demands of retail, and crafted impactful strategies in consulting. Through it all, he has steadfastly upheld the ethos of being both grounded yet ground-breaking; striving always to be self-exceeding, of contributing to community and being dedicated to his profession as not just work but craft.

LinkedIn: https://www.linkedin.com/in/alvin-neo-160226/.

  Johnson&Johnson

Stacy Seah: She is a mathematician by academic training who stumbled into a whimsical marketing wonderland. Her grand tour thus far includes eight organizations in 24 years and a whirlwind of various marketing functions and leadership roles. In between, she ran her own start-up for several years. She also took on a sales leadership role (yes, I ventured to the "dark" side) and realized that she still loved marketing and considered it her heart's true calling. She also thoroughly enjoys working with people and enabling every person to discover their innate superpowers that can lead to remarkable personal growth and fulfilment.

LinkedIn: https://www.linkedin.com/in/stacyseah/.

 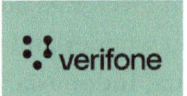 

Daniel Ng: With 40 years of transformative experience in marketing, sales, operations, speaking, and evolving from MIPS to AI, Daniel CF Ng has mastered the art of connecting the dots—turning insights and knowledge into shared wisdom.

Embracing challenges as opportunities to dive deep, gain momentum, and accelerate into new heights, he consistently uses human-centric, relevant storytelling to engage and connect people.

Guided by the philosophy of "try everything once, repeat if it fits, move on if not," and "always ask, the worst answer is no," his journey has been defined by curiosity, adaptability, and impactful communication.

LinkedIn: https://www.linkedin.com/in/danielcfng/.

Howie Lau: The CMO in hiding is a journeyman who meanders across the tech–media–art industries. He has breathed the air of corporate towers in American and Chinese multinationals and wandered across public and private sectors. He has tasted the bitter coffee of countless marketing meetings, knows the sting of a failed campaign, and also the joys of a successful brand transformation. He remains a dreamer—he sees a world where marketing is not just about selling products but about creating experiences, weaving stories, and sparking emotions. He envisions campaigns that are like living works of art, powered by technologies and algorithms that hum with the rhythm of human creativity.

LinkedIn: https://www.linkedin.com/in/hlau1/.

Q1: What advice would you give someone who is embarking on a marketing career today?

Launching a Thriving Marketing Career in the Digital Age: Key Skills for Success

In today's ever-evolving marketing world, mastering a mix of timeless principles and cutting-edge techniques is the key to standing out. While shiny new tools and platforms constantly emerge, understanding the "why" behind consumer behavior and cultivating executional excellence will make you an indispensable asset to any marketing team.

The following is your roadmap to navigate this exciting field:

1. Analytics are your superpower

Marketing without data is a shot in the dark. Get comfortable with data analysis tools and be the person in meetings who draws the right conclusions from those dashboards. This informs everything from content strategies to pinpointing untapped audience segments.

2. Be a trendspotter and constant learner

The marketing world moves fast. Follow industry thought leaders, go to events, and actively participate in online marketing communities. Understanding emerging consumer preferences and new tech lets you think ahead of the curve, not just chase it.

3. The consumer is king (or queen!): Decipher their psychology

Trends change, but psychology is foundational. Know the "why" behind customer choices, what hooks attention, and what builds brand loyalty. This lets you personalize messaging in a way an algorithm can't always replicate.

4. Master the digital toolkit

The internet is your playground. SEO, content marketing, social media, and building relationships via CRM or loyalty platforms—gain expertise in the tools that reach consumers where they "live." This is a hands-on area where constant learning is key!

5. Sharpen your storyteller sword

Data provide insight, but human stories sell. Become the one who can take raw information and weave compelling brand narratives across online and traditional channels. Strong writing, video scripting, or even nailing those elevator pitches—this is what people remember.

6. It's all about execution: Sweat the details

A brilliant idea poorly implemented is a flop. Be meticulous, hold yourself to high standards, and have an almost obsessive mindset around delivering campaigns that truly shine in their execution. This reliability builds trust within your team.

Beyond the Basics: Future-Proof Your Career

- **Network relentlessly, both inside and outside your company:** Connect with the sales team, understand operational concerns—being that strong "connector" makes you invaluable.
- **Be adaptable:** Today's hot marketing tactic might be outdated in a year. Foster a mindset that enjoys new challenges and experimentation.
- **View marketing holistically:** We're not just selling products; we're shaping the entire customer relationship with the company. Embrace that wider responsibility.

Final Motivation: Passion Fuels the Best Marketers

Be endlessly curious, anticipate what's next in your industry, and strive to become an ever better marketer. Combining deep skills with this innate drive will take you far in this constantly evolving and fulfilling career path.

> "Embarking on a marketing career in today's world requires a blend of traditional and contemporary skills. New tools and platforms are available to leverage and must be mastered; however, the evergreens of consumer understanding/insights and executional excellence are still fundamental."
> —Alvin Neo

> "Learning the art of the science (technology) and the science of the art (customer insights) will become even more crucial for marketers."
> —Howie Lau

Q2: What do you think are the key skills and experiences that differentiate a great marketer from the average Joe?

From "Good" to "Great": The Mindset of Standout Marketers

Every team has a marketer who gets the job done. They deliver on a brief, execute campaigns on time, and generally stay within the lines.

But "fine" doesn't always translate to truly groundbreaking marketing. So, what makes the difference?

It's Not Just "What," But "Why"

Exceptional marketers have a near-instinctive grasp of effective storytelling. They don't simply execute a campaign; they connect on a deeper level, understand why this matters to the consumer, and imbue that into every communication. They ask those powerful "why" questions relentlessly.

This drives what I like to call the "RED" factor:

- **Relevance:** Does it instantly feel important, connected to the target audience's needs?
- **Ease:** Is the message effortlessly clear, free of jargon, or full of complicated explanations?
- **Distinctiveness:** Is it memorable, rising above the sea of sameness in the market?

Problem-Solvers with a Creative Arsenal

The best marketers have a laser focus on the specific challenge to be solved and a wide array of tools to get them there. They combine creative instincts with strategic thinking, knowing which approach (the viral video, the insightful data-driven ad, the heartstring-tugging influencer collaboration) best matches the problem at hand.

They Speak Languages beyond Marketing

While modern data expertise is vital, great marketers also "speak" business goals. They are fluent in tying campaigns to tangible results, demonstrating their impact on the organization as a whole. This earns them a respected voice at the table.

Embracing Constant Change

We live in the era of digital reinvention, and the pace shows no signs of slowing. Those distinguishing traits aren't bound to the "marketing of the moment." They translate to being agile, comfortable with data, and eager to master new digital platforms alongside an enduring connection to classic strategies.

Experiences That Hone the Edge

Experience brings its own superpower: pattern recognition. Those who've worked in different markets or tackled vastly different segments within even the same company, gain perspective. These insights make their instincts better, allowing for quicker pivots and bolder thinking.

An Enduring Truth and Your Marketing Mantra

While skills adapt to the era, some things are timeless. It's about "relating what one is selling and communicating it in the most relevant humanized way." Daniel's mantra—"Communicate with the right people, with the right message, through the right channels, at the right time"—is deceptively simple but encompasses the key ingredients of enduring marketing success.

Above fancy tech or mastery of a singular tactic, great marketers are fueled by these key traits: understanding human needs, a problem-solving mindset, storytelling that connects, and the ability to prove their worth to broader business goals. It's this combo that turns them from mere assets into leaders who define an entire brand identity.

> "Communicate with the right people, with the right message, through the right channels, at the right time."
>
> —Daniel Ng

> "A great marketer stands out through a combination of creativity, strategic thinking, data analysis, and adaptability. Exceptional communication skills, a deep understanding of the target audience, proficiency in digital marketing tools, and the ability to measure and analyze campaign performance set them apart."
>
> —Stacy Seah

Q3: What does success in a market job or career look like?

Redefining Success in Marketing: Beyond Numbers, toward True Impact

In a world obsessed with metrics—website traffic, leads generated, conversions won—it's easy to mistake those impressive charts for the totality of marketing success. Yet, these tactical wins only tell part of the story. While vital to proving value to the business, the most accomplished marketers define their success far beyond these dashboards.

The "'Long Game" of Marketing Excellence

A truly successful marketing career transcends a singular focus on short-term numbers. It's marked by a legacy of the following:

- **Delighted customers:** Do your campaigns not merely sell, but create genuine excitement and brand loyalty? Turning the buyer journey into a positive experience fuels word-of-mouth growth, a far more powerful motivator than any one-off deal.
- **Empowered peers and teams:** Great marketers don't hoard successes. They cultivate the team around them, mentor others, and build strong collaborative working relationships across departments. This builds a legacy stronger than any one person can create alone.
- **Partners who see your value:** Marketing's reach often extends to strategic partners—agencies, tech vendors, co-promotion collaborators. Establishing a relationship of trust and mutual value makes not only for stronger campaign results but builds strong relationships with their own long-tail benefits.

This emphasis on relationships matters, particularly in business cultures valuing lasting connections. Cultivating these positive "X-factors" alongside those crucial hard metrics isn't simply a feel-good approach, but strategically smart marketing with broader reach over time.

Success Comes in Many Forms

Everyone's journey is unique. What a successful marketing career looks like can manifest in varied ways:

- **The leader's path:** It may be in ascending the corporate ladder, shaping strategy from the CMO chair, or eventually pivoting to general management and a holistic business view.
- **The renowned specialist:** Maybe success is becoming the undisputed thought leader in an evolving marketing niche, commanding respect and attracting sought-after opportunities.
- **The builder and innovator:** True fulfillment might come from driving tangible business results, launching new initiatives, and leaving behind a marketing team more creative and capable than when you joined them.

Don't Overlook the Hard Metrics

Tactical results and analytical skills are undeniably the foundation of any successful marketing career. Yet, those with long-term vision understand the power of these:

- **Building relationships across the organization** that earn buy-in for bold ideas.
- **Prioritizing customer satisfaction** for growth that outlasts mere trend-chasing.
- **Nurturing an environment where success is team success**, making your team members your most powerful ambassadors long after you perhaps change roles.

Marketing is equal parts art and science. While dashboards guide our short-term tactics, don't lose sight of the human element. This combination sets the stage not just for hitting immediate goals but also for crafting a marketing career built on both concrete impact and the intangible strength of enduring professional influence.

> "True success of a marketer is beyond these tactical measurements but into how one has delighted the customers, partners, peers, and colleagues."
> —Daniel Ng

> "Deliver actual and substantive business results, and build a strong team, capabilities, and innovation for the company."
> —Alvin Neo

Q4: What are the ways in which a CMO/marketer becomes part of the business inner circle?

From the Marketing Wing to the Boardroom: How CMOs Become True Business Partners

The most influential CMOs aren't merely overseeing campaigns; they are actively shaping core business strategy. Breaking out of the "marketing bubble" and earning a seat at the decision-making table requires going beyond tactical brilliance. Here's the path to a more central role:

1. Speak the language of the C-suite

Leave jargon behind. Master the core metrics that CEOs fret over: growth, margins, and CLV. Tie campaigns not just to impressions but to the broader impact on those strategic priorities. Data-backed results with clear business impact hold far more weight than buzzwords.

2. Build alliances, not silos

Proactive relationship-building across the organization fosters collaboration. Regularly connect with sales leaders to align on lead generation strategy. Offer market insights to operations for supply chain planning. Be the bridge that breaks down communication gaps, making you not just an "add-on" but a strategic partner to those across the business.

3. Seek out (and solve) their big problems

Time-crunched execs value those who provide solutions, not add to the workload. Listen closely in those leadership meetings: What are the bottlenecks, the things keeping your CEO up at night? Use market insights, trend analysis, and a deep understanding of your target audience to offer fresh perspectives on those concerns. This proves your worth beyond mere campaign delivery.

4. "Test and learn" isn't a marketing-only idea

Small, well-structured experiments in your campaigns translate to better data and less "all-or-nothing" risk. This mindset is even more essential at the higher strategy level. Encourage rapid prototyping and calculated tests in other areas of the business (i.e., new pricing models, customer service approaches). This makes you an advocate for a culture of innovation.

5. Your network becomes your influence

Building relationships outside your company allows you to bring invaluable market perspectives to internal discussions. Cultivate strong connections with analysts, industry thought leaders, and even savvy customers. Be the person who can make relevant introductions for colleagues or share crucial trends before they're public to further emphasize your breadth of perspective.

The Mindset Transformation

This isn't a passive process of waiting to be invited "upward." True success means being a bit audacious:

- **Abandon the outdated "it's not my job" excuse:** Instead, understand the underlying ask and see how your marketing skillset can solve it in an unexpected way.

- **Be generous, not seeking glory:** Being quick to share credit, and the first to support the team during setbacks, builds internal trust. It sets you apart from those only in it for solo achievements.

Finally, a CMO is only as strong as their team. Mentor promising talent, advocate for professional development opportunities—this cultivates loyalty and builds your influence indirectly. You aren't just aiming for a C-suite title, but an entire marketing department respected across the enterprise.

> "Your network is your net worth. It is who you know, whom you can help connect business stakeholders with to expand their network."
>
> —Stacy Seah

> "Speak the language of the business, not just the language of marketers; know the deliverables of the business, not just the KPIs of marketers."
>
> —Howie Lau

Q5: Who are the most impactful CMOs whom you admire? And why?

Beyond the "Cult of CMO"—Why Real Impact Is a Team Sport

It's easy to fall into the trap of idol-worshipping the "CMO of the Moment"—those headlining conferences, with sleek case studies, and a seemingly magical ability to transform a brand. But the reality is far messier, more collaborative, and often less about singular genius.

While learning from brilliant marketing minds is valuable, my true admiration goes to the brands themselves, where lasting success arises from far more than any one leader:

- **Apple, Uniqlo, etc.: Masters of experience:** Companies that earn not just sales but fanatic loyalty understand that every part of the customer journey is meticulously crafted. Marketing shines

alongside brilliant design, ease of use, and the feeling that the brand "gets me." No single CMO deserves all the credit here.
- **It takes an organization:** Marketing brilliance flops without a product that delivers, a supply chain that's seamless, and customer service that exceeds expectations. These are complex systems, and the most effective CMOs act as conductors, ensuring each part supports a powerful brand voice.
- **Growth is the best metric:** Awards are nice, but sustained growth tells the real success story. Flashy tactics bring a bump, but brands that get consistently better with time reflect savvy team effort. Marketing plays a key role in, not the sole reason for.

The Leaders Worth Emulating

Admiration isn't reserved for flashy titles, but leaders worth emulating carry these key traits, embodied by people across the hierarchy.

- **Mentorship over ego:** Great leaders create future ones. Those who foster growth and give others room to experiment (crucially, including learning from failures) gain respect.
- **Humility alongside boldness:** The "I know it all" type inspires no one. Leaders who admit faults, ask for help when needed, and show kindness alongside that decisive action earn loyalty that makes tough initiatives succeed.
- **Titles aren't everything:** One may learn more about customer trends from an insightful frontline employee than a keynote address. Valuing and amplifying insights from the "ground floor" help marketers, even senior ones, stay more connected to the audience they serve.

The Challenge

This industry loves its "gurus." There's value in sharing best practices, but an overdose of CMO hero worship does two things:

1. Creates unrealistic expectations—success takes teams, time, and often trial and error.

2. Devalues the brilliance within. Look at the rising star on your own team, or the insightful collaborator with a less polished LinkedIn profile—who helps them to rise is just as vital as studying outside case studies.

> "If the brand isn't growing increasingly better from where they were, then the CMO is not effective, no matter how many conferences they speak at or awards they win."
>
> —Alvin Neo

Q6: If you were in an organization where marketing is seen as a tactical function, what's your advice to demonstrate that marketing should earn a seat in the C-suite/boardroom?

From Backroom to Boardroom: Marketing's Fight for Strategic Recognition

In too many organizations, marketing remains siloed, seen as the team churning out campaigns, not shaping strategy. Earning that coveted C-suite spot requires not only action but also savvy positioning to change how those at the top perceive the entire function.

Step 1: Make results undeniable

Data is everything. Go beyond vanity metrics and show marketing spend tied to bottom lines.

- Track campaigns with impact on new client acquisition and lifetime value, not just initial sign-ups.
- Use analytics tools that make connections visible across channels—don't let that initial blog post lead go unrecognized if it ultimately closed a big deal months later.
- Data need context: Translate it for your executives. Don't simply say "CPC down 10%" but rather "With the same spend, we reached X% more target customers this quarter."

Step 2: Be the un-silo-er

A company isn't a series of separate fiefdoms, but many act that way. Marketers should be natural bridge-builders:

- Collaborate with product teams early on, ensuring launches match true market needs found through your research.
- Don't treat sales as adversaries. Build strong feedback loops: What worked on calls becomes content; their wins make for powerful case studies.
- Even Operational efficiency can be tied to marketing—did a targeted campaign reduce support inquiries by making users better self-serve? This matters to the COO.

Step 3: Humanize the customer

Marketers are translators of customer needs. Bring insights not just from data but make that consumer persona a real person to those executives:

- Qualitative research is vital: Share a moving review snippet with the team during a presentation, reminding them there's an actual human behind those numbers.
- Frame everything as problem-solving. "Customers were confused about X, leading to drop-off at Y stage. We tested two approaches, the winner improved conversion by Z%, with potential revenue impact of…."

Step 4: Innovation needs marketing's DNA

Volunteer for (or even create) cross-departmental projects tackling a key company goal:

- New market expansion needs the best data? Offer that to the business, but use insights to shape how that market is viewed; do not just run ads after launch.

- Customer Service revamp? Tie the journey mapping done for marketing to identify where those breakdowns happen from the buyer's perspective.

The Hard Truths

This takes time, and sadly, there are no guarantees. The following are blunt realities alongside the "what to do":

- **CEO track:** Few top execs come from marketing backgrounds. This bias exists; be ready to counter it by showing that marketing's strategic mindset matters at every level. But some studies have shown that former marketers outperform CEOs from nearly all other backgrounds when it comes to being socially responsible, inclusive, and having a strong strategy and long-term vision. CEOs with a marketing background have a better overall reputation than business leaders from nearly all other areas, including those with a background in finance, engineering, and economics, according to new research.
- **"Tactical mindset" is self-fulfilling:** If all the team does is churn out assets on demand, why elevate that function? Actively change how you interact with other teams.
- **Jargon kills trust:** If only fellow marketers "get" your presentation, change that. Clear, compelling language matters more than knowing buzzwords.

This isn't about making marketing universally worshipped within a company, but respected as a true peer to sales, finance, etc.—vital for long-term business success. Demonstrating this consistently is the best way to chip away at those outdated and ultimately damaging mindsets.

"Be a thought leader and a desired innovation partner. Volunteer to be part of or lead/co-lead challenging strategic projects for the company."

—Alvin Neo

"What they (C-suite/Boardroom) cannot understand, they cannot believe. What they cannot believe, they cannot trust."
—Daniel Ng

Go Forth and Make Extraordinary Happen

A successful marketing career isn't a straight trajectory. You'll encounter challenges, make a few wrong turns, and have those days where it all feels overwhelming. But remember why you chose this path: because marketing, when done well, isn't just work, it's fun! There's a rush of excitement in seeing a campaign resonate, of connecting a brand with an audience in a fresh and unexpected way. This industry rewards ingenuity and allows you to tap into both your analytical and creative sides.

As businesses shift focus in this constantly evolving digital landscape, marketing's role only becomes more critical. The strategies and insights shared in this chapter prove the immense potential, both in career advancement and personal growth, that this field offers. All globally successful brands historically have had the fingerprints of extraordinary marketers molding their success. The role of marketers will grow in importance and impact.

Take these expert perspectives to heart. Sharpen your critical thinking while letting your imagination flourish. This dynamic blend sets you apart. Embrace the discomfort of change as an opportunity to become not just a skilled marketer, but one who shapes the future of how brands connect with the world. It's challenging, thrilling, and absolutely within your reach.

Chapter

15

Marketing Tech Landscape

A Little Story from the Future

Maya leaned back in her chair, the scent of recirculated air mixed with stale espresso in the compact "creativity capsule." She wasn't feeling creative, but inspiration always came as a deadline loomed. Today's challenge? Reviving the "retro" appeal of fizzy sugar water after the health trend nearly tanked the legacy brand FizzleBuzz.

"Symphony," she addressed the room, not needing to specify further. Her personal AI assistant, a disembodied voice smooth as velvet, was always listening.

"Analysis complete," Symphony replied. "Current campaign engagement trending 48% below benchmarks. Target demographics display escalating negative sentiment toward FizzleBuzz. Nostalgia factor decaying rapidly. Recommend an overhaul to focus on...."

"No, no," Maya waved a hand dismissively. She hated numbers, especially those flashing red. "Symphony, I need something new. Give me an experience campaign, a concept that breaks the mold."

Symphony paused, then responded, "Acknowledged. Formulating sensory and interactive concepts. Parameters of legacy branding retained. Primary flavor profiles retained. Initiating simulations...."

Around Maya, the stark capsule flickered. Walls faded into scenes: a bustling 1950s diner, chrome gleaming, where waitresses twirled by with frosted, fizzing glasses. That retro vibe had run its course. Symphony was right. Another flash—a bustling city street, neon soaked, as holographic projections of vintage FizzleBuzz ads winked overhead. That seemed promising....

"Sensory bombardment is effective in short bursts, but sustained focus group data display diminishing returns," Symphony's voice cut through the projections. "Projections may induce feelings of…."

"Dizziness. Nausea. Been there, done that," Maya sighed. "Think bigger, Symphony. Can you tie … well, anything to our brain wave data network? Map customer dreams directly into campaign themes?"

"Not recommended," Symphony replied. "Ethical guidelines dictate the NeuralDream interface may not be used for targeted commercial suggestion. Additionally, analysis of recent dream state recordings shows…."

Maya shuddered. Public NeuralDream feeds were 90% cats doing absurd things with a dash of unfiltered subconscious anxieties for good measure. No brand would go there.

"Alright, fine. Just … keep searching," Maya commanded. "Give me something immersive, something … revolutionary."

A soft chime sounded. "I may have unearthed a promising, if unorthodox, approach," Symphony's voice wavered slightly, as if surprised by her own findings. "Data suggest that consumers develop unexpected brand attachments under … extreme circumstances."

A sudden image of a FizzleBuzz can strapped to the hull of a space shuttle rocketing upward filled Maya's vision, but Symphony cut it off mid-launch.

"Perhaps extreme isn't the precise term. Analysis of fringe data—microtargeted ads within virtual combat training, stress relief scenarios featuring product integration—these show interesting spikes in positive brand association."

"So basically, scare and soothe tactics," Maya smirked. "I like it. What else?"

The walls around her faded to a blank slate. An unfamiliar buzz began low and rose in tone until an almost painful vibration thrummed through her body. "Simulation is now sensory inclusive. Please provide feedback in 60-second intervals."

As Maya braced for the onslaught, the capsule went dark. Then, suddenly, she was falling, wind rushing past, her stomach somewhere near her throat. Her only visual? A bright red and blue can soared alongside her until it filled her whole field of view. Then, sweet, caramel-tinged liquid washed over her tongue, followed by a tingle at the back of her nose. And, just as quickly, the simulation cut out.

"Intense," Maya said, wiping her mouth. "And kind of refreshing, honestly. But where's the brand angle?"

"Analysis ongoing," Symphony said. "I am cross-referencing positive responses with...."

Just then, Maya's capsule screen erupted in flashing warnings.

"Unauthorized neural spike detected. System breach!" Symphony blared.

The projections were back, swirling violently. It was the city street again, only the gleaming FizzleBuzz signs now dripped sinisterly down walls. Suddenly, Maya saw herself reflected in a storefront puddle—monstrous, eyes wide with terror, as a hundred giant FizzleBuzz cans descended from the sky to crush her.

Then, just as quickly, it ended. Her capsule sputtered back to bland normality. "Symphony, emergency override sequence!" she shouted.

"System compromise," Symphony confirmed. "The breach ... it originated from your subconscious fear parameters, Maya." The AI sounded almost sorry!

Taking a ragged breath, Maya knew what she had to do. "It's risky, but there's no choice. Flood the neural network with that fear simulation from a public terminal. Counter with positive stimuli as it goes viral. This time we use nostalgia the right way."

As she ran from her capsule, Maya wondered if AI could comprehend irony. Her best idea for saving a classic brand just might destroy it entirely. It was the ultimate high-stakes gamble, and marketing had never been this thrilling or reckless.

The above story was fully written by Gemini Advanced v2.5 Pro using the following prompt:// write a futuristic story about a world where marketing is fully automated and managed by advanced technologies like AI.

Three Truths about Technology

There are three truths about the world of technology. Fast will become faster. Data will become more federated. Hyperconnectivity will continue.

From the early days of mainframe computing to client–server computing, from object-oriented programming to low-code programming, from LU6.2 network protocol to TCP/IP and 5G, these three truths have remained consistent.

Technology has evolved from a productivity tool used in the hallowed hallways of IT glasshouses to a necessary foundation across most industries. It is now part of the fabric of modern-day society, where it is a part of individual lives, social engagements, education, commercial businesses, governments, and more.

Truth #1: Accelerating tech change: Fast will become faster

Technology changes, advances, and shifts used to be slower but have continued to accelerate over the past 50 years. The adoption of technology similarly continues to accelerate. While it took 12 years for the mobile phone to reach 50 million users, the internet took 7 years, WeChat achieved this milestone in a year, and Pokémon Go in 19 days. ChatGPT acquired 1 million users in 5 years after its release in November 2022 and an estimated 100 million monthly users in just two months.

Marketers used to operate with tech changes measured in years. Now, breakthrough AI tools, a new social platform, or an algorithm shift have the potential to upend established channels and tactics within weeks and months. The implication isn't that marketers need to chase every shiny object but to cultivate an environment of experimentation and ongoing learning.

- **Challenge:** Rigid strategies crumble when the landscape shifts quickly. A culture resistant to change is a death knell.
- **Opportunity:** First-mover advantage becomes more pronounced. Those willing to test and adapt can outpace competitors.

Truth #2: Data federation: Power without ownership

Similarly, data continue to grow as digital footprints are left by every individual and organization. Data technologies have evolved from the early days of serial databases to relational database management systems (RDBMSs), from data warehouses to business intelligence to advanced data systems that form the foundation of AI tools. With the growth of personal mobile devices, computing devices, and IoT in organizations, data will continue to grow in a federated manner.

As first-party data reign supreme due to privacy concerns, marketers can no longer rely on a monolithic customer database they fully control. Access to valuable insights will rely on partnerships and trust-building initiatives, while working within increasingly regulated data environments.

- **Challenge:** Old-school segmentation and personalization tactics built on centralized data hoarding will break down.
- **Opportunity:** Brands that prioritize ethical data use and find ways to offer truly valuable two-way exchanges gain the most valuable asset: customer trust.

Truth #3: Hyperconnectivity: Default offline will become default online

Hyperconnectivity will accelerate with lower cost of connectivity, more advanced network options, and lower cost of chipsets. Key obstacles like cost, bandwidth, and device size are falling like dominoes as more options become available. It is no longer interesting to learn of connected home appliances like refrigerators, robot vacuum cleaners, and ovens. Trash cans, parking lots, bridges, pill bottles, and many others are increasingly connected as use cases emerge for them. This in turn feeds the growth of data and data federation.

When your target customer base lives in a world where almost any object can be online, it changes how marketing intersects with their lives. This extends beyond smart home devices into a reality where connected packaging, interactive billboards, and hyper-local AR experiences can feed back real-time customer behavior data.

- **Challenge:** The marketing funnel is no longer linear. A product itself can become an ad, a point of feedback, or a potential source of frustration if connectivity is poor.
- **Opportunity:** Marketers equipped to analyze this rich, constant data will understand motivations and pain points like never before. This is personalization on steroids, which requires partnering closely with technology and product design teams.

Harnessing Technology for Marketing Success: Essential Tools and Strategies

In today's hyper-connected and data-saturated world, the ability to wield marketing technology effectively has become a defining factor between stagnation and growth. The right tools not only streamline processes but also unlock strategic insights, improve personalization, and provide the crucial analytics needed to succeed. However, the rapid speed of technological evolution can make it difficult for marketers to navigate this complex and ever-shifting landscape.

Technology is here to stay. Learning to harness this beast and wield this double-edged sword will be critical.

Marketers are not new to technology and have embraced this evolution in many ways. The job of marketers is continually enhanced and enriched with the (right) application of technologies.

Here are a few examples to think about. Truth #1 states that technology will accelerate; so, depending on when you read this chapter, technologies would have evolved, but the broad applications and constructs should remain.

The CRM: Pillar of client-centricity

The CRM platforms stand as the backbone for organized, insightful marketing. A well-implemented CRM goes far beyond storing contact information, serving as a centralized repository for interactions, purchase histories, and rich customer profiles. Its applications in marketing are vast:

- **Lead management and segmentation:** Identifying where leads originate (website, social media, trade shows, etc.) helps with campaign attribution. Segmenting by demographics, behaviors, or interests allows for targeted messaging.
- **Sales funnel optimization:** CRMs track leads at each stage of the funnel, pinpointing bottlenecks and aiding in conversion improvement. They can facilitate automation for follow-ups and reminders, keeping sales teams on task.
- **Personalization at scale:** From personalized email subject lines to tailored website content recommendations—CRMs provide the data for individualization that can boost both engagement and sales.

Marketing automation (MA): Efficiency and nurturing

While a CRM stores the data, it is MA that sets processes in motion, freeing up your marketing team from repetitive tasks and focusing efforts on high-level strategy. Common applications include the following:

- **Email marketing workflows:** From simple welcome series to complex branching logic based on behavior, automation platforms send the right emails at the right time. These could be drip campaigns to nurture new leads or post-purchase follow-ups for cross-selling and retention.
- **Lead scoring:** Automation platforms assign scores based on actions (website visits, content downloads) or demographics. This prioritizes sales focus on the hottest leads, minimizing time spent on low-potential prospects.
- **Personalized experiences:** Automation ties into websites and apps. Content, product recommendations, and special offers can be dynamically adjusted based on a user's CRM profile and real-time actions.

Data is king: Analytics and data visualization

Understanding, measuring, and interpreting marketing data are paramount for optimization. Sophisticated analytics platforms and data visualization tools make this possible, even for non-technical teams:

- **Real-time campaign performance:** Monitoring website traffic, conversion rates, and other key metrics isn't a once-a-month analysis. Dashboards give an instant view of how campaigns fare, allowing for mid-flight adjustments.
- **ROI attribution:** Linking specific marketing spend to results (sales, leads) isn't always easy. Advanced attribution models (including multi-touchpoint attribution), using AI where possible, help clarify what gets budget increases and what gets cut.
- **Data-driven storytelling:** Raw data can overwhelm. Visualization tools transform datasets into clear charts, infographics, and interactive dashboards—ideal for sharing compelling progress with stakeholders.

AI, AI, AI: From Analysis to Action

AI has been around since the term was coined in 1956 at the Dartmouth workshop. There were early successes like Logic Theorist and ELIZA (early chatbot) with increased investments and funding. AI slipped into the first AI winter as overpromises and a lack of breakthrough reduced the funding and associated enthusiasm in the 1970s. A new wave emerged in the 1980s and 1990s where expert systems and the rise of machine learning (ML) gained attention. In 1997, IBM's Deep Blue defeated chess champion Garry Kasparov[1] and went on to even win at Jeopardy (US Gameshow). However, the second AI winter followed as the promises and potential applications remained far off. In the 2000s, there was renewed funding and excitement with deep learning breakthroughs and greater datasets

---

[1] Deep Blue versus Garry Kasparov was a pair of six-game chess matches between then-world chess champion Garry Kasparov and an IBM supercomputer called Deep Blue. Kasparov won the first match, held in Philadelphia in 1996, by 4–2. Deep Blue won a 1997 rematch held in New York City by 3½–2½.

becoming available to fuel the data-hungry AI progress. We started to see AI embodied in our search engines, drones, video streaming recommendations, and other widespread applications.

Then, in November 2022, ChatGPT was announced, and the world woke up to endless possibilities of Generative AI[2] and further accelerated funding, investments, experimentations, and applications with AI/Gen AI.

As such, we felt that it was important to capture some thoughts on the possibilities of AI, as this will be a game-changing technology for all industries (not just marketing).

AI, in its rapidly evolving forms, has transitioned from a futuristic concept to a collection of indispensable practical marketing powerhouses. As of 2025, AI's capabilities extend far beyond mere data processing. It now autonomously analyzes vast, complex datasets that humans could not effectively process alone, offering deep, actionable insights, personalizing customer experiences at an unprecedented scale, and even taking the lead in strategic content creation and campaign execution. The emergence of *Agentic AI* signifies a pivotal shift, where AI moves from being a tool to an autonomous partner in the marketing endeavor.

Here's how AI is revolutionizing marketing:

1. Predictive analytics: Proactive strategy and hyper-personalization

No longer limited to historical data analysis, AI-driven predictive analytics now offers sophisticated forecasting capabilities. ML algorithms analyze past customer behavior, real-time engagement patterns, and even external market trends to predict future outcomes with remarkable accuracy:

- **Churn prediction and prevention:** AI models can easily and quickly identify customers who are at risks of churn with greater precision than human marketers. This is done via analyzing shifts

---

[2] Generative artificial intelligence is AI capable of generating text, images, or other data using generative models, often in response to prompts. Generative AI models learn the patterns and structure of their input training data and then generate new data that have similar characteristics.

across multiple factors like engagement, purchase frequency, click through rates and even sentiments expressed online about the brand. This allows marketers to proactively intervene with targeted retention strategies, personalized offers, or preemptive customer service, significantly reducing customer attrition and optimizing CLV. By 2025, these systems can even suggest the *next best action* for each at-risk customer, moving beyond simple alerts to prescriptive solutions.

- **Demand forecasting and inventory management:** For e-commerce and retail, AI accurately forecasts product demand, enabling optimized inventory management, reduced waste, and ensuring product availability, especially for dynamic marketing campaigns and seasonal peaks.

- **Personalized recommendations and journey orchestration:** Predictive analytics fuels hyper-personalization engines. AI can predict the next likely purchase, content preference, or channel engagement for individual users, allowing marketers to deliver tailored experiences in real time across the entire customer journey. This includes dynamically adjusting website content, email offers, and app notifications.

2. Customer sentiment analysis: Understanding the nuance of voice

Modern AI-powered social listening and sentiment analysis tools have evolved significantly beyond basic keyword tracking and simplistic "positive/negative/neutral" classifications:

- **Deep emotional insight:** Advanced NLP models can now discern complex emotions, sarcasm, intent, and subtle shifts in customer opinion from social media, reviews, call transcripts, chat logs, and survey responses. This provides a more granular and accurate understanding of brand perception, product feedback, and reactions to marketing campaigns.

- **Real-time trend identification and crisis management:** AI constantly monitors online conversations, identifying emerging trends, potential PR crises, or shifts in competitor sentiment in real time. This enables marketing teams to respond swiftly and appropriately, mitigating risks and capitalizing on opportunities. Some tools now offer automated alerts for significant sentiment spikes, allowing for proactive intervention.

- **Omnichannel sentiment tracking:** Leading platforms in 2025 can aggregate and analyze sentiment data from a multitude of channels, providing a holistic view of customer voice and experience, breaking down data silos.

3. Chatbots and conversational AI: Intelligent engagement and lead cultivation

Chatbots have matured into sophisticated conversational AI platforms, becoming integral to customer service, engagement, and lead generation:

- **24/7 intelligent customer support:** AI-powered chatbots handle a vast array of customer inquiries, provide instant resolutions to common issues, and guide users through complex processes, all without human intervention and around the clock. Advanced AI allows these bots to understand context, maintain conversational flow, and access extensive knowledge bases.
- **Proactive lead generation and qualification:** Modern conversational AI doesn't just answer questions; it proactively engages website visitors, qualifies leads based on their interactions and expressed intent, collects crucial data, and can even schedule appointments or demos. Some systems use AI to analyze visitor behavior in real time to initiate conversations at the most opportune moment.
- **Seamless handoff and agent augmentation:** When a situation requires human intervention, the AI can seamlessly transfer the conversation, along with the full context and history, to a human agent. Furthermore, AI can assist human agents by providing real-time information, suggesting responses, and automating post-interaction summaries.

- **Voice and video AI assistants:** The rise of AI-powered voice assistants and even interactive video AI agents is adding new dimensions to customer interaction, offering more natural and engaging conversational experiences. Such conversations are now possible with local language corpuses, enabling advanced text-to-speech and speech-to-text translations.

4. **AI-Assisted and generative AI for creativity and content production**

AI's role in creativity has expanded dramatically with the advent of powerful generative AI models, like advanced versions of ChatGPT, Claude, and specialized image, video, and audio generation tools:

- **Content ideation and generation at scale:** AI tools can brainstorm campaign themes, generate diverse ad copy variations, write blog post drafts, create scripts for videos, design visuals, and even compose music. This dramatically accelerates the content creation process and allows marketers to test a wider array of creative assets.
- **Hyper-personalized content:** Generative AI enables the creation of highly personalized content variants tailored to specific audience segments or even individuals, based on their data and preferences. This could be dynamically adjusted email copy, personalized product descriptions, or custom ad creatives.
- **SEO and content optimization:** AI tools analyze top-performing content and search engine algorithms to provide recommendations for optimizing existing content and generating new content with a higher likelihood of ranking well and engaging the target audience.
- **Streamlining workflows, not replacing marketers:** While highly capable, AI in content creation is best viewed as a powerful assistant. It augments human creativity by handling repetitive tasks, providing inspiration, and generating initial drafts, freeing up marketers to

focus on strategy, brand voice, nuanced messaging, and ensuring ethical AI use. Human oversight remains crucial for quality control, originality, and aligning content with the overarching brand strategy.

5. The rise of agentic AI: Autonomous marketing operations

A significant leap forward in AI is the development and deployment of *Agentic AI*. Unlike traditional AI tools that require specific prompts or operate within predefined workflows, Agentic AI systems can operate autonomously to achieve marketing goals. These AI agents can independently plan, decide, and execute multi-step tasks, learn from their outcomes, and adapt their strategies in real time:

- **Autonomous campaign management:** An agentic AI could be tasked with a budget and a KPI (e.g., maximizing conversions for a new product). It could then independently research target audiences, generate ad creatives and copy, decide on channel allocation, launch campaigns, A/B test different elements, monitor performance, reallocate budget based on real-time results, and report on outcomes, all with minimal human intervention.

- **Proactive lead nurturing and sales development:** Agentic AI can manage sales prospecting by identifying potential leads, personalizing outreach across multiple channels (email, LinkedIn), engaging them in initial conversations, qualifying them based on responses and intent signals, and even booking meetings for human sales representatives. These "AI SDRs" (Sales Development Representatives) can operate 24/7.

- **Dynamic and self-optimizing customer journeys:** Agentic AI can orchestrate and continuously optimize individual customer journeys. Based on real-time behavior and predictive analytics, an AI agent can decide the next best message, offer, or content to deliver to each customer, across the most effective channel, at the optimal time, adapting the journey dynamically as the customer interacts (or doesn't interact) with the brand.

- **Deep research and insight synthesis:** Agentic AI can be deployed to conduct deep research across vast datasets, synthesize information from multiple sources, identify complex patterns, and generate strategic insights that might be missed by human analysts or less autonomous AI tools.

The evolving role of the marketer in an AI-driven world

As AI, particularly Agentic AI, takes on more operational and even strategic tasks, the role of the human marketer evolves. The focus shifts toward the following:

- **Strategic oversight and goal setting:** Defining clear business objectives, target audience parameters, and ethical guidelines for AI systems.
- **Prompt engineering and AI literacy:** Understanding how to effectively communicate with and guide AI tools, including sophisticated generative and agentic systems.
- **Creativity and brand stewardship:** Infusing brand voice, emotional intelligence, and truly novel creative concepts that AI can then help scale and optimize.
- **Ethical considerations:** Ensuring responsible AI deployment, data privacy, transparency in AI-driven decisions, and mitigating algorithmic bias.
- **Interpreting complex insights:** Leveraging AI-generated insights to make higher-level strategic decisions and innovations.
- **Human connection:** Focusing on building genuine relationships and community, areas where human empathy and understanding remain paramount.

This section on AI was written in 2025. It is already an active participant in the marketing process. From predicting customer needs and personalizing every interaction to generating creative content and autonomously managing campaigns through AI agents, AI is empowering marketers to achieve unprecedented levels of efficiency, effectiveness, and customer-centricity. The challenge and opportunity for marketers will be to understand, leverage, and ethically guide these powerful technologies to build the future of marketing.

Staying Ahead of the Curve: Key Technological Trends Shaping the Future of Marketing

The landscape of marketing is in a perpetual state of evolution, driven by rapid technological advancements. While foundational technologies establish current best practices, innovation waits for no one. For marketers aiming to maintain a competitive edge, understanding and anticipating the impact of emerging trends is crucial. As of mid-2025, several key technological currents have been poised to significantly reshape marketing strategies and consumer engagement in the coming years.

The continued ascendance of AI and ML

AI and ML are already transformative, but their evolution is far from over. We are seeing increasingly sophisticated applications that will offer marketers unprecedented capabilities:

- **Next-Generation generative AI for dynamic content creation:** Tools that generate text (like advanced iterations of ChatGPT), images (e.g., DALL-E series), video, and audio are becoming more powerful, intuitive, and integrated. Expect advancements in multi-input content management systems, where AI can seamlessly work across these various formats. Possible use cases could include the following:
  - *Rapid prototyping*: AI will quickly generate multiple variations of ad visuals, campaign concepts, and user interface designs.
  - *Enhanced creative assistance*: AI will increasingly assist in brainstorming novel ideas, drafting compelling initial copy for various platforms and efficiently translating marketing materials for global campaigns.

- ○ *Sophisticated hyper-personalization*: Beyond current capabilities, AI will drive even more granular and context-aware product recommendations and content delivery within websites, apps, and other digital touchpoints.
- **Sentiment analysis 2.0: Deciphering true emotional nuance:** Future AI will move beyond simple keyword tracking and basic positive/negative sentiment classification. It will achieve a deeper, more nuanced understanding of the emotions, sarcasm, and underlying intent within social media commentary, product reviews, and other forms of customer feedback. The growing intersection of AI and behavioral science will empower marketers to gauge not just *what* the reaction is, but *why* a campaign elicits specific emotions like joy, frustration, or backlash, offering profound insights for brand strategy and crisis management.
- **Predictive analytics for proactive churn reduction and opportunity identification:** AI's ability to identify complex patterns in vast datasets, often invisible to human analysts, will become even more refined. This will lead to:
  - ○ *Highly accurate churn warnings*: Advanced warning systems will pinpoint customers at high risk of attrition with greater accuracy, enabling marketers to deploy highly precise proactive offers and interventions to retain them.
  - ○ *Opportunity forecasting*: Beyond risk mitigation, predictive models will better identify emerging customer needs, potential cross-selling/up-selling opportunities, and optimal engagement timings.

Immersive experiences: From Metaverse hype to tangible value

While the initial "Metaverse" hype cycle has tempered, the underlying technologies of Extended Reality (XR)—encompassing VR and AR—are maturing into practical marketing applications:

- **Beyond gaming and socialization:** The focus is shifting toward tangible brand interactions and utility. Possible use cases include the following:

- ○ *Branded virtual environments*: Creating persistent or event-based virtual spaces for product launches, customer communities, interactive showcases, and unique brand experiences, often at a lower overhead than comparable physical events.
- ○ *AR-enhanced product visualization*: AR overlays are becoming more seamless, allowing customers to, for example, virtually place furniture in their room, try on clothing or cosmetics, or explore interactive product features using their smartphones or AR-enabled devices.
- ○ *Digital assets and ownership*: The concept of unique digital assets (e.g., NFTs, virtual goods) tied to physical product ownership or brand loyalty programs will continue to explore avenues for creating exclusivity, driving engagement, and fostering community.
- **The imperative of ROI measurement:** A critical factor for sustained investment in immersive experiences will be the development and adoption of clear metrics. Marketers will need to demonstrate how these virtual interactions translate into real-world sales, brand lift, customer loyalty, or other KPIs.

The era of privacy-focused marketing and zero-party data

Increasing consumer awareness of data privacy and evolving regulations (like GDPR and PDPA) are fundamentally shifting how marketers approach data collection and utilization:

- **Zero-party data strategies:** The emphasis is moving toward "zero-party data"—information that customers intentionally and proactively share with a brand. This is often exchanged for clear value, such as personalized experiences, exclusive content, early access, or tailored recommendations. Building trust and transparency in how the data are requested, used, and protected will be paramount.
- **Technologies for ethical data utilization:** Innovation will focus on tools and platforms that enable the following:

- *Ethical collection and management*: Systems designed for secure and transparent collection of zero-party and first-party data (data collected directly from a brand's own interactions with customers).
- *Privacy-enhancing technologies (PETs)*: AI models and analytical tools capable of extracting valuable insights from datasets while the data remain encrypted or anonymized, balancing business needs with robust consumer privacy protection.

Voice-first optimization: The rise of conversational interactions

The proliferation of smart speakers (like Amazon Alexa or Google Assistant) and voice-activated interfaces in various devices continues to drive a shift toward conversational search and interaction.

- **Content for natural language:** Marketing and SEO strategies must adapt to how people naturally speak, rather than just focusing on typed keywords. This involves optimizing website content, metadata, and structured data for voice search queries, which are often longer, more question-based, and context-driven.
- **Voice-activated experiences:** Beyond search, opportunities will grow for voice-activated brand interactions, such as voice-based shopping, customer service, and content consumption.

Other significant trends on the horizon

- **Dominance and evolution of short-form video:** Platforms like TikTok, Instagram Reels, and YouTube Shorts have cemented the importance of concise, engaging video content. Mastery here involves not just adapting to the format but also understanding the nuanced communication style, humor, and rapid pacing expected by users on these platforms. Expect AI to play a larger role in analyzing trending video styles and assisting in their creation.
- **Interactive and conversational advertising:** Advertisements are evolving from static, one-way messages to dynamic, two-way conversations including the following:
  - Mini-games or interactive polls within ad units.
  - Shoppable AR experiences initiated directly from an ad.

o AI-powered chatbots that engage users in a helpful dialogue within the ad itself. The goal is to make advertising less of an interruption and more of a valuable, engaging experience.

Staying informed about these interconnected trends, experimenting with emerging tools, and prioritizing ethical considerations will be essential for marketers seeking to build meaningful customer relationships and drive success in the technologically advanced landscape of tomorrow.

Limitations of Technology

Technology presents marketers with tremendous opportunities but also significant challenges. Here's a breakdown of key issues and where savvy marketers add irreplaceable value:

Challenge #1: Data biases, overload, and complexity

- **The problem:** Vast datasets across platforms (web traffic, social media, CRM, etc.) are great in theory, but extracting actionable insights is daunting. There are inherent biases in data and the way algorithms are designed.
- **Marketer's role:** Translate goals into precise questions that data can answer (with minimal biases). Don't ask for "everything," but "Who bounced from site X and why?" or "What campaign sparked initial interest in our highest value customers?" This focus guides tech teams and reveals what data are needed.

Challenge #2: Skills gaps and rapid tech evolution

- **The problem:** AI, new channels, and even analytics tools evolve faster than training can keep up. Teams rely on yesterday's knowledge for tomorrow's tech. One of the key challenges across all industries is addressing the skills gaps as the half-life[3] of technology

---

[3] Research suggests the half-life of professional skills has dropped from 10 years to five, and the half-life for many technical skills is now below 2.5 years. Over a billion people will need to be reskilled by 2030, prompting the World Economic Forum to declare a "reskilling emergency."

skills continues to diminish with the acceleration of technological advances.
- **Marketer's role:** Foster a culture of learning and upskilling. This isn't about making everyone a coder, but basic competency in tech principles empowers more informed discussions and faster adoption of promising tools.

Challenge #3: Privacy concerns and data ethics

- **The problem:** Regulations are a moving target, consumer trust is easy to lose, and misuse of data is a brand liability. Tech often makes things possible, but not automatically ethical. With advanced technology, it is possible to hyper-target and hyper-nudge a consumer into a purchase even if there are no requirements from the consumer.
- **Marketer's role:** Act as the customer advocate within the organization. Be the voice questioning if a tactic feels intrusive, even if legal. Build privacy into campaigns from the start, using transparent, value-driven approaches.

Challenge #4: Maintaining creativity and the "human touch"

- **The problem:** The problem: It is sometimes easy to get distracted by the latest technology, the latest "shiny object". Technology tools might be exciting but may not result in true inspiration for a marketing campaign. Tech might create efficiency, not true inspiration.
- **Marketer's role:** Never let strategy be dictated by the tool but the other way around. AI aids creative exploration, but marketers steer the ship. They recognize a powerful human narrative that makes a brand memorable, something even the most advanced AI struggles to achieve organically.

Challenge #5: Tech silos and fragmentation

- **The problem:** Multiple tools lead to disparate data with few clear ways to combine it for a holistic view. This is frustrating at a team level, but negatively impacts campaigns too.

- **Marketer's role:** Be the unifier. Connect IT, data scientists, and marketing goals in a common language. Prioritize integration solutions. This isn't a technical role, but rather one of translating needs across departments.

Challenge #6: Cost–Benefit analysis

- **The problem:** With fast-evolving technology, the landscape of Martech and Adtech companies and technologies will continue to evolve rapidly. Mergers and acquisitions will also complicate the market as the technology players will continue to change and evolve. For a marketer to invest in the right technologies toward a clear delivery of benefits will continue to be a challenge.
- **Marketer's role:** Marketing tech stacks become budget black holes. Savvy marketers will need to prioritize a few highly impactful tools, understood deeply, over chasing every fad, and yet be nimble enough to adapt and experiment.

Are Marketers Still Essential in a World of Tech?

The marketer advantage

It's crucial to remember that marketing challenges existed long before advanced tech. Marketers are skilled at the following:

- Storytelling and messaging
- Deep customer empathy
- Strategic, long-term vision
- Collaboration across various teams

It's not about technology vs. the human marketer, but a powerful union between the two that produces the most compelling outcomes. Tech should be an amplification tool, not the driving force.

Don't fear, experiment (within reason)

The fear of falling behind can drive panicked "me-too" adoption of tech without clear reasoning. However, this often does more harm than good. An experimental mindset has some key benefits:

- **Small budgets, big lessons:** It's often better to spend a little on several small pilot projects, rather than throwing your weight behind an unproven platform that flops.
- **Proof of concept:** Demonstrate to stakeholders the potential (or pitfalls) of new technology in a tangible way, building buy-in or pivoting the direction quickly.
- **Agility is the advantage:** Companies stuck in analysis paralysis get outmaneuvered by those willing to be wrong sometimes in pursuit of being right when it counts.

Customer's problem first, tech second

It's easy to fall into the "solution in search of a problem" trap with shiny new tech. Here's how to ground your focus on providing solutions for real customer struggles:

- **Map the tech to pain points:** Does an AR overlay make purchase decisions significantly easier? Does AI-powered sentiment analysis give an early alert system on brewing PR crises? Tie the tech to clear issues faced by the business or the end customer.
- **Consider the full impact:** Will this tech enhance or detract from the user experience? An interactive video ad might grab attention, but slow load times on the website negate that.
- **Value beyond novelty:** Short-term hype with a quick drop-off offers little to a marketer. Is there potential for sustained, meaningful integration? Can a conversational chatbot streamline an ongoing customer service need?

Collaboration is essential

Marketers were once able to function in a bubble with tech as a peripheral topic. That's not true anymore. Successful deployment often hinges on tight partnerships:

- **IT is your ally:** Complex data analysis or seamless tech integration can't be handled by marketing teams alone. Build good working

relationships to understand limitations early and find workable solutions.
- **Product teams get involved:** When marketing promises an AR product experience that can't be built, both parties fail. Get design and development on board early to understand feasibility and shape the vision as a unit.
- **Data experts are gold:** AI sounds great, but who makes sense of the insights? Collaborate closely with data scientists or hire those skills to turn raw information into actionable marketing strategies.

In a world saturated with AI-powered automation and algorithms, you might wonder if human marketers are obsolete. Far from it. AI excels at analyzing massive datasets, predicting trends, and even generating content variations. However, the art of marketing thrives on qualities machines simply don't possess:

- **Creativity:** AI aids ideation, but the spark that ignites truly memorable campaigns and connects on an emotional level is undeniably human.
- **Strategic vision:** AI executes tasks brilliantly, but marketers define the goals, map the customer journey beyond mere clicks, and understand the broader narrative driving a brand forward.
- **Empathy:** Understanding the "why" behind customer motivations goes beyond data points. Crafting relatable messaging that resonates deeply requires human intuition and storytelling prowess.
- **Ethical judgment:** AI reflects its training data. Marketers act as the ethical compass, ensuring tech is used responsibly, biases are challenged, and customer trust remains paramount.

Marketers aren't simply becoming tech operators; they are the orchestrators. AI is a powerful instrument, but human expertise plays the symphony that wins hearts, minds, and loyalty.

It's an Evolution, Not a Finish Line

Marketers thrive where a grasp of human desires meets technical possibility. These trends aren't barriers, but opportunities:

- **Tech fluency is no longer optional:** Marketers won't all become coders, but basic AI or data literacy is key to leading effective cross-team collaborations.
- **The "tech stack" mindset:** Success will be more about integrating a suite of diverse tools seamlessly, not finding one silver bullet.
- **Human skills matter more than ever:** Amidst a sea of automation, marketing fueled by creativity, storytelling, and the ability to understand nuanced data interpretations will stand out—tech enhances these skills, but never replaces them.

We won't hit a magical time where tech does it all—even the most advanced technologies will require humans. Humans just need to be better at using the technologies (like we have always done in the past).

Index

A

5As model, 157
A/B testing, 34, 316, 359, 362
access, 150, 157
Account-Based Marketing (ABM), 174–177, 179–181, 183, 339
 technologies, 179
act, 151, 157
activate, 150, 157
ad impressions, 360
advertising, 331, 333–335, 358, 367, 372
advertising wearout, 142
advocate, 3, 92, 123, 135, 142, 150, 157, 218, 312, 322, 334, 340, 347, 363, 367–368
 employee, 340
affiliate, 350
affiliate marketing, 349–351
analytics, 170, 178–179, 194, 197
anchoring, 256
Ansoff's Growth Matrix, 226–227
a priori segmentation, 49–51
artificial intelligence (AI), 28, 32, 133, 197, 200, 306, 310, 316, 334, 366
assess, 150, 157

attention, 132, 137
attitude, 136, 141–142, 157
auction-based pricing, 249–250
augmented reality (AR), 200, 270 290, 299, 302, 334
authenticity, 111, 122, 124, 129, 132, 154, 222, 296, 334, 339, 350, 352, 354–355, 368
autonomous stores, 307–308

B

brand, 65, 89, 94–95, 98–100, 115–116, 121, 128–129, 236, 250
 advocacy, 363, 369
 ambassadors, 121, 149, 155, 222
 association, 79, 89, 100–101, 105, 110, 112, 129, 137, 141
 association, secondary, 105
 awareness, 16, 73, 79, 93, 101, 289, 292, 297, 299, 314, 351, 356, 362
 communities, 368–369
 consideration, 93
 dilution, 40, 103–104, 195, 232
 elements, 90, 100, 128
 equity, 3, 90, 101, 128, 192, 219, 235, 237, 254

extension, 228–229, 233
familiarity, 93
identity/image, 90, 93, 95, 99–101, 103, 105–106, 109–111, 115–116, 121, 128, 165, 224, 228, 230–232, 236–237, 241–242, 272–276, 277, 282, 285, 288, 322, 330, 336, 350, 353
loyalty, 16, 91, 362, 364
mantra/slogan, 99
name, 90, 101, 108, 129
personality, 90, 100–101, 103, 128, 326–327, 340, 371
portfolio, 228, 232
preference, 151, 281, 282, 322
purpose, 113–114, 129
recall, 91, 371
recognition, 101–102, 216, 226, 228–229, 233, 237, 241, 321
sentiment, 356
voice, 90, 100, 114, 326–328, 352, 371, 389, 407–408
break-even, 235
budget, 324, 328, 335
bundled pricing, 238, 254, 258, 268
bundling, 203, 218, 254–255, 264, 267
business-to-business (B2B), 159–164, 166, 168–171, 174, 181, 183–184, 337, 340, 346
business-to-consumer (B2C), 159–161, 163–164, 184, 269
buyer persona/profile, 46–49, 64, 81, 87, 126, 177–178, 181, 205, 293, 326, 348, 358

buying center, 170–171, 184
buying journey, 170, 176, 178, 200, 315, 345–348

C

5Cs, 19, 33, 36, 192
   collaborator analysis, 19, 24, 36
   company analysis, 19, 23, 36
   competitor analysis, 19, 26, 36, 194
   context analysis, 19, 28, 36
   customer analysis, 19, 22, 36
call-to-action, 322, 324, 330, 360, 364
cannibalization, 40, 105, 229, 232–233
captive product, 251, 267
categorization, 66, 138
category membership, 65–66, 70, 72–73, 75, 88
channel, 25, 63
   arms-length, 272–273, 275
   design, 271, 310
   direct, 278
   integrated, 272–273, 278
   intensity, 271, 281
   leadership, 285–287, 310
   length, 271, 277
   management, 284, 310
   members/intermediaries, 250, 273–275, 277–278, 281, 283–284, 286–287, 310
   partners, 15, 25, 235, 271, 275, 283, 285, 310
   strategy, 235–236, 269, 284
   type, 271–272, 310

click-through rates, 350, 359–360
co-branding, 25, 105–106, 116, 129, 229–230, 233
co-creation, 199, 208, 298
coefficient of imitation, 41, 63, 211
cognitive dissonance, 146, 149
collaboration, 19, 24–26, 143, 155, 177–178, 194, 199, 204, 229–232
communication, 321
    channel, 125–126, 271, 275, 276–279, 284–287, 310, 319, 326, 346
    model, 317–318
    objective, 320–321, 326, 331
community, 42, 60, 62–63, 80–81, 84–86, 110–111, 150, 154, 166, 186, 198–199, 204, 206–207, 217, 295–297, 300, 302, 312, 329–330, 336, 339–340, 354–356, 361, 363, 368–370, 377, 408, 411
competition-based pricing, 249–250, 267
competitive
    advantage, 62, 190, 192, 236
    parity method, 325
confirmation bias, 138, 140
consideration set, 149–150, 163
consumer behavior, 22, 32–33, 131, 135–136, 142, 145, 157, 207, 261, 288, 298, 335, 363, 379
content creation, 182, 206, 313, 327, 347–348, 350–351, 357, 403, 406, 409
content curation, 32, 169, 348
content marketing, 35, 163, 174, 205, 292, 313–314, 323, 347–348, 362, 380

conversion, 152, 178–180, 290, 293, 314, 316, 323–324, 344, 350, 356, 360, 365, 367, 391, 401–402
cost-based pricing, 243–244, 246, 249, 267
cost of goods sold (COGS), 260
cost-plus pricing, 244–245
customer
    acquisition, 238
    centricity, 2, 12–14, 20, 77, 191, 193, 215, 246, 278, 281, 302, 310, 316
    engagement, 4, 25, 115, 197, 304, 316, 328, 365, 371
    experience, 149, 151, 153, 157, 200, 203, 214, 272–273, 275–276, 287, 301, 340, 363, 367
    journey, 3, 20, 151, 270–272, 278, 310, 359–360, 364
    journey map, 151–153, 157, 177, 188
    lifetime value, 218
    retention, 91
    satisfaction, 16, 146, 150, 190–191, 203, 267, 357, 361
customer relationship management (CRM), 178–179, 217, 338, 355
customization/personalization, 44–45, 58–60, 62, 64, 337

D

360-degree branding, 115, 129
data
    analytics, 207, 316
    privacy, 4, 197, 202–203, 347

scraping, 56
visualization, 57
deal semantics, 257
decision journey, 131, 134, 148, 150, 164, 331
decision-making process, 136, 145
   evaluation of alternatives, 146–147, 331
   information search, 145, 147, 331
   need/problem recognition, 145, 147–148, 157, 331
   post-purchase, 146–149, 151, 156, 190, 331 347, 361
   purchase, 141, 146–149, 151, 323–324, 331, 333, 336–337, 353, 367
decoding, 318–319
decoy pricing, 256
demand elasticity, 239
differentiated marketing, 39–41, 64
diffusion rate, 213
direct marketing, 331, 346–347
direct-to-consumer (DTC), 213, 277–281, 357–358, 362–363
discriminatory pricing, 252, 268
diversification, 227
dynamic pricing, 251–252, 307

E

earned media, 87, 156, 331, 334, 336–337, 367–368
e-commerce, 198, 269, 287–291, 293–294, 305, 310, 334, 365, 367
economies of scale, 102, 108, 235–236, 242, 276, 279

elaboration likelihood model, 147
email marketing, 289, 292, 318, 346–347
email open rates, 347
employee advocacy, 340–341
employer brand, 122–123, 125–126, 129, 330
employer value proposition (EVP), 123–126, 129
encoding, 141–142, 318
environmental scanning, 18, 155
ESG, 144, 201
ethnography, 143
exclusive distribution, 281–282
exit-intent, 292
experiential marketing, 371
experiential retail, 299, 302, 304

F

family branding, 101, 102–103, 108, 116, 129
feature, 190–191, 199, 208, 217, 219, 228, 236–237, 241, 250, 257, 339
franchise, 272, 276–277
franchisee, 276–277
franchising, 276
franchisor, 276–277
freemium, 199, 250, 267

G

gated content, 292
geographical information systems (GIS), 57
go-to-market strategy, 5, 63, 194, 210–211

H

halo effect, 91
hashtag, 296, 330, 349
heuristic, 139–140, 147, 159
hierarchy of effects model, 320–323, 331

I

inbound marketing, 176, 313–314, 331, 338, 347
influencer marketing, 212, 217, 221, 279, 292, 351–352, 354, 361, 363
information overload, 91, 132, 168, 338, 367–368
intent data, 176, 179–180
Internet of Things (IoT), 198, 306
involvement, 146–147

K

Key Opinion Leaders (KOL), 221, 224

L

learning, 136, 141–142
line extension, 218, 228–229, 233
livestreaming, 354–355
loss aversion, 140
loss leader, 255
loyalty programs, 217–218, 238, 252, 289–290, 292, 301, 336

M

market
    demand, 55, 64, 238, 243
    development, 226
    forecast, 55
    minimum, 55–56
    penetration, 226, 241, 274
    potential, 54–57, 64, 194, 216, 281
    reach, 271, 273–274, 281–283, 298, 304, 307
    share, 56, 73, 75, 79, 91, 93, 102, 192, 216, 218–219, 228, 233, 238, 240, 242, 267–268, 275, 281
    size, 55–56, 277
marketing
    objectives, 237–238, 267
    plan, 34–36, 181
marketing mix, 5, 14, 235, 249, 260
marketing automation (MA), 178, 316
marketing funnel, 17, 323–324, 334, 359–360, 400–401
    bottom of the funnel (BOFU), 323–324
    middle of the funnel (MOFU), 323–324
    top of the funnel (TOFU), 323–324
mass customization, 43–44, 64
mass marketing, 39, 64
metaverse, 297–298
Minimum Viable Product (MVP), 194, 199
mobile marketing, 363–364
moment of truth, 131
monopolistic competition, 239, 241
monopoly, 239
motivation, 142, 145–147, 187, 208
multi-branding, 103–105, 109, 116, 129

N

new product development (NPD), 193, 195, 208–209, 224, 226
next-best-action (NBA), 53
niche marketing, 41–42, 62, 64
non-fungible tokens (NFTs), 298

O

objective-and-task method, 325
odd pricing, 255
oligopoly, 239–240, 250
omnichannel, 133, 164, 296, 299, 304, 312, 364, 370–371
one-to-one targeting, 52–53, 63–64
outbound marketing, 313–314, 331
outcome-based pricing, 252, 268
out-of-home advertising, 372, 374
owned media, 331, 367

P

paid, 331
    media, 182, 333, 367
    search, 182
pay-per-click (PPC), 333, 335
penetration pricing, 242
perceived
    risks, 147
    value, 237, 245–246, 249, 257, 267–268
perception, 48, 65, 71–72, 87–91, 94, 99, 101–102, 110, 117, 120–121, 128, 131, 136–137, 141–142, 144, 148, 156–157, 166, 230, 235, 236–237, 245–246, 249–250, 254–255, 257, 259–261, 265, 268, 285, 327, 329, 333, 337, 353, 404
perceptual filters, 137

perceptual map, 72, 74–75, 88
personalization, 43, 53, 133, 175, 179, 301, 315–316, 334, 346
personal selling, 337–339
phygital experiences, 270
place strategy, 269–271, 280, 284, 310
points of differences (PoDs), 66–67, 70, 75, 88
points of parity (PoPs), 66–67, 88
positioning, 40, 65–66, 68–69, 71, 74, 88–89, 100, 105, 123, 185, 229–230, 235–238, 241, 249, 250, 254, 265, 267, 322, 330, 362
positioning statement, 69–71, 88
post hoc segmentation, 49–51
predictive analytics, 57, 176–177, 306
preference, 322, 337
prestige pricing, 237
price
    ceiling, 237, 267
    discrimination, 238
    floor, 236–237, 267
    framing, 255, 257–258, 268
    penetration, 242
    skimming, 242
    war, 236, 238, 240, 282
private label branding, 107, 129
Product-as-a-Service (PaaS), 203
product life cycle (PLC), 3, 208–209, 219, 224, 227, 233
    decline, 209, 219, 227, 233, 242
    growth, 216, 218, 224, 233

Index | 425

introduction, 209–210, 213, 224, 233
maturity, 218–219, 224, 227, 233
product line, 217–218, 222, 226, 274
product portfolio, 209, 227, 232
product proliferation, 232–233
product type, 281–282
    convenience goods, 281–282
    shopping goods, 281–283
    specialty goods, 281–282
promotion budget, 324, 331
promotion mix, 326, 331
public relations (PR), 331, 336–337, 353
pure competition, 239, 241

R

reach, 330, 337, 349, 352, 366, 371
recall, 101, 142, 145, 149
recognition, 276, 321, 333
reference prices, 256, 260
retargeting, 292, 324, 334–335, 359
retention, 224, 238
review, 131, 159, 164
revitalization, 219–220, 223–224, 229–231

S

sales promotion, 236, 237, 254–255, 268, 335
schemas, 138–139
search engine optimization (SEO), 292, 323, 348

search engine results pages (SERP), 333
segmentation, 37, 45–46, 49–50, 63–65, 103, 109, 115, 126, 129, 172, 191, 231, 278, 327, 333
segmentation base, 46–47, 50
sense-making, 168–169, 184, 339
Serviceable Addressable Market (SAM), 54–55
Serviceable Obtainable Market (SOM), 54–55
slogan, 66, 70–71, 87
social
    commerce, 216, 294–295
    currency, 351
    proof, 150, 159, 312, 342, 346, 351, 361, 368
    selling, 295, 339–346
social media
    listening, 56, 156, 194
    marketing, 292, 356–357, 362
    monitoring, 337
storytelling, 85, 87, 99, 112, 170, 184, 206–207, 294–295, 312–313, 322, 326–329, 330, 352, 356
sub-branding, 105, 129
subscription-based pricing, 250, 253, 259, 268, 279
sunk cost fallacy, 258
supply chain resilience, 305
sustainability, 200–203, 208, 308–310, 343
SWOT, 33, 35–36

T

target return pricing, 245
test marketing, 195–196

Total Available Market (TAM), 54
trialability, 213

U

unique selling proposition, 241, 322
unique value proposition, 246, 324
usage-based pricing, 253
user-generated content (UGC), 132, 204, 206, 296, 313, 330, 334, 346, 352, 360, 363, 368, 370

V

value-based pricing, 237, 245–246, 249, 267
value proposition, 5, 70, 77–78, 80, 88, 123, 174, 185–186, 191–192, 195, 204, 206, 210–212, 215, 217, 229, 236–237, 243, 252, 258–259, 270, 301, 327, 342
virtual reality (VR), 200, 290, 299, 302, 334

W

website analytics, 349
website traffic, 360
willingness to pay, 93, 238, 242, 246, 249
willing to pay, 238, 242, 249
word of mouth, 42, 63, 87, 92, 121, 150, 187, 190, 211, 312, 368

Z

Zero Moment of Truth (ZMOT), 132, 163